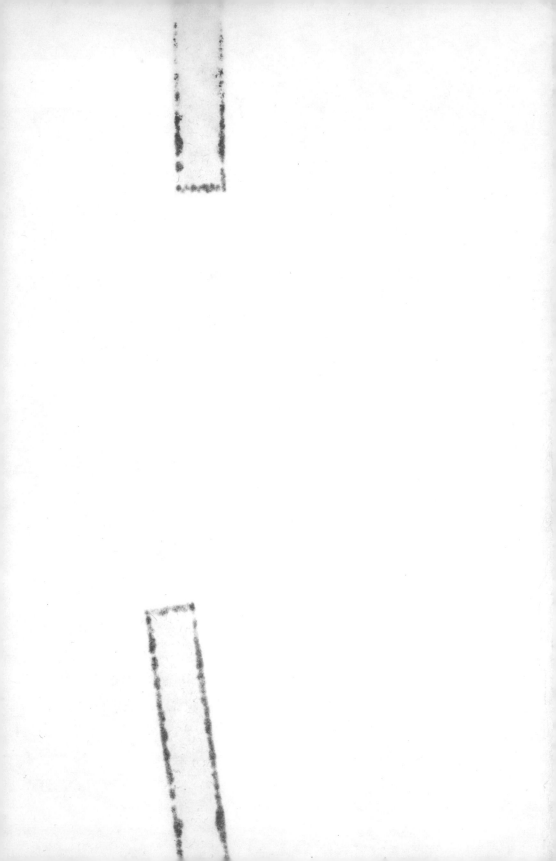

OUR INDIAN WARDS

*Is Not the Government Strong Enough to Keep its
Agreements with Us?*

—Chief Ouray

OUR INDIAN WARDS

By George W. Manypenny

New Foreword by Henry E. Fritz
Saint Olaf College

DA CAPO PRESS • NEW YORK • 1972

Library of Congress Cataloging in Publication Data

Manypenny, George Washington, 1808-1893.
    Our Indian wards.

    1. Indians of North America—Government relations.
2. Indians of North America—Wars. I. Title.
E93.M29   1972   970.5   68-54844
    ISBN 0-306-71140-0

First published by Robert Clarke & Co., Cincinnati, 1880.
Republished, 1972, with a new foreword and a documentary appendix.

Reproduced by permission from a copy of the first edition
in the collection of the Enoch Pratt Free Library, Baltimore, Maryland.

© 1972 Da Capo Press, Inc.
A Subsidiary of Plenum Publishing Corporation
227 West 17th Street, New York, New York 10011

Manufactured in the United States of America

OUR INDIAN WARDS

CONTENTS.

CHAPTER VI.

CHAPTER VII.

CHAPTER VIII.

CHAPTER IX.

CHAPTER XV.

CHAPTER XVI.

CHAPTER XVII.

CHAPTER XVIII.

CHAPTER XIX.

APPENDIX

FOREWORD

The publication of *Our Indian Wards* in 1880 was the climax of more than a quarter century of reform effort in behalf of American Indians by George W. Manypenny. As Commissioner of Indian Affairs throughout the administration of Franklin Pierce (1853–1857), Manypenny had defended the reservations of the West against encroachment and spoliation by white citizens, a notable case being that of the Kaw tribe in Kansas. In 1854, not content with official reports from agents and superintendents, he had visited many of the agencies east of the Rocky Mountains in order to gain an intimate knowledge of Indian problems. More than anything else, his administration became known for resistance to fraudulent claims upon Indian annuities, and for this he incurred the enmity of prominent western politicians.

A letter written to Senator Thomas Hart Benton in 1855 reveals Manypenny as a man of considerable energy, intelligence, honesty, and courage in the public service. In the *National Intelligencer*, Benton had attacked the Commissioner's practice of requiring vouchers and receipts in support of claims payable by the government from Indian funds. In a lengthy reply, Manypenny asserted that he would not yield to anyone, however influential, who demanded that subordinates of the Indian Bureau not be required "to present their accounts and vouchers for disbursements," and that he would endeavor to protect the treasury against improper transactions in Kansas, California, and elsewhere. He informed the Senator that a claim for $981,818. submitted by the Superintendent for California was "as transparent a humbug as any ever got up by either you or Barnum"; and he supported this statement with information obtained from the office of the surveyor general in California showing that a field of wheat included in the claim at an estimated value of $684,000. could not have been worth more than $53,856.

To correct abuses that hindered the preparation of Indians for incorporation into Anglo-American society, Manypenny suggested that the government adopt a policy of dealing with Indians as wards and cease its recognition of chiefs as spokesmen for quasi-independent nations. He was a champion of this point of view more than a decade and a half before the practice of making treaties with Indian tribes was ended in 1871. For him it was a matter of humanity, Christianity, and national honor that penal laws forbid the pilfering of Indian annuities, that contracts between Indians and private persons be declared null and void, and that government personnel found guilty of participation in such transactions be instantly dismissed. As a first step toward teaching Indians to farm their land, he advocated an end to removals from one location to another and the enactment of more stringent penal legislation against the encroachment of white settlers upon reservations.

Manypenny was generally opposed to punitive expeditions led by officers of the Army against Indian tribes. His attitude here was apparent as early as 1855 when General William S. Harney humbled the Brulé Sioux in the battle of Ash Hollow near Fort Laramie. Harney was avenging the massacre the previous year of Lieutenant Grattan's company which occurred during an attempt to arrest a Miniconjou Sioux for killing a stray cow belonging to Morman immigrants. This tragedy had been the result of an unfortunate combination of circumstances: any stray animal was fair game by Indian standards; the offender had taken refuge in the Brulé camp; Lieutenant Grattan, although lacking experience in dealing with Indians, was anxious to make a record for bravery; Grattan's interpreter, intoxicated and bearing a personal grievance against the Brulé, was undiplomatic; and the Indians were upset by the invasion of their country. Hence, Manypenny's condemnation of Harney's military campaign is easy to understand, particularly since he believed that good relations could have been maintained from the beginning by using Indian funds to reimburse the Mormons for their loss. Furthermore, Manypenny considered the attack on the Brulé illegal in that it had not been authorized by the Secretary of the Interior or his subordinates—jurisdiction over Indian affairs had been transferred from the War Department to Interior in 1849.

Although biographical information concerning Manypenny is
scarce,[1] he identified with that group of Protestant reformers who
wanted to employ persuasion instead of military force to bring
nomadic Indians upon reservations where they might be taught civilized ways under the supervision of agents appointed by the religious
denominations. This outlook was one of two major forces that produced the so-called Peace Policy of the Grant administration. From a
humanitarian standpoint, the other major force was less appealing.
Like the reformers, some high-ranking military officers were interested
in civilizing Indians, but they preferred to eradicate primitive habits
at the point of the rifle and the bayonet. General William T. Sherman
wanted the Indian Bureau returned to the War Department in order
to give the Army jurisdiction over Indian affairs both on and off the
reservations. This would solve the problem of having the reservations
used as sanctuaries for Indian marauders who raided farms, ranches,
and lines of communication. At the same time, Indian agents would
have the support of troops in their efforts to inculcate civilized habits
among the tribesmen.

Neither the reformers nor the military officers were entirely realis-
tic. Persuasion had little effect upon recalcitrant Indians who were
intent upon continuing their ancient custom of life by the chase; military force was usually needed to confine them within a reservation.
On the other hand, the presence of soldiers adjacent to agencies led to
moral degradation among Indian women, thus hindering the efforts of

---

1. Born in Uniontown, Pennsylvania, in 1808, Manypenny lived for most of his
   adult life in Ohio. He came to Washington, Ohio, in 1826 to edit the Washington *Republican*. Four years later, he purchased the St. Clairsville *Gazette*
   and turned it into an important newspaper. In 1840, he served as contractor
   for building the dam at Zanesville, and he continued to live in Zanesville until
   his appointment as Commissioner of Indian Affairs. From 1841 through 1846,
   Manypenny was Clerk of Common Pleas for Muskingum County, and in 1850,
   he became a member of the Board of Public Works. He was active as a devel-
   oper of real estate and as a speculator in town lots. After his term as Commissioner of Indian Affairs, Manypenny moved to Columbus and in 1859, with
   Thomas Miller, purchased the *Ohio Statesman*, becoming editor of the paper.
   From 1861 to 1873, he served as Ohio's General Manager of Public Works.
   Manypenny died in 1893.

the missionary teachers. Although many other qualifications were desirable, the religious denominations could at least supply personnel with good moral habits who were committed to bringing the gospel and the work ethic to primitive people. In the end, the need for a compromise between the reformers and the military became apparent.

That compromise, known as the Peace Policy, was accomplished during the Indian crisis on the Great Plains that followed the Civil War. Frontier movements westward from the prairies of the mid-continent and eastward from the Pacific slope rendered obsolete the removal policy begun in the Jacksonian era. Settlers, surveyors, and immigrants were in danger from war parties seething with resentment toward white men who disregarded treaty obligations. Great herds of buffalo, the main support of plains-Indian culture, were being slaughtered by hide hunters and by sportsmen who came to the region in the relative comfort of railway cars. The Army lacked sufficient troops to cope with the guerrilla warfare carried on by Indians mounted on fleet ponies and supplied with firearms and whiskey by illicit traders. Under these circumstances the government had little choice but to reduce the number of roving bands by providing places of refuge for Indians who were inclined toward peace and by promising them rations together with the vocational instruction necessary for assimilation into white society.

The Peace Policy was adopted on the advice of the Board of Indian Commissioners, a body representing the Protestant churches which was established by Congress in 1869 under pressure from Quaker and Episcopalian lobbyists. On the one hand, it provided for the appointment of all agency personnel by the religious denominations; on the other, it gave the Army jurisdiction over Indians who chose to remain outside the reservations. The nature of this policy was made clear in an order issued by General Philip H. Sheridan, commander of the Missouri Military Division, on June 29, 1869:

> All Indians when on their proper reservations are under the exclusive control and jurisdiction of their agents. They will not be interfered with in any manner by military authority, except upon requisition of the special agent resident with them, his superintendent, or the Bureau of

> Indian Affairs in Washington. Outside the well defined
> limits of their reservations they are under the original and
> exclusive jurisdiction of military authority...All Indians
> ...who do not immediately remove to their reservations,
> will be...treated as hostile, wherever they may be found,
> and particularly if they are near settlements or the great
> lines of communication.

It can be said quite accurately that under this arrangement the government offered the Indians three alternatives: first, assimilation into the culture that was displacing their own; second, a parasitic existence in confinement; third, extermination. As matters turned out, the majority went the middle way; in part through the lack of appropriations sufficient to support efforts toward assimilation.

Manypenny was opposed to that feature of the Peace Policy which gave the Army jurisdiction over Indians outside of reservations. He felt that the Interior Department had been given exclusive authority over Indian affairs by the congressional act of 1849 which took the Indian Bureau away from the War Department. In 1867, more than two years before the positions of Protestant reformers and military officers were compromised in the Peace Policy, Manypenny had fought the proposal of a Senate committee to transfer the Indian Bureau back to the Department of War. As an alternative, he argued that Congress should create a Department of Indian Affairs and give its Secretary full rank in the Cabinet. In his view, the Army should not go into the Indian country unless invited there by a civil authority for the purpose of dealing with a great emergency.[2]

Manypenny's experience with Indian administration and his keen interest in Indian welfare led to his appointment to several commissions established to negotiate with the tribes. He served as chairman of the Sioux Commission in 1876 and of the Ute Commission in 1880. His work on the former was important for at least three reasons. First, it occurred during the great public clamor following the Custer mas-

---

2. *Letter of Hon. George W. Manypenny* [to the Cincinnati *Gazette*] *in Regard to Treatment of the Indians,* [dated at Columbus, Ohio] *January 31, 1867.* Reprinted as the Appendix to the present volume.

sacre for the use of naked force until the Indians were thoroughly
humbled and made incapable of further resistance. Second, it met
stern opposition from Army officers of high rank who hoped to take
advantage of public resentment to gain complete control over Indian
affairs. Finally, it brought Manypenny into contact with Episcopal
Bishop Henry B. Whipple of Minnesota, another member of the Commission, who had been a champion of Indian rights and of assimilation in accordance with the wardship theory since 1859.

It seems certain that Manypenny was prompted to write *Our Indian
Wards* in response to his experiences as chairman of the Sioux Commission, and as a means of keeping the cause of justice for Indians
alive during a period when public opinion was adverse to reform. He
was strongly antagonistic toward the military officers who were assigned the task of disarming and dismounting the Sioux. (It angered
him to learn of their taking control of the agencies after the Sioux
commission had completed its work.) He had hoped that the report of
his commission would serve to revive interest in reform but was disappointed when the press gave it slight coverage. Finally, in 1877,
his concern over the "deadness in the Church," which reflected the
general climate of opinion in reference to the Indian problem, was
almost as great a motivation to write a book as his antipathy toward
General Sherman.

The war with the Sioux was accompanied by a new effort to transfer the Indian Bureau to the War Department. It began shortly before
the massacre of Custer's regiment and gained considerable strength
in the emotionally charged atmosphere of the late seventies. Manypenny was fearful that a bill to that effect before the House of Representatives in 1878 would become law. In correspondence with Bishop
Whipple, he again stated a preference for a Department of Indian
Affairs; and, very likely, preparation of *Our Indian Wards* was hastened by publication that year of Lt. Col. Elwell S. Otis' *The Indian
Question.*

Colonel Otis' volume created the impression that the military
branch of the government could do a far better job of managing
Indian affairs than the Interior Department. It contended that eight
years of the Peace Policy had brought no progress in preparing Indians

for assimilation, and asserted that the Indian Bureau continued to
be notoriously corrupt. It made many constructive recommendations,
especially in respect to the need for a criminal code of law applicable
to the reservation, and suggested that "a strong, efficient force would
be required to fully inaugurate these innovations in our system of
Indian management." The first step was to place hostile bands at the
agencies, where, "under the vigilant eye of an energetic police or military power, they would be obliged to check their passions" and would
become accustomed "to fixed abodes, cultivated fields, and productive
labor."

So far as the specifics of a program for Indian assimilation into
white society were concerned, Otis' reccommendations were quite similar to those of the leading reformers who sought supremacy for civil
authority. But Manypenny was offended by arguments for an approach
he had resisted for twenty-five years. In the Colonel's words:

> Government has finally learned the necessity of localizing
> the tribes, in order to advance their condition, but the more
> necessary measure of enforced repression does not seem
> to be appreciated. Should a tribe today break into rebel-
> lion, the ministers of peace would be sent out to purchase
> submission. There is danger now that the Sioux nation may
> be paid or hired to settle down under its mere promise to
> desist from robbery and murder. Far better would it be for
> its ultimate welfare, should hostilities continue until it is
> obliged to beg for mercy, . . . even though it be at the ex-
> pense of all its possessions and a large fraction of its num-
> bers. A misconceived spirit of . . . philanthropy would stay
> the hand engaged in teaching it the rudimentary lesson
> of modern civilization. . . .

Through *Our Indian Wards*, Manypenny set out to prove that from
the time of earliest settlement in America, Indian wars had been caused
by the white man's rapacity; and to illustrate from the historical record that the Army was unsuited to take control of Indian affairs.
(Because of his strong prejudice against those officers whose forces
had defeated the Sioux, he seemed to admire the defiant spirit of Sitting
Bull.) Simultaneously, he proposed land-in-severalty legislation to make
homesteaders of Indians within reservations. Thus his book was part

of that reform literature which brought about the passage of the Dawes Individual Allotment Act of 1887. As an appeal to humanitarian sentiment, it deserves to be compared with Helen Hunt Jackson's *Century of Dishonor*, which was published a year later.

Saint Olaf College   HENRY E. FRITZ
Northfield, Minnesota

INTRODUCTORY.

In the preparation and publication of this work the author has been moved by a sincere desire to render service in the amelioration of the condition of our Indian population, now numbering about two hundred and seventy-five thousand souls. The condition of this population, and the relations existing between the Indians and the white people dwelling on the border, is not satisfactory. This fact no intelligent man will deny. There is diversity of opinion as to the causes which produce the discontent and disorder that prevail, as well as the wars that result therefrom. These border wars began at a very early period, and may be traced through our whole history, and the record is a sickening detail of outrage, robbery, and murder. The careful student of history should have no difficulty in discovering the origin of our Indian complications, as well as the causes that have stimulated conflicts between the white and red man, and which have formed such sad chapters in our annals.

It can not be denied, that from the period when the first infant settlements were made upon the Atlantic sea-board by European colonists, until the present time, there have been constant, persistent, and unceasing efforts on the part of the white man to drive the Indian from his hunting ground and his home. When the encroachments of the former became unbearable, they were forcibly resisted by the latter. This was the only mode left to the Indian by which to redress his wrongs, since he had no standing in the civil tribunals of the colonies, and even to this day we have practically denied him the benefit of our courts. Unless we expect from the savage more forbearance than from the civilized man under like circumstances, there should be no surprise that he has resisted the aggressions made upon him. That he was willing, under proper treatment, to have lived in amity with the white man, there is abundant evidence.

In 1607, the first permanent settlement in our country was commenced at Jamestown, Virginia, by a colony of Englishmen. A few years thereafter, in a conversation between Captain John Smith, one of the original councilmen in the colony, and Powhatan, the principal chief of the Indians residing in southern Virginia, the latter said:

"I am an old man, and must soon die, and the succession must descend in order to my brothers, and then to my two sisters and their daughters. I wish their experience was equal to mine, *and that your love to us might not be less than ours to you. Why should you take by force from us that which you can obtain by love? Why should you destroy us, who have provided you with food?* What can you gain by war? We can hide our provisions, and fly into the woods, and then you must, consequently, almost famish by reason of wronging your friends. You see us unarmed and willing to supply your wants, if you will come in a friendly manner, and not with swords and guns, as to invade an enemy. I am not so simple as not to know that it is better to eat good meat, be well, and sleep quietly with my women and children, to laugh and be merry with the English, and, being their friend, to have copper hatchets and whatever else I want, than to fly from all, to lie cold in the woods, feed upon acorns, roots, and such trash, and to be so hunted that I can not rest, eat, or sleep, and so, in this miserable manner, to end my miserable life; and, Captain Smith, *this might soon be your fate too, through your rashness and unadvisedness. I therefore exhort you to peaceable counsels."*

It will, in a few years, be three centuries since the chief Powhatan had the talk with Captain Smith, from which this extract is taken. If the views expressed by the chief, had governed the intercourse between the races from that period until the present time, much of the suffering, torture, and premature death that accompanied the colonizing and settlement of our country would have been spared, the civilization of the Indian assured, and the white and red man have dwelt together in harmony and peace. It was no fault of the natives that relations of peace and good will were not successfully cultivated.

On this occasion, and in behalf of his race, Powhatan *solved the Indian problem;* and William Penn justified this solution when he assumed direction of affairs in his province, and established such relations with the Indians that peace and friendship prevailed for more than two-thirds of a century, during which time the Friends held power. In the second chapter of this work, the conduct of this great and good man, in his intercourse with, and his opinion of the native race, will be found, and to the same the reader is respectfully referred.

In view of the pacific disposition of the natives, as attested by Powhatan, and the fact that the followers of William Penn lived so many years with the Indians without a single serious disturbance in his province, coupled with the pledge in the ordinance of 1787 that "the utmost good faith shall be observed toward the Indians; their lands and property shall never be taken from them without their consent; and in their property, rights, and liberty they shall never be invaded or disturbed, unless in just and lawful wars authorized by Congress," there is in the ever recurring and never ending conflicts between the white man and the Indian, cause for the deepest humiliation.

From the organization of the government until the year 1871, the extinction of Indian title to lands was acquired by treaty, and by the same process the new home set apart from time to time for the residence of the tribe was assured to it, with the covenant in the treaty that such new home should be the permanent home of the tribe FOREVER. Such covenants, though solemnly entered into by the government, were not regarded. Whenever the progress of settlement brought the white man's residence near the Indian's home, another treaty was demanded. If the tribe was unwilling to surrender this " permanent home," and no other means were found adequate to bring the Indians into negotiation, in due time, through complications of some sort, there was what was termed an " Indian outbreak," rapidly followed by a conflict, terminating in another removal.

The effect of these removals, so often repeated, has at all times worked injury to the Indians, and proved fatal to their advancement. Under the operation some tribes have yielded in despair. Others that survived did not recover from or overcome the fatal results for generations. Communities of our own race could not undergo like trials without serious loss in numbers as well as vitality ; and, if repeated, as in the case of the Indians, who have so often been removed, they would relapse into a very low grade of civilization. When the facts are considered, there should be no surprise that our Indian wards have not advanced more rapidly.

Superadded to the affliction growing out of these frequent removals, other and numerous difficulties have been placed in the path of the Indians. Even the most beneficent measures of the government looking to his advancement have, in many cases, been counteracted by the agencies employed to execute them; agents have frequently proved faithless, and soldiers sent to protect the tribes have not only been cruel and vindictive, but often have introduced demoralization and carried disease among them. In fact (though it may seem paradoxical), it is yet true, that the white man's conduct and example, instead of aiding, has been the chief obstacle in the way of the civilization of the Indian.

In 1826, the then secretary of war said this Indian question was a most solemn one, and that it addressed itself "to the American people, whose answer was full of responsibility. . . Shall we go on quietly in a course which, judging from the past, *threatens their extinction, while their past sufferings and future prospects so pathetically appeal to our compassion?*" Twenty years later, the attorney-general of the United States said "there is nothing in the whole compass of our laws so hard to bring within any precise definition, or logical or scientific arrangement, as the relation in which the Indian stands toward the United States." And the report of the peace commission, of the date of January 7, 1868, said: "Nobody pays any attention to Indian matters. This is a deplorable fact. Members of Congress understand the negro question, and talk learnedly on finance and political economy, but when the progress of settlement reaches the Indian's home, the only question considered is 'how best to get his lands.' When they are obtained, the Indian is lost sight of. While our missionary societies and benevolent associations have annually collected thousands of dollars from the charitable to send to Asia and Africa, for the purposes of civilization, scarcely a dollar is expended or a thought bestowed on the civilization of the Indians at our very doors."

Is it not time that a change should take place? Is it not time that the government and people of the United States should resolve that justice and fair dealing shall be substituted for that coldness, sordid selfishness, and cruelty which the native race has endured in all the years of the past? The Indian is not only entitled to justice at our hands, but we should extend to the race our earnest sympathy and aid. Our wards should have our best efforts for the amelioration of their condition. There are among them many men of worth, with natural gifts equal to those possessed by our own race; and, with a fair and equal chance in the battle of life, there should be no doubt as to the willingness of the Indian to accept our civilization, or of his capability to become a useful member of society. Let the red man have what he never has had, appropriate protection and support, and fair opportunity. Let him be emancipated from every evil and adverse influence, and lifted up and pressed forward in the new life. Let us deal with him as we would be dealt by. In short, let us admit that he is a MAN, and treat him as such, not spasmodically, but persistently, constantly, and in every relation of life.

To begin, let him have a fixed and settled home. This is imperative. Let him be distressed no more with the fear and apprehension that this home will be taken from him. Many of the reservations on which the Indians now reside are not suitable as to location or the quality of the land embraced within them. They have been selected in exigencies arising at the time, and without any regard to their adaptability to the uses intended. However afflicting it may be, there is an absolute necessity that some of these reservations be recast. This is demanded by the true interests of both races. Some tribes have tracts so barren, that, no matter how desirous they may be to engage in cultivation, they must be debarred the privilege; others are so located as to expose them at all times to trespass from the whites, and, thus disturbed, they must fail in their efforts. There are in the Western States and Territories nearly an hundred different reservations, in all aggregating about 180,000,000 acres of land. The report of the Indian office, for 1878, estimates that, of this land, about 18,000,000 of acres are tillable. It is believed this estimate of tillable land is too large. There is, however, too much territory in a number of the reservations, and it is clear that there are too many of them. In recasting and reducing the number, by consolidation or otherwise, the greatest care should be taken, since the change and re-location of those whose true interests require it, should be final. In discussing this phase of the Indian question, in the *North American Review*, in 1873, Francis A. Walker, a former commissioner of Indian affairs, said :

" It is manifest, therefore, that the next five or ten years must witness a general recasting of the scheme of Indian reservations. This is not to be accomplished by confiscating the Indian title, but by exchange, by concession, by consolidation. Let Congress provide the necessary authority, under proper limitations for the executive departments, and the adjustment desired can be reached easily and amicably." Six years have passed since this suggestion was made, but Congress has taken no step looking to the consummation of the work. It should be done at once, and with the utmost care. No tribe should have assigned to it, for a permanent home, a reservation that does not contain sufficient tillable land. On this point there should be absolute certainty, and the title to the tract assigned should be as perfect and good as that by which the government conveys its quarter sections to actual settlers. This done, and a great point will be gained. The mind of the Indian will, for the first time, be at rest on a question that has disturbed his ancestor as well as himself. To each head of a family there should, within the reservation, be assigned a homestead. The number of acres in it should be sufficiently large, but not excessive. He should be taught that he is the proprietor, with the right to exercise jurisdiction over his farm, and be secured in the enjoyment of all he produces upon it. The title to the land should remain in the tribe, since the Indians are generally not prepared for fee-simple titles. In years to come, these may be granted.

When the tribe is permanently located on the reservation, and the integrity of the same is placed beyond question, and when those disposed to intrude upon the possessions of the red man understand, that if done, it is at their peril, and that certain and swift punishment will follow, the work of the agent may be successfully prosecuted. This should be confided to none but men of the highest character for integrity, of good executive ability, and industrious habits. Such men will not have, among their subordinates, any who are unworthy. At times, indeed too often, the Indians have suffered much for want of agents with proper qualifications. While firm in the discharge of their duties, both the agent and his employes, when engaged in the instruction and direction of the Indian in his work and labor, will do well to offer to the savage the reason why this thing be done and the other omitted. He is the pupil; they the instructors. In this most important matter a military agent will always fail. His education, training, and discipline are not in the right direction to qualify him to discharge the duties of an Indian agent. From the highest to the lowest in rank, it is the duty of the subordinate to obey orders. The reason why a particular command is given is not explained. To the soldier this is not necessary or proper; but the instruction of the savage is quite a different thing, and the Indian agent who, on all proper occasions, devotes a few minutes in unfolding to the mind of the Indian why he should do as instructed, will find

it time well spent. Firmness and kindness should go hand
in hand. This will not interfere with reformatory discipline.
In all cases where Indians can be utilized about the labor of
the agency it should be done, and no white employes, except
such as can not be dispensed with, should be in the service.
The young men of the tribe will gladly take hold of and discharge the duties assigned them, and they will be trustworthy and faithful. Competent men, to act as Indian
agents, are to be found in many tribes, and it would be well
to give some of these positions as such.

The Indian women must cease to do the outdoor work, and
confine themselves to domestic duties and the cares of the
house and the family. The labor in the garden and the field
must be done by the men and boys. To the nomad, this
change will be a great innovation; but the step being taken
by one, others will follow, and, with proper prompting and
encouragement, accessions will continually be made to the
ranks of labor. The methods that succeed in one case may,
for the time, seem to fail in another. The reason will be
found in the surrounding circumstances. Every phase of the
problem must be studied by the agent in charge, and, if faithful, diligent, and patient, he will soon surmount all difficulties. That the Indians who are well advanced in years will
desire to adhere to their savage customs may be expected.
Many of these will yield, and, when the change comes, such
will embrace the pursuits of civilized life with earnestness,
and succeed admirably. As the habit of roaming must cease,
and all Indians have their fixed homes, the young of both
sexes will always be within reach, and then an inviting and
interesting field will be open, not only for the work of the
agent, but for the Christian missionary. With reference to
missionary work among the Indians, it may be stated that
the various religious denominations in the United States, dur-

ing the year 1877, contributed for educational and other purposes, among all the tribes except the Cherokee, Choctaw,
Chickasaw, Creek, and Seminole Indians, the sum of $70,114,
as follows: For education, $33,950; for all other purposes,
$36,164. The statistics in the annual report of the Indian
office, for the year 1877, are authority for this statement.

From the same report, it is shown that many tribes have
not a single missionary among them. Those thus situate number, in the aggregate, from 60,000 to 70,000 souls! This is
a sad story. The annual contributions made for missionary
purposes, by the membership of the various religious denominations in the United States, amount to millions of dollars.
The mere statement of this fact, in connection with the other
fact—that, of the vast sum contributed, the mission boards of
the various denominations set off barely $70,000 per year for
school and mission work among our native heathen—is well
calculated to produce profound surprise. That such cold indifference should exist in the Christian world toward these
hapless people, is a source of deep regret.

With reference to the protection of the person and property of each Indian, and to provide for the punishment of
such members of the tribe as trespass upon his farm, as well
as for the punishment of minor offenses committed by one
Indian against another, within the reservation, a brief and
simple code of regulations, with proper penalties, prepared
by the department, and adopted by the Indians in council,
will be all sufficient; and an Indian police, limited in number,
will suffice to give efficiency and force to them; and thus
order will be preserved. Then, Congress should, in good
faith, by appropriate legislation, fulfill the pledge made in the
ordinance of 1787, and pass such laws, "founded in justice
and humanity," as may be necessary to protect the Indian
race "in their property, rights, and liberty." Every senti-

ment of justice demands that this be done at once.   The fact
that nearly a century has passed since this ordinance was
adopted, and that no adequate legislation has been provided,
in pursuance of it, to guarantee to the Indian his rights, is a
burning shame.   Let there be no further delay.   The present
laws for the protection of the Indians from intrusion, trespass,
and personal injury by lawless whites, are wholly inadequate.
The attention of Congress has repeatedly been called to this
fact.   It is true that it is made the duty of the military arm,
in certain cases, to remove intruders from the Indian lands,
but this duty is seldom discharged.   On the contrary, the
troops have been frequently used to punish the Indians, because they did not quietly submit to wrong and oppression,
and the invasion of their rights and territory.   Unlawful expeditions into the Indian reservations have been made, under
the protection and escort of our troops—such, for instance, as
the invasion of the Black Hills, in 1874, guarded by troops,
with Gattling guns, under command of Gen. Custer.   He
acted under the authority of his superiors, and with the
knowledge of the interior department.   This expedition was
not to put down any insubordination among the Sioux, nor
was it authorized by Congress.   It was simply a gold-hunting
invasion, and invited miners into the Hills.   The next year,
owing to the dissatisfaction of the Sioux, Gen. Crook was
sent there to drive out the intruders, who, by the bad example set them in 1874, had rushed in; but his sympathies were
with the invaders, and his troops were finally turned upon
the Indians; and thus began the Sioux war of 1876.

To obtain from Congress appropriate legislation, and the
passage of such laws as will effectually protect our Indian
wards in all their personal and property rights, will be a difficult matter.   If the people, however, who are the source of
power, take hold of the subject with that earnestness which

its importance demands, and make known to their servants what their wishes are, the result will be accomplished. To give force and vigor to the administration of Indian affairs, the bureau should be emancipated from the interior as well as the war department. The secretary of the interior is now burdened with the vast business and duties of five distinct bureaus, viz., pension, land, patent, education, and Indian. He can not give to the latter that patient attention, and bestow upon it the labor, its importance demands, and which is absolutely necessary. Of themselves, the business and duties of the Indian bureau are sufficient to engross the entire time, attention, and labor of one possessed of the highest grade of executive ability. No other work should disturb his mind, or occupy his time. On this subject, the peace commission of 1867–8 said :

" We believe the Indian question to be one of such momentous importance, as respects both the honor and the interests of the nation, as to require for its solution an undivided responsibility. The vast and complicated duties now devolved upon the secretary of the interior, leave him too little time to examine and determine the multiplicity of questions necessarily connected with the government of a race. The same may be said of the secretary of war. As things now are, it is difficult to fix responsibility. When errors are committed, the civil department blames the military; the military retort by the charge of inefficiency and corruption against the officers of the bureau. The commissioner of Indian affairs escapes responsibility by pointing to the secretary of the interior, while the secretary may well respond that, though in theory he may be responsible, practically he is governed by the head of the bureau. We, therefore, recommend that Indian affairs be committed to an independent department."

The Sioux commission of 1876, in referring to the evils existing in the management of Indian affairs, said :

" We submit that the remedy for these evils is not to be found by again placing the care of the Indians in the war department. It had this duty for near three-quarters of a century, and during the whole period there is no page in the history of our Indian management upon which our recollection can linger with emotions of pleasure. . . . Our Indian affairs should be managed by an independent department. It ought to have at its head one of the first men of the nation, whose recommendations would be heeded, and who, as a member of the cabinet, could confer with the heads of the war and interior departments, and devise such wise and just plans as would equally protect the rights of the Indians and our own citizens. . . . The head of the interior department is now burdened with five distinct bureaus. He can not give to Indian affairs that patient attention which is necessary to success. The war department, as its name indicates, is unsuited for the work of civilization. Officers of the army are not fitted, by inclination or training, to teach Indian children to read and write, or Indian men to sow and reap."

In the tables of statistics, accompanying the report of the commissioner of Indian affairs, for 1878, it is stated that the number of Indians who wear citizen's dress is 127,450. Of these 61,467 are males, and 65,983 are females. The number of houses occupied by Indians is 23,060. Of schools, there are among the Indians 60 boarding and 306 day schools. The number of scholars attending these schools is 12,222. Of these, 6,631 are males and 5,591 are females. The number of children of school age is estimated at 49,200. In· this estimate some tribes are not reported. The actual number of school age in all the tribes is probably 55,000. The number of Indians who can read is stated at 41,300.   There was expended for education during the year $353,125.   Of this sum, the five civilized tribes appropriated $137,775.   The number of church buildings, including those among the five civilized tribes, in the " Indian Territory," is 219 ; and the number of missionaries, including such as are among the five tribes referred to, is 226.

The five civilized tribes cultivated during the year 245,000 acres of land ; the product from which was 494,400 bushels of wheat, 2,642,000 bushels of corn, 201,000 bushels of oats and barley, 320,000 bushels of vegetables, and 116,500 tons of hay.   They own 40,000 horses, 4,750 mules, 236,000 cattle, 173,000 hogs, and 25,500 sheep.

Other Indian tribes than the five referred to cultivated during the year 128,018 acres of land ; the product from which was 266,100 bushels of wheat, 971,303 bushels of corn, 172,697 bushels of oats and barley, 315,585 bushels of vegetables, 36,943 tons of hay, 193 tons of melons, and 697 tons of pumpkins.   There were 22,319 acres of new land broken during the year, and 128,056 rods of fencing made.   There were during the year 2,351 allotments of land made to full-blooded Indians.   The Indians other than the five tribes owned 176,766 horses, 4,479 mules, 52,867 cattle, 27,671 hogs, and 510,674 sheep.

Other results from Indian labor were 8,100,630 feet of lumber sawed, 132,888 cords of wood cut, 200,600 shingles made, 387,000 pounds of maple sugar made, 146,000 pounds of wild rice gathered, 17,000 woolen blankets and shawls made, 2,530 willow baskets made, 3,800 cords of hemlock bark peeled for sale, 211,000 pounds of wool sold, and 3,600 barrels of fish sold.

When we call to mind the fact that by the treaties of 1867–8 with the Sioux, Cheyenne, Arapahoe, the Comanche,

Kiowa, and other wild tribes, who had always lived by the chase, it was left with such of them as chose to do so to lead the life of nomads, and that this wild life was sanctioned by Congress, and specific appropriations made for the benefit of such as roamed and hunted, and the further fact that the lands in the reservations of a number of tribes are not susceptible of cultivation, the statistics given, with the product of the labor of those engaged in agricultural and pastoral life, should be sufficient to satisfy the most skeptical that our Indian wards can be made self-supporting, and that with proper care and attention this result may be reached in a very few years.

The opinion that the Indian population is destined in a brief period to disappear prevails to a very great extent among the masses of our people. This is regarded as the unavoidable result of contact with civilization. A careful study of the census of this population through a series of years, with an examination of vital statistics for the past four years, will satisfy the reader that this opinion must be modified, and the conclusion will be reached that the Indians, instead of vanishing, are destined to be and remain with us for ages to come. It is undoubtedly true that from a multiplicity of causes many of the weaker tribes have ceased to exist as such, while the more favored, as well as the more robust ones, have passed through the fearful ordeal, and are slowly increasing in numbers. In 1825 the population of the Cherokee nation, including the half-breeds among them, was 15,000. Between that period and the time of their removal to their present reservation they suffered loss from wars and other causes. In the process of removal they lost nearly one-fourth of their number, and during our late civil war Cherokee troops were engaged in the conflict, and hence suffered loss; and yet by the census of 1878 it is seen that the Cherokees have a population of 21,072. The Chickasaws numbered 2,000 more in 1878 than in 1825. The Delawares now in the Indian Territory show a slight increase over their number in 1854. The population of the Iroquois in New York and Canada in 1877 was 13,668, which considerably exceeds any previous trustworthy estimate of their number for more than a century. Other tribes show a like result. On the other hand, some tribes show a decline in their numbers, the causes for which the careful student of the Indian problem will have no difficulty in reaching. It is a fact that all wild Indians, for a period after the process of civilization begins, diminish in numbers. The use of the white man's food, the restraint from roaming, and the ill-ventilated huts in which they dwell, increases disease, and checks for the time being procreation. In the present state of transition, it is said some Dakota families bear no children. There is one source of diminution by which the census of Indian tribes is reduced which is not real. It is not uncommon at this day for Indian families, who have advanced in civilization more rapidly than their fellows, to sever the tribal relation and become merged with the population in the white settlements. Among the Minnesota Sioux this process is going on with some force.

Within a few years the matter of vital statistics has had considerable attention from the Indian office, and the results are encouraging. From these Mr. S. N. Clark, of the bureau of education, has compiled a table of births and deaths in those tribes whose reports contain information on the subject for the years 1874, 1875, and 1876. The result is as follows: 1874, births, 2,152; deaths, 1,490; 1875, births, 1,985; deaths, 1,601; 1876, births, 2,401; deaths, 2,215. According to the same reports, the number of Indians that received medical treatment, in 1874, was 27,553; in 1875, 46,594; in 1876, 37,232. To attempt to deduce a ratio from these figures would, said Mr. Clark, yield false results, since the tribes that reported births and deaths from year to year varied. With this explanation, Mr. Clark gives the following figures : In 1874, the births in tribes numbering 48,000 were 1,495 ; the deaths in tribes numbering 63,772 were 1,047 ; in 1875, the births in tribes numbering 74,417 were 1,905 ; and the deaths in tribes numbering 99,309 were 1,566; in 1876, the births in tribes numbering 81,734 were 2,386; and the deaths in tribes numbering 90,590 were 2,195. While this data may not warrant any definite conclusions as to the tendency and ratio of increase, there is sufficient in the figures to dispel the theory, which is so commonly held, that the Indian race is vanishing, and, from natural causes, will soon disappear.

To such of our fellow-citizens as do not feel impelled by the promptings of their better natures and the feelings of humanity to take an interest in the proper solution of the Indian question, the fact that these wards of ours, and their descendants, are destined to be and remain upon the soil for generations, should, from a selfish standpoint, attract their most serious attention. The amount of money disbursed in the payment of annuities and for rations, clothing, and all else connected with the legitimate expenditures of the Indian department, is much less than the amount drawn from the treasury to carry on unjust and cruel wars against the Indians. These wars are exceedingly expensive. As an instance : in 1835, a war was begun with the Seminole Indians, in Florida. A few years preceding, Gen. Porter, then secretary of war, estimated the population of these Indians at 4,000. In 1835, Gen. Jackson, then president, was of the opinion that their military strength was about 500 warriors, while Gen. Cass, his secretary of war, estimated the warriors at 750. Lieut. C. A. Harris, then on duty in the Indian service, reported to the war department that the entire Seminole nation, their negroes included, did not exceed 3,000, and could not bring into the field more than 500 efficient warriors. Gen. Scott, then commanding the troops operating against the Seminoles, in a report, made on the 30th of April, 1836, said : " I am more than ever persuaded that the whole force of the enemy, including negroes, does not exceed 1,200 fighting men. It is probably something less." In 1837, the Indian office gave the number of " Florida Indians," east of the Mississippi, and " under treaty stipulations to remove," at 5,000. During the war the Seminoles had some accessions from the Creeks and from fugitive slaves who had joined them, but the number of both was not large. The war lasted seven years. The whole available force of the regular army was engaged in the combat, and Generals Scott, Clinch, Gaines, Eustis, Jessup, and Worth, with many other experienced and distinguished officers, were on duty. It was in this war that Col. Zachary Taylor, who, in 1848, was elected President of the United States, suggested the use of blood-hounds to accompany the troops operating against the Seminoles. The suggestion was approved, and the animals were brought into use to hunt down the Indians ! In addition to the whole force of the regular army, a portion of the navy, and in the aggregate, during the war, more than 20,000 volunteers, were brought into service. In the second year of the war (1836), Gen. Jessup entered the field at the head of one column of 8,000 troops, well provided with all the materials and equipments of war. He had as allies several battalions of Creek Indian warriors. Choctaws and Delawares also joined his standard. This one single Indian war cost upwards of forty millions of dollars ! In this war the losses among the troops in the regular army and in the navy were 1,555, and among the volunteers the losses were equal, if they did not exceed that number ; making the aggregate of our losses more than three thousand men.

The losses of the Seminoles were not known. Indians always strive to carry off their dead from the battle-field, and conceal the number. Some years after the close of this war, the Seminole Indians were removed to the Indian Territory, in which, on a portion of the Creek reservation, they now dwell. A remnant remained in Florida, and still dwells there, and number about 500, and those in the Indian Territory now number 2,500. This Seminole war was inaugurated to drive the Indians out of Florida, when, by an expenditure of a quarter of a million of money, a peaccable removal, without the intervention of the military arm, could, without any doubt, have been effected.

In the preparation of this work there has been no attempt to present a continuous history of the Indian race, or the conflicts with it from the time of the discovery of America. In the most condensed form, such a narrative would fill volumes, and would, in some sense, be a mere repetition, since the story of one Indian war is the story of all. In what is narrated in the several chapters, it has been the object of the author to adhere to facts, and to give a faithful relation of the various forms in which complications with the Indians arise, and the manner in which the civil as well as the military authorities deal with the wards of the government. In what is stated in relation to the assumptions and conduct of the military arm toward the Indian tribes, there is nothing extenuate nor aught set down in malice. It is submitted that the facts given ought to silence, now and hereafter, the clamor in which military officers have indulged against the civil administration of Indian affairs, and forever dispose of the question of the restoration of the Indian bureau to the war department—a theme on which these officers (with but few exceptions) have indulged, with an assurance amounting to audacity.

Should the work have any agency in arousing the public mind, and quickening the conscience of the people, to the end that our Indian wards may, in some degree, have that attention which is demanded by every sentiment of justice and every impulse of humanity, so that oppression and cruelty shall give place to just and fair treatment, and thus their path of life be made not only bearable, but strewn with such aid, instruction, and sympathy as will win them from their wild life, and induce them to accept the comforts of civilization and a settled home, the writer will be abundantly repaid for his labor. That a better and brighter day may speedily come to the despised Indian, should be the aspiration and prayer of every man and woman in our broad land, and all should earnestly and faithfully labor for such reforms as will secure exact justice in our dealings with, and thus assure the civilization of, our Indian Wards.

GEO. W. MANYPENNY.

January 20, 1880.

OUR INDIAN WARDS.

CHAPTER I.

THE early explorers that visited the "New World" were
met by the native inhabitants in the most friendly manner.
The utmost confidence was reposed in the strangers, and such
rude hospitalities as the natives possessed were freely extended
to them. All early annals are agreed on this fact. The kindness and confidence of the natives was not reciprocated. The
adventurers, whether Spanish, French, Dutch, or English, did
not, in their intercourse with the Indians, so conduct themselves as to confirm the good will bestowed upon them. They
were from the very beginning distrustful, exacting, and over-
bearing, and there was scarcely a vessel that left on its return
trip that did not carry off some of the natives, who were frequently forcibly seized for that purpose.

The voyagers, whether among the natives on our shores, or
on their vessels homeward bound, frequently acted like demi-
savages toward such Indians as were in their power, and very
early the practice of kidnaping them to sell them into slavery
was commenced. Some pretended that they only seized and
carried off the natives as trophies of the voyage, or to serve as
guides for future expeditions, and while this may be true in
exceptional cases, the chief purpose was to traffic in them as
chattels. Others were ready on the slightest provocation, or
even without provocation, to take the lives of the Indians
whenever opportunity offered.

Such conduct was well calculated to and did destroy the
confidence of the Indians, and distrust, and finally hatred, took
its place, and they were ready to avenge the wrongs suffered

by their kindred whenever opportunity offered, and upon such
of the white race as fell in their way. Their mode of retaliation was of course barbarous, such as all savage people practice. It must not, however, be forgotten that they were not
the aggressors, and that their provocation was great.

The native population was sparse, and the country, vast in
extent, was in a state of nature, if we except the very slight
modification made by the rude dwellings in the Indian villages and the fields and gardens adjacent. These villages
were generally surrounded by palisades of logs and brush-
wood. In addition to the product of the chase, the food of
the Indian was fish, maize, pumpkins, beans, wild rice, and
roots. Their arms were the bow and arrow, the war club and
spear. Their implements of husbandry were of the rudest
kind. Each village had its chiefs, and frequently a number
of villages in the same locality formed a sort of confederacy,
with superior chiefs exercising authority over the whole.
The inhabitants of the villages were, in their intercourse,
sociable and friendly. Disputes were rare. Their chief subjects of conversation were tribal affairs, and hunting and
fishing. No one thought of interrupting his neighbor when
speaking. All were glad to receive visitors. No profane
language was used. Indeed, the Indians had no words applicable to profanity. When a stranger took refuge among
them, it was regarded a sacred duty to extend hospitality to
such an one, and to refuse succor or relief was a grave offense.
In war, their conduct toward their enemies was barbarous.
Their wardrobe was scanty, and made of the skins of animals.

Such, in brief, was the condition of the Indian population
near the Atlantic coast at the time of the discovery of North
America. As from time to time the Indians became accustomed to the ways and manners of the Europeans, they admitted the superiority of the latter in the arts, but expressed
contempt for them because they submitted to laborious em-
ployments. They thought their advantages in hunting and
fishing gave them precedence over the Europeans, and that in
their moral conduct they were superior to the refinements
which the latter brought with them. They were quite loathe
to exchange their modes of living for such as were introduced

by the new comers, and maintained that it was not in accordance with the design of the Great Spirit that they should do so.

The reports which the explorers carried home in relation to the value of the newly discovered lands, in time had its effect upon the different European powers, and they set about to possess them. Each endeavored to excel in founding colonies in the "New World." It was at that time held by the Christian states of Europe that newly discovered countries belonged to the discoverer, and that while exceptions might be made in favor of the native inhabitants who were Christians, such natives as were not Christians were regarded as proper subjects, not only for conquest, but for plunder. The commission granted by the English king to Cabot, was somewhat similar to that previously granted to Columbus by Ferdinand and Isabella, except that in the latter case Spain bore the expense of the outfit and voyage, while England left Cabot to provide the means himself. Cabot's commission authorized him, or either of his sons, their heirs or deputies, to sail with a fleet in search of islands, or regions inhabited by infidels, and hitherto unknown to Christendom, to take possession of the same in the name of the king of England, " and as his vassals to conquer, possess, and occupy the same, enjoying for themselves, their heirs and assigns forever, the sole right of trading thither, paying to the king in lieu of customs and imposts a fifth of all net profits." It would be interesting to incorporate the various patents granted by European monarchs to the differents explorers who came out to possess the " New World," as well as the proceedings which took place at the ostentatious dedication of each particular tract of country, together with the conduct of the colonists toward the natives who happened to reside in regions where the first settlements were made. A single example in each case will have to suffice. Sparks has given from the " Proces-Verbal" in the French archives, the procedure of La Salle on the banks of the Mississippi, near its mouth, in appropriating a vast country and vesting the title in the same to France. After preparing a column and affixing to the same a cross and the arms of France, with an appropriate inscription, the whole party under arms chanted the *Te Deum*, the *Exaudiat*, the *Domine Salvum fac Regum*, and then, after a salute of fire-arms and cries of *Vive le Roi*, the column was erected by M. de La Salle, who, standing near it, said :

"In the name of the most high, mighty, invincible, and victorious Prince, *Louis the Great*, by the grace of God, King of France and of Navarre, fourteenth of that name, I, in virtue of the commission of his majesty, which I hold in my hand, and which may be seen by all whom it may concern, have taken, and do now take, in the name of his majesty, and of his successors to the crown, possession of this country of Louisiana, the seas, harbors, ports, bays, adjacent straits, and all the nations, peoples, provinces, cities, towns, villages, mines, minerals, fisheries, streams, and rivers comprised in the extent of said Louisiana, from the mouth of the great river St. Louis, on the eastern side, otherwise called Ohio, Allighan, Scipo, or Chickagua, and this with the consent of the Chavarons, Chickasaws, and other people dwelling therein, with whom we have made alliance; also along the river Colbert, or Mississippi, and rivers which discharge themselves therein, from its source beyond the country of the Kiows, or Nadouessious, and this with the consent of the Montantees, Illinois, Mesigameas, Natchez, Koroas, which are the most considerable nations dwelling therein, with whom, also, we have made alliance, either by ourselves or others in our behalf, as far as its mouth at the sea, or Gulf of Mexico, about the twenty-seventh degree of the elevation of the north pole, and also to the mouth of the river Palms ; upon the assurance which we have received from all these nations, that we are the first Europeans that have descended or ascended the said river Colbert, hereby protesting against all those who may in future undertake to invade any or all of these countries, peoples, or lands above described, to the prejudice of the right of his majesty, acquired by the consent of the nations herein named. Of which, and all that can be needed, I hereby take to witness those who hear me, and demand an act of the notary, as required by law."

To which the whole assembly responded with shouts of *Vive le Roi* and with salutes of fire-arms. Moreover the said Sieur de La Salle caused to be buried at the foot of the tree, to which the cross was attached, a leaden plate, on one side of which was engraved the arms of France, with a Latin inscription. La Salle then remarked that his majesty, as the eldest son of the church, would not annex any country to his crown without making it his chief care to establish the Christian religion therein, and its symbol must now be planted, which was accordingly done at once by erecting a cross, before which the *Vesilla* and *Domine Salvum fac Regum* were sung, to all which his associates, thirteen in number, attached the certificate " required by law," one of them acting as notary. And thus the foundation of the claim of France to the Mississippi valley was laid " fairly," according to the usages of European powers. Sparks observes that " there is an obscurity in this enunciation of places and Indian nations, which may be ascribed to an ignorance of the geography of the country, but it seems to be the design of Sieur de La Salle to take possession of the whole country watered by the Mississippi, from its mouth to its source, and by the streams flowing into it on both sides." As a matter of course, conflicts grew out of these appropriations of the territory of the " New World," some of which were only settled by the force of arms, and all of which resulted disastrously to the Indians.

Anterior to the grant by France to La Salle, James I. of England granted a charter by which the American coast between the thirty-fourth and forty-fifth degrees of north latitude was set apart to be colonized by two rival companies—one composed chiefly of adventurers from London ; the other from those residing in the west of England, known as the Plymouth and Bristol company. James' motive, as alleged in the charter, was the advancement of the divine glory, " by bringing the Indians and savage residents of those parts to human civility and a settled and quiet government." These companies were known as the London and Plymouth companies. The first was designated as the first Virginia colony, and permitted to occupy and plant anywhere between the thirty-fourth and forty-second degrees of north latitude. The Plymouth was designated as the second Virginia colony, and might occupy and plant anywhere between the thirty-eighth and forty-fifth degrees of north latitude, but neither was to occupy any country within a hundred miles of the first settlement previously made by the other. Each colony was to extend along the coast fifty miles either way from the point first occupied, and from the same point inward or seaward one hundred miles. Each company was authorized to search for mines, paying the king for the yield thereof, one-fifth of all gold and silver, and one-fifteenth of all copper. It was made the especial duty of the councils governing these colonies to provide that "the true word and service of God, according to the rites and service of the Church of England, be preached, planted, and used in the colonies, and among the neighboring savages." In process of time, and after many complications, the London, or first Virginia company, obtained a new charter, and was created a corporation, under the title of "The Treasurer and Company of Adventurers and Planters of the City of London, for the first colony of Virginia." In the new charter a distinct and separate grant of territory was provided for. Subsequently the Plymouth company applied for a similar grant, but this was opposed by the London company. After years of solicitation the Plymouth company succeeded in obtaining a new charter, known as the "Great Patent." By this charter all North America, from the fortieth to the forty-eighth degree of north latitude, excepting only such places as were then actually possessed by any other Christian prince or people was granted, with exclusive right of jurisdiction, settlement, and traffic, and incorporated as "The Council established at Plymouth, in the county of Devon, for the Planting, Ruling, Ordering, and Governing of New England in America." In the interval between the granting of the first and second patents to the London and Plymouth companies, disorder was prevalent among the colonists, the Indians suffered sadly, and as opportunity offered they retaliated.

In the progress of time and growing out of religious dissensions in England, a body of men known as the Pilgrims determined to remove, and had actually escaped to Holland, where they resided for some years. They did not, however, like the manners and customs of the Dutch, and determined to emigrate to Virginia, provided they were allowed a settlement to themselves, where they could arrange religious matters to suit their own views and ideas. Two of their principal men went to England as agents, and through their efforts the company agreed to give the Pilgrims a grant of land, but other guarantees were not obtained. After further negotiation they decided to emigrate, leaving John Robinson, one of their preachers, at Leyden, with such of his congregation as were not ready to embark, or not thought fit for pioneers. After a fast and religious service, under Brewster, one of the ruling elders, the adventurers took passage on the Speedwell, to Southampton. Here they were joined by Cushman, in the Mayflower, which was hired for the voyage, to convey the outfit and provisions. They immediately embarked, distributing the passengers between the vessels, but the Speedwell proved unseaworthy and was discharged. Some of her passengers went on board the Mayflower. About twenty, including Cushman, unwillingly remained behind. They had a tedious voyage of more than two months, when the ship entered Cape Cod harbor. The colonists, finding they were not in the limits of the Virginia company, whose grant they had obtained, thought it fit before landing, in view of the fact that there were some indications of insubordination, to draw up an agreement for their social government. Before it was executed they offered up thanksgiving for their preservation on the voyage, and prayers for future guidance. By the agreement which they signed, they mutually promised to obey such "just and equal laws and ordinances" as from time to time should be thought necessary and for the common good. The colony consisted of one hundred and one persons. John Carver was chosen to act as governor for one year. It was the 10th of November, 1620, when the Mayflower entered Cape Cod harbor. A month intervened before the colonists disembarked. The interval was occupied in coasting along the shore. Exploring parties occasionally landed and were sent inland to make explorations. Frequently these parties found deserted Indian wigwams, and at one point a quantity of corn, in baskets, buried in the sand. This was taken possession of and served for seed the next spring. Occasionally,

Indians were seen, and at one time, probably incensed at the loss of the corn, some of them showed signs of hostility, but disappeared without molesting the Pilgrims. The natives in the region of Cape Cod were not without previous experience with the whites. Both French and English adventurers had been there, and their intercourse with the natives was not such as to impress these simple people favorably. A single instance of perfidy, out of many committed by the whites, will satisfy the reader that the Indians had cause to look upon the Europeans with suspicion. It occurred in 1614, and is narrated by Captain John Smith, who, after stating that they spent a long time in trying to catch whales, without success, and as for finding gold, " it was rather the master's device to get a voyage that projected it." He says that for trifles they got " near 1,100 beaver skins, 100 martin, and many otters, the most of them within the distance of twenty leagues." On his departure for Europe, the captain remarks thus: " The other ship stayed to fit herself for Spain with dried fish, which was sold at Malaga for four rials the quintal, each hundred weight two quintals and a half. But one Thomas Hunt, the master of this ship (when I was gone), thinking to prevent that intent I had to make there a plantation, thereby to keep this abounding country still in obscurity, that only he and some few merchants more might enjoy wholly the benefit of trade and profit of this country, betrayed four and twenty of these poor salvages aboard his ship, and most dishonestly and inhumanly, for their kind usage of me and all our men, carried them with him to Malaga, and there for a little private gain, sold these silly salvages for rials of eight; but this vile act kept him. ever after from any more employment to those parts."

The great event in the history of New England, *the landing of the Pilgrims*, took place on the 11th December, 1620. On the 7th of December the boat's crew of explorers, who had " gone ranging up and down till the sun began to draw low," hastened out of the woods and returned to their shallop. About midnight some Indians appeared, and the event is thus described in their journal: " About midnight we heard a great and hideous cry, and our sentinel called *arm! arm!* so we bestirred ourselves and shot off a couple of muskets, and the noise ceased. We concluded that it was a company of wolves and foxes, for one of our company told us that he had heard such a noise in Newfoundland. At five o'clock in the morning (December 8) we began to be stirring. Upon a sudden we heard a great and strange cry, which we knew to be the same voices, though they varied their notes. One of our company being ashore came running and cried, ' *They are men!* *Indians! Indians!'* and withal their arrows came flying among us. Our men ran out with all speed to recover their arms. The cry of our enemies was dreadful, especially when our men ran out to recover their arms. Their note was after this manner, ' *Woach, woach, ha ha, hach, woach.*' Our men were no sooner come to their arms but the enemy was ready to assault them. There was a lusty man, and no whit less valliant, who was thought to be their captain, stood behind a tree within half a musket shot of us, and there let his arrows fly at us. He stood three shots of a musket. At length one of us, as he said, taking full aim at him, he gave an extraordinary cry and away they all went." It was not known that any blood was shed in this first " battle," but presumed that the lusty man was wounded. The "conquerors" gathered up the trophies of their " victory," in all sixteen arrows, some of which were " headed with brass, some with hart's horn, and others with eagle's claws." These were all sent by the Pilgrims to their friends in England.

In speaking of an event that occurred previous to this attack, Morton says: " The Indians got all the powaws in the country, who for three days together, in a horrid and devilish manner, did curse and execrate them with their conjurations, which assembly and service they held in a dark and dismal swamp;" and adds, " Behold how Satan labored to hinder the Gospel from coming into New England."

Some time after the landing of the Pilgrims, a Wampanoag Indian, named Samoset, came to Plymouth. He could speak some broken English, having been much among the whites who came to fish at Monhiggon. His first salutation was: " *Welcome, Englishmen! Welcome, Englishmen!*" He gave the colonists much information. His residence was not in that region, but some five days' journey therefrom. "He told us (they say) the place where we now live is called Pautuxet, and that about four years ago all the inhabitants died of some extraordinary plague, and there is neither man, woman, nor child remaining, as indeed we have found none; so there is none to hinder our possession or lay claim to it."

After this singular people had sailed for America, James, their oppressor, had caused a charter to issue to them. Before they left home they had permission from this monarch to go out and settle in the wilderness, and they did not appear to have any scruple about taking possession of the country where they landed, although it was not within the limits of the Virginia colony. In the charter of James I. to the Pilgrims, which has become known as "*The Grand Plimouth Charter*," he said, "that he had been given certainly to knowe, that within these late years there hath, by God's visitation, reigned a wonderfull plague, together with many horrible slaughters and murthers, committed amongst the sauages and brutish people there heretofore inhabiting, in a manner to the utter destruction, deuastacion, and depopulacion of that whole territorye, so that there is not left, for many leagues together in a manner, any that do claime or challenge any kind of interest therein."

Thus assured by the charter of King James, and informed by Samoset that all the inhabitants of the region for "many leagues" had died of a great plague, and that neither man, woman, nor child remained, the good Pilgrims felt that they were providentially seized and possessed of a country wherein they could establish a system of religious worship such as they could not enjoy in their own native land. As the years passed and accessions were made to the English settlements, difficulties between the colonists and the natives frequently occurred, often resulting in the loss of life on both sides. In commenting upon these Drake says: "These affairs call for no commentary; that must accompany every mind through every step of the relation. It would be a weakness, as appears to us, to attempt a vindication of the rash conduct of the English." When Robinson, one of the fathers of the Plymouth Church, heard how his people (the Pilgrims) had conducted these affairs with the Indians, he wrote them to consider of the disposition of one of their number (Captain Standish), "who was of a warm temper," but he hoped that the Lord had sent him among them for a good end, if they used him as they should. "He doubted," he said, "whether there was not wanting that tenderness of the life of man, made after God's image," which was so necessary, and above all, that "it would have been happy if they had converted some before they had killed any."

In 1637, it was resolved in the Massachusetts colony to raise troops to make war on the Pequod Indians. Previous to this period there had been many conflicts with these Indians, in which the colonists were as barbarous in their mode of warfare as the Indians. Dr. Mather's writings contain such items as the following: "Some of Uncas' men being there at Saybrook, in order to assisting the English against the Pequods, espied seven Indians, and slily encompassing them, slew five of them, and took one prisoner and brought him to the English fort, which gave great satisfaction and encouragement to the English. . . . When the prisoner was executed, his limbs were by violence pulled from one another, and burned to ashes." Again, Dr. M. says, in sailing westward from Saybrook, "the wind not answering, they cast anchor. Some scattering Pequods were then taken and slain, as also the Pequod sachem, before expressed, had his head cut off, whence that place did bear the name of Sachem's Head."

The contemplated expedition against the doomed Pequods met with some delay after the troops were raised, and some had gone forward under Underhill to Fort Saybrook. There seemed to be no doubt in the minds of the colonists about the justness of the war, but it was thought the army "was too much a covenant with works." The expedition finally got ready to move, and "by a solemn public invocation of the word of God," a leader was designated by lot from among the magistrates. Stoughton was chosen as such, and a chaplain was also selected. While the Massachusetts party procrastinated, the Connecticut towns had sent forward a force which had been joined by those at Fort Saybrook, and led by Mason and Underhill, the Pequods were attacked while within their

fort or village, and asleep in their wigwams, and literally
annihilated. " The barking of a dog," says Drake, " was the
first notice they had of the approach of the enemy, yet very
few knew the cause of the alarm, until met by the naked
swords of the foe. The fort had two entrances at opposite
points, into which each party of the English were led, sword
in hand." Such was the surprise of the Indians "that they
made very feeble resistance. Having only their own missile
weapons, they could do nothing at hand to hand with the
English rapiers. They were pursued from wigwam to wigwam, and slaughtered in every secret place. Women and
children were cut to pieces while endeavoring to hide under
their beds. At length fire was set in the mats that covered
the wigwams, which furiously spread over the whole fort, and
the dead and dying were together consumed. A part of the
English had formed a circumference upon the outside, and
shot such as attempted to fly. Many ascended the pickets to
escape the flames, but were shot down by those stationed for
that purpose. About six hundred Pequods were supposed to
have perished in this fight, or perhaps I should say *massacre*.
There were but two English killed, and but one of these by
the enemy, and about twenty wounded. Sassacus himself
was in another fort, and being informed of the ravages of the
English, destroyed his habitations, and with about eighty
others fled to the Mohawks, who treacherously beheaded him
and sent his scalp to the English." Underhill, although engaged in the affair, says the colonists, " bereaved of pity, and
without compassion, kept up the fight within the fort, while
their Indian allies, forming a circle around, struck down every
Pequod who attempted to escape." He adds: " Great and
doleful was the bloody sight to the view of young soldiers, to
see so many souls lie gasping on the ground, so thick you
could hardly pass along."

Morton thus describes the termination of this massacre:
" At this time it was a fearful sight to see them thus frying in
the fire, and the streams of blood quenching the same, and
terrible was the stink and scent thereof, but the victory seemed
a sweet sacrifice, and they gave the praise thereof to God,
who had wrought so wonderfully for them, thus to inclose

their enemies in his hands, and give them so speedy a victory over so proud, insulting, and blasphemous an enemy." Dr. Mather, in speaking of the event, says: "It is supposed that no less than five or six hundred Pequod souls were brought down to hell that day."

The colonists believed that they were perfectly justified in this and other like acts against the Indians, and that their success was sufficient evidence that they had the divine approval for the destruction of the "bloody heathen." Underhill wrote: "We had sufficient light from the word of God for our proceedings;" and Mason, after reciting with exultation some portions of the Psalms, exclaimed: "Thus the Lord was pleased to smite our enemies in the hinder parts, and to give us their land for an inheritance." There were still a few Pequods remaining who were not in the fort. (This fort was situate near the present town of Groton, Connecticut.) Stoughton, with his forces, appeared about a fortnight after the slaughter, and, joined by Mason, set out to finish up the work. The Indians were hunted from swamp to swamp. At one place about one hundred were captured, twenty-two of whom were men. These were put to death; thirty women and children were given to the Narragansetts (then the allies of the colonists), and about fifty others sent to Boston, and from thence distributed as slaves to some of the principal colonists. Quite a number of adult male persons, that had from time to time fallen into the hands of the colonists, were sent to the West Indies and sold into slavery, and the women and children of such were made slaves at home. During Stoughton's campaign, he wrote the governor of Massachusetts as follows: "By this pinnace you shall receive forty-eight or fifty women and children, unless they stay here to be helpful, etc., concerning which there is one I formerly mentioned that is the fairest and largest that I saw among them, to whom I have given a coate to clothe her. It is my desire to have her for a servant, if it may stand with your good likeing, else not. There is a little squaw that steward Calicut desireth, to whom he hath given a coate. Lieut. Davenport also desireth one, to wit, a small one that hath three strokes upon the stomache. He desireth her if it shall stand with your good likeing." Thus were the Pequods exterminated. They were regarded by the Puritans as belonging to the " cursed race of Ham;" fit only to be rooted out and destroyed.

The feeling of the colonists toward the Pequods and the barbarous treatment and cruel murder of the entire tribe, discloses the general feeling of the whites toward the Indians at that period. Comparatively ignorant of the views and intentions of the Indians, the whites were distrustful, and hence in their intercourse with them they were from the beginning exacting and vindictive. As time advanced, the opinion grew among the colonists that the Indian was a cumberer of the ground; that he stood in the way of Christian civilization, and that they were justified in destroying him. It is true that there were exceptions among the whites, and a few men, of whom Eliot was a type, believed that the Indian, though a savage, was a man, and these labored among the natives with the spirit of true missionaries. Such men had a heavy burden to carry, but they labored incessantly to reclaim the savage and teach him the Christian faith. Under the teachings of these devoted men, there were by the beginning of what is known as King Philip's War about ten to twelve hundred converts, who were known as the " Preying Indians." Eliot, who managed the missionary funds, was admonished by the Puritans that they feared lest the converts " should only follow Christ for loaves and outward advantage." It was only by constant effort and importunity that he was enabled to overcome this suspicious fear, and obtain liberty from the colonists to organize a church at his Indian town. He, however, received but little aid for this enterprise from the colonists, and was compelled to rely mainly on contributions from friends in England to support it. When it is remembered that in the grants from European powers to their subjects who came out to plant colonies in North America, one avowed purpose was to propagate the gospel among the heathen, and that the New England colonists felt that the duty of laboring to convert the natives was obligatory on them, what actually occurred seems more like fiction than truth. The conduct of the colonists toward the natives was such as to precipitate conflicts, and hence the respect, and even veneration, manifested by the natives on the landing of the whites was rapidly transformed into distrust, hatred, and revenge. The extension of the settlements, and the traffic which followed, put fire-arms into the hands of the Indians, and thus they were enabled to resist oppression with fearful effect. The colonial records, and the journals of many of the actors, burden our early annals with sad chapters, which, when read, fill the heart with sorrow and pain.

In the conflicts which in the progress of time grew up between European powers, touching their territorial rights in the new country, the savages were enlisted and took up arms, and in our colonial disturbances, and in the Revolutionary War, the Indians were involved in like manner. Thus their thirst for war was cultivated, and the efforts of devoted men, who from time to time appeared among them as missionaries, were rendered almost fruitless.

In the conflicts which prevailed between the natives and the frontier settlers, growing out of the aggressions of the latter upon the hunting grounds of the former, human life was most fearfully sacrificed. These conflicts produced a most bitter state of feeling on both sides. The Indians regarded the white man with abhorrence. They believed that his design was not only to despoil them of their lands, but to destroy them as a people; and the whites regarded the Indian as an irreclaimable savage, who, without remorse and in the most barbarous manner, killed the innocent and unoffending settlers without regard to age or sex. The cruel wrongs inflicted on the Indians were never forgotten, but transmitted from parent to child, and to be avenged when opportunity offered. And the injuries sustained by the whites at the hands of the Indians inflamed the friends and relatives of those who suffered, and they in turn inflicted punishment on the savages wherever possible. Thus began an irrepressible conflict, which, in some form, has continued from generation to generation, even until the present time.

CHAPTER II.

The intercourse and dealings of William Penn with the Indians.—The impression made upon them.—Penn's description of the Indians as he found them.

The dealings between William Penn and the Indians are an exception to the general statement in the preceding chapter, standing out isolated and alone in our early history. That great man resolved that in the management of his affairs with the natives in the Province of Pennsylvania, which he held by a royal charter, strict justice should at all times govern his conduct. He was, by his charter, made true and absolute lord of the province. He had authority to raise troops, make war, pursue his enemies by land and sea, and, "by God's assistance, to vanquish and take them." He sent over a colony in 1681, to take possession of the province, and followed himself in 1682. His first care was to establish friendly relations with the Indians. In this regard, he dealt justly and with great kindness. He did not ignore the rights of the natives, and rely upon his grant, sweeping as it was, for a perfect title to the country, but purchased it from the Indians, and paid them for it. In a treaty made under the "Old Elm Tree," on the banks of the Delaware, he established such relations, and thereafter lived up to them in such good faith, as preserved peaceful and friendly intercourse for more than half a century. During all this time, there was not a fort built or a hostile gun fired.

In commenting on this treaty, Voltaire said it was the only one made without an oath, and the only one that had not been broken. Penn's conduct toward the natives was such as to give him an affectionate remembrance among all the Indian nations. Many, to this day, refer to it. He did more than satisfy the Indians for their lands. He paid for some of them twice. At a conference held at Lancaster, Pennsylvania, in 1744, upward of sixty years after Penn's treaty with the Indians on the Delaware, one of the chiefs of the Six Nations said :

"When our brother Onas (the name given to Penn by his red brothers), a great while ago, came to Albany to buy the Susquehannah lands from us, our brother, the governor of New York, who, as we supposed, had not a good understanding with our brother Onas, advised us not to sell him any land, for he would make a bad use of it; and, pretending to be our friend, he advised us, in order to prevent Onas, or any other persons, imposing on us, and that we might always have our land when we wanted it, to put it into his hands; and he told us he would keep it for our use, and never open his hands, but keep them close shut, and not part with it, but at our request. Accordingly, we trusted him, and put our lands into his hands, and charged him to keep them safe for our use. But, some time after, he went to England and carried our land with him, and there sold it to our brother Onas for a large sum of money. And when, at the instance of our brother Onas, we were minded to sell him some lands, he told us we had sold the Susquehannah lands already to the governor of New York, and that he had bought them from him in England; though, when he came to understand how the governor of New York had deceived us, he very generously paid us for our lands over again."

Red Jacket, a Seneca chief, was one of a delegation of New York Indians that visited Philadelphia in 1792. These were received and welcomed by the governor of Pennsylvania, and addressed by him at the council chamber. There was suspended on the wall a fine picture of William Penn, and to it the governor referred in his speech in an appropriate manner. This delegation was some time in the city, and, some days after the reception, there was a second interview, at which several of the chiefs spoke in response to the speech of welcome. Red Jacket spoke as follows:

"Brother Onas, governor (the Indians continued this name, and applied it to Penn's successors), open unprejudiced ears to what we have to say. Some days since, you addressed us, and what you said gave us great pleasure. This day, the

2

Great Spirit has allowed us to meet you again in this council chamber. We hope that your not receiving an immediate answer to your address will make no improper impression on your mind. We mention this, lest you might suspect that your kind welcome and friendly address has not had a proper effect upon our hearts. We assure you it is far otherwise. In your address to us the other day, in this ancient council chamber, where our fathers have often conversed together, several things struck our attention very forcibly. When you told us this was the place in which our fathers often met on peaceable terms, it gave us sensible pleasure, and more joy than we could express. Though we have no writings, like you, yet we remember often to have heard of the friendship that existed between our fathers and yours. The picture to which you have drawn our attention (the portrait of Penn) brought fresh to our minds the friendly conferences that used to be held between the former governors of Pennsylvania and our tribes, and showed the love which your forefathers had for peace, and the friendly disposition of our people. It is still our wish, as well as yours, to preserve peace between our tribes and you, and it would be well if the same spirit existed among the Indians to the westward. Your disposition is that for which the ancient Onas governors were remarkable. As you love peace, so do we also; and we wish that it could be extended to the most distant part of this great country. We agreed in council, this morning, that the sentiments I have expressed should be communicated to you before the delegates of the Five Nations, and to tell you that our cordial welcome to this city, and the good sentiments contained in your address, have made a deep impression on our hearts, and given us great joy; *and from the heart I tell you so.* This is all I have to say."

This speech was made one hundred and ten years after the date of Penn's treaty, and though the Indians "have no writings" by which events are recorded, and thus kept fresh in the minds of those who succeed the actors in them, Red Jacket showed that he was not ignorant of what transpired in 1682, between William Penn and the Lenni Lenapes and other Indians, on the banks of the Delaware, more than one hundred years previous. Some twenty-five years since, a venerable chief of the Delawares, Capt. Ketchem, in a conversation with the author in the (then) country of those Indians, in relation to the events of the past, said: "We have no books like our white brothers in which to record these things, but they are written on our hearts, and are transmitted to our children, and by them to theirs, and thus they are preserved." In the same conversation the old chief referred to Penn's council on the Delaware, and to the treaty made with his ancestors by the United States, at Fort Pitt, when the "thirteen fires (the United States) were young" (1778), and the pledge of the Indians to aid and assist by supplies and warriors in the revolutionary war. At the close of a very interesting and earnest conversation, the venerable man said with deep feeling: "When you return to Washington, say to our Great Father, that we desire him and his white children so to act toward us red men, who are also his children, that when all have done acting here (pointing to the earth), we shall meet up yonder" (pointing to the heavens).

Having referred to the dealings of William Penn with the Indians in the province of Pennsylvania, and the harmony that existed between him and his successors and them for more than half a century, it seems appropriate in this connection to embody the principles which governed him in his intercourse with the natives, as well as his opinion of them. Having obtained his grant from the king, he appointed his relative, William Markham, temporary deputy governor, and the latter, in the fall of 1681, set sail with three ships loaded with colonists and supplies for Pennsylvania. Penn did not come over until the following year. He designed Markham for his secretary when he himself should visit the country. From the colonists he selected judicious commissioners, who had instructions to form a league with the Indians on their arrival. They were directed to be just and candid with the natives, and they were intrusted with an open letter addressed to the Indians, of which the following is a copy:

"LONDON, 18*th of* 8*th mo.*, 1681.

" MY FRIENDS :—There is a great God and power that hath made the world and all things therein, to whom you, and I,

and all people, owe their living and well-being, and to whom
you and I must one day give an account for all that we do in
the world. This great God hath written his law on our
hearts, by which we are taught to love and help one another.
Now this great God hath been pleased to make me concerned
in your part of the world; and the king of the country where
I live hath been pleased to give me a great province therein,
but I desire to enjoy it with your love and consent, that we may
always live together as brothers and friends, else, what
would the great God do to us, who hath made us, not to de-
vour and destroy one another, but to live soberly and kindly
in the world. Now I would have you well observe that I am
very sensible of the unkindness and injustice that hath been
too much exercised toward you by the people of these parts,
who have sought themselves, and to make great advantages
of you, rather than to be examples of goodness and patience
unto you, and caused your grudging and animosity, sometimes to the shedding of blood, which has made the great
God angry. But I am not such a man, as is well known in
my own country. I have great love and regard for you, and
desire to win and gain your love and friendship by a kind,
just, and peaceable life, and the people I send to you are of
the same mind, and shall, in all things, behave themselves
accordingly; and if in anything, any shall offend you, or
your people, you shall have a speedy satisfaction for the same
by an equal number of just men on both sides, that by no
means you shall have just cause of being against them. I
shall shortly come to you myself, at which time we may more
fully confer together and discourse this matter; in the meantime I have sent my commissioners to treat with you about
land, and to form with you a firm league of peace; let me
desire you to be kind to them and their people, and to receive
these *presents* and *tokens* which I have sent you as a token of
my *good* will to you, and my resolution to live justly, peaceably, and friendly with you.

"I am your loving friend,

"WILLIAM PENN."

During the fall of 1681, in writing to a particular friend in
England, in relation to his enterprise, Penn said: "For my

country (Pennsylvania), I eyed the Lord in obtaining it, and more was I drawn inward to look to him, and to it more to his hand and power, than to any other way. I have so obtained it and desire so to keep it, that I may not be unworthy of his blessing; but do that which may answer his kind providence, and serve his truth and people, that an example may be set up to the nations; there may be some there, though not here, for such a holy experiment."

Penn arrived in his colony in July, 1682, and took legal possession and assumed authority and jurisdiction as governor of the same. He immediately convened an assembly, at which certain laws and regulations, agreed upon in England, with some additional ones for the government of the colony, were adopted and promulgated. Among these were the following:

"Inasmuch as it is usual with planters to overreach the poor natives of the country in trade, by goods not being good of the kind, or debased with mixtures, with which they are sensibly aggrieved, it is agreed that whatever is sold to the Indians, in consideration of their furs, be sold in the market place, and there suffer the test, whether good or bad; if good, to pass; if bad, not to be sold for good, that the Indians may not be provoked nor abused.

"That no man shall, by any ways or means, in word or deed, affront or wrong any Indian, but he shall incur the same penalty of the law as if he had committed a wrong against his fellow-planter; and if any Indian shall abuse, in word or deed, any planter of this province, that he shall not be his own judge upon the Indians, but he shall make his complaint to the governor of the province, his lieutenant or deputy, or some inferior magistrate near him, who shall, to the utmost of his power, take care, with the king of the said Indians, that all reasonable satisfaction be made to the said injured planter.

"That all differences between the planters and the natives shall also be ended by twelve men, that is, by six planters and six natives; that so we may live friendly together, as much as in us lieth, preventing all occasions of heart-burnings and mischiefs.

"That the Indians shall have liberty to do all things relat-

ing to improvements of their grounds, and providing sustenance for their families, that any of the planters may enjoy."

When the time had arrived at which Penn and the Indians
had agreed to meet personally, to confirm the treaty of peace,
and the purchase of the land which his commissioners had bar-
gained for, and the transaction was now to be publicly ratified,
"he proceeded, accompanied by his friends of both sexes, to
Coaquannuck, the Indian name of the place where Philadelphia now stands. On his arrival he found the chiefs and their
people there assembled. They were seen in the woods as far
as the eye could reach, and looked frightful, both on account
of their number and their arms. The Quakers are reported
to have been but as a handful in comparison, and these without any weapons, so that dismay and terror had come upon
them, had they not confided in the justice of their cause. In
relation to this event, Chalkley, in his life of Penn, says:

"It is much to be regretted, when we have accounts of
minor treaties between William Penn and the Indians, that
in no history can be found an account of this, though so many
make mention of it, and though all concur in considering it
the most glorious in the annals of the world.

"There are, however, relations in Indian speeches, and
traditions in Quaker families, descended from those who
were present on the occasion, from which we may learn
something about it. It appears that though the parties were
to assemble at Coaquannuck, the treaty was made a little
higher up, at Schackamaxon. Upon this Kensington now
stands, the houses of which may be considered in Philadelphia. William Penn appeared in his usual clothes. He had
no crown, scepter, mace, sword, halberd, nor any insignia
of office. He was distinguished only by wearing a sky-blue
sash around his waist, which was of silk net-work, and
which was of no longer apparent dimensions than an officer's
military sack, and much like it in color. On his right was
Colonel Markham, his relation and secretary, and on his left
Friend Pearson. After followed a train of Quakers. Before
him was carried various articles of merchandise, which, when
they came near the sachems, were spread upon the ground.
He held a roll of parchment containing a confirmation of the

treaty of purchase and amity in his hand. One of the sachems, who was the chief of them, then put upon his own head a kind of chaplet, in which appeared a small horn. This, as among the primitive eastern nations, and according to scripture language, was an emblem of kingly power, and whenever the chief who had a right to wear it put it on, it was understood that the place was made sacred, and the persons of all present inviolable. Upon putting on this horn the Indians threw down their bows and arrows, and seated themselves around the chiefs, in the form of a half moon, upon the ground. The chief sachem then announced to William Penn, by means of an interpreter, that the Indians were ready to hear him. Having been called upon, Penn began thus :

"The great God who made him and them, who ruled in heaven and earth, and who knew the inmost thoughts of men, knew that him and his friends had a hearty desire to live in peace with them, and to serve them to the utmost of their power. It was not their custom to use hostile weapons against their fellow-creatures ; for which reason they came unarmed. Their object was not to do injury, and thus provoke the Great Spirit, but to do good. They were. then met on the broad pathway of good faith and good-will ; so that no advantage was to be taken on either side, but all was to be openness, brotherhood, and love."

After these and other words, he unrolled the parchment, and by means of the same interpreter, conveyed to them, article by article, the conditions of the purchase, and the words of the compact there made for their perpetual union. Among other things, even in the territory they had alienated, they were not to be molested in their lawful pursuits, for it was to be common to them and the English. They were to have the same liberty to do all things therein, relating to the improvement of their grounds, and providing sustenance for their families, which the English had. If any disputes should arise between them, they should be settled by twelve persons, half of whom should be English and half Indians.

"He then paid them for their land, and made them many presents beside, from the merchandise which had been spread before them.   Having done this, he spread the roll of parchment on the ground, observing again that the ground should be common to both people.   He added, that he would not do as the Marylanders did, that is, call them children, or brothers only, for often parents were apt to whip their children too severely, and brothers sometimes would differ ; neither would he compare the friendship between them to a chain, for the rain might rust it, or a tree might fall and break it ; but he should consider them as the same flesh and blood with the Christians, and the same as if one man were to be divided into two parts.   He took up the parchment and presented it to the sachem who wore the horn and chaplet, and desired him and the other sachems to preserve it carefully for three generations, that their children might know what had passed between them, just as if he remained with them to repeat it.

" That William Penn must have done and said a great deal more on this interesting occasion than has now been repeated, there can be no doubt.   What I have advanced (continues Chalkley) may be relied upon, but I am not warranted in going further.   It is also to be regretted that the speeches of the chiefs on this memorable day have not come down to us. It is only known that they solemnly pledged themselves, according to their country manners, to live in love with Penn and his children as long as the sun and the moon shall endure."

In commenting on this transaction, Abbe Reynol says :

" Penn thought it right to obtain an additional right, by fair and open purchase from the aborigines, and thus to signalize his arrival by an act of equity which made his person and principles equally beloved.   Here it is that the mind rests with pleasure upon modern history, and feels some kind of compensation for the disgust, melancholy, and horror which the whole of it, but particularly that part which relates to the European settlements in America, inspires."

Noble says, " Penn occupied his domain by actual bargain and sale with the Indians.   This act does him infinite honor, as no blood was shed, and the Christians and barbarians met as brothers.   Penn has thus taught us to respect the lives and property of the most ignorant nations."

Proud, in his history of Pennsylvania, says that "Penn, being now returned from Maryland to Coaquannuck, purchased land from the Indians, whom he treated with great justice and sincere kindness. It was at this time, when he first entered into that personal friendship with them, which ever afterward continued between them, and which, for the space of more that seventy years, was never interrupted, or so long as the Quakers retained power in Pennsylvania. His conduct in general to the people, was in engaging his justice in particular so conspicuous, and the counsel and advice he gave them were so evidently for their advantage, that he became thereby very much endeared to them, and the sense thereof made such deep impressions on their minds, that his name and memory will scarcely be effaced while they continue a people."

The great Elm Tree, under which the Penn treaty was confirmed, became historic. During our revolutionary war, when the British forces under General Simcoe were quartered at Kensington, and his troops were cutting down the trees in the neighborhood for firewood, he guarded it with sentinels, with orders not to permit a branch to be cut from it. This tree, in 1811, yielded to a storm and was blown down, when the wood was used for cups and various other articles, to be preserved as memorials.

The habits, manners, and customs of the Indians, in their wild state, at the time Penn came among them, he has transmitted to us, and they are but little different from such as attach to the uncivilized Indians of a later date. He says:

" The natives I shall consider in their persons, manners, language, religion, and government, with my sense of the original. For their persons, they are generally tall, straight, well built, and of singular proportions. They tread strong and clever, and mostly walk with a lofty chin; of complexion dark, but by design, as the gypsies in England. They grease themselves with bear's oil clarified; and using no defense against sun or weather, their skins must needs be swarthy. Their eye is little and black, not unlike a straight Jew; the thick lip and flat nose, so frequent with the East Indian and the blacks are not common to them, for I have seen as comely,

European-like faces among them, of both sexes, as on the other side of the sea; and truly an Italian-like complexion hath not much more of the white, and the nose of many of them hath much of the Roman.

"Their language is lofty, yet narrow; but like the Hebrew, in signification—full, like shorthand in writing, one word serveth in the place of three, and the rest are supplied by the understanding of the hearer; imperfect in their tenses, wanting in their moods, participles, adverbs, conjunctions. I have made it my business to understand the language, that I might not want an interpreter on any business, and I must say that I know not a language spoken in Europe, that hath words of more sweetness or greatness, in accent and emphasis, than theirs; for instances, Oc-to-co-chau, Kan-co-cas, Oric-tou, Schack, Po-ques-com, all which are names of places, and have grandeur in them. Of words of sweetness, Anna, is mother; Inemas, is brother; Nitcap, is friend; Ur-gue-vut, is very good; Pa-nee, is bread; Met-sa, eat; Mettah-ne-hattah, to have; Paya-ta-camis, Sas-pas-sin, Pas-se-gan, the names of places. Tar-ma-nee, Se-ca-nee, Ma-nau-see, Sa-ca-torious, are the names of persons.

"If one ask them for any thing they have not, they will answer, Mettah-ne-Hattah, which to translate, means *is not I have*, instead of I have not.

"Of their manners and customs there is much to be said. I will begin with children. So soon as they are born they wash them in water, and while very young, and in cold water to choose, they plunge them in the river, to harden and embolden them. Having wrapped them in a cloth, they lay them on a straight thin board, a little more than the length and breadth of the child, and swaddle it first upon the board, to make it straight—wherefore all Indians have flat heads—and thus they carry them at their backs. The children go very young, at nine months old, commonly; they use only a small cloth round their waist till they are large; if boys, they go a fishing till ripe for the woods, which is about fifteen; then they hunt, and after giving some proofs of their manhood, by a good return of skins, they may marry, else it is a shame to think of a wife. The girls stay with their mothers, and help to hoe the ground, plant corn, and carry burdens; and they do well to use them young, which they must do when they are old, for the wives are the true servants of the husbands, otherwise the men are very affectionate to them.

" When the young women are fit for marriage, they wear something on their heads for an advertisement, but so as their faces are hardly seen but when they please. The age they marry at, if women, is about thirteen or fourteen; if boys, seventeen or eighteen; they are seldom older.

" Their houses are mats or barks of trees, set on poles, in the fashion of English barns, out of the power of the winds, for they are hardly higher than a man; they lie on reeds or grass; in traveling they lie in the woods, about a great fire, with the mantle of duffles they wear by day wrapped about them, and a few boughs stuck around them.

" Their diet is maize or Indian corn, divers ways prepared; sometimes roasted in the ear in ashes, sometimes beaten and boiled with water, which they call hominy; they also make cakes, not unpleasant to eat; they have likewise several sorts of beans and peas that are good nourishment, and the woods and rivers are their larder.

" If a European comes to see them, or calls for lodging at their house or wigwam, they give him the best place, and the first cut. If they come to visit us, they salute us with an 'Itah,' which is as much as to say, *good be to you,* and set them down, which is generally on the ground; it may be they speak not a word, but observe all that is passing. If you give them any thing to eat or drink, well, for they will not ask; and be it little or much, if it be with kindness, they are well pleased, else they go away sullen, but say nothing.

" They are great concealers of their own resentment, brought to it, I believe, by the revenge that hath been practiced among them; in either of these they are not exceeded by the Italians.

" But in liberality they excel; nothing is too good to set for a friend; give them a fine gun, coat, or other thing, it may pass twenty hands before it sticks; light of heart, strong affections, but soon spent. The most merry creatures that live; they feast and dance perpetually, almost; they never have much, nor want much; wealth circulateth like the blood;

all parties partake, and none shall want what another party hath, yet exact observers of property. Some kings sold, others presented me with several tracts of land; the pay or presents I presented them were not hoarded by the particular owners, but the neighboring kings and their class being present when the goods were brought out, the parties chiefly consulted what and to whom they should give them. To every king, then, by the hands of a person for that work appointed, is a portion sent, so sorted and folded, and with that gravity which is admirable. Then the kings subdivide it in like manner among their subjects, they hardly leaving themselves an equal share with one of their subjects, and be it on such occasions as festivals, or at their common meals, the kings distribute, and to themselves last. They care for little, because they want but little, and the reason is, a little contents them; in this, they sufficiently revenge on us; if they are ignorant of our pleasures, they are free from our pains.

" They are not disquieted with bills of lading and exchange, nor perplexed with chancery suits and exchequer reckonings. We sweat and toil to live; their pleasure feeds them. I mean their hunting, fishing, and fowling, and this table is spread anywhere; they eat twice a day, morning and evening; their table and seats are the ground. Since Europeans came into these parts, they are grown great lovers of strong drink, rum especially, and for it exchange the richest of their skins and furs. If they are heated with liquor, they are restless till they have enough to sleep; that is their cry, some more, and I will go to sleep; but when drunk, one of the most wretched spectacles in the world.

" In sickness, impatient to be cured, and for it give any thing, especially for their children, to whom they are extremely natural. They drink at those times a teran, or concoction of roots in spring water, and if they eat any flesh, it must be the female of any creature. If they die, they bury them with their apparel, be they men or women, and the nearest of kin fling in something precious with them, as a token of their love; their mourning is blacking of their faces, which they continue for a year; they are choice of the graves of their dead, least they should be lost by time, and fall to common use; they pick off the grass that grows upon them, and heap up the fallen earth with great care and exactness.

"These poor people are under a dark night in things relating to religion; to be sure, the traditions of it they have only; yet they believe in a God and immortality, without the help of metaphysics; for, say they, there is a great King that made them, and that the souls of the good shall go thither, where they shall live again. Their worship consists of two parts—sacrifice and cantico; their sacrifice is their first fruits; the first and the fattest buck they kill goeth to the fire, where he is burnt, with the mournful ditty of him that performeth the ceremony, but with such marvelous fervency and labor of body, that they will even sweat to a foam. The other part is their cantico, performed by round dances, sometimes words, sometimes songs, then shouts; two being in the middle, that begin, and by singing and drumming on a board, direct the chorus. Their postures in the dance are very antique and differing, but all keep measure. This is done with equal earnestness and labor, but great appearances of joy. In the fall, when the corn cometh in, they begin to feast one another. There have been two great festivals already, to which all come that would; I was at one myself. Their entertainment was a great seat by a spring, under some shady trees, and twenty-five bucks, with hot cakes of new corn, both wheat and beans, which they make up in square form, in the leaves of the stem, and bake them in the ashes; and after that they fall to dancing. But they that go must carry a small present, in their money; it may be sixpence, which is made of the bone of a fish; the black is with them as gold, the white silver; they call it all wampum.

"Their government is by kings, which they call sachema, and those reign by succession, but always of the mother's side; for instance, the children of him who is now king will not succeed, but his brother, by the mother, or the children of his sister, whose sons (and after them the children of her daughter,) will reign, for no woman inherits. The reason they render for this way of descent is that their issue may not be spurious.

"Every king hath his council, and that consists of all the

old and wise men of his nation, which number, perhaps, two hundred people; nothing of moment is undertaken, be it war or peace, selling of land or traffic, without advising with them, and, which is more, with the young men too. It is admirable to consider how powerful the kings are, and yet how they move by the breath of their people. I have had occasion to be in council with them upon treaties for land, and to adjust the terms of trade; their order is this: The king sits in the middle of a half moon, and his council, the old and wise on each hand; behind them, at a little distance, sit the younger part, in the same figures. Having consulted and resolved their business, the king ordered one of them to speak to me; he stood up, came to me, and in the name of the king saluted me, then took me by the hand and told me that he was ordered by his king to speak to me, and now it was not he but the king that spoke, because what he should say was the king's mind. He first prayed me to excuse them that they had not complied with me the last time; he feared there might be some fault in the interpreter, being neither Indian nor English; beside, it was the Indian custom to deliberate, and take up much time in council, before they resolved, and that if the young people and owners of the land had been as ready as he, I had not met with so much delay. Having thus introduced his matter, he fell to the bounds of the land they had agreed to dispose of, and the price which is little and dear, that which would have bought twenty miles, not buying now two. During the time that this person spoke, not a man of them was observed to whisper or smile; the old were grave, the young reverend in their deportment; they speak little, but fervently, and with elegance. I have never seen more natural sagacity, considering them without (I was going to say) the spoil of tradition; and he will deserve the name of 'man' that outwits them in a treaty about a thing which they understand. When the purchase was agreed on, great promises were made, on both sides, of kindness and good neighborhood, and that the English and the Indians must live in love, as long as the sun gave light; which done, another made a speech to the Indians, in the name of all the sachamahens or kings; first, to tell them what was done;

next, to charge and command them to love the Christians, and particularly to live in peace with me; that many governors had been in the river, but that no governor had come himself to live and stay here before; and having now such a one that treated them so well, they should never do him or his people any wrong. At every sentence of which they shouted and said, 'Amen,' in their way.

" The justice they have is pecuniary. In case of any wrong or evil fact—be it murder itself—they atone by feasts and presents of their wampum, which is proportioned to the offense or person injured, or of the sex they are of; for, in case they kill a woman, they pay double, and the reason they render is that she can raise children, which men can not do. It is rare that they fall out, if sober; and, if drunk, forgive it, saying it was the drink and not the man that abused them.

" We have agreed that, in all differences between us, six of each side shall settle the matter. Do not abuse them, but let them have justice, and you win them. The worst is that they are the worse for the Christians, who have propagated their views, and yielded them tradition for ill and not for good things. But, as low an ebb as these people are at, and as inglorious as their own condition looks, the Christians have not outlived their right, with all the pretensions to a higher manifestation. What good, then, might not a good people ingraft, where there is so distinct a knowledge left between good and evil ?

" I beseech God to incline the hearts of all who come into these parts to outlive the knowledge of the natives by fixed obedience to the greater knowledge of the will of God; for it were miserable, indeed, for us to fall under the just censure of the poor Indians' consciences, while we make professions of things so far transcending.

" For the original, I am ready to believe them of the Jewish race ; I mean of the stock of the ten tribes—and that for the following reasons : *First.* They were to go to a land not planted or known, which, to be sure, Asia and Africa were, if not Europe ; and he that intended that extraordinary judgment upon them, might make the passage not uneasy to them, as it is not impossible in itself, from the eastermost part of

Asia to the westermost part of America.   In the next place,
I find them of like countenance, and their children of so
lively resemblance that a man would think himself in Duke's
place or Berry street, in London, when he seeth them.   But
this is not all.   They agree in rites; they reckon by moons;
they offer their first fruits; they have a kind of feast of
tabernacles; they are said to lay their altar upon twelve
stones; their mourning a year; customs of women; with
many other things that do not now occur."

CHAPTER III.

EVENTS IMMEDIATELY PRECEDING AND FOLLOWING THE TREATY OF PARIS, IN 1763.—CESSIONS BY FRANCE AND SPAIN OF THEIR RIGHTS TO TERRITORY EAST OF THE MISSISSIPPI.—CONSPIRACY OF PONTIAC.—TROOPS RAISED IN PENNSYLVANIA AND VIRGINIA.—BOUNTY FOR INDIAN SCALPS.—WHITES OCCUPY THE OHIO VALLEY.—ENTER KENTUCKY AND THE NORTHWEST TERRITORY.—RUPTURE BETWEEN GREAT BRITAIN AND HER COLONIES.—BEGINNING OF THE REVOLUTIONARY WAR, ETC.

As the colonies grew in numbers and increased in population, complications and wars with the Indian tribes increased. The peaceful relations existing in the Province of Pennsylvania between the races, from 1682 to about 1740, are an exception. In all the other provinces or colonies the Indian was regarded as an undesirable neighbor. His lands were coveted and wrested from him. To trace in the briefest detail the various conflicts that arose between the whites and Indians, from the time of the landing of the Pilgrims to our Revolutionary era, would fill a massive volume. It is not deemed necessary that these early annals be reproduced in order to a proper understanding of the Indian question.

We shall not go further back than the end of the struggle in which the French and English were engaged in war in relation to their territorial possessions in America. We should not go back thus far, were it not to allude to a remarkable character that appeared among the Indians at that time, and made a masterly effort in their behalf.

By the treaty of Paris, concluded February 10, 1763, the war between France and England terminated, and France renounced all pretensions to the possessions she had claimed east of the Mississippi, and made over the same to Great Britain. About the same time Spain ceded Florida to England, and thus the latter was vested with the ownership and sovereignty, so far as that depended on the consent of her rivals, of the entire eastern half of North America. In all the

3

years in which controversies and conflicts existed between
European powers, touching their territorial rights on this continent, the Indians were involved, their natural love of war
cultivated, and, as a consequence, they were demoralized.
The few who sought their reclamation and civilization were
powerless.

After the fall of Fort Du Quesne, in 1759, settlers from
Pennsylvania, Maryland, and Virginia began to press across
the mountains to possess themselves of the lands on the eastern or southern shore of the Ohio river and the valleys
bordering on its tributaries, many looking ultimately to a
home in Kentucky or in the " Territory northwest of the
river Ohio." With the reverses of the French, the Iroquois
went over to the side of the English, while numerous tribes
in the west, who had fought on the side of the French, retired into the forest and remained on their hunting grounds.
Hence, the settlers referred to were emboldened to go out
and found new homes. There were many adverse claims to
the lands, by companies holding under grants from the crown,
or claiming on contracts of various kinds, and there were
soldiers' claims under the proclamation of Dinwiddie, governor of the colony of Virginia. Notwithstanding these
facts, thousands were preparing and in motion to go out and
possess the country, taking no notice of the rights of the Indians inhabiting it. At the same period there was an incipient movement among the various western tribes, who, in
the war, had followed the fortunes of France, to recover the
possessions which England had won from her. This was
called the "*Conspiracy of Pontiac.*" This man was an Ottawa
chief, and one of the most remarkable men that appeared in
his time. By his skill, ability, and strategy, he had pre-
arranged a combined movement upon the military and trading
posts at Detroit, Michilimackinac, Lebeuf, Presque Isle, Sandusky, Miami, St. Joseph, Green Bay, Niagara, Fort Pitt, and
other frontier posts, and had enlisted in the enterprise the
Miamis, Ottawas, Chippewas, Wyandots, Pottawatomies, Delawares, Shawnees, and other tribes. The attack was to be
made about the last of May, 1763. Each tribe was to surprise the garrison or post in its own locality, slaughter the

soldiers and other inmates, and then all were unitedly to turn upon the frontier settlements. The messengers of Pontiac bore from him to the different tribes the following speech: "Why, says the Great Spirit, do you suffer these dogs in red clothing to enter your country and take the land I have given you? Drive them from it! Drive them! When you are in distress I will help you."

In the language of the author of the *Annals of the West*: "This voice was heard, but not by the whites. The unsuspecting traders journeyed from village to village; the soldiers in the forts shrunk from the sun of early summer, and dozed away the day; the frontier settler, singing in fancied security, sowed his crop, or, watching the sun set through the girdled trees, mused upon one more peaceful harvest, and told his children of the horrors of the ten years' war, now, thank God, over. From the Alleghanies to the Mississippi the trees had leaved, and all was calm, life, and joy. But through that great country, the bands of sullen red men were journeying from the central valleys to the lakes and eastern hills. Bands of Chippewas gathered about Michilimackinac. Ottawas filled the woods near Detroit. The Maumee post, Presque Isle, Niagara, Pitt, Legonier, and every English fort was hemmed in by mingled tribes, who felt that the great battle drew nigh which was to determine their fate, and the possession of their noble lands. At last the day came. The traders every-where were seized, their goods taken from them, and more than one hundred of them put to death. Nine British forts yielded instantly, and the savages drank the blood of many a Briton. The border streams of Pennsylvania and Virginia ran red again. We hear, says a letter from Fort Pitt, ' of scalping every hour.' In western Virginia and Pennsylvania more than twenty thousand people were driven from their homes. . . . Fort Pitt, Niagara, and Detroit were attacked, but not taken. [These were regular fortified forts. Pontiac commanded in person at Detroit, and would undoubtedly have taken it, but the plot was communicated to the commander in advance by an Indian girl, and hence he was prepared to defend his position. Pontiac, however, environed the fort for several months, keeping the troops within the fortifications, and only abandoned the siege when advised that heavy reinforcements were near at hand for its relief.] Pontiac resided near Detroit. He was one of those heroic men who stamp their character on their country and their age. No American savage 'has shown a more marked character, in forming great and comprehensive plans, or in executing them with energy and boldness."

In Tuttle's Border Wars, he says that "although the Indians of the Northwest were poorly qualified to engage in a war with the English, they had good reasons for commencing it. A defeat could not be much worse than the insults to which they were every day subjected, and to stand quietly by and see their best hunting grounds invaded by the English settlers, was not to be endured by Indian warriors who could boast as brave and sagacious a leader as Pontiac. The French missionaries and fur-traders who had formerly come among them, gave but little cause for alarm. These adventurers were, for the most part, satisfied with the proceeds of a traffic with the savages, or with telling them the story of the cross; but it was not so with the Englishman. He was essentially a husbandman, and for half a league around his little hut, he claimed exclusive rights to the resources of the territory. When the Indian invaded these limits he was treated with haughty opposition and ordered away. Thus the red men beheld the rapidly approaching ruin of their race, and hastened to avert it. Pontiac, whose penetrating mind could reach farthest into coming events, warned those around him of the danger of allowing the English to make permanent settlements in their country, and counseled the tribes to unite in one great effort against the common foe. He did not support the common idea which prevailed among the infuriated Indians, of driving the English into the Atlantic ocean, for he well knew their military skill and power; but being persuaded by the French, that the king of France was at that time advancing up the St. Lawrence with a mighty army, he resolved to lead the warriors to battle, with a view to restoring the French power in Canada, and to check the English in their progress westward.

"Resolved on this course, Pontiac, at the close of the year

1762, sent out deputies to all the tribes. They visited the country of the Ohio, passed northward to the region of the Upper Lakes and the wild borders of the river Ottawa, and far southward to the mouth of the Mississippi, bearing with them the belt of wampum, broad and long as the importance of the message demanded, and the tomahawk stained red in token of war. They went from camp to camp, and village to village, and wherever they appeared the sachems and old men assembled to hear the words of the great Pontiac. The head chief of the embassy flung down the tomahawk on the ground before them, and holding the war belt in his hand, delivered with vehement gesture, word for word, the speech with which he was charged. Every-where the speech was received with approval, the hatchet taken up, and the auditors stood pledged, according to the Indian custom, to aid in the projected war. At this period the western wilderness presented an interesting scene. Every-where the Indians were preparing for war. The war dance was celebrated in a hundred villages, and chiefs and warriors, painted and adorned, stood ready for the onset. To begin the war, however, was reserved by Pontiac as his own special privilege. In the spring of 1763 his great conspiracy was mature, and he summoned the chiefs and warriors of all the tribes of the newly formed league to a war council. The sachems met on the banks of the Ecories river, near Detroit, whither Pontiac had gone to welcome them. Band after band of painted warriors came straggling in, until the forest was alive with restless savages for nearly a mile up and down the little stream. It was, indeed, an important event for the red man. At frequent intervals during the year just past he had heard of the words of the great Ottawa chief, as delivered by his deputies. Now they had met this wonderful man face to face. He who, through his diligent ambassadors, had united all the tribes of the Algonquin family under a confederacy equal in democratic scope to that of the far famed Six Nations, was now to speak to many of his subjects for the first time. He was to tell them in true Indian eloquence, the story of their approaching ruin; he was to uncover the selfish policy of the English, and point to the only means by which they could revive their declining prowess; he was to stand forth before his savage auditors, and verify, by matchless power of word and gesture, the thrilling story of his greatness, which had been passed from village to village on the tongues of his light-footed messengers. Truly the occasion was an exciting one for the assembled tribes. All waited patiently to hear the words of the famous Ottawa chief.

"The council took place on the 27th of April, 1763. On that morning several old men, the heralds of the camp, passed to and fro among the lodges, calling the warriors, in a loud voice, to attend the meeting. In accordance with the summons they came issuing from their cabins—the tall, naked figures of the wild Ojibwas, with quivers slung at their backs and light clubs resting in the hollow of their arms; Ottawas, wrapped in their gaudy blankets; Wyandots, fluttering in painted shirts, their heads adorned with feathers and their leggins garnished with belts. All were soon seated in a wide circle upon the grass, row within row, a mighty and warlike assembly. Each savage countenance wore an expression of gravity. Pipes with ornamental stems were lighted and passed from hand to hand, until all had smoked together in harmony.

"Then Pontiac came forth from his lodge, and walked forward into the midst of the council. He was a man of medium height, with a grandly proportioned muscular figure, and an address well calculated to win the admiration and respect of the savage heart. His complexion was rather dark for an Indian, and his features wore a bold and stern expression while his bearing was imperious and peremptory. His only attire was that of a primitive savage—a scanty cincture girt about his loins, and his long black hair flowing loosely at his back—excepting the plumes and decorations of the war dress."

In his address, his voice was loud and impassioned, his gestures fierce, and at every pause his auditors manifested their assent in deep, guttural ejaculations. His exposure of the English policy toward the Indians was eloquent and exhaustive. He complimented the French extravagantly, and contrasted them with the "red coats." He gave a summary of the many insults and injuries which he and his followers had received at the hands of the English commandant at Detroit, and ably portrayed the danger to be apprehended if the British were allowed to maintain their settlements in the country. He said they had conquered Canada, and were now about to turn upon and slaughter the Indians. Already they had invaded their best hunting grounds, and if not checked, it would not be long until the Indians would be driven from their homes. He threw down a broad belt of wampum, saying, " that he had received it from his great father, the king of France, in token that he had heard the voice of his red children, and was on his way to aid them in a war against the English." All present listened to his speech with marked attention, and at its close each warrior was eager to attack the British fort. But the chief counseled them to desist for the present. He wished to establish order and method at the beginning, and thus insure success.

The news that so many forts and posts had fallen into the hands of the Indians, caused great alarm among the whites, and the appearance of parties of Indians on the frontier of Pennsylvania and Virginia filled the people with consternation. It seemed as though all the Indian tribes east of the Mississippi were in a hostile attitude. Colonel Bouquet, having raised a force at Philadelphia to go to the relief of Fort Pitt, found when he arrived at Carlisle, early in July, the whole country in a panic. The settlers in Sherman's valley, and on the Tuscarora, suffered; and those on the Juniata did not escape. Carlisle was filled with fugitives, and many left that place, and pressed on to Lancaster, and even to Philadelphia. In fact, all the frontier settlers in the English colonies were in a desperate condition. Troops were raised in Pennsylvania and Virginia to repel and punish the Indians. Some columns met with misfortune, others were successful and victorious. In turn the Indians suffered sadly. Many were barbarously killed, and instances were frequent where Indian prisoners in large numbers were deliberately massacred. Under the excitement, the Moravian mission Indians, on the Susquehannah, were attacked, and many of them, men, women, and children, were cruelly murdered. Such as escaped fled to Lancaster, and were, for their security, lodged in jail.

A military organization, called the "Paxton Boys," broke open the doors of the jail, and perpetrated a new massacre of the inmates. The fury of the mob—one thousand strong —was so great that they went on to Philadelphia, to destroy some friendly Indians who had taken refuge there. The mob, through the intervention of Franklin and a large volunteer force raised in the city, was prevented from accomplishing its bloody work; but there was no power in the province adequate to punish it. Those Indians—called the Christian Indians—then moved higher up the Susquehannah, and from thence, in a few years, to Ohio, a portion of them, to suffer other outrages, and finally massacre, at Gnaudenhutten   About this period the English governor of the Province of Pennsylvania offered a bounty for Indian scalps. The Colony of Massachusetts had years before done this.

On a second expedition, Bouquet made a temporary treaty with the Delawares, Shawnees, and some other Indians, by which about two hundred white prisoners were given up to him, and it was agreed that all the tribes involved would arrange for a meeting with Sir William Johnson, with whom a permanent treaty should be made. Subsequently a treaty was executed, as agreed upon, between the Indians and Sir William, who represented the English government, one of the stipulations of which was that the Indians should join the English army in its march into the Illinois country, for the purpose of aiding them in getting possession of the forts there. Shortly before this treaty was executed, the British government issued a proclamation (October, 1763), which was designed to allay the fears of the red men, and had it been faithfully observed, would, no doubt, in the future have had a most salutary effect. The following extracts will disclose the character of the document:

"And, whereas, it is just and reasonable, and essential to our interests, and the security of our colonies that the several nations or tribes of Indians with whom we are connected, and who live under our protection, should not be molested or disturbed in the possession of such parts of our dominions and territories, as, not having been ceded to or purchased by us, are reserved to them, or any of them, as their hunting grounds; we do, therefore, with the advice of our privy council, declare it to be our royal will and pleasure, that no governor or commander-in-chief, in any of our colonies of Quebec, East Florida, or West Florida, do presume, on any pretext whatever, to grant warrants of survey, or pass any patents for lands beyond the bounds of their respective governments, as described in their commissions; as, also, that no governor or commander-in-chief of our other colonies or plantations in America do presume for the present, and until our further pleasure be made known, to grant warrants of survey, or pass patents for any lands, beyond the heads or sources of any of the rivers which fall into the Atlantic ocean from the west or northwest; or upon any lands whatever, which, not having been ceded to or purchased by us, as aforesaid, are reserved to said Indians or any of them.

" And we do further declare it to be our royal will and pleasure, for the present, as aforesaid, to reserve under our sovereignty, protection, and dominion, for the use of the said Indians, all the land and territories not included within the limits of our said three new governments, or within the limits of the territory granted to the Hudson's Bay Company; as also all the lands and territories lying to the westward of the sources of the rivers which fall into the sea from the west and northwest, as aforesaid; and we do hereby strictly forbid, on pain of our displeasure, all our loving subjects from making any purchases or settlements whatever, or taking possession of any lands above reserved, without our special leave and license for that purpose first obtained.

" And we do further strictly enjoin and require all persons whatever, who have either willfully or inadvertently seated themselves upon any lands within the countries above described, or upon any other lands, which, not having been ceded to or purchased by us, are still reserved to the said Indians, as aforesaid, forthwith to remove themselves from such settlements.

" And, whereas, great frauds and abuses have been committed in purchasing lands from the Indians, to the great prejudice of our interests, and to the great dissatisfaction of the Indians; in order, therefore, to prevent such irregularities in the future, and to the end that the Indians may be convinced of our justice, and determined resolution to remove all reasonable cause of discontent, we do, with the advice of our privy council, strictly enjoin and require that no private person do presume to make any purchase from the said Indians, or of any lands reserved to the said Indians, within these parts of our said colonies where we have thought proper to allow settlements; but that, if at any time, any of the said Indians should be inclined to dispose of the said lands, the same shall be purchased only for us, in our name, at some public meeting or assembly of the said Indians, to be held for that purpose, by the governor or commander-in-chief of our colony, respectively, within which they shall lie; and in case they shall be within the limits of any of the proprietaries, conformable to such directions as we or they shall think proper to give for that purpose; and we do, by the advice of our privy council, declare and enjoin that the trade with said Indians shall be open to all of our subjects whatever: *Provided*, that every person who may incline to trade with said Indians do take out a license for carrying on such trade, from the governor or commander-in-chief of any of our colonies, respectively, where such person may reside; and also give security to observe such regulations as we shall at any time think fit, by ourselves, or commissioners to be appointed for this purpose, to direct and appoint, for the benefit of the said trade; and we do hereby authorize, enjoin, and require the governors and commanders-in-chief of all our colonies, respectively, as well those under our immediate government as those under the direction and government of proprietaries, to grant such licenses without fee or reward, taking especial care to insert therein a condition that such license shall be void, and the security forfeited, in case the person to whom the same is granted, shall refuse or neglect to observe such regulations as we shall think proper to prescribe as aforesaid."

In 1765, Col. Grogan, by an order from Sir William Johnson, descended the Ohio river to conciliate the Indians. He was accompanied by deputies from the Senecas, Shawnees, and Delawares. From the mouth of the Wabash he proceeded into the Illinois country, and then made his way to Niagara. He failed to accomplish any thing. The Indians felt restless and dissatisfied, since the prairies and valleys of which they had held undisputed possession, were now claimed by the English on the strength of a treaty of which they were ignorant. The British were coming to take their country, and though protection was promised them from the incursion of white settlers, they felt there was no confidence to be placed in these promises. And these fears were realized. Neither the governors nor individuals regarded the warnings of the royal proclamation or the promises made by Sir William Johnson. Settlers were crossing the mountains and entering the country in the Northwestern Territory. Gen. Gage, the commander of the king's forces, admonished the settlers in some sections that they must remove, but they gave no heed to his admonition. Many schemes for colonization were afloat, resulting in rivalry among those engaged in them, and consequent disorder.

The Indians were anxious that a definite boundary line should be established between them and the English. To this end Sir William Johnson was authorized to treat with them. The council for that purpose was held at Fort Stanwix, in the fall of 1768. Parties from New Jersey, Virginia, and Pennsylvania were present. Sir William Johnson and his assistants, accompanied by the agents of the traders who suffered in the war which closed in 1763, were on hand, and the Indians were represented by deputies from the Six Nations, the Delawares, and Shawnees only. The most important matter was to determine the line which should separate the western Indians from the English *in all future time*, and this line the Indians claimed should be the Ohio river. A boundary line, adopting the Ohio to its source from the mouth of the Tennessee river, and from the source of the Ohio up the Alleghany to Kittanning, and thence across to the Susquehannah, was adopted. Thus the country south of the Alleghany and east of the Ohio was, by virtue of this treaty, regarded as belonging to the British. But the Cherokee Indians claimed that part south of the Kenhawa. Grants for the country were speedily made. The work of settlement, which had been for some time checked, began to revive, and it was but a short time until scattering colonies were planted on the Ohio, in Kentucky, and even in regions northwest of the Ohio. The savages, of course, became dissatisfied, and this dissatisfaction was cultivated by the French traders. Emigration continued, and the best lands of the Indians were taken. Indians were killed at various points along the Ohio river. Washington, who had made a journey to the Ohio, noticed this dissatisfaction, and recorded it in his journal in 1770. The elder Indians urged their tribes to submit to what seemed inevitable, and for a time their advice was not wholly lost, but hatred naturally filled the breasts of the natives, and the continued aggressions upon them caused them to thirst for revenge.

It is needless to detail the events which followed, up to the time of the rupture between the mother country and her colonies, culminating in the declaration of American independence. Suffice it to say that conflicts continued; and among the incidents that served most to inflame the Indians was the killing of the family of the chief Logan. By this act this chief, who had been the friend, was made a deadly foe of the white man.

In the latter part of the year 1775, and the first half of 1776, the Indians seemed to be inactive. Excursions against those who were invading their hunting grounds nearly ceased. They had not given up the contest; but were preparing, in connection with British agents in the Northwest, to act with energy against the colonists. It had been in contemplation, by both the English and the colonists, even before the war of the Revolution, in the event of an open rupture, to make use of the Indians in the struggle. The example was set by the French and English in their war, and it was generally held that such alliance was unavoidable. It is charged that the English took the first step to enlist the Indians as allies in the war with the colonies. The first mention of it by the colonists was in the address of the Massachusetts congress, to the Iroquois, in 1775, in which it was said they had heard that the British were inciting the savages against the colonists; and they requested the Six Nations to aid them or stand neutral. Later, in the same year, an agent from the Virginia house of burgesses visited

the western Indians, and, in a council with them, found that
Governor Carlton had been there before him, and offered the
Indians the alliance of England. Thus, it would seem that
both parties, even before the battle of Lexington, had sought
an alliance with the savages. The Congress of the United
Colonies, during the year 1775, advocated a policy that looked
chiefly to an effort to keep the Indians out of the contest en
tirely; but England, both by promises and threats, endeavored
to enlist them. In her efforts, in this respect, she had but
little success until her first victories in the north, and then the
Indians began to take her side. In 1778, Congress authorized
the employment of Indians in the service of the United
States. Some of our histories say that authority was given to
employ them in 1776, and that the commander-in-chief was authorized to employ them in such service as he pleased, and to
offer them a bounty for prisoners taken by them. During the
war the English went further, and gave the Indians a
bounty for scalps. The northwestern Indians, angered by
the constant invasion of their country by hunters, chiefly
from Carolina and Virginia, and being accessible to the English by the lakes, became enlisted in their behalf, and committed many atrocities, chiefly in Kentucky.

As the war progressed, great uneasiness was felt on the frontiers of Pennsylvania and Virginia, because of rumors of coming troubles from the savages. The tribes nearest the American settlements were pressed upon by more distant bands.
Even the settlers on the Mohawk and Susquehannah were in
constant dread of incursions. The Shawnee chief, Cornstalk,
was a faithful friend of the colonists, and his voice and influence were for peace, and his efforts in that behalf were very
valuable. Cornstalk, owing to the confusion and trouble by
which he was surrounded, went across the Ohio river in 1777,
to talk matters over with the commander of a post at the mouth
of the Big Kenhawa. He was a man of great energy, courage, and good sense, and very reliable. The Americans there,
believing that the Shawnees were inclined to unite with the
British, determined to retain him and Red Hawk, a subordinate chief who was with him. Cornstalk talked freely of
the condition of affairs, and said to Captain Arbuckle, in

command, that unless he and his friends could have assurances of protection from the " Long Knives," they might be compelled " to go with the stream." This visit, made as a friend, worked a different result from what he expected. They did not permit him to depart. The day passed by, and on the next morning an Indian on the opposite shore hailed the fort. He was brought over, and was the son of Cornstalk, who was anxious about his father, since he had not returned home. The son was also secured as a hostage. A few days thereafter two Indians, who were unknown to the whites, killed a white hunter. The cry was instantly raised, " Kill the red dogs in the fort." Arbuckle attempted, it is said, to prevent this, but his life was threatened. The mob rushed to the fort where the captive Indians were. Cornstalk met them at the entrance and was pierced by seven bullets. His son and Red Hawk were also slain. Dodridge, in his Notes, says, " from that hour peace was not to be hoped for."

About this time a congress of Indians was gathering at Otsego, stimulated by the English, to arrange " to eat the flesh and drink the blood of the Bostonians." Other atrocities on the part of the whites were committed. All these occurrences aroused the savages, and then the settlers suffered in return, in the loss of life and destruction of property. Such was their condition, by reason of the movements of the Indians, that their cornfields were not cultivated. The events of this period were of the most touching character, and full of thrilling incidents.

The oppressive acts of Great Britain anterior to the revolt of the colonies, and preceding the odious stamp act, and the feeling of discontent thereby produced, had induced that government to take preparatory steps to resist the outbreak which seemed inevitable, and she had her emissaries among the savages, inciting them to take up arms. Indeed, it was apprehended that several tribes were then in a hostile attitude by reason of the conduct of the troops, who were engaged in the hostilities known in our colonial history as Dunmore's war. On the first of June, 1775, a petition from the people of that part of Augusta county, Virginia, west of the Alleghany mountains, was laid before the Continental Congress. The petitioners expressed "fears of a rupture with the Indians, on account of Lord Dunmore's conduct," and desired "commissioners from the colony of Virginia and province of Pennsylvania, to attend a meeting of the Indians at Pittsburg on behalf of these colonies." On the 30th of the same month a number of letters and speeches from the Stockbridge Indians were laid before the Congress and read, and the Committee on Indian Affairs was directed to prepare proper talks to the several tribes of Indians, for engaging the continuance of their friendship and neutrality in the existing unhappy dispute with Great Britain. It was also resolved "that the securing and preserving of the friendship of the Indian nations appears to be a subject of the utmost moment to these colonies; that there was too much reason to apprehend that the British will spare no pains to excite the several Indian nations to take up arms against the colonies, and that it became them to be very active and vigilant, in exercising every prudent means to strengthen and confirm the friendly disposition toward the colonies, among the northern tribes, which has so long prevailed, and which has been lately manifested by some of those to the southward." The Congress at the same time made provision for the appointment of boards of commissioners to superintend Indian affairs in behalf of the colonies. It designated three Indian departments—the northern, southern, and middle; the first to embrace all the Six Nations, and all the Indians northward of those; the second to extend so far north as to include the Cherokees, and all the Indians south of them; and the third to include the Indian nations that lie between the other two departments. It gave authority and power to the commissioners to treat with the Indians in their respective departments, in the name and on behalf of the colonies; the object being to preserve peace and friendship with the Indians and to prevent their taking any part in the present commotions. The commissioners were empowered to seize any of the king's superintendents, their deputies or agents, who were found stirring up or inciting the Indians to become inimical to the colonies, and to keep them in safe custody until such order is taken in the premises as to the Congress may seem proper. Other powers and duties were conferred upon the commissioners, and money appropriated to be expended by them in making treaties and supplying presents to the Indians.

This was the first legislation of the Continental Congress creating an official board to administer Indian affairs. During the remainder of the year 1775, many resolves were adopted by the Congress giving advice and aid to the Commissioners of Indian Affairs in the several departments, and looking to the securing of an alliance with the Indian nations. On the 27th of January, 1776, Congress—

"*Resolved*, That in order to preserve the confidence and friendship of the Indians, and to prevent their suffering for want of the necessaries of life, a suitable assortment of Indian goods, to the amount of forty thousand pounds sterling, be imported on account and risk of the United Colonies.

"That said goods, when imported, be divided among the different departments, in the following proportions, viz: for the northern department, comprehending Canada, thirteen thousand three hundred and thirty-three pounds, six shillings and eight pence sterling; for the middle department, the like value; and the residue for the southern department.

"That in order to pay for the said goods, a quantity of produce of these colonies be exported to some foreign European market, where it will sell to the best advantage.

"That the secret committee be empowered to contract with proper persons for importing said goods, and for exporting produce to pay for the same.

"That said goods, when imported, be delivered to the Commissioners of Indian Affairs, for the respective departments, or their order, in the proportion before mentioned.

"That the respective commissioners, or such of them as can conveniently assemble for that purpose, shall, as the goods arrive, fix a price, adding to the first cost, interest, the charge of insurance, and all other charges, and also a commission not exceeding two and one-half per cent. on the first cost, for their own care and trouble in receiving, storing, and selling them to the Indian traders; but such commissioners as are at the same time members of Congress shall not be burdened with this part of the business, nor receive any part of the aforesaid commission.

"That no person shall be permitted to trade with the Indians without license from one or more of the commissioners of each respective department.

"That all traders shall dispose of their goods at such stated reasonable prices as shall be fixed and ascertained by the commissioners, or a majority of such as can conveniently assemble for that purpose, in each respective department, and shall allow the Indians a reasonable price for their skins and furs, and take no unjust advantage of their distress and intemperance; and to this end they shall respectively, upon receiving their licenses, enter into bond to the commissioners, for the use of the United Colonies, in such penalty as the acting commissioners, or commissioner, shall think proper, conditioned for the performance of the terms and regulations above prescribed.

"That to such licensed traders only, the respective commissioners shall deliver the goods, so to be imported, in such proportions as they shall judge will best promote a fair trade, and relieve the necessities of the Indians.

"That every trader on receiving the goods shall pay to the commissioners, in hand, the price at which they shall be estimated; and the commissioners shall, from time to time, as the money shall come to their hands, transmit the same to the Continental treasurers, deducting only the allowance for their trouble, as aforesaid.

"That the trade with the Indian nations shall be carried on at such posts and places only, as the commissioners for each department shall respectively appoint.

"That these resolutions shall not be construed to prevent or deter any private person from importing goods for the Indian trade, under the restrictions herein expressed."

On the 15th of February, 1776, the Congress—

"*Resolved*, That a friendly commerce between the people of the United Colonies and the Indians, and the propagation of the gospel and the cultivation of the civil arts among the latter, may produce many and inestimable advantages to both,

4

and that the Commissioners of Indian Affairs be directed to consider of proper places, in their respective departments, for the residence of ministers and schoolmasters, and report the same to Congress."

During the remainder of this year (1776) and through the year 1777, many resolves were passed by the Congress, all looking to the preservation of friendly intercourse with the Indian nations. It was a period of deep solicitude, since British agents and emissaries were at work among them, striving to enlist them against the United States, in the war then in progress. In the month of March, 1778, the Congress—

"*Resolved*, That General Washington be empowered, if he thinks it prudent and proper, to employ in the service of the United States a body of Indians, not exceeding four hundred, and that it be left to him to pursue such measures as he judges best for procuring them, and to employ them, when procured, in such way as will annoy the enemy, without suffering them to injure those who are friends to the cause of America."

At the same time the Congress—

"*Resolved*, That Brigadier McIntosh be directed to assemble at Fort Pitt as many Continental troops and militia as will amount to fifteen hundred, and proceed without delay to destroy such towns of the hostile tribes as he, in his discretion, shall think will most effectually tend to chastise and terrify the savages, and to check their ravages on the frontiers of these states."

The first of these resolutions was no doubt induced by the fact, then notorious, that the British had Indians employed in their military service; while the second, levying troops to destroy the towns of the hostile Indians, was prompted by the incursion into Wyoming, by the Seneca Indians, "aided by tories and other banditti," from the frontiers of New York, New Jersey, and Pennsylvania, and rumors that expeditions of a like character were contemplated. The board of war was directed to take prompt measures in the premises. During the progress of the struggle for independence, many of the inhabitants of the colonies were tortured and killed by the Indians, and many Indians were killed by the whites, and there was no time when there was not fear and apprehension because of the temper of many of the Indian tribes, who, through the influence of British agents and emissaries, were made actively hostile. Moreover, both parties had enlisted them in the military service, and thus their savage propensities and love of war were cultivated, their passionate love of strong drink gratified, and at the close of the contest the Indians generally were left in a very demoralized condition.

CHAPTER IV.

EVENTS FOLLOWING THE TREATY OF PEACE.—THE EFFECT UPON THE INDIANS.—
THE FRONTIER POSTS REMAIN IN THE HANDS OF THE BRITISH.—COMPLICA-
TIONS RESULTING THEREFROM.—MILITARY EXPEDITIONS AGAINST THE IN-
DIANS.—INTERVIEW, AT NIAGARA, BETWEEN UNITED STATES COMMISSION-
ERS AND DEPUTATIONS FROM THE INDIAN NATIONS, ETC.

AMONG the pressing duties which forced themselves on the
Congress of the United States, at the close of the Revolutionary war, none were more imperative than some satisfactory adjustment with the Indian nations. Not long after the
cessation of hostilities, and the treaty of peace, the Congress,
in May, 1783—

"*Resolved*, That the secretary of war take the most effective
measures to inform the several Indian nations on the frontiers
of the United States, that preliminary articles of peace have
been agreed on, and hostilities have ceased with Great Britain,
and to communicate to them that the forts within the United
States, and in possession of the British troops, will speedily
be evacuated; intimating, also, that the United States are disposed to enter into friendly treaty with the different tribes,
and to inform the hostile Indian nations that unless they immediately cease all hostilities against the citizens of the United
States, and accept of these friendly proffers of peace, Congress
will take the most decided measures to compel them thereto."

When the treaty of Paris was concluded, in 1763, the French
had not extinguished the Indian title to the lands in the western country, and, in fact, owned only a few small tracts about
her various forts situate therein. No transfer of territory
came from Pontiac's war, or from that of Dunmore. The
New York Indians, it is true, had, at the treaty of Fort Stanwix, in 1763, ceded to the English their lands south of the
Ohio river. Hence, " when, at the close of the Revolution,
in 1783, Great Britain made over her western lands to the
United States, she made over nothing more than she had received from France, excepting the title of the Six Nations

and the southern Indians to a portion of the territory south
of the Ohio river. But this was not the view that the Congress of the United States took of the affair. This body, it
would seem, conceived that it had, under the treaty with
England, a full right to all the lands embraced in the territory
thereby ceded, and, regarding the Indian title as forfeited by
the Revolution, assumed that the government would not purchase lands from the Indians, but grant them peace, and dictate terms as to the boundary lines of territory allowed."

In the treaty with the Delawares, in 1778 (the first formal
treaty made by the United States with any Indian tribe), the
lands of the Indians are not referred to by any given boundaries. It was simply stated that the most practicable way for
the troops of the United States, to the posts and forts of the
British on the lakes and other places, "is by passing through
the country of the Delawares;" and the Indians agreed "to
give a free passage through their country to the troops aforesaid."

In 1782, the year before the treaty of peace, Congress had
under consideration a cession of land from the State of New
York to the United States, and the committee to whom the
subject was referred, on the first of May of that year, recommended the acceptance of the cession, for the following
reasons:

" 1. It clearly appeared to your committee that all the
lands belonging to the Six Nations of Indians and their tributaries have been, in due form, put under the protection of the
crown of England, by the said Six Nations, as appendant to
the late government of the colony of New York, so far as respects jurisdiction only.

" 2. That the citizens of the said colony of New York have
borne the burden, both as to blood and treasure, of protecting
and supporting the said Six Nations of Indians and their
tributaries, for upward of one hundred years last past, as the
dependents and allies of the said government.

" 3. That the crown of England has always considered and
treated the country of the said Six Nations and their tributaries, inhabited as far as the forty-fifth degree of north latitude, as appendant to the government of New York.

" 4. That the neighboring colonies of Massachusetts, Connecticut, Pennsylvania, Maryland, and Virginia have also, from time to time, by their public acts, recognized and admitted the said Six Nations and their tributaries to be appendant to the government of New York.

" 5. That by Congress accepting this cession, the jurisdiction of the whole western territory, belonging to the Six Nations and their tributaries, will be vested in the United States, greatly to the advantage of the Union."

The committee of Congress assume, in their report, a right in the Six Nations to lands in the western territory which had no foundation in fact. The government commissioners, Oliver Walcott, Richard Butler, and Arthur Lee, who made the treaty of the 22d of October, 1784, with the Six Nations, at Fort Stanwix, certainly entertained no such opinion. The provisions of the treaty are sufficient evidence on this subject. The first article gives peace to the Senecas, Mohawks, Onondagas, and Cayugas, and the United States receives and gives them protection on the following conditions: Six Indian hostages are to be given to the commissioners by the said Indians, to remain in possession of the United States, till all the prisoners, white and black, which were taken by the Senecas, in the late war, shall be given up; and the Oneidas and Tuscaroras are to be secured in the possession of the lands on which they are settled. The third article reads thus:

" Art. 3. A line shall be drawn beginning at the mouth of a creek about four miles east of Niagara, called Oyonwayea, or Johnson's landing place, upon the lake, named by the Indians Oswego, and by us Ontario; from thence southerly, always four miles east of the carrying path, between Lake Erie and Ontario, to the mouth of Tehoreroran, or Buffalo creek, on Lake Erie; thence south to the north boundary of the State of Pennsylvania, thence west to the end of the said north boundary, thence south along the west boundary of said state to the river Ohio, the said line, from the mouth of the Oyonwayea to the Ohio, shall be the western boundary of the Six Nations; that the Six Nations shall and do yield to the United States all claims to the country west of the said boundary, and then they shall be secured in the peaceable possession of the lands they inhabit, east and north of the same, reserving only six miles square round the Fort of Oswego to the United States, for the support of the same."

The fourth and last article of the treaty says that " the commissioners, in consideration of the present circumstances of the Six Nations, and in the execution of the humane and liberal views of the United States, upon the signing of the above articles, will order goods to be delivered to the said Six Nations, for their use and comfort."

The Six Nations had, on many occasions previous to that time, operated in Canada, and westward along the lakes; they had driven the Hurons and other tribes infesting the borders of the lakes before them; had made incursions to the south and southwest on hostile expeditions; the French, on divers occasions, had felt their power, and years before our revolutionary period they had organized their confederacy, and it was said that when the colonies were discussing the matter of forming some sort of a league or union, the Iroquois chiefs and orators held up their confederation as an example for imitation.

It is not to be presumed that such a people, if they considered they had valid claims to such a vast country as the western territory would yield all right to it, simply for a few goods to be delivered to them for their use and comfort, at the time of signing the Fort Stanwix treaty.

In the month of January, 1789, another treaty was made with the Six Nations at Fort Harmer. Arthur St. Clair, then governor of the Northwest Territory, was the commissioner on the part of the United States. The Six Nations (except the Mohawks, who did not attend) confirmed the boundary line established by the treaty of 1784, and gave a release and quitclaim to all lands west of said boundary to the United States, and the parties mutually pledged to each other peace and friendship.

The original instructions for the government of the commissioners appointed in 1783, to make treaties with all the Indian nations, provided for one convention with all the tribes, but these were amended the following March, so as to authorize treaties with tribes separately, as far as possible.

On the 21st of January, 1785, a treaty was made at Fort McIntosh, between the United States and the Wyandots, Delawares, Chippewas, and Ottawas. George Rogers Clark, Richard Butler, and Arthur Lee represented the government. The Indians agreed to give up all prisoners taken by them, and acknowledged themselves and all their tribes to be under the protection of the United States, and no other sovereign whatever. The third article reads as follows:

"Art. 3. The boundary line between the United States and the Wyandot and Delaware nations shall begin at the mouth of the river Cuyahoga, and thence up said river to the portage between that and the Tuscarawas branch of the Muskingum; thence down the said branch to the forks at the crossing place above Fort Lawrence (Laurens), thence westwardly to the portage of the Big Miami, which runs into the Ohio, at the mouth of which branch the fort stood which was taken by the French in 1752; thence along said portage to the Great Miami, or Ome river (Maumee), and down the southeast side of the same to its mouth; thence along the south shore of Lake Erie to the mouth of the Cuyahoga, where it began."

By the fourth article all the lands contained within the said boundary lines were confirmed to the Wyandot and Delaware nations, and to such of the Ottawas as live thereon, saving and reserving for the establishment of trading posts reservations of six miles square, at the mouth of the Miami, or Ome (Maumee) river; at the portage on the branch of the Big Miami, which runs into the Ohio, and the same on the lake at Sandusky, where the fort formerly stood, and two miles square on each side of the lower rapids of Sandusky river, "which posts and lands shall be to the use and under the government of the United States." Reservations were also excepted at the posts of Detroit and Michilimackinac.

The fifth article stipulates, that if any citizen of the United States, or other person, not being an Indian, shall attempt to settle on any of the lands allotted to the Wyandot and Delaware nations, except the lands reserved, "such persons shall forfeit the protection of the United States, and the Indians *may punish him as they please.*" The Indians acknowledge that the territory east, west, and south of the lines described in the third article, so far as *they* formerly claimed the same, belong to the United States, and none of their tribes shall presume to settle upon the same.

On the 9th day of January, 1789, a treaty between the United States, by Governor Arthur St. Clair, and the sachems and warriors of the Wyandot, Delaware, Ottawa, Chippewa, Pottawatomie, and Sac nations, was concluded, at Fort Harmer, for removing all causes of controversy, regulating trade, and settling boundaries. By this treaty the boundary line between the United States and said Indian nations, as defined in the treaty of Fort McIntosh (January 21, 1785), was confirmed, except as follows: In the boundary line from the portage to that branch of the Miami river which runs into the lake, as described in the Fort McIntosh treaty, the words, if strictly construed, would carry the line over to the Auglaize, which was neither the intention of the commissioners nor the Indians, " therefore it is hereby declared that the line shall run from said portage directly to the first fork of the Miami river, which is to the southward and eastward of the Miami village, thence down the main branch of the Miami to said village, thence down that river to Lake Erie, and along the margin thereof to the place of beginning."

In consideration of former presents, and goods then delivered, the Indians renewed and confirmed the said boundary line, to the end that the same may remain a division line between the lands of the United States of America and the lands of said Indian nations *forever*. And said Indians relinquished and ceded to the United States all the land east, south, and west of the boundaries designated, so far as they formerly claimed the same. The Indians are prohibited from disposing of their lands to any sovereign power, except the United States. They are to occupy their lands as they see fit, and are to be permitted to hunt within the ceded territory, without hindrance or molestation, so long as they demean themselves peaceably, and offer no injury or annoyance to any of the subjects or citizens of the United States. They are to give up all prisoners, and all parties or persons committing murder or robbery, either Indians or whites, are to be delivered up for trial according to the laws of the territory; and "if any person or persons, citizens or subjects of the United States, or any other person, not being an Indian, shall *presume* to settle upon the lands confirmed to the said nations, he and they shall be out of the protection of the United States, and the Indian nations *may punish him or them in such manner as they see fit*."

A separate treaty with the Shawanoe nation was entered into on the northwest bank of the Ohio river, at the mouth of the Great Miami river, on the 31st of January, 1786. In it, the Indians acknowledged the United States to be the sole and absolute sovereign of all the territory ceded to them by the treaty of peace between them and the king of Great Britain, which treaty was ratified January 14, 1784; and the United States granted peace to the Shawanoe nation, and agreed to receive the Indians into their friendship and protection.

Article sixth is in these words: "The United States do allot to the Shawanoe nation lands within their territory, to live and hunt upon, beginning at the south line of the lands allotted to the Wyandot and Delaware nations, at the place where the main branch of the Great Miami river, which falls into the Ohio, intersects said line; thence down the river Miami to the fork of that river next below the old fort which was taken by the French in 1752; thence due west to the river De la Panse; thence down that river to the river Wabash, beyond which lines none of the citizens of the United States shall settle, nor disturb the Shawanoes in their settlements and possessions; and the Shawanoes do relinquish to the United States all title, or pretense of title, they ever had to the lands east, west, and south of the east, west, and south lines before described."

In the seventh and last article it is stipulated that "if any citizen of the United States shall presume to settle upon the lands allotted to the Shawanoes by this treaty, *he or they shall be put out of the protection of the United States*."

By the terms of the treaty of peace, Great Britain was to evacuate all the posts and forts held by her without delay. From complications not then anticipated, she held the frontier posts for a number of years. This fact left the impression among the Indians that the controversy was not yet closed, and their minds were poisoned by those about the posts. The British Indian superintendent, John Johnson, thus wrote to Brant in 1787 :

" Do not suffer an idea to have a place in your mind that it will be for your interest to sit still and see the Americans attempt the posts. It is for your sakes chiefly, if not entirely, that we hold them. If you become indifferent about them, they may, perhaps, be given up ; what security would you have then ? You would be left at the mercy of a people whose blood calls aloud for revenge ; whereas, by supporting them, you encourage us to hold them, and encourage the new settlements, already considerable, and every day increasing by numbers coming in who find they can not live in the States. Many thousands are preparing to come in. This increase of his majesty's subjects will serve as a protection to you, should the subjects of the States, by endeavoring to make further encroachments on you, disturb your quiet." The same year the British commandant at Detroit wrote Brant that the governor was sorry to learn " that while the Indians were soliciting his assistance in their preparations for war, some of the Six Nations had sent deputies to Albany to treat with the Americans, who, it is said, have made a treaty with them, granting permission to make roads for the purpose of coming to Niagara ; but that, notwithstanding these things, the Indians should have their presents, as they are marks of the king's approbation of their former conduct. In future, his lordship wishes them to act as best for their interests ; he can not begin a war with the Americans, because some of their people encroach and make depredations on part of the Indian country, but they must see it is his lordship's intention to defend the posts ; and that while these are preserved, the Indians must find great security therefrom, and consequently the Americans have greater difficulty in taking possession of their lands ; but should they (the Americans) once become masters of the posts, they will surround the Indians, and accomplish their purpose with but little trouble. From a consideration of all which it remains with the Indians to decide what is most for their interest, and to let his lordship know their determination, that he may take measures accordingly; but whatever their resolution is, it should be taken as by one and the same people, by which means they will be respected and become strong; but if they divide, and act one part against the other, they will become weak, and help to destroy each other. This is a substance of what his lordship desired me to tell you. . . . It is well known that no encroachments ever have or ever will be made by the English upon the lands or property of the Indians, in consequence of possessing the posts. How far that will be the case if ever the Americans get into them, may very easily be imagined from their hostile perseverance, even without this advantage, in driving the Indians off of their lands and taking possession of them."

The condition of things in the Western Territory at this time—the intrusion of the whites and their trespassing on the Indian lands and the conflicts that occurred—were well calculated to and did prepare the minds of the Indians to receive favorably the suggestions that came to them from the British posts, and to attach them to the English. In view of existing facts, a military expedition was organized and placed under the command of Gen. Harmer. He penetrated the country to the Miami villages on the head-waters of the Maumee, in 1790. He had two unimportant skirmishes with the Indians in the month of October, and destroyed several of their towns, and about twenty thousand bushels of corn in the ear. The Indians abandoned their villages before his army reached them.

In 1791, by authority of the government, a body of mounted volunteers was raised in Kentucky to operate against the Indians on the Wabash. Many Indians were killed, their villages burned, and about four hundred acres of their corn destroyed. Harmer did not reach the upper Indian towns on the Wabash. The government had been for several years impressed with a desire to establish a strong military post at the junction of the St. Mary's and St. Joseph's rivers, and these expeditions were in some degree prompted by this desire.

In the spring of the same year (1791) another expedition was fitted out and placed under the command of Governor Arthur St. Clair, who had been appointed a major-general in the United States army. In the instructions to St. Clair, the secretary of war informed him that one object of the campaign was to establish a strong and permanent military post at the Miami village, and after the defeat of St. Clair, the secretary, in his official report of the affair, made December 26, 1791, said : " The great object of the campaign was to establish a strong military post at the Miami village." St. Clair's army reached a stream which he supposed was the St. Mary of the Maumee, but in fact a branch of the Wabash, on the 3d of November, 1791. At this point, which he supposed to be about fifteen miles from the village, he determined to throw up a slight work in which to deposit the men's knapsacks and all else not of absolute necessity, and then to have moved on " to attack the enemy as soon as the first regiment came up ; " but he was not allowed to do either, since on the 4th, about half an hour before sunrise, and when the men had just been dismissed from the morning parade, St. Clair reported that " an attack was made upon the militia. These gave way in a very little time and rushed into camp (through Major Butler's battalion which, together with a part of Clark's, they threw into considerable disorder, and which, notwithstanding the exertions of both these officers, was never altogether remedied). The fire, however, of the front line checked the Indians; but, almost instantly, a very severe attack began upon that line, and in a few minutes it was likewise extended to the second. The great weight of it was directed against the center of each, where the artillery was placed, and from which the men were repeatedly driven with great slaughter." The conflict was terrible. The artillery was silenced, every officer but one being killed. Every officer of the second regiment except three fell, and more than one-half of the army was destroyed. The remnant made an effort to regain the road, which done " the militia took along it, followed by the troops." In his report of this unhappy affair, St. Clair said : " The retreat, in those circumstances, was, as you may be sure, a precipitate one. It was in fact a flight. The camp and the artillery were abandoned, but that was unavoidable, for not a horse was left alive to have drawn it off, had it otherwise been practicable. But the most disgraceful part of the business is, that the greatest part of the men threw away their arms and accouterments, even after the pursuit, which continued about four miles, had ceased. I found the road strewed with them for many miles, but was not able to remedy it, for having had all my horses killed, and being mounted upon one that could not be pricked out of a walk, I could not get forward myself; and the orders I sent forward, either to halt the front or to prevent the men from parting with their arms, were unattended to. The flight continued to Fort Jefferson, twenty-nine miles, which was reached a little after sun-setting." Out of an army of fourteen hundred men, the killed and wounded amounted to eight hundred and ninety, in an attempt " to establish a strong military post at the Miami village," which " was the great object of the campaign." Other forts were contemplated in addition to this one, connecting it with Fort Washington, on the Ohio. Before St. Clair set out, he was advised by the secretary of war that the establishment of a fort at the Miami village " is considered an important object of the campaign, and is to take place in all events. In case of a previous treaty, the Indians are to be conciliated upon this point, if possible, and it is presumed good arguments may be offered to induce their acquiescence." When we remember that Governor St. Clair was the United States commissioner and party to the treaty of Fort Harmer, made January 9, 1789, less than three years before the overwhelming defeat of his army, and by that treaty a line was established to be and remain " a division line between the lands of the United States and the lands of said Indian nations *forever*," and that the village was in the territory confirmed to the Indian nations forever, by the treaty, with assurances that " if any person or persons, citizens or subjects of the United States, or any person not being an Indian, shall presume to settle upon the lands confirmed to the said nations, he and they shall be out of the protection of the United States, *and the said Indian nations may punish him or them in such manner as they see fit*"—there appears to be in this sad tragedy matter for the most serious reflection. Various tracts of land were, by the treaty, reserved for posts and forts, but there is no provision for any reservation at the Miami village, for any purpose whatever, notwithstanding the existence of the village was known before the treaty was made, and in fact is specifically referred to in the treaty.

Before St. Clair's army set out on its ill-fated expedition, a talk was sent to various Indian nations, inviting them to a peace conference, proposed to be held with them, at the rapids of the Maumee. Subsequently, the place of meeting was changed to Sandusky. Benjamin Lincoln, Beverly Randolph, and Timothy Pickering were appointed commissioners. When these gentlemen were at Niagara, the guests of Governor Simcoe, the Mohawk chief, Brant, with some fifty other Indian deputies, who came from the Maumee, called on them, and, through Brant, in the presence of the governor, thus addressed them:

" *Brothers:* We have met to-day our brothers, the Bostonians and the English; we are glad to have the meeting, and think that it is by appointment of the Great Spirit. Brothers of the United States: We told you the other day, at Fort Erie, that, at another time, we would inform you why we had not assembled at the time and place appointed for holding the treaty with you. We now inform you that it was because there was so much of the appearance of war in that quarter. Brothers: We have given the reasons for our not meeting you; and now we request an explanation of those warlike appearances. Brothers: The people you see here are sent to represent the Indian nations who own the land north of the Ohio as their common property, and who are all of one mind, one heart. Brothers: We have come to speak to you for two reasons—one, because your warriors, being in our neighborhood, have prevented our meeting at the appointed place; the other, to know if you are properly authorized to run and establish a new boundary line between the lands of the United States and the Indian nations? We are still desirous of meeting you at the appointed place. Brothers: We wish you to deliberate well on this business. We have spoken our sentiments in sincerity, considering ourselves in the presence of the Great Spirit, from whom, in time of danger, we expect assistance."

On the succeeding day, the commissioners made the following reply :

" *Brothers:* You have mentioned two objects of your coming to meet us at this place. One, to obtain an explanation of the warlike appearances on the part of the United States, on the northwestern side of the Ohio ; the other, whether we have authority to run and establish a new boundary line between your lands and ours. Brothers : On the first point, we can not but express our regret that any reports of warlike appearances on the part of the United States should have delayed our meeting at Sandusky. The nature of the case irresistibly forbids all apprehensions of any hostile incursions into the Indian country north of the Ohio, during the treaty at Sandusky. Brothers : We are deputed by the Great Chief and the Great Council of the United States to treat with you of peace ; and is it possible that the same Great Chief and his Great Council could order their warriors to make fresh war, while we were sitting round the same fire with you, in order to make peace ? Is it possible that our Great Chief and his Great Council would act so deceitfully toward us, their commissioners, as well as toward you ? Brothers : We think it not possible ; but we will quit arguments, and come to facts. Brothers : We assure you that our Great Chief, General Washington, has strictly forbidden all hostilities against you, until the event of the proposed treaty at Sandusky shall be known. Here is the proclamation of his head warrior, General Wayne, to that effect. But, brothers, our Great Chief is so sincere in his professions for peace, and so desirous for preventing every thing which would obstruct the treaty and prolong the war, that besides giving the above order to his head warrior, he has informed the governors of the several states adjoining the Ohio, of the treaty proposed to be held at Sandusky, and desired them to unite their power with his to prevent any hostile attempts against the Indians north of the Ohio, until the result of the treaty is made known. These governors have accordingly issued their orders strictly forbidding all such hostilities.

The proclamations of the governors of Virginia and Pennsylvania, we have here in our hands.   Brothers: If, after all these precautions of our Great Chief, any hostilities should be committed north of the Ohio, they must proceed from a few disorderly people, whom no considerations of public good can restrain.   But we hope and believe that none such can be found.

" *Brothers:* After these explanations, we hope you will possess your minds in peace, relying on the good faith of the United States that no injury is to be apprehended by you during the treaty.   Brothers: We now come to the second point: Whether we are authorized to run and establish a new boundary line between your lands and ours.   Brothers: We answer explicitly that we have that authority.   Where this line should run, will be the great subject of discussion at the treaty between you and us; and we sincerely hope and expect that it will then be fixed to the satisfaction of both parties.   Doubtless some concessions must be made on both sides.   In all disputes and quarrels both parties usually take some wrong steps; so that it is only by mutual concessions that a true reconciliation can be effected.   Brothers: We wish you to understand us clearly on this head; for we mean that all our proceedings shall be made with candor.   We therefore repeat, and say explicitly, that some concessions will be necessary on your part as well as on ours, in order to establish a just and permanent peace.   After this great point of the boundary shall be fully considered at the treaty, we shall know what concessions and stipulations it will be proper to make, on the part of the United States; and we trust they will be such as the world will pronounce reasonable and just.   Brothers: You told us you represented the nations of Indians who owned the lands north of the Ohio, and whose chiefs are assembled at the rapids of the Maumee.   Brothers: It would be a satisfaction for us to be informed of the names of those nations, and of the number of chiefs of each so assembled.   Brothers: We once more turn our eyes to your representation of warlike appearances in our country.   To give you complete satisfaction on this point, we now assure

5

you that as soon as our council at this place is ended we will send a messenger on horseback to the great chief of the United States, requesting him to renew, and strongly repeat, his orders to his head warrior, not only to abstain from all hostilities against you, but to remain quietly at his post until the event of the treaty shall be known."

Much more was said by the commissioners, which may be omitted in this connection, since in the communcation of the Indians, in reply to the speech of the commissioners, the former have embodied the most important statements of the latter, with their comments on them. In reply to the inquiry of the commissioners, as to the tribes then at the rapids, Brant said : " Yesterday you expressed a wish to be informed of the names of the nations, and number of chiefs, assembled at the Maumee; but, as they were daily coming in, we can not give you exact information. You will see for yourself in a few days. When we left it the following nations were there, to wit: Five Nations, Wyandots, Delawares, Shawanoes, Munsees, Miamies, Chippewas, Ottawas, Pottawatomies, Nantikokies, Mingoes, Cherokees. The principal men of them .were there. "

The reader will remember that the treaty of Fort McIntosh, made January 21, 1785, was with the Wyandot, Delaware, Chippewa, and Ottawa nations only; and St. Clair's treaty, of January 9, 1789, was with the above named and the Pottawatomies and Sac nations only. The Miami, Kickapoo, Eel River, Wea, Piankashaw, Kaskaskia, and other tribes northwest of the Ohio river, had no lot or part in either. The St. Clair, or Harmer treaty, was made about eighteen months after the adoption of the ordinance of 1787. In that ordinance the following provision is found: " The utmost good faith shall always be observed toward the Indians; their lands and property shall never be taken from them without their consent; and in their property, rights, and liberty they shall never be invaded or disturbed unless in just and lawful wars, authorized by Congress; but laws, founded in justice and humanity, shall, from time to time, be made for preventing wrongs being done to them, and for preserving peace and friendship with them."

The talk of the United States commissioners, in reply to the speech of Brant and his associates, at the Niagara meeting, was made in July, 1793. The final reply to this talk was adopted in a general council of the confederate Indian nations, held at the foot of the rapids of the Maumee, on the 13th of August, 1793. Its importance will be perceived on the perusal of the document itself. It is as follows:

" To the Commissioners of the United States:

" *Brothers:* We have received your speech, dated the 31st of last month, and it has been interpreted to all the different nations. We have been long in sending you an answer, because of the great importance of the subject. But we now answer it fully, having given it all the consideration in our power.

" *Brothers:* You tell us that after you had made peace with the king, our father, about ten years ago, 'it remained to make peace between the United States and the Indian nations who had taken part with the king. For this purpose commissioners were appointed, who sent messengers to all those Indian nations, inviting them to come and make peace;' and after reciting the periods at which you say treaties were held at Fort Stanwix, Fort McIntosh, and Miami, all which treaties, according to your own acknowledgment, were for the sole purpose of making peace, you then say: 'Brothers: The commissioners who conducted these treaties in behalf of the United States, sent the papers containing them to the general council of the States, who supposing them satisfactory to the natives treated with, proceeded to dispose of the lands thereby ceded.'

" *Brothers:* This is telling us plainly what we always understood to be the case, and it agrees with the declarations of those few who attended those treaties, viz: that they went to your commissioners to make peace, but through fear were obliged to sign any paper that was laid before them; and it has since appeared that deeds of cession were signed by them, instead of treaties of peace.

" *Brothers:* You then say, 'after some time it appears that people in your nations were dissatisfied with the treaties of Fort McIntosh and Miami; therefore, the council of the

United States appointed Governor St. Clair their commissioner, with full power, for the purpose of removing all causes of controversy, relating to trade and settling boundaries between the Indian nations in the northern department of the United States. He accordingly sent messengers inviting all the nations concerned to meet him at a council fire to be kindled at the falls of the Muskingum. While he was waiting for them some mischief happened at that place, and the fire was put out; so he kindled a council fire at Fort Harmer, where nearly six hundred Indians of different nations attended. The Six Nations then renewed and confirmed the treaty of Fort Stanwix; and the Wyandots and Delawares renewed and confirmed the treaty of Fort McIntosh; some Ottawas, Chippewas, Pottawatomies, and Sacs were also parties to the treaty of Fort Harmer.' Now, brothers, these are your words, and it is necessary for us to make a short reply to them.

" *Brothers :* A general council of all the Indian confederacy was held, as you well know, in the fall of the year 1788, at this place; and that general council was invited by your commissioner, Governor St. Clair, to meet him for the purpose of holding a treaty, with regard to the lands mentioned by you to have been ceded by the treaties of Fort Stanwix and Fort McIntosh.

" *Brothers :* We are in possession of the speeches and letters which passed on that occasion, between those deputed by the confederated Indians and Governor St. Clair, the commissioner of the United States. These papers prove that your said commissioner; in the beginning of the year 1789, and after having been informed by the general council of the preceding fall, that no bargain or sale for any part of these Indian lands would be considered as valid or binding, unless agreed to by a general council, nevertheless, persisted in collecting together a few chiefs of two or three nations only, and with them held a treaty for the cession of an immense country, in which they were no more interested than as a branch of the general confederacy, and who were in no manner authorized to make any grant or concession whatever.

" *Brothers :* How, then, was it possible for you to expect to enjoy peace, and quietly to hold these lands, when your commissioner was informed long before he had the treaty of Fort Harmer, that the consent of a general council was absolutely necessary to convey any part of these lands to the United States? The part of these lands which the United States now wish us to relinquish, and which you say are settled, have been sold by the United States since that time.

" *Brothers:* You say 'the United States wish to have confirmed all the lands ceded to them by the treaty of Fort Harmer, and also a small tract at the rapids of the Ohio, claimed by General Clark, for the use of himself and his warriors. And in consideration thereof, the United States would give such a large sum of money or goods, as was never given at any one time, for any quantity of Indian lands, since the white people first set their feet on this island. And because these lands did every year furnish you with skins and furs, with which you bought clothing and other necessaries, the United States will now furnish the like constant supplies. And, therefore, beside the great sum to be delivered at once, they will every year deliver you a large quantity of goods, as are best fitted to the wants of yourselves and your women and children.'

" *Brothers:* Money to us is of no value, and to most of us unknown; and as no consideration whatever can induce us to sell our lands on which we get sustenance for our women and children, we hope we may be allowed to point out a mode by which your settlers may be easily removed, and peace thereby obtained.

" *Brothers:* We know that these settlers are poor, or they never would have ventured to live in a country which has been in continual trouble ever since they crossed the Ohio. Divide, therefore, this large sum of money, which you have offered to us, among these people. Give to each, also, a proportion of what you say you would give to us, annually, over and above this large sum of money; and as we are persuaded, they would most readily accept of it, in lieu of the land you sold them. If you add, also, the great sums you must expend in raising and paying armies, with a view to force us to yield our country, you will certainly have more than sufficient for the purpose of repaying these settlers, for all their labor and all their improvements.

"*Brothers:* You have talked to us about concessions. It appears strange that you should expect any from us, who have only been defending our just rights, against your invasions. We want peace. Restore to us our country, and we shall be enemies no longer.

"*Brothers:* You make one concession to us by offering us your money, and another by having agreed to do us justice, after having long and injuriously withheld it; we mean in the acknowledgment you have made, that the king of England never did, nor never had a right to give you our country, by the treaty of peace. And you want to make this act of common justice a great part of your concessions; and seem to expect that, because you have at last acknowledged our independence, we should, for such a favor, surrender to you our country.

"*Brothers:* You have talked, also, a great deal about preemption, and your exclusive right to purchase Indian lands, as ceded to you by the king, at the treaty of peace.

"*Brothers:* We never made any agreement with the king, nor with any other nation, that we would give to either the exclusive right of purchasing our lands; and we declare to you that we consider ourselves free to make any bargain or cession of lands, whenever and to whomsoever we please. If the white people, as you say, made a treaty that none of them but the king should purchase of us, and that he has given that right to the United States, it is an affair which concerns you and him, and not us; we have never parted with such a power.

"*Brothers:* At our general council held at the Glaize last fall, we agreed to meet commissioners from the United States, for the purpose of restoring peace, provided they consented to acknowledge and confirm our boundary line to the Ohio, and we determined not to meet you until you gave us satisfaction on that point; that is the reason we have never met.

"We desire you to consider, brothers, that our only demand is the peaceable possession of a small part of our once great country. Look back and review the lands from whence we have been driven to this spot. We can retreat no farther, because the country behind us barely affords food for its inhabitants; and we have, therefore, resolved to leave our bones in this small space to which we are now confined.

" *Brothers:* We shall be persuaded that you mean to do us justice, if you agree that the Ohio shall remain the boundary line between us. If you will not consent thereto, our meeting will be altogether unnecessary. This is the great point, which we hoped would have been explained before you left your homes, as our message, last fall, was principally directed to obtain that information. Done in general council, at the foot of the Maumee rapids, the 13th day of August, 1793."

This document was signed by the deputies of the nations who were in the general council that adopted it. They were the Wyandots, Miamis, Monhicans, Seven Nations of Canada, Ottawas, Connoys, Pottawatomies, Messagoes, Delawares, Senecas of the Glaize, Chippewas, Nantakokies, Shawanoes, Munsees, Creeks, and Cherokees. To it, the United States commissioners made no reply. Indeed, they could not, since the most telling points in it could not be controverted. The government was extremely anxious to compose existing difficulties, and was disposed to be liberal in the terms of accommodation, provided the promises its commissioners were prepared to make should, in the event of a treaty, be carried out. The Indians, however, smarting under the wrongs they had suffered, and, no doubt, prompted by the enemies of the United States, and believing, as they did, that such a natural boundary line as the Ohio river was absolutely necessary to be established between their lands and those of the whites, made it the *sine qua non* to any treaty arrangements, and thus staked their very existence upon a contest which must inevitably follow; for, in the condition of affairs as they then were, the settlements already made by the whites northwest of the Ohio rendered it impossible to conclude a treaty with that river as the boundary line, and hence there seemed to be no alternative but a resort to arms, to settle the pending difficulty. Anterior to the first expedition, under Harmer, doubts were expressed by Washington as to the justice as well as the policy of offensive operations against the Indian tribes in the Northwest Territory. If, at an earlier day, and before any settlements were made in the Western Territory, the government had operated through commissioners of high character, proper arrangements might probably have been made with the Indian nations for the occupation of a portion of the country by the white people, and thus much of the suffering, and many of the terrible events which make such sad chapters in our early annals, might have been averted. In contemplating these events, it is only natural that our sympathies become deeply enlisted in behalf of those of our own race who struggled and suffered, and even met death, in the conflict to open up the wilderness and found new states; but we should not forget that the red man, whom our fathers found here, had his sufferings and trials also. He had not the means to write and publish them as they occurred, but sufficient is known to command for the Indian race our sincere sympathy.

It can not be denied that the invasion and occupation of the territory northwest of the Ohio river was made anterior to any arrangement with the natives for that purpose. Had the Indian nations been civilized communities of our own race, but subjects or citizens of a foreign state, mankind would have admitted the justice of their cause, and such an address from them as the one sent by the confederate tribes to the United States commissioners, on the 13th of August, 1793, would have taken rank with the Declaration of Independence. Being "savages," the arguments and facts presented by them to our commissioners were not answered and refuted, but, by military power, the Indians were confronted, and, being unable to make successful resistance, the red men were compelled to yield the boundary they had contended for, and submit to irresistible force.

CHAPTER V.

St. Clair's defeat communicated to Congress.—Another campaign projected.—Gen. Wayne assigned to command it.—The Indians defeated.
—Treaty of Greenville.—A boundary or division line adopted.—
More territory demanded from the Indians.—Subsequent treaties and
their effect.—Rupture between Tecumseh and Gen. Harrison.—Battle of Tippecanoe.—Tecumseh joins the British, and is killed at the
battle of the Thames, etc.

On the 9th of November, 1791, General St. Clair made report to the secretary of war, communicating the sad disaster
that befell his army on the 4th of the month. On the 12th of
December of the same year, the information was communicated to Congress, and on the 26th of December, the secretary submitted to the president a communication, in which
suggestions and recommendations were made as to future
operations. After discussing the policy of the government
toward the Indians, the futility, in his opinion, of all attempts
to preserve peace, and the justice of the claim of the United
States, he says: " Hence it would appear the principles of
justice as well as policy, and it may be added the principles
of economy, all combine to dictate that an adequate military
force should be raised as soon as possible, placed upon the
frontiers, and disciplined according to the nature of the service, and, in order to meet with the prospect of success, the
greatest possible combination of the Indian enemy." The
secretary recommended while this army was being organized
the temporary employment of mounted volunteers, such as
had in the border wars given fame to Kentucky, to operate
in a desultory way against the Indians, thus occupying them
in the protection of their own families and preventing " them
from spreading terror and destruction along the frontiers."
He further suggested " the expediency of employing the Indians in alliance with us against the hostile Indians. The
justice of engaging them (he said) will depend upon the justice of the war. If the war be just upon our part, it will

certainly bear the test of examination to use the same sort of means in our defense as are used against us." In his official report of St. Clair's defeat to Congress, the secretary said that " the great object of the campaign was to establish a strong military post at the Miami village, which was to be connected by posts to Fort Washington and the Ohio." The reply of the confederate Indian nations from their general council at the foot of the rapids of the Maumee, to our commissioners, was: " Restore to us our country, and we shall be enemies no longer." However imperative the necessity for some military operations for the protection of the settlers in the Western Territory, at the time, it is difficult to see how the war could be called a just war. However, after the defeat of St. Clair, another and more formidable military expedition was a foregone conclusion. St. Clair resigned, and his place was supplied by the appointment of Anthony Wayne, who, in June, 1792, moved westward, making Pittsburgh, for a time, his headquarters, where he commenced organizing an army which, it was said, " was to be the ultimate argument of the Americans with the Indian Confederation." While Wayne was organizing and drilling his troops, which he denominated the Legion of the United States, Gen. Washington had instructed peace talks to be sent among the Indian nations. In the spring of 1793, Wayne's army arrived at Fort Washington (near Cincinnati), and remained there until after the rejection by the Indian Confederation of the propositions made by our commissioners for a treaty. Early in October, 1793, he moved from Cincinnati; and on the 25th of the month a portion of his army occupied the field of St. Clair's defeat. Here he immediately erected a fort, called Recovery, which was garrisoned and placed under a proper commander. On this field were found about six hundred human skulls, which were gathered up and buried. One of the officers wrote: " When we went to lay down in our tents at night, we had to scrape the bones together and carry them out." These were the sad memorials of the conflict between St. Clair's troops and the Indians. At this period the British were stimulating the Indians, and promising them assistance. Some Pottawatomie Indians told Wayne that Governor Simcoe was stimulating and urging the Indians to war; that the speeches they "received from him were as red as blood; all the wampum and feathers were painted red, and even the tobacco was painted red." Wayne himself remained at Greenville during the winter and spring. On the 30th of June, 1794, Fort Recovery was attacked by a large Indian force under the chief Little Turtle, who was the successful commander in the battle with St. Clair's troops. It was supposed that when he attacked Wayne's troops that he had from ten to fifteen hundred men, not all, however, Indians. He was repulsed. On the 26th of July, Wayne was joined by about sixteen hundred mounted volunteers from Kentucky. On the 8th of August, his army was at Grand Glaize, and proceeded to build Fort Defiance. The Indians, on hearing of Wayne's movements, abandoned their towns before he reached the Glaize. While engaged on Fort Defiance, Wayne received full information as to the strength of the Indians, the probable aid they would get from Detroit, and all circumstances necessary to be known, and decided to march forward without delay. Before doing this, however, he sent out a message to the Indians for compromise and peace, by a man named Miller, who had lived among the Shawanoes, and who had but recently been taken prisoner by one of Wayne's spies. He addressed this message: "To the Delawares, Shawanoes, Miamis, and Wyandots, and to each and every of them, and to all other Indian nations, northwest of the Ohio, whom it may concern. As commander-in-chief of the army and commissioner plenipotentiary of the United States of America, for settling the terms upon which a permanent and lasting peace shall be made with each and every of the hostile Indians northwest of the Ohio," he assured them that he was actuated by the purest principles of humanity, and urged by pity for the errors into which bad and designing men had led them, he once more from the head of his army extended the friendly hand of peace toward them, and invited them to appoint deputies to meet him without delay, on his march, to settle the preliminaries of a *lasting peace*, which would eventually and soon restore to them, "the Delawares, Miamis, Shawanoes, and all other tribes and nations lately settled on the margins of the Miami of the Lake and Auglaize rivers, your late grounds and possessions, and preserve you and your distressed and helpless women and children from danger and famine during the present fall and ensuing winter." He assured them that the arm of the United States was strong and powerful, but they loved mercy and kindness more than war and desolation. He pledged his honor for the safe return of any deputies they might appoint to meet him. Miller started with this message on the 13th of April, 1794, and, not having returned on the 15th, Wayne, on the 16th, put his army in motion, and on that day met Miller on his way back, with a message from the Indians, who desired Wayne to remain ten days at the Glaize, and in the meantime they would decide for peace or war. To this he made no reply, but kept his army moving forward. After proceeding about five miles, his advance received a severe fire from the Indians, who were secreted in the woods and high grass. The savages were formed in three lines, within supporting distance of each other, and extending for near two miles at right angles with the river. They were in full force and in possession of their favorite ground. The battle was pressed with vigor, but an impetuous charge by the troops drove the savages and some Canadian militia, who were in the action, from their coverts in a short time. It was supposed the Indians and their allies numbered two thousand. Wayne's force engaged in the affair was less than that. Indeed, it is said it did not much exceed one thousand, but it was skillfully handled. The Indians were put to the rout, and took to flight, leaving Wayne's legion in full possession of the field. Every officer, from the generals down to the ensigns, received the commendation of the commander. The woods were strewn for a considerable distance with the dead bodies of Indians and their white auxiliaries, the latter armed with British muskets and bayonets. The army remained for three days on the banks of the Maumee, during which time all the houses of the Indians were consumed by fire, and the corn-fields destroyed for a considerable distance both above and below Fort Miami. Even within pistol-shot of the British garrison, at that place, the inmates were compelled to remain tacit spectators of the general conflagration and devastation. The houses, stores, and property of the British Indian agent, Col. McKee, a principal stimulator of the Indians to war, were destroyed.

The army returned by easy marches to Fort Defiance, laying waste the villages and corn-fields of the Indians on each side of the Maumee for a distance of fifty miles. From thence Wayne reported the result of his campaign, and said, "there remains yet a great number of villages and a great quantity of corn to be consumed and destroyed upon the Auglaize and the Maumee, above this place, which will be effected in a few days." Wayne remained at Fort Defiance until the 14th of September, when he set out for the Miami village, at the junction of the St. Joseph and St. Mary, to build the fortress which he called Fort Wayne. This was completed October 22, 1794. There was much sickness among the troops during this time, and they were short of rations. On the 28th of October the legion began its return march to Greenville. Here the volunteers were mustered out. The British agents and officials continued, after the army left the Maumee, to tamper with the Indians in order to induce them to abstain from any treaty arrangements with General Wayne. A Canadian who had purchased three American prisoners from the Indians, came to Fort Wayne to exchange them for some of his relatives, and while there stated that Governor Simcoe, Colonel McKee, and Captain Brant arrived at Fort Miami on the 30th ult. (September.) Brant had with him one hundred Mohawks and Massagoes. Governor Simcoe sent for the chiefs of the different hostile Indians, and invited them to meet him at the mouth of the Detroit river to hold a treaty. Simcoe, Colonel McKee, and Captain Brant, together with Blue Jacket, Buckengales, Little Turtle, Captain Johnny, and other chiefs of the Delawares, Miamis, Shawanoes, Torwas, and Pottawatomies, set out accordingly for the place assigned for the treaty, about the first of October. The Indians, he said, were well and regularly supplied with provisions from the British magazines, at a place called Swan Creek, near the lake.

General Wayne learned from some friendly Wyandots, that on the 10th of October the Indians met the British at the Big Rock, and were advised that their griefs were laid before the king, and Governor Simcoe insisted that they should not listen to any terms of peace from the Americans, but to propose a truce or suspension of hostilities until spring, when a grand council or assemblage of all the warriors and tribes of Indians should take place, for the purpose of compelling the Americans to cross to the east side of the Ohio, and in the interim advise every nation to sign a deed of conveyance of all their lands on the west side of the Ohio to the king, in trust for the Indians, so as to give the British a pretext or color for assisting them, in case the Americans refused to abandon all their posts and possessions on the west side of the Ohio river, and which the Indians should warn them to do immediately after they were assembled in force in the spring; and to call upon the British to guarantee the lands thus ceded in trust, and to make a general attack on the frontiers at the same time; that the British would be prepared to attack the Americans also, in every quarter, and would compel them to cross the Ohio, and give up the lands to the Indians. Captain Brant also told them to keep a good heart and be strong; to do as their father advised; that he would return home for the present with his warriors and come again early in the spring, with an additional number, so as to have the whole summer before them to fight, kill, and pursue the Americans, who could not possibly stand against the force and numbers that would be opposed to them; that he had been always successful and would insure them victory; that he would not attack the Americans at this time, as it would only put them on their guard, and bring them upon the Indians in this quarter during the winter. Therefore, he advised the Indians to amuse the Americans with a prospect of peace, until they should collect in force to fall upon them early in the spring, and when least expected.

At this time the Indians were in a pitiable condition. The crops and dwellings of all who lived in the Maumee and Auglaize valleys had been destroyed. They were in a strait for subsistence. Whether the whites were subjects of Great Britain or citizens of the United States, their treatment of the red men was not such as to induce them to place implicit confidence in their promises. They were, however,

aware that by the treaty of peace the English had renounced
all their authority and rights in the western country, and
notwithstanding the intrigues of Governor Simcoe many
were inclined to make peace. Some were impressed with
this feeling before Wayne's army came into the country.
Such Indians from time to time advised Wayne of their desire for peace. The necessities of the Indians during the
winter of 1794–5 were very great, and they were dependent
on the English, who did not supply their wants. Their
cattle perished, and their dogs died, and they were suffering
for food—in fact, in a starving condition. Under such circumstances, and the absence of aid from the British, the Indians began to yield and sue for peace. In the latter part of
winter there was an exchange of prisoners, and with some
tribes preliminary arrangements were made for a definite
treaty in the following June. Early in this month deputies
from the northwestern tribes began to arrive at Greenville,
and on the sixteenth of the month the first formal council
was held, with such of the deputies as were then present.
Other chiefs and deputies continued to arrive, and the council
continued to deliberate until the 30th of July, on which day
the parties united upon the basis of an agreement *which was
to bury the hatchet forever.* Between that day and the third of
August it was engrossed, and on the last named day signed
by "Anthony Wayne, Sole Commissioner on the part of the
United States, and the Wyandot, Delaware, Shawanoe, Ottawa, Chippewa, Pottawatomie, Miami, Eel River, Wea,
Kickapoo, Piankashaw, and Kaskaskia nations of Indians, by
the deputies of those nations respectively."

By the first article of this treaty, all hostilities were hence-
forth to cease, and peace, which *was to be perpetual,* was established, and a friendly intercourse between these Indian tribes
and the United States was to take place. By the second article all prisoners were to be restored.

The following general boundary line between the lands of
the United States and the lands of these Indian tribes, was established by the third article of the treaty, viz: Beginning " at
the mouth of the Cuyahoga river, and running thence up the
same to the portage, between that and the Tuscarawas branch

of the Muskingum; thence down that branch to the crossing place above Fort Lawrence (Laurens); thence westerly to a fork of the branch of the Great Miami river, running into the Ohio, at or near which fork stood Loramie's store, and where commences the portage between the Miami of the Ohio and St. Mary's river, which is a branch of the Miami, which runs into Lake Erie; thence a westerly course to Fort Recovery; thence southwesterly in a direct line to the Ohio, so as to intersect that river opposite the mouth of the Kentucke or Cuttawa river." The same article of the treaty has this stipulation in it: " In consideration of the peace now established; of the goods formerly received from the United States; of those now to be delivered; of the yearly delivery of goods now stipulated to be made hereafter; and to indemnify the United States for the injuries and expenses they have sustained during the war, the said Indian tribes do hereby cede and relinquish forever, all their claims to the lands lying eastwardly and southwardly of the general boundary line now described; and these lands, or any part of them, shall never hereafter be made a cause or pretense, on the part of the said tribes, or any of them, of war or injury to the United States, or any of the people thereof." In addition to the territory thus ceded to the United States, " as an evidence of the returning friendship of said Indian tribes, and of their confidence in the United States, and desire to provide for their accommodation, and for that convenient intercourse which will be beneficial to both parties," they cede to the government some fifteen separate pieces of land, in quantities ranging from two to twelve miles square, together with the posts of Detroit and Michilimackinac, with considerable land attached to each. Some of these reservations were adjacent to the Mississippi, and all in the unceded country. A free passage by land and water was guaranteed to the people of the United States, through the Indian country, to these posts, as well as the free use of the harbors and mouths of rivers along the lakes adjoining the Indian lands, for sheltering vessels and boats, and liberty to land their cargoes when necessary for safety.

In consideration of the peace established, and the cessions

and relinquishments of lands made by the Indians in the third article, it was stipulated in the fourth article of the treaty, that in order to manifest the liberality of the government, and as a means of rendering this peace *strong and perpetual,* " the United States *relinquished* their claims to all other Indian lands northward of the river Ohio, eastward of the Mississippi, and westward and southward of the great lakes and the waters uniting them, according to the boundary line agreed on by the United States and the king of Great Britain, in the treaty of peace made between them in the year 1783." There was, however, excepted from this relinquishment a tract of one hundred and fifty thousand acres, near the falls of the Ohio, which had been assigned to General Clark, for the use of himself and his warriors, the post of Vincennes, on the Wabash, and the lands adjacent, to which the Indian title had been extinguished; the lands at such other places in possession of the French people, and other white settlers among them, to which the Indian title was also extinguished, and the post of Fort Massac, toward the mouth of the Ohio; to all which parcels of land so excepted the Indians relinquished all the title and claim which they, or any of them, ever had.

Goods to the amount of twenty thousand dollars were delivered to the Indian tribes, and the receipt thereof acknowledged by them, and it was covenanted that " henceforward, every year, *forever,* the United States will deliver at some convenient place northwest of the Ohio, like useful goods, suited to the circumstances of the Indians, of the value of nine thousand five hundred dollars, reckoning that value at the first cost of the goods, in the city or place in the United States where they shall be procured. Such goods to be divided thus: To the Wyandots, Delawares, Shawanoes, Miamis, Ottawas, Chippewas, Pottawatomies, each one thousand dollars; and to the Kickapoos, Weas, Eel Rivers, Piankashaws, and Kaskaskias, each, five hundred dollars. To prevent any misunderstanding about any of the Indian lands, to which the United States relinquished all claim in the fourth article of the treaty, it was in the fifth article thereof " explicitly declared that the

6

meaning of that relinquishment is this : The Indian tribes who have a right to these lands, are quietly to enjoy them, hunting, planting, and dwelling thereon, so long as they please, without any molestation from the United States ; but when those tribes, or any of them, shall be disposed to sell their lands, or any part of them, they are to be sold only to the United States ; and until such sale the United States will protect all the said Indian tribes in the quiet enjoyment of their lands, against all citizens of the United States, and against all other white persons who intrude upon the same." The sixth article provides that " if any citizen of the United States, or any other white person or persons, shall presume to settle upon the lands now relinquished by the United States, such citizen, or other person, shall be out of the protection of the United States, and the Indians, on whose land the settlement shall be made, may drive off the settler, or punish him in such manner as they shall think fit ; and because such settlements, made without the consent of the United States, will be injurious to them as well as to the Indians, the United States shall be at liberty to break them up, and remove and punish the settlers as they shall think proper, and so effect that protection of the Indian lands hereinbefore stipulated."

By the treaty, the Indians were allowed to hunt upon the lands ceded to the United States, without hindrance or molestation, so long as they demeaned themselves peaceably and offered no injury to the people of the United States ; stringent provisions for trade with the Indians were incorporated ; and it was agreed that, for injuries done by individuals, on either side, no private revenge or retaliation should take place ; but instead thereof, complaint shall be made by the party injured to the other, and such prudent measures then be pursued as will be necessary to preserve peace and friendship unbroken, until the great council of the United States shall make equitable provision in the case, to the satisfaction of both parties. Other beneficial and precautionary provisions were incorporated in this treaty. There are but few of the many Indian treaties that we have made with the red man, that are so painstaking and comprehensive in their provisions as Wayne's treaty of Greenville. Withal, it was deceptive, and very soon worked injury to the Indians, who supposed they had a full guaranty to the country relinquished to them. The fatal point was in this—while it guaranteed to the Indians the unmolested occupancy of the lands north, west, and south of the general boundary line described in the treaty, the numerous reservations set apart in this country thus guaranteed, with the right of way to each, virtually opened the Indian country to invasion by the whites, who were not slow in improving the opportunity thus offered to intrude on the Indian lands. It was, however, effective in this—it left the citizens of the United States in the possession and enjoyment of all the lands lying eastwardly and southwardly of the general boundary line described in the third article. There is one noticeable fact connected with this "general boundary line," and that is, by it the Miami village, the establishment of a strong military post at which was the prime object of General St. Clair's campaign in 1791, is left in the country relinquished by the United States to the Indian tribes.

The experience of General Washington, and his personal knowledge of border wars that took place years before our war for independence, between the Indians and parties that sought to make settlements on their lands, caused him to give the matter of the public domain, and the settlement of the same, much thought, and in 1783, in a letter written to James Duane, then in Congress, he unfolded the difficulties that lay in the way of occupying and settling the lands acquired by the treaty of peace. Many schemes were suggested by enterprising and speculative characters, for disposing of the public lands, looking to their absorption in large grants, without regard to the rights of the Indian population. In his letter, Washington insisted that settlements should be made compact; that it should be made felony to survey or settle on any lands west of a line to be designated by Congress; that no land should be purchased from the Indians, except by the sovereign power; and prophesied the renewal of border wars, ending in great sacrifice of life and expenditure of money, if stringent measures were not adopted. The events following proved the wisdom of his suggestions, although they were not carried out. The Congress of the Confederation did, it is true, pass some resolutions and adopt some ordinances of a salutary nature, but they were not regarded. The result was an Indian war of some years' duration, which, however desirous we may be to palliate it, can not be justified.

At the close of Wayne's campaign, the Indians were reduced and impoverished. Those inhabiting the Maumee and Auglaize valleys were left destitute. In one of the letters Wayne wrote from Grand Glaize, he said: "The margins of these beautiful rivers, the Miami of the Lake and Auglaize, appear like one continued village for a number of miles, both above and below this place; nor have I ever before beheld such immense fields of corn in any part of America, from Canada to Florida." All these were destroyed, simply and only to gratify the rapacity of the white man. For several years after the treaty of Greenville, but few difficulties occurred between the Indians and the whites. The former in a good degree remembered the covenants of the treaty, and there seemed to be land sufficient in the ceded country to satisfy, for the time, the avarice of the latter. But as settlements extended and began to approach the boundary line, it was deemed necessary to request our red "brothers" to enter into treaty relations again. More land was demanded; and on the 7th day of June, 1803, General William Henry Harrison, "Governor of Indiana Territory, Superintendent of Indian Affairs, and Commissioner Plenipotentiary of the United States, for concluding any treaty or treaties which may be found necessary with any of the Indian tribes northwest of the river Ohio, of the one part, and the tribes of Indians called the Delawares, Shawanoes, Pottawatomies, Miamis, and Kickapoos, by their chiefs and head warriors, and those of the Eel Rivers, Weas, Piankashaws, and Kaskaskias, by their agents and representatives, Tuthinipee, Winnemar, Richardville, and Little Turtle (who are properly authorized by said tribes), of the other part," convened at Fort Wayne, and entered into a treaty. As early as 1788, the Indians in the Northwest Territory notified the United States government that, by a regulation of their confederation or league, no treaty for a cession of territory would be binding, unless all the Indian nations belonging to the confederacy united in the agreement. It was because of the absence of deputies from many of the Indian nations belonging to the confederacy that the validity of the treaties of Fort McIntosh and Fort Harmer were denied. To enforce these treaties was one of the objects of the campaigns of Harmer and St. Clair; and in 1794, the Indians, on this account, refused to meet the government commissioners, and hence the campaign of General Wayne. It is to be presumed that when Wayne entered into negotiations, in 1795, at Greenville, he had present delegates representing all the nations in the Indian confederacy, and that they were parties to the agreement. It is observed that the Chippewas and Ottawas, two very important tribes who were parties to the treaty of Greenville, were not parties to the treaty of Fort Wayne. Moreover, several of the tribes who were parties to this treaty, appear to have been there only by agents or representatives.

On the 22d day of August, only two months after the execution of the Fort Wayne treaty, Governor Harrison made another treaty at Vincennes; the Indian tribes represented being the Eel River, Wyandot, Piankashaw, and Kaskaskia nations, and also the Kickapoos, "by their representatives, the chiefs of the Eel River nation." The Delawares, Shawanoes, Ottawas, Chippewas, and Miamis were absent.

On the 4th of July, 1805, Charles Jowett, as commissioner on the part of the United States, made a treaty at Fort Industry, with the Wyandots, Ottawas, Chippewas, Munsees, Delawares, Shawanoes, and Pottawatomies. The Kickapoos, Weas, Piankashaws, and Kaskaskias were absent.

On the 25th of August, 1805, Governor Harrison made a treaty at Grouceland, near Vincennes, with the Delawares, Pottawatomies, Miamis, Eel Rivers, and Weas. The Wyandots, Shawanoes, Ottawas, Chippewas, Piankashaws, and Kaskaskias were absent.

On the 17th of November, 1807, Governor William Hull, of the Michigan Territory, made a treaty at Detroit, at which only the Chippewas, Ottawas, Pottawatomies, and Wyandots were represented.

On the 25th of November, 1808, Governor Hull made a treaty at Brownstown, at which only the Chippewas, Ottawas, Pottawatomies, Wyandots, and Shawanoes were represented.

On the 30th of September, 1809, Governor W. H. Harrison made a treaty at Fort Wayne, in which only the Delawares, Pottawatomies, and Miamis were represented.

All these treaties were for cessions of land; and thus in the space of fifteen years it is seen that Wayne's treaty of 1795, with all its excellent provisions for the government and protection of the Indians, was not only substantially obliterated, and vast bodies of the lands assured by it to the Indian nations were transferred to the white man, the original proprietors dispossessed, and wherever found were a broken-down, disheartened, and miserable people.

As cession after cession of land was obtained from the Indians, by this process of almost continual treaty-making, Tecumseh and his brother, the Prophet, as well as other leading Indians, became alarmed, and set about to revive the confederacy and form a union of the tribes to prevent further cessions as well as settlements on their lands. Another purpose they had in view was to attempt a reformation of the habits of the Indians, many of whom, through despondency, had become much addicted to the use of liquor, by which they were made unfit for intelligent action.

By the treaty of 1809, at Fort Wayne, certain lands on the Wabash were ceded to the United States. Tecumseh entered a bitter protest against these treaties, and notably against this Fort Wayne treaty. The land ceded by this treaty was in the valley of the Wabash, and while the length of the cession could not be determined by the language of the treaty, it is provided that the tract shall not be less in width, at the narrowest point, than thirty miles. In an interview with Governor Harrison, after this treaty was made, Tecumseh insisted that there must be no more cessions of land acquired by treaties made with but a fragment of the Indian nations interested, and that the petty village chiefs were not the parties authorized to make treaties. He insisted that the principle must be recognized that no purchase could be made unless sanctioned by a council representing all the tribes parties to the Wayne treaty of 1795, as one nation. He had been charged to the governor with having threatened to kill the chiefs who signed the treaty of 1809, and this he admitted to be true. He recited in an earnest manner the aggressions of the whites upon the Indians and the wrong done them; and while he disclaimed any intention of making war on the people of the United States, he declared it to be his unalterable resolution to oppose any further incursions of the whites upon the domain of the Indians. When it is remembered that the Shawanoes were among the most influential of the tribes parties to the treaty of 1795, and that they were specially interested in the land on the Wabash, ceded by the treaty of 1809, and yet that there is not the name of a single Shawanoe attached to that treaty, it would seem that Tecumseh had good cause to express dissatisfaction. It would have required more than ordinary grace to have restrained the wrath of a representative of a civilized community, and induced him to patiently submit under like circumstances. Tecumseh was, strictly speaking, neither a war nor a peace chief, but withal was regarded a sagacious and brave warrior and a wise and efficient counselor. In the reply of Governor Harrison to the speech of this chief, at the interview referred to, the interpreter was interrupted by the Indian, who said that all that the governor stated was false, and that he and the Seventeen Fires (the United States) had cheated and imposed upon the Indians. The governor did not attempt to explain—indeed, it is not seen how he could; but told the chief that he was a bad man, and that he would hold no further communication with him, and thus the interview ended. For some time previous to this interview which closed so abruptly, Governor Harrison had, in view of the movements of Tecumseh and his brother, been looking to a conflict as probable, and immediately after the chief left Vincennes proceeded to prepare for a contest, by strengthening the militia and posting the regular troops that were with him. Tecumseh had said that the lands ceded by the treaty of 1809 must be given up and no more treaties made with village chiefs, and unless this was acceded to, his effort to unite all the Indians in hostility would be continued, and hence war seemed to be a foregone conclusion. At this juncture sundry deputations, from such of the natives as felt their weakness, came and promised peace and compliance, but Governor Harrison put his troops in the field, and on the 5th of October, 1811, was on the Wabash, about sixty-five miles above Vincennes, where he built Fort Harrison. On the 31st of the month he was at the mouth of the Vermillion, where he built a block-house; from thence he advanced for the Prophet's town, and without interruption, on the 6th of November reached its vicinity. Here he was met by Indian embassadors, whom he informed that he had no hostile intentions if the Indians were true to existing treaties. Of course he meant the treaties made subsequent to the treaty of 1795, all of which were made by only portions of tribes parties to that treaty, and hence not in the judgment of many of the Indians binding upon them. Harrison encamped that night on a piece of dry oak land, indicated by the chiefs, who, he said before they left, united with him in a mutual promise for a suspension of hostilities, "until an interview could be had on the following day." His camp was near the Indian town, and the Indians doubting his profession that he had no hostile intent in invading their country with an army, attacked him on the morning of the 7th of November, before day, and after a vigorous contest were repulsed and driven by the infantry and dragoons into a marsh, where they could not be followed. The Americans lost in the battle thirty-seven killed, and had one hundred and fifty-one wounded, twenty-five of whom were mortally wounded. Forty Indians were killed; the number of wounded unknown. There was no further operation by the troops, and on the 4th of December, Governor Harrison wrote that the frontiers never enjoyed more perfect repose.

In Tuttle's history of Michigan (1873), when speaking of the events which occurred about this period, it is said: "These new troubles were indeed nothing more than the Americans might have expected. The Indians saw a new power encroaching upon the inheritance handed down to them from their ancestors. It was not difficult, therefore, to unite them in one last desperate effort to resist this usurping power. Their titles had been only partially extinguished, and they complained that where this had been done, the treaties had been unfairly conducted; that the Indians had been deceived; that they were in a state of intoxication at the time they signed away their lands, and that even under those circumstances, only a part of the tribes had given their consent."

Tecumseh was absent among the southern Indians at the time of the battle of Tippecanoe, and on his return reproached his brother, the Prophet, for his indiscretion. By his imprudence in attacking Harrison's army, at Tippecanoe, the Prophet had, in the judgment of Tecumseh, ruined the scheme of the projected confederacy. He, however, immediately sent word to Harrison, that he had returned home from the south, and was prepared to make a visit to Washington, to see the president, which had some time before been proposed. The governor gave him permission to go, but not to conduct a party of Indians, which was desired. The proposed visit on these terms was declined, and all intercourse terminated. At Fort Wayne, some time after this, Tecumseh disavowed to the Indian agent any intention to make war on the United States, and reproached Governor Harrison for invading his country with troops, during his absence in the south. To the reply of the agent, the chief listened with great indifference, and thereafter departed for Malden, in Upper Canada, and went into the British service. This gave him power to do much injury, and he was active. As an evidence of this it may be stated that as soon as Hull had retreated out of Canada, and Mackinac had fallen into the hands of the British, Tecumseh sent a messenger to the Pottawatomies, then residing near Fort Dearborn (Chicago), informing them of the fact, and urging them to arm immediately. The sad fate of the troops then in the garrison there is known to all; and the conflicts in the Northwest, during the war of 1812, in which the British had as allies numerous bands of the Indian nations, who were parties to Wayne's treaty of 1795, and the aid they rendered the British cause, are matters of history. In the month of October, 1813, at the battle of the Thames, in Canada, a novel charge was made by the Kentucky cavalry, and this produced a panic, under which the main body of the British troops yielded at once;

but their Indian allies fought with great courage. In the contest, Tecumseh, the great Shawanoe chief, fell.

After the defeat of Hull and the victories gained by the British and Indians in the Northwest, the people in the Western states became much excited, especially against the Indians. No one stopped to inquire how the denizens of the forest had become involved in the war; it was sufficient to know that they were engaged in it. The fact that they were not all on one side seemed not to be considered. Governor Edwards, of Illinois, was soon engaged in organizing troops and fitting out an expedition to operate against the Indians on the Illinois river. Colonel Russell, of the 17th U. S. regiment, was engaged in raising troops, called rangers, to co-operate with Governor Reynolds; and General Hopkins, a revolutionary veteran, was in command of Kentucky troops. He was to move up the Wabash to Fort Harrison, with a large force, destroying all the Indian villages on or near the river; thence to cross over to the Illinois country, and down the Sangamon and the Vermillion, laying waste and destroying all Indian villages on his route, and then join Edwards, and destroy the villages on the Illinois river. He wrote, on the 29th September, to Governor Shelby, of Kentucky, and said: "My present intention is to attack every settlement on the Wabash, and destroy their property, then fall upon the Illinois, and I trust in all the next month to perform much of it." Insubordination among his troops prevented him from effecting much of this. Governor Reynolds' expedition was more successful, but many of the Indian villages which he destroyed were abandoned by the inhabitants, and hence their lives were not at his mercy. Many sad incidents occurred, but it is not necessary to chronicle them. What is stated is sufficient to show the temper of the superior race toward the natives.

At the close of the war a treaty was held at Greenville, with the Wyandots, Delawares, Shawanoes, and Senecas, who adhered in the war to the United States. General Harrison and Governor Cass represented the United States. Among the provisions of the treaty was one giving peace to the Miamis, Weas, and Eel River Indians, and portions of the Pottawatomies, Ottawas, and Kickapoos, who were engaged in the British service; and all these tribes agreed to aid the Americans, should the war continue. Happily it was at an end. This period was one in which the Indian population in the Northwest suffered sadly. Some tribes were almost annihilated, and all were badly demoralized; and none were favorably impressed with the civilization of the white man. The impressions of an unfavorable character remained fresh in the memory of the Indians during the lives of the actors, and were transmitted by them to their children.

CHAPTER VI.

EARLY TREATIES WITH THE CHEROKEES, CHOCTAWS, CHICKASAWS, AND CREEKS.—
MESSAGE OF PRESIDENT MONROE, AND VIEWS OF JOHN C. CALHOUN, SECRE-
TARY OF WAR, RECOMMENDING THE REMOVAL OF THE INDIAN NATIONS RE-
SIDING EAST OF THE MISSISSIPPI RIVER TO THE WEST SIDE.—VIEWS OF
JAMES BARBOUR, SECRETARY OF WAR, ON THE SAME SUBJECT.—MESSAGE OF
PRESIDENT JACKSON RECOMMENDING THIS REMOVAL.—ACT OF CONGRESS PRO-
VIDING FOR THE SAME PASSED MAY 28, 1830.

THE first treaty made with an Indian nation, within the
territory south of the Ohio and east of the Mississippi, was
with the Cherokees. This country was designated as the
Territory of the United States south of the river Ohio. The
treaty is known as the treaty of Hopewell. By it a definite
boundary between the Indian lands and those of " the citizens
of the United States, within the limits of the United States,"
was fixed, and it was stipulated that if any citizen of the
United States, or other person, not being an Indian, " shall
attempt to settle on any of the lands westward or southward
of the said boundary, or having already settled on, and will
not remove from the same, within six months after the ratification of the treaty, such person shall forfeit the protection
of the United States, and the Indians may punish him or not
as they please." From their peculiar situation certain persons who had settled between the French Broad and Holstein
rivers were excepted from this penalty. It was stipulated in
the treaty " that the hatchet shall be buried *forever*, and the
peace given by the United States, and the friendship re-established between the said States on the one part, and all the
Cherokees on the other, shall be universal;" and that " the
Indians may have full confidence in the United States, respecting their interests, they shall have the right to send a
deputy of their choice, when they think fit, to Congress."
This treaty was executed on the 28th of November, 1785.

On the 2d of July, 1791, another treaty with the Cherokees
was entered into " on the bank of the Holstein, near French

Broad, within the limits of the United States." William
Blount, governor of the territory south of the river Ohio, was
the commissioner on the part of the United States. By this
treaty a new "boundary between the citizens of the United
States and the Cherokee nation" was established, and in
order to preclude *forever* all disputes relative to the said
boundary, it was agreed that "the same shall be ascertained
and marked plainly, by three persons appointed by the
United States, and three Cherokees, on the part of their
nation." For a consideration named, the Indians did release
and quitclaim, relinquish and cede to the United States all
the land to the right of the boundary line described; and
"the United States *solemnly* guaranteed to the Cherokees all
their lands not hereby ceded." It was also again provided
that "if any citizen of the United States, or other person, not
being an Indian, shall settle on any of the Cherokees' lands,
such person shall forfeit the protection of the United States,
and the Cherokees may punish him or not, as they please."
It was in this treaty further stipulated that "no citizen or inhabitant of the United States shall attempt to hunt or destroy
the game on the lands of the Cherokees; nor shall any citizen
or inhabitant go into the Cherokee country without a pass-
port first obtained from the governor of some one of the United
States, or territorial districts, or such other person as the
president may designate."

Between July 2, 1791, and February 27, 1819, twelve additional treaties were made with the Cherokees, being at the
rate of one for every two and a half years. In the fall of the
year 1808, a deputation of Cherokees, representing both the
upper and lower towns, visited Washington City; the first
named to inform the President of their great desire to engage
in the pursuits of agriculture and civilized life, in the country
then occupied by them, and to advise him that as all the
nation could not be induced to join them in this new life,
that it was desired by them to establish a division line between the upper and lower towns, and thus by concentrating
their society within narrow limits, they proposed to begin the
establishment of fixed laws and regular government; the deputies of the lower towns to make known their desire to con-

tinue the hunter life, and also the scarcity of game where they then lived, and their wish to remove across the Mississippi, on some vacant lands of the United States. To this the president said : "The United States, my children, are the friends of both parties. Those who remain may be assured of our patronage, or aid and good neighborhood. Those who wish to remove, are permitted to send an exploring party to reconnoiter the country on the waters of the Arkansas and White rivers, and the higher up the better, as they will be the longer unapproached by our settlements." In process of time those who wished to emigrate did do so, and settled on lands of the United States on the Arkansas and White rivers.

On the 8th of July, 1817, deputies from the Cherokee nation east, as well as deputies from those who had removed to the Arkansas, met at the Cherokee agency, within the Cherokee nation, General Andrew Jackson and Joseph McMinn, governor of Tennessee, to execute a treaty relinquishing to the United States all the right, title, and interest of the western Cherokees, to all lands of right belonging to them as a part of the nation, "which they have and are about to leave, proportioned to their numbers, including with those then on the Arkansas, those about to leave, and also to make an equal distribution of the annuities due to the whole nation." These objects effected, the treaty provided for a census to be taken; a new boundary line was established, by which the United States acquired a portion of the Cherokee territory, and guaranteed aid to those who removed. Other provisions beneficial to the Cherokees who remained, as well as to those who removed, were incorporated in this treaty. The new boundary line between the lands ceded to the United States and those remaining to the Indians, was to be run by United States commissioners, accompanied by such commissioners as the Cherokees may appoint, and the faith of the government given to prevent the intrusion of any of its citizens into the Cherokee lands. The treaty of 1819 provided that the annuity due the Cherokee nation should be paid, two-thirds to the Cherokees east of the Mississippi, and one-third to the Cherokees west of that river, and reiterated the pledge that the boundary line to designate the lands ceded by it should be run by joint commissioners, and " that all white people who have intruded or may hereafter intrude on the lands reserved for the Cherokees, shall be removed by the United States."

The first treaty between the Choctaw nation of Indians and the United States was made at Hopewell, on the 3d day of January, 1786. By it a boundary line defining the limits of · the Choctaws was established, and it was provided, that " if any citizen of the United States, or other person, not being an Indian, should attempt to settle on any of the lands allotted to the Indians, such person should forfeit the protection of the United States, and the Indians might punish him, or not, as they pleased ; the hatchet was buried *forever;*" and it was affirmed, that " the peace given by the United States, and friendship re-established between the said states and the Choctaw nation, shall be universal." Between that date and the 20th of January, 1825, seven additional treaties were made with the Choctaws. The second one was made on the 17th December, 1801. In it, the contracting parties agreed, " that the old line of demarcation heretofore established by and between the officers of his Brittanic majesty and the Choctaw nation, shall be retraced, and plainly marked in such a way and manner as the president may direct, in the presence of two persons to be appointed by the said nation ; and that the said line shall be the boundary between the settlements of the Mississippi Territory and the Choctaw nation." By the same treaty, the Indians did relinquish to the United States and quitclaim forever, all their right, title, and pretension to the land lying between the said line and the Mississippi river. All white persons residing within the Choctaw country were to be removed outside of the same toward the Mississippi river, together with their slaves, household furniture, tools, materials, and stock, and the cabins or houses erected by such persons were to be demolished.

James Wilkinson, commissioner on the part of the United States, accompanied by Mingo Pooscoos and Alatta Hooma, Choctaw commissioners, did run and distinctly mark this division line, and reported their proceedings on the 31st of

August, 1803. Their report concludes thus: " And we, the said commissioners plenipotentiary, do ratify and confirm the said line of demarcation, and do recognize and acknowledge the same to be the boundary which shall separate and distinguish the land ceded to the United States, between the Tombigbee, Mobile, and Pascagola rivers, from that which has not been ceded by the said Choctaw nation."

By the treaty made in November, 1805, the Choctaws ceded a portion of their country to the United States; by the treaty made in October, 1816, another portion is ceded; by the treaty of October 18, 1820, for and in consideration of a cession of another portion of the Choctaw country to the United States, there was ceded to said nation a tract of country west of the Mississippi river, situate between the Arkansas and Red rivers, the boundary lines of which were to be ascertained and distinctly marked, by commissioners to be appointed for that purpose, to be accompanied by such person as the Choctaws may select; and for the purpose of assisting such of the Choctaws as wish to remove to the country west, aid was to be given them on the journey, and for one year after their arrival at their new home.

By the treaty of January 20, 1825, the Choctaws ceded another portion of their land, east of the Mississippi, to the United States.

The first treaty between the United States and the Chickasaw nation was made at Hopewell, on the 10th of January, 1786. By this treaty a boundary line was established between the lands allotted to the Chickasaws and those set apart to the Cherokees and Choctaws, and those in possession of the Creeks; and it was provided, that " the hatchet shall be buried *forever*, and the peace given by the United States of America and the friendship re-established between the said states and the Chickasaw nation shall be universal." It was also stipulated, that if any citizen of the United States, or other person, not being an Indian, shall attempt to settle on any of the lands hereby allotted to the Chickasaws, such person shall forfeit the protection of the United States, and the Indians may punish him, or not, as they please. Between the date of this treaty and October 19, 1818, the Chickasaws made four additional treaties, in some of which cessions of land were conveyed to the United States.

The first treaty made with the Creek Indians was on the 7th of August, 1790. By this treaty a boundary between the citizens of the United States and the Creek nation was established; and, to prevent disputes, this line was to be ascertained by an able surveyor, on the part of the United States, assisted by three old citizens of Georgia and three old Creek chiefs, appointed for that purpose; and that said boundary be rendered distinct, it was agreed that, where necessary, it should be marked by a line of felled trees, at least twenty feet wide. All claims of the Creeks to other lands were extinguished forever. The United States *solemnly* guaranteed to the Creeks all their land defined by the established boundary; and provided that if any citizen of the United States, or other person, not being an Indian, should attempt to settle on any of the Creek lands, such person should forfeit the protection of the United States, and the Creeks might punish him or not, as they please. It is declared that there shall be perpetual peace and friendship between all the citizens of the United States, and all the individuals, towns, and tribes, of the upper, middle, and lower Creeks, and Seminoles, composing the Creek nation of Indians. Between the date of this treaty and the 12th of February, 1825, seven additional treaties were made with these Indians. These, with but one exception, were for the cession of additional territory to the United States. One of them, made on the 9th of August, 1814, was with General Andrew Jackson, the commander of the United States troops, then engaged in a war with the Creeks, and was an agreement and capitulation. By it they ceded to the United States a large body of land, as an equivalent for the expenses of the war; and the United States guaranteed to them the integrity of the residue of their country. The articles of the treaty were to constitute the basis of a *permanent* peace between the government and the Creek nation. By the eighth and last article of the treaty the Creeks ceded to the United States all their lands within the State of Georgia, and also all other lands which they

7

then occupied, or to which they made claim, lying north and west of a line to be run from the first principal falls upon the Chattahooche river, above Cowetan town, to Ockfuskee Old Town, upon the Tallapoosa; thence to the falls of Coosaw river, at or near a place called the Hickory Ground; and the United States agreed to give, in exchange for this cession, the like quantity of land, acre for acre, westward of the Mississippi river, on the Arkansas river, and to pay them for their improvements, their losses in removal, and for the purchase of supplies in their new home, the sum of four hundred thousand dollars.

After the close of the war of 1812, there was a constant pressure for the extinguishment of the Indian title to lands in the territory northwest of the river Ohio. But little effort was made by the government to resist this pressure. Indeed, it seemed, in order to appease it, that the services of William Henry Harrison, Lewis Cass, Duncan McArthur, John Graham, Benjamin Park, Ninian Edwards, William Clark, Augustus Chouteau, Solomon Sibly, Jonathan Jennings, and many others, were in almost constant demand as commissioners, on the part of the United States, to negotiate with tribe after tribe of the Indian population, with a view to obtain cessions of their lands.

In the progress of these events, and nearly fifty years after the declaration of our independence, and more than forty years after our treaty of peace in 1783, with England, the president of the United States, on the 27th of January, 1825, then near the close of a term of eight years' service, in a message to Congress, urged the removal of the Indian tribes, from the lands then occupied by them within the several states and organized territories, to the west of the Mississippi river, notwithstanding the United States had in some form, in its treaties with these tribes, guaranteed to each of them *forever* a portion of the territory on which it then resided. This message was induced by the demand of the State of Georgia, that the title of the Cherokee Indians to their lands in that state should, without delay, be extinguished. In the compact of 1802, between Georgia and the United States, the latter had agreed to extinguish the Indian title so soon as it could be done "peaceably and on reasonable terms." The Indians were not a party to the compact, and by the treaty of Hopewell, in 1785, between the government and the Cherokees, the limits of their lands within the State of Georgia, and elsewhere, were defined, and it was stipulated that if any citizen of the United States, or other person, not being an Indian, should attempt to settle in the Cherokee country, or having so settled will not remove within the space of six months after the ratification of the treaty, such an one "shall forfeit the protection of the United States, and the Indians may punish him or not, as they please." By the treaty of Holstein, in 1791, this boundary was reaffirmed, and in 1797, the lines were ascertained and marked, in pursuance of the provision of the treaty of 1791. At the time of the compact of 1802, between Georgia and the United States, all these facts were known. No such compact existed between the United States and any other state.

In his message, President Monroe said: "Experience has clearly demonstrated that, in their present state, it is impossible to incorporate them [the Indians] in such masses, in any form whatever, into our system. It has been demonstrated with equal certainty, that, without a timely anticipation of, and provision against, the dangers to which they are exposed, under causes which it will be difficult, if not impossible, to control, their degradation and extermination will be inevitable. The great object to be accomplished is, the removal of those tribes to the territory designated, on conditions which shall be satisfactory to themselves and honorable to the United States. This can be done only by conveying to each tribe a good title to an adequate portion of land to which it may consent to remove, and providing for it there a system of internal government, which shall protect their property from invasion, and, by regular progress of improvement and civilization, prevent that degeneracy which has generally marked the transition from one to the other state." The president continued thus: "I transmit herewith a report from the secretary of war, which presents the best estimate which can be formed from the documents in that department, of the number of Indians within our states and territories, and of the amount of land held by the several tribes within each; of the state of the country lying northward and westward thereof, within our acknowledged boundaries; of the parts to which the Indian title has been extinguished; and of the conditions on which other parts, in an amount which may be adequate to the objects contemplated, may be obtained. By this report, it appears that the Indian title has already been extinguished to extensive tracts in that quarter, and that other portions may be acquired, to the extent desired, on very moderate conditions. Satisfied, I also am, that the removal proposed, is not only practicable, but that the advantages attending it, to the Indians, may be made so apparent that all the tribes, even the most opposed, may be induced to accede to it.

" The digest of a government, with the consent of the Indians, which should be endowed with sufficient power to meet all the objections contemplated, to collect the several tribes together in a bond of unity, and preserve order in each; to prevent intrusions on their property; to teach them, by regular instruction, the arts of civilized life; and make them a civilized people, is an object of very high importance. It is the powerful consideration which we have to offer to these tribes, as an inducement to relinquish the lands on which they now reside, and to remove to those which are designated. It is not doubted that this arrangement will present considerations of sufficient force to surmount all their prejudices in favor of the soil of their nativity, however strong they may be. Their elders have sufficient intelligence to discern the certain progress of events, in the present train, and sufficient virtue, by yielding to momentary sacrifices, to protect their families and posterity from inevitable destruction. They will also perceive that they may thus attain an elevation, to which, as communities, they could not otherwise aspire.

" To the United States the arrangement offers many important advantages, in addition to those which have been enumerated. By the establishment of such a government over these tribes, with their consent, we become, in reality, their benefactors. The relation of conflicting interests, which has heretofore existed between them and our frontier settle--

ments, will cease. There will be no more wars between them and the United States. Adopting such a government, their movement will be in harmony with us, and its good effect be felt throughout the whole extent of our territory, to the Pacific. It may fairly be presumed, that, through the agency of such a government, the condition of all the tribes inhabiting that vast region may be eventually improved; that permanent peace may be preserved with them, and our commerce be much extended. With a view to this important object, I recommend it to Congress to adopt, by *solemn declaration*, certain fundamental principles, in accord with those suggested, as the basis of such arrangements as may be entered into with the several tribes, to the strict observance of which the faith of the nation shall be pledged. I recommend it also to Congress, to provide, by law, for the appointment of a suitable number of commissioners, who shall, under the direction of the president, be authorized to visit, and explain to the several tribes the objects of the government, and to make with them, according to instructions, such arrangements as shall be best calculated to carry these objects into effect."

The report of the secretary of war, which accompanied this message, stated that the number of Indians contemplated to be transplanted by the scheme was about ninety-seven thousand, who then resided in North Carolina, Georgia, Alabama, Tennessee, Ohio, Indiana, Illinois, Missouri, New York, and the territories of Arkansas and Michigan, and where located occupied about seventy-seven million of acres of land. The secretary thought that the Indians in New York, the Ottawas of Ohio, and those in Indiana and Illinois, and the peninsula of Michigan, might be removed to the country west of Lake Michigan and north of Illinois. He also thought that the Indians in Florida need not go west, since they had ceded to the United States all the northern part of the territory, and were residing out of the way in the southern part of the peninsula, and thus reduced the number to be provided for west of Missouri and the Territory of Arkansas to about eighty thousand.

The secretary said that no arrangement for their removal

ought to be made which did not regard the interests of the Indians as well as our own; that almost all of the tribes proposed to be afflicted by the arrangement were more or less advanced in the arts of civilized life, there being scarcely one of them which has not the establishment of schools in the nation, affording at once the means of moral, religious, and intellectual improvement. He added, that there was another point which it was indispensable should be guarded, in order to render the condition of the Indians less afflicting: " One of the greatest evils to which they are subject (said the secretary) is that *incessant pressure* of our population, which forces them from seat to seat, without allowing time for that moral and intellectual improvement for which they appear to be naturally eminently susceptible. To guard against this evil, so fatal to the race, there ought to be the *strongest and most solemn assurance that the country given them should be theirs, as a permanent home, for themselves and their posterity, without being disturbed by the encroachments of our citizens.*" The secretary made many suggestions as to a system of government and laws that should be provided for them in their new home, which he thought would prove to the Indians and their posterity a permanent blessing. He said they should have a permanent and solemn guaranty for their possessions, and receive the countenance and aid of the government for the gradual extension of its privileges to them, in which event there would be among all the tribes a disposition to accord with the views of the government, and great confidence was felt that the basis of a system might be laid which, in a few years, would entirely effect the object in view, to the mutual benefit of the government and the Indians, " and which, in its operation, would effectually arrest the calamitous course of events to which they must be subjected without a radical change in the present system." The subject-matter contained in the message of the president, and the report of his secretary, were laid before Congress, but no action was at that time taken.

In January, 1826, Hon. John Cocke, the chairman of the Indian committee in the House of Representatives, inclosed a prepared " bill for the preservation and civilization of the

Indian tribes within the United States," to the Hon. James Barbour, then secretary of war, for such suggestions, or the forming of another bill for the same purpose, as to the secretary might seem proper. Mr. Barbour framed a new bill, and sent it with a report in "elucidation of its purposes" to Mr. Cocke, on the 3d of February, 1826. In his report, Mr. Barbour said : "The condition of the aborigines of this country, and their future destiny, have long engaged the attention of the philosopher and statesman, inspiring an interest correspondent to the importance of the subject. The history of the past presents but little on which recollection lingers with satisfaction. The future is not more cheering, unless resort be speedily had to other counsels than those by which we have heretofore been governed. From the first discovery of America to the present time one master passion, common to all mankind, that of acquiring land, has driven, in ceaseless succession, the white man on the Indian. The latter, reluctantly yielding to a force he could not resist, has retired from the ocean to the mountains, and from the mountains to more inhospitable recesses, wasting away by sufferings and wars, foreign and intestine, till a wretched fragment only survives of the numerous hordes once inhabiting this country, whose portion it is to brood in grief over their past misfortunes, or to look in despair on the approaching catastrophe of their impending doom. It were now an unprofitable task to inquire on what principle the nations of Europe were justified in dispossessing the native proprietor of his birthright. They brought with them their own maxims, which recognized power as the only standard of right, and fraud and force as perfectly legitimate in the acquisition of territory. It has been done, and time has confirmed the act.

"In the contest for dominion the milder qualities of justice and clemency were disregarded. But that contest has long since ceased in the United States, where, on the one side, are seen a great people, familiar with arts and arms, whose energies are increased by union, and directed by an efficient government; on the other, a few ignorant and divided tribes of barbarians. It is necessary for the former only to express its will, to receive or enforce immediate submission from the latter.   The suggestions of policy should no longer stifle the claims of justice and humanity.   It is now, therefore, that a most solemn question addresses itself to the American people, and whose answer is full of responsibility.   Shall we go on quietly in a course, which, judging from the past, threatens their extinction, while their past sufferings and future prospects so pathetically appeal to our compassion?   The responsibility to which I refer, is what a nation owes to itself, to its future character in all time to come.   For next to the means of self-defense and the blessings of free government, stands in point of importance the character of a nation.   Its distinguishing characteristics should be justice and moderation. To spare the weak is its brightest ornament.   It is, therefore, a source of the highest gratification that an opportunity is now offered the people of the United States to practice these maxims, and give an example of the triumph of liberal principles, over that sordid selfishness which has been the fruitful spring of human calamity.

"It is the province of history to commit to its pages the transactions of nations.   Posterity look to this depository with the most intense interest.   The fair fame of their ancestors, a most precious inheritance, is to them equally a source of pride and a motive of continued good action.   But she performs her province with impartiality.   The authority she exercises in the absence of others, is a check on bad rule. The tyrant and the oppressor see in the character of their prototypes, the sentence posterity is preparing for them. Which side of the picture shall we elect?   For the decision is left to ourselves.   Shall the record transmit the present race to future generations, as standing by, insensible to the progress of desolation which threatens the remnant of this people; or shall these unfriendly characters give place to a generous effort which shall have been made to save them from destruction?   While deliberating on this solemn question, I would appeal to that high Providence, whose delight is justice and mercy, and take counsel from the oracles of his will, revealed to man, in his terrible denunciation against the oppressor.

"In reviewing the past, justice requires that the humane

attempts of the federal government, coeval with its origin, should receive an honorable notice. That they have essentially failed, the sad experience of every day but too strongly testifies. If the original plan, conceived in the spirit of benevolence, had not been fated to encounter that as yet unabated desire to bereave them of their lands, it would, perhaps, have realized much of the hopes of its friends. So long, however, as that desire continues to direct our councils, every effort must fail. A cursory review is all that is necessary to show the incongruity of the measures we have pursued, and the cause of their failure. Missionaries are sent among them to enlighten their minds, by imbibing them with religious impressions. Schools have been established by the aid of private as well as public donations, for the instruction of their youths. They have been persuaded to abandon the chase —to locate themselves and become cultivators of the soil—implements of husbandry and domestic animals have been presented them, and all these things have been done, accompanied with professions of disinterested solicitude for their happiness. Yielding to these temptations, some of them have reclaimed the forest, planted their orchards, and erected houses, not only for their abode, but for the administration of justice and for religious worship. And when they have so done, *you* send *your* agent to tell them they must surrender their country to the white man, and recommit themselves to some new desert, and substitute as the means of their subsistence the precarious chase for the certainty of cultivation. The love of our native land is implanted in every human bosom, whether he roams the wilderness, or is found in the highest state of civilization. This attachment increases with the comforts of our country, and is strongest when these comforts are the fruits of our own exertions. Can it be matter of surprise that they hear with unmixed indignation of what seems to them our ruthless purpose of expelling them from their country, thus endeared? They see that our professions are insincere—that our promises have been broken, that the happiness of the Indian is a cheap sacrifice to the acquisition of more lands; and when attempted to be soothed by the assurance that the country to which we propose to send them is desirable, they emphatically ask us, what new pledges can you give us that we shall not again be exiled when it is your wish to possess these lands? It is easier to state than to answer this question. A regard for consistency, apart from any other consideration, requires a change of measures. Either let him retain and enjoy his home, or, if he is to be driven from it, abstain from cherishing illusions we mean to disappoint, and thereby make him to feel more sensibly the extent of his loss."

As a relief for existing evils, the secretary had some doubts of the efficacy of removing the Indians to the west of the Mississippi. He suggested many difficulties, and, moreover, expressed apprehensions that if removed " the same propensity which has conducted the white population to the remote regions they (the Indians) now occupy, will continue to propel the tide, till it is arrested only by the distant shores of the Pacific." He, however, prepared a bill, and submitted it with his report, the outlines of which were as follows:

First. The country west of the Mississippi, and beyond the states and territories, and so much on the east side of the Mississippi as lies west of Lakes Huron and Michigan, to be set apart for the exclusive abode of the Indians.

Second. Their removal by individuals, in contradistinction to tribes.

Third. A territorial government to be maintained by the United States.

Fourth. If circumstances shall eventually justify it, the extinction of tribes, and their amalgamation in one mass, and a distribution of property among the individuals.

Fifth. Leaves the condition of those who do not emigrate unaltered.

The secretary concludes his exhaustive report thus: " I will add, that the end proposed is the happiness of the Indian— the instrument of its accomplishment—their progressive, and, finally, their complete civilization. The obstacles to success are their ignorance, their prejudices, their repugnance to labor, their wandering propensities, and the uncertainty of the future. I would endeavor to overcome these by schools; by a distribution of land in individual right; by a permanent social establishment which should require the performance of social duties; by assigning them a country of which they are never to be bereaved, and cherishing them with parental kindness." The report and bill of the secretary did not receive the favorable consideration of Congress. During the remainder of the administration of John Q. Adams the government was perplexed with the Indian problem. The states in which the Indians held reservations were urging that the Indian title be extinguished, and the Indians removed to the west of the Mississippi. Georgia was impatient for the fulfillment of the compact of 1802, and the removal of all Indians from that state. That portion of the Cherokees who declined to emigrate had organized a government of their own, within the State of Georgia, and the controversy growing out of this act became national; the people in every state were discussing it in their political assemblies; it pervaded Congress, and engaged the attention of the Supreme Court of the United States, Georgia having by legislation sought to repress the Indian government set up within her limits.

Thus matters stood at the time of the inauguration of President Jackson. In his first annual message, December 8, 1829, he dealt with the subject at considerable length, and especially with the existing aspect of affairs between the State of Georgia and the Cherokees. The president said: "The condition and ulterior destiny of the Indian tribes within the limits of some of our states have become objects of much importance. It has long been the policy of the government to introduce among them the arts of civilization, in the hope of gradually reclaiming them from a wandering life. This policy has, however, been coupled with another, wholly incompatible with its success. Professing a desire to civilize and settle them, we have, at the same time, lost no opportunity to purchase their lands, and thrust them further into the wilderness. By this means they have not only been kept in a wandering state, but been led to look upon us as unjust and indifferent to their fate. Thus, though lavish in its expenditures on the subject, government has continually defeated its own policy; and the Indians, in general, receding farther and farther to the west, have retained their savage habits. A portion, however, of the southern tribes, having mingled

much with the whites, and made some progress in the arts of
civilized life, have lately attempted to erect an independent government within the limits of Georgia and Alabama.   These
states claiming to be the only sovereigns within their respective
territories, extending their laws over the Indians, induced the
latter to call upon the United States for protection.   Under
the circumstances, the question presented was, whether the
general government had a right to sustain these people in their
pretensions?   The constitution declares, that ' no new state
shall be formed or erected within the jurisdiction of any other
state,' without the consent of its legislature.   Georgia became a member of the confederacy which eventuated in our
federal union, as a sovereign state, always asserting her claim
to certain limits, which having been originally defined in her
colonial charter, and subsequently recognized in the treaty of
peace, she has ever since continued to enjoy, except as they
have been circumscribed by her own voluntary transfer of a
portion of her territory to the United States, in the articles of
cession of 1802.   Alabama was admitted into the Union on the
same footing with the original states, with boundaries which
were prescribed by Congress.   There is no constitutional,
conventional, or legal provision which allows them less power
over the Indians within their borders than is possessed by the
people of Maine or New York.   Would the people of Maine
permit the Penobscot tribe to erect an independent government within that state?   And unless they did, would it not
be the duty of the general government to support them in
resisting such a measure?   Would the people of the State of
New York permit each remnant of the Six Nations within her
limits to declare itself an independent people under the protection of the United States?   Could the Indians establish
a separate republic on each of their reservations in Ohio?
And if they were so disposed, would it be the duty of the government to protect them in the attempt?   If the principle
involved in the obvious answers to these questions be abandoned, it will follow that the objects of the goverment are re-
versed, and that it has become a part of its duty to aid in
destroying the states which it was established to protect.
Actuated by this view of the subject, I informed the Indians

inhabiting parts of Georgia and Alabama, that their attempt
to establish an independent government would not be coun-
tenanced by the executive of the United States; and advised
them to emigrate beyond the Mississippi, or submit to the
laws of those states." In the further discussion of the subject, President Jackson submitted to Congress, " the interesting question, whether something can not be done, consistently
with the rights of the states, to preserve this much injured
race?" And added: "As a means of effecting this end, I
suggest for your consideration the propriety of setting apart
an ample district west of the Mississippi, and without the
limits of any state or territory now formed, to be *guaranteed*
to the Indian tribes as long as they shall occupy it, each tribe
having the distinct control over the portion designated for its
own use. There they may be secured in the enjoyment of
governments of their own choice, subject to no other control
from the United States than such as may be necessary to preserve peace on the frontier and between the several tribes.
There the benevolent may endeavor to teach them the arts of
civilization; and by promoting union and harmony among
them, to raise up an interesting commonwealth, destined to
perpetuate the race, and to attest the humanity and justice of
the government."

Congress took hold of the subject, and in February, 1830,
both the Senate and House Committees on Indian Affairs made
reports in favor of the policy of the removal of the Indians
to the west of the Mississippi river; and before the close of
the session, a law was passed, entitled " an act to provide for
an exchange of lands with the Indians residing within any of
the states or territories, and for their removal west of the river
Mississippi." This was approved by the president, May 28,
1830.

The first section authorized the president of the United
States to cause so much of any territory belonging to the
United States, west of the river Mississippi, and not included
in any state or organized territory, and to which the original
Indian title was extinguished, as he might judge necessary, to
be divided into a suitable number of districts, for the reception of such tribes or nations of Indians as may choose to ex-

change the lands where they now reside, and remove to the west.

The second section authorized the president to exchange the lands embraced in any such districts with any tribe or nation of Indians then residing within the limits of any of the states or territories, for the land claimed and occupied by them within such states or territories.

The third section authorized the president to *solemnly* assure the tribes with whom the exchange was made, that the United States would *forever* secure and guarantee to them, and their heirs or successors, the country so exchanged with them, and, if they prefer it, the United States would cause a patent or grant to be made and executed to them for the same.

The fourth section authorized the president to ascertain such improvements on the lands of the Indians as added value to the same, and cause such value to be appraised, and to pay the amount of the same to the parties rightfully claiming such improvements.

The fifth section authorized the president to render such aid as was necessary and proper, to enable the emigrants to remove to and settle in their new home ; and such aid as was necessary for their support for one year after their removal.

The sixth section authorized the president to cause each tribe that emigrated to be protected at their new residence, against all interruption or disturbance from any other tribe of Indians, or from any other person or persons whatever.

The seventh section provided for the same superintendence and care in their new home that was extended to them where they then resided.

The eighth and last section appropriated the sum of five hundred thousand dollars to enable the president to give effect to the law.

CHAPTER VII.

DEDICATION OF THE COUNTRY WEST OF THE MISSISSIPPI RIVER FOR A PERMANENT
HOME FOR THE INDIANS RESIDING EAST OF IT.—GUARANTEES THAT THIS
NEW HOME SHOULD NEVER BE EMBRACED WITHIN THE LIMITS OF ANY OR-
GANIZED STATE OR TERRITORY.—THE TRIBES THAT EMIGRATED.—THEIR
" LOST MONEY."—THE ANNEXATION OF TEXAS AND OTHER ACQUISITIONS.—THE
EFFECT UPON THE INDIANS.—DEMANDS THAT THE COUNTRY SHOULD BE OPENED
TO THE SETTLEMENT OF THE WHITE PEOPLE.—ORGANIZATION OF THE TERRI-
TORY OF KANSAS.—ITS EFFECT ON THE EMIGRATED TRIBES—TREATIES OF
1854.—INTRUSION OF THE WHITES.—MILITARY OFFICERS AT FORT LEAVEN-
WORTH SYMPATHIZE WITH THE " SQUATTERS."—THE RESERVATIONS OF THE
CHEROKEES, CHICKASAWS, CHOCTAWS, ETC.

SEVERAL years previous to the passage of the act of 1830,
the United States acquired, by treaty with the Kansas and
Great and Little Osage Indians, the territory west of Missouri and Arkansas, south of the Great Nemehaw and north
of Red river, and bounded on the west by a line drawn from
the head source of the Nemehaw to the source of the Kansas
river, and thence southwardly through the Rock Saline to the
Red river, and this country was dedicated for the future but
permanent homes of the Indian tribes or nations to be transplanted to it, upon their removal from their lands on the east
side of the Mississippi. It required several years to accomplish the transfer of such of the Indians east, as were pur-
suaded to remove. Finally, the Cherokees, Creeks, Choctaws, Chickasaws, Delawares, Shawanoes, Miamis, Kickapoos,
Pottowatomies, Chippewas of Rouch de Bœuf, Sacs and
Foxes, Weas and Piankashaws, Kaskaskias and Peorias, were
located west of the States of Missouri and Arkansas. In
time a portion of the Seminoles were also removed and placed
within the territory assigned to the Creeks. None of these
Indian tribes were exempt from the sacrifices, suffering, and
loss of life incident to Indian removals. It is doubtful
whether a like number of our own race could, under similar
circumstances, have sustained themselves as well.

In the tract granted to the Cherokees, it was estimated that there were within the boundaries defined, about seven millions of acres of land; and in addition thereto, they were guaranteed a perpetual outlet west, as far as the sovereignty of the United States and their right of soil extended, with a free and unmolested use of all the country west of their western boundary. Letters patent were to be issued to them for the tract specified, and it was covenanted and agreed by the United States, " that the lands ceded to the Cherokee nation, in the foregoing articles, shall, *in no future time, without their consent*, be included within the territorial limits or jurisdiction of any state or territory; but they (said states) shall secure to the Cherokee nation the right, by their national councils, to make and to carry into effect all such laws as they may deem necessary for the government and protection of the persons and property within their own country belonging to their people, or such persons as have connected themselves with them." It was further stipulated that the Cherokees should be entitled to a delegate in the House of Representatives of the United States, whenever Congress should make provision for the same.

The tract granted to the Creeks was estimated to contain over five millions of acres, and the United States covenanted with them, that the same " shall be solemnly guaranteed to the Creek Indians, *nor shall any state or territory ever have a right to pass laws for the government of such Indians*, but they shall be allowed to govern themselves, so far as may be compatible with the general jurisdiction which Congress may think proper to exercise over them; and the United States will defend them from the unjust hostilities of other Indians, and will, as soon as the boundaries of the tract are ascertained, cause a patent or grant to be executed to the Creek tribe for the same."

The original grant to the Choctaws, of a home west of the Mississippi, was made as early as 1820. The boundaries of this grant were modified by the treaty of January 20, 1825. After the act of Congress of May 28, 1830, another treaty was made with these Indians, to wit, on the 27th of September, 1830, in which it is provided that the United States, under a grant specially to be made by the president of the United States, shall cause to be conveyed to the Choctaw nation a tract of country west of the Mississippi, *in fee simple* to them and their descendants, to inure to them while they shall exist as a nation, and live on it. [Here the country is described by metes and bounds.] This stipulation is in the fourth article: "The government and people of the United States are hereby obliged to secure to the said Choctaw nation of red people, the jurisdiction and government of the persons and property that may be within their limits west, *so that no territory or state* shall ever have a right to pass laws for the government of the Choctaw nation of red people and their descendants; and that no part of the land granted them *shall ever be embraced in any territory or state;* but the United States shall forever secure said Choctaw nation from and against all laws, except such as from time to time may be enacted in their own national councils, not inconsistent with the constitution, treaties, and laws of the United States; and except such as may, and which have been enacted by Congress, to the extent that Congress, under the constitution, are required to exercise legislation over Indian affairs." The tract granted to the Choctaws was estimated to contain over nine millions of acres of land.

The Chickasaw nation purchased from the Choctaws, within the limits of the latter, on the 17th January, 1837, a district of country, for which they paid the Choctaws the sum of five hundred and thirty thousand dollars. In the treaty, the country purchased is described by metes and bounds, and denominated the Chickasaw district of the Choctaw nation, to have an equal representation in the Choctaw council with any other district in the same, and placed on an equal footing with the other districts of said Choctaw nation, and to be subject to the same laws as the Choctaws.

By the provisions of a treaty proclaimed April 12, 1834, the Seminole Indians had assigned to them for their *future residence forever*, a tract of land in the territory of the Creeks, west of the Arkansas Territory.

By a supplementary article to the treaty of January 15, 1819, with the Delaware Indians, dated March 24, 1831, they were assigned, as a permanent home west of the Mississippi,

8

guaranteed to them by the treaty of 1819, the country in the forks of the Kansas and Missouri rivers, extending up the Kansas to the Kansas (Indian) line, and up the Missouri to Camp Leavenworth, and thence by a line drawn westwardly, leaving a space ten miles wide, north of the Kansas (Indian) boundary line, for an outlet, "the same to be conveyed and *forever* secured to the Delaware nation as their permanent residence."

The Shawnees, then residing in Missouri, were, by the treaty of December 30, 1825, granted, for themselves and those of their brethren then residing in Ohio, a tract of land equal to fifty miles square, west of the State of Missouri; and the same was afterward confirmed by a patent issued to them by the United States.

In a treaty, concluded with the Miamis on the 6th November, 1838, the United States stipulated " to possess the Miami tribe of Indians, and *guarantee to them forever*, a country west of the Mississippi, to remove to and settle on," the same to be in a region contiguous to that in the occupation of the tribes which had emigrated from Ohio and Indiana; and the United States agreed to protect " the said tribe, and the people thereof, in their rights and possessions, against the injuries, encroachments, and oppressions of any person or persons, tribe or tribes, whatsoever."

Without further recapitulation of the grants and covenants to other tribes that were transplanted, under the act of May 28, 1830, it may be stated that the United States, in some form, guaranteed to each and all that the new home should be the *permanent* residence of the Indian tribes and their posterity; that patents should issue to them, and that the country to which they removed should never be embraced within the limits of any organized state or territory.

In this new home the Indians were to be relieved from all the embarrassments, trials, and difficulties by which they were beset east of the Mississippi, and which had proved so fatal to the race. As a rule, the tribes which were, by this process of emigration, located west of Missouri, had not such aids among their own people as those located west of Arkansas. They were in small communities, and had comparatively but few educated men among them, and of these there were some who, previous to their removal, were dissolute in their habits; and all such, at their new homes, had ample opportunity to indulge in dissipation. Missions and schools were, however, established among them, and numbers began to cultivate the soil and raise stock. But there was no fixed policy adopted by the government for the reclamation and civilization of these Indians after they were transplanted. It appeared that each individual acted on his own motion, and elected to be a nomad or a farmer. It was not far to the buffalo range, and game was plentiful; hence the temptation to roam and hunt was very strong. Large numbers of each tribe were in the habit of making two hunts during the year, occupying, in each, from two to three months. The product of the hunt was valuable, not only in the supply of food, but of robes and skins. The government did not attempt to restrain the Indians in their habit of hunting. Indeed, it seemed rather to encourage them in it.

In the process of time, several manual labor schools were established among these Indians, under the patronage of the Presbyterians, Baptists, Methodists, Catholics, and Friends, and many of the Indian children were instructed at these schools. At some period, probably during the Mexican war, the annuities due to some of these tribes, for purposes of civilization, were withheld, and hence there were balances in their favor due and unpaid. This' fact set a number of sharpers after the Indians, who, by various devices, obtained from the chiefs authority to collect this " lost money," as it was termed; the Indians agreeing to allow, in many cases, as a fee, one-half of the sum obtained. How far government agents and military officers had knowledge of these trans-actions, and participated in the spoil, can not be definitely stated; but there was abundant reason to believe that some were corruptly engaged in them. Some of the chiefs were also corruptly involved. As the facts became known they produced discontent among the Indians.

Following the annexation of Texas, and the acquisition of our possessions on the Pacific coast, emigration commenced. Numberless caravans began to cross the plains, and these

necessarily passed through the Indian reservations west of
Missouri.   These intrusions had a very bad influence on the
Indians.   They were regarded by them as violations of their
treaty stipulations.   Moreover, the emigrants were not mindful of the rights of the Indians.   Depredations were committed upon them; they were despoiled of their property,
personally abused, and frequently shot down.   The reports
made by these emigrants of the character of the lands in the
Indian reservations induced many whites to invade them.
The fact that the Indian occupant had a " solemn " guaranty
from the government that this land he lived upon should be
to him and his posterity a permanent home " forever " was
not respected.   Even statesmen became uneasy because the
Indian territory was not thrown open to occupation and settlement by the white man, some averring that it was an outrage that a country so fine should be occupied by hordes of
savages, to the exclusion of the white race.   The " unabated
desire to bereave " the Indians of their lands, of which the
secretary of war spoke in 1826, when urging that the very
country now occupied by these tribes should be set apart for
the permanent homes of the Indians then residing in the
states, was now manifested more strongly than ever.   The
pledge of the United States to every tribe that they should
be protected in the quiet enjoyment of the country assigned
them was derided and held of no avail.   It was said that the
Indian was a treacherous barbarian; that he had none of the
feelings or instincts of civilization; that these could never be
imparted to him; that he was in the way of progress, and
must stand aside and give room for the development of the
energies of those who were yearning to possess and subdue
the land.   The agitation worked fearfully on the minds of the
Indians.   But this fact did not disturb those who clamored
for the extinction of the Indian title.   The contagion finally
entered Congress, and the same body which, in 1830, authorized the president, by a law then passed, to procure this
country and assign it to the tribes that he might persuade to
emigrate to it, with the pledge that it should be to them and
their posterity a permanent home *forever*, in 1852, entertained
a bill and passed it through the House of Representatives to

organize the Territory of Nebraska, embracing many of these Indian tribes within the limits of the same. The bill failed in the Senate, but at the next session, in lieu of such bill, there was inserted in the civil and diplomatic bill a clause appropriating the sum of $50,000, to enable the president to negotiate with the Indians, and obtain their consent to the establishment of a territorial government west of Missouri and Arkansas, and to embrace within its limits the lands in their reservations.

In the month of August, 1853, the commissioner of Indian affairs, by direction of the president, visited the Indian country to confer with the various tribes, as a preliminary measure, looking to negotiations with them for the purpose of procuring their assent to a territorial government, and the extinguishment of their title, in whole or in part, to the lands owned by them. He found, when he reached the borders of the Indian country, the people discussing, with some warmth, the question whether portions of the land within it, were not then open to settlement by the whites; in fact, at that time there were those who, holding the right in the whites to settle in the territory, had gone over the border to explore the same with the intention of locating in it. Some months previously Thomas H. Benton had made a publication, taking the ground that a large portion of the country was then subject to the occupancy of the whites, without the consent of the Indians or the aid of congressional legislation. He had gone so far as to cause a map to be prepared and lithographed, which he designated as an official map of "Nebraska," prepared by the commissioner of Indian affairs, at the request of Colonel Benton, and published to show the lands open to settlement therein. This map the commissioner found in the hands of exploring parties, and in a note published in a paper at Independence, Missouri, denounced it, stating that he had never prepared a map for any such purpose, and that in his judgment there was no land within what was then known as Nebraska open to settlement. These discussions and explorations had a very unfavorable influence on the Indians. Reports reached them that bodies of white men were coming into their country, to take possession of and drive them from it. In this condition of things it was found very difficult to quiet the Indians and restore them to a tranquil condition. Some were for lighting up their fires "after the old Indian fashion," and confederating for defense. As a general thing the elder Indians, who had been transplanted, retained a vivid recollection of the promises made to them at the time of their removal, and the assurance that their present should be their permanent homes, and that the white race should never interfere with them or their possessions, was prominently dwelt on by their speakers in every council. Indeed, some of them displayed an earnest eloquence when referring to the subject.

The commissioner visited the Omahas, Ottoes and Missourias, Iowas, Sacs and Foxes of the Missouri, Kickapoos, Delawares, Wyandots, Shawnees, Pottawatomies, Sacs and Foxes of the Mississippi, Chippewas of Swan creek and Black river, Ottawas, Peorias and Kaskaskias, Weas and Piankashaws, and Miamis, all of whom, except the Omahas, and Ottoes and Missourias, were Indians who had been transplanted by the government, in pursuance of the law of 1830. He did not find these Indians as prosperous or as far advanced in civilization as he had been led to expect from the reports made from time to time of their condition. There were many specimens, "noble specimens," he termed them, who had fully adopted civilized pursuits, and were laboring to reclaim and regenerate their race. He found a number of good farmers among them, with the improvements, conveniences, and comforts of the white man; others, and in greater numbers, who had rude dwellings and fields, but with few of the comforts usual among civilized people, while there were some who were unwilling to submit themselves to labor, and sought every opportunity to indulge to excess in the use of whisky. In the various schools there were found groups of interesting children, and from examination and the opinion of the teachers, the commissioner came to the conclusion that these children were capable of equal mental culture with white children, and learned as rapidly. Every thing about the schools appeared in good order, and in them the children obtained a fair education in the ordinary branches. In addition to the school training, the female children were taught needle-work as well as ordinary house-work, and the boys were taught to labor on the farm. The commissioner came to the conclusion that the administration of the affairs of the Indians was not wholly free from abuses, and that such of the Indians as resided near Fort Leavenworth and the Missouri line, were more demoralized than those who lived in localities more distant.

In 1854, treaties were made with the Omaha, Ottoe and Missouria, Sac and Fox of the Missouri, Iowa, Kickapoo, Delaware, Shawnee, Kaskaskia, Peoria, Wea, Piankashaw, and Miami Indians, and the Territories of Kansas and Nebraska were organized. All of the lands of the Indians, except in the aggregate about one million three hundred thousand acres, reserved for their homes, were ceded to the government. Some of the tribes made their cessions in trust, the net proceeds of the lands when sold to be paid them; others made unconditional cessions.

In negotiating with the Indians, the commissioner had considerable difficulty, owing to the fact that outside influences, seeking to mold the treaties to suit their views and interests, were at work. As a case in point, the negotiations with the Shawnees may be mentioned. The treaty was made at Washington City. The tract owned by the Shawnees, and for which they held the patent of the government, was estimated to contain sixteen hundred thousand acres of land. The lowest figure placed on this land, reserving from the tract a reservation of moderate dimensions for their home, was eight hundred and twenty-nine thousand dollars, and this to be paid cash in hand. After discussing the matter for perhaps one week, the Indians consented to accept the sum named in eight annual payments. The commissioner on the part of the government desired the Indians to invest the principal in six per cent. bonds, yielding annually nearly fifty thousand dollars interest, and endeavored to convince them that this sum would be sufficient annuity, and with the yield of their farms, if properly cultivated, would place them in an independent position. But no argument could move them, being, as it was quite apparent they were, under the control of those professing to be friendly to them, but in fact only scheming to have a large sum paid down, to the end that they could reach it. The commissioner informed the government of the state of the negotiations, and expressed the opinion that it was not consistent with the interests of the Shawnees (there were only eight hundred and fifty of them) to have a hundred thousand dollars per year paid them, and advised that the negotiations cease, and the delegation be sent home, since it was probable that at some future time a more appropriate and satisfactory arrangement, and one more in harmony with the true interests of the Indians, could be made. But such was the incessant clamor for opening the country and letting in the white people, that the treaty, by direction of superior authority, was concluded. With a view to protect the Indians from the arts and wiles of those who had become quite expert in manipulating Indian matters, and getting up "national obligations" for groundless claims against the Indians, a clause was inserted in the treaty with the Shawnees to this effect: "No portion of the money stipulated by this instrument to be paid to the Shawnees, shall be taken by the government of the United States, by its agents or otherwise, to pay debts contracted by the Shawnees, as individuals, nor any part thereof for the payment of national debts or obligations contracted by the Shawnee council." When the treaty was under consideration in the Senate for its ratification, the following amendment was added to the clause above quoted: "*Provided*, that this article shall not be construed to prohibit the council from setting apart a portion of any annual payment for purposes strictly national in their character, and for the payment of national or tribal debts, first to be approved by the president." The Indians had under a former treaty a perpetual annuity, ample for any sum that the council might need, and yet the Senate saw fit, without any request from the Indians or from any true friend of theirs, but through the influence of those who sought to, and did control them as to the period in which the purchase money should be paid, to make this amendment, and thus open wide the door to the very abuse which the original clause sought to guard against. The fact is simply noticed here to show that the Senate of the United States was not free from improper influences, when dealing with Indian affairs.

In the annual report of the commissioner of Indian affairs, dated November 25, 1854, the condition of affairs, as they then existed, and the effect upon the Indians likely to be produced, was dwelt on at some length. Among other things the commissioner said : " In view of the facts above stated, I am constrained to submit a few suggestions in relation to the emigrated tribes in Kansas Territory, who, by the policy of the government, adopted nearly thirty years ago, and reluctantly acquiesced in by them, were removed to, and became inhabitants of, the country now embraced in this territory. Already many of them have ceded, and it is expected that others will cede, the larger portion of their lands to the United States, for the use and occupation of our citizens. The faith of the nation was pledged in the most solemn form, before these tribes were removed to the west of the Mississippi, that they should have the undisputed possession and control of the country, and that the tracts assigned to them therein, should be their permanent homes. It was called ' the Indian Territory,' and the intercourse act made it unlawful for white men to go into it, except on a license obtained and for special purposes ; and in this secluded home, it was believed that the efforts of the government and the philanthropist to civilize the red man, would be more successful than ever before. Such, however, was not the case. Our population advanced rapidly to the line which was to be the barrier, and with the emigration consequent upon our acquisitions from Mexico, and the organization of our new territories, necessarily subjected the Indian to that kind of contact with the whites, which was sure to entail on them the vices, while deprived of the good influences of civilization.

" In the recent negotiations for their lands the Indians dwelt upon the former pledges and promises made to them, and were averse generally to the surrender of any portion of their country. They said that they were to have the land ' as long as grass grew or water run,' and they feared the result if they should consent to yield any part of their possessions. When they did consent to sell, it was only on the condition that each tribe should retain a portion of their tract as a permanent home. All were unitedly and firmly opposed to another removal. So fixed and settled was this idea, that propositions clearly for their interests were rejected by them.

"The residences of the tribes who have recently ceded portions of their lands, should, therefore, be considered (subject in a few cases to a contraction of limits) as permanently fixed. Already the white population is occupying the lands between and adjacent to the Indian reservations, and even going west of and beyond them, and at no distant day, all the country immediately to the west of the reserves, which is worth occupying, will have been taken up. And then the current of population (until within a few years flowing only from the east,) now comes sweeping like an avalanche from the Pacific coast, almost overwhelming the indigenous Indians in its approaches. It is, therefore, in my judgment, clear, beyond doubt or question, that the emigrated tribes in Kansas Territory are permanently there—there to be thoroughly civilized, and to become a constituted portion of the population, or there to be destroyed and exterminated. What a spectacle for the view of the statesman, philanthropist, Christian! With reservations dotting the eastern portion of the territory, there they stand, the representatives and remnants of tribes once as powerful and dreaded, as these are now weak and dispirited. By alternate persuasion and force, some of these tribes have been removed step by step, from mountain to valley, and from river to plain, until they have been pushed half way across the continent. They can go no further. On the ground they now occupy, the crisis must be met, and their future determined. Among them may be found the educated, civilized, and converted Indian, the benighted and inveterate heathen, and every intermediate grade. But there they are, and as they are, with outstanding obligations in their behalf, of the most solemn and imperative character, voluntarily assumed by the government. Their condition is a critical one; such as to entitle them not only to the justice of the government, but to the most profound sympathy of the people. Extermination may be their fate, but not of necessity. By a union of good influences, and a proper effort, I believe they may, and will be saved, and their complete civilization effected.

"Be that as it may, the duty of the government is plain. It should fulfill with the greatest promptness and fidelity, every treaty stipulation with these Indians; frown down at the first dawning, any and every attempt to corrupt them; see that their ample annuities are directed faithfully to their education and improvement, and not made the means of their destruction; incessantly resist the efforts of the selfish and heartless men, who, by specious plans and devices for their own gain, may seek to distract and divide them; require diligence, energy, and integrity in the administration of their affairs, by the agents who may be intrusted with their interests and welfare; and visit the severest penalties of the law on all who may violate its salutary provisions in relation to them. Let these things be done, and the co-operation of the civil officers, magistrates, and the good citizens of the territory secured, and the most active efforts of the friends of the benevolent institutions now existing among them be brought into exercise for their moral culture; and by harmonious and constant effort and action, a change may, and it is believed will be, brought about, and Kansas become distinguished as a land in which the complete and thorough civilization of the red man was worked out and accomplished."

A few months previous to the date of the report from which the above is quoted, it was discovered that an association of persons had seized upon a piece of land fronting on the Missouri, below Fort Leavenworth, and laid out a town thereon, called the city of Leavenworth. This act was in direct violation of the treaty with the Delaware Indians; yet the unlawful proceeding took place under the eyes of the military officers stationed at the fort. Indeed, some of them were active agents in the transaction. The Indians were disturbed at what was transpiring, and complained to the Indian office about it. The example set in seizing the site of the city of Leavenworth was contagious, and parties entered the Delaware tract, and placed upon the land, at various points, such monuments as would, as they hoped, give them, under the custom of "squatters" on the public land, a right of pre-emption. The commissioner advised the Indians that all such persons were acting unlawfully, and could derive no advantage by their acts. He at the same time requested that all intruders should be expelled by the military force at the fort. He said this was due to the Indians, and if neglected, they would become dispirited and lose confidence in the public authorities, in which event all efforts to improve their condition must be unavailing. Instead of his efforts in this direction being met with in a proper spirit, the military became quite indignant; denounced the commissioner, and defended the squatters, and the influence of city lots in Leavenworth (the future great city of the West, as it was called) reached even to Washington, and found favor in the halls of Congress. In the annual report of November, 1855, the commissioner thus refers to the condition of things then existing in the territory, and its effect on the Indians:

" The peculiar condition of the emigrated tribes in Kansas Territory was stated at some length in the last annual report. They were removed thither under the most solemn assurances and guarantees that the country assigned them should be to them and their descendants a permanent home forever. In retroceding large bodies of land to the United States, by which portions of the territory were lawfully opened to the occupation and settlement of its citizens, neither the government nor the Indians sought to change the guarantees and stipulations of former treaties; but they were recognized as obligatory and binding within the tracts of land reserved for the permanent homes of the Indians. The organic act of the territory so regarded them, and it was expressly declared that nothing in the act should ' be construed to impair the rights of persons or property now pertaining to the Indians in said territory, so long as such rights shall remain unextinguished by treaty between the United States and such Indians.' The peaceful possession and quiet enjoyment of the tracts reserved by the Indians for their homes are guaranteed and secured to them by the faith of treaties and the laws of the land, and it is to be regretted that, in different sections of the territory, persons have trespassed upon their rights, by committing waste, and even locating within and making improvements upon the Indian lands. As cases have been reported, the agents have been instructed to notify the wrong-doers that their acts were in violation of the law and the faith of treaties, and that they must cease their trespasses, and retire outside of the Indian reservations. Many of the intruders have wholly disregarded the admonitions and warnings of the officers of the Indian service, and to compel obedience, and to vindicate the good faith and authority of the government, in this behalf, the military arm has been invoked and called into requisition ; and under instructions recently issued, by direction of the president, it is expected that all persons remaining unlawfully upon any of the Indian reservations in Kansas Territory, after a period to be fixed, and of which they will have notice, will be forcibly ejected therefrom. However disagreeable it may be to resort to this extreme measure, the condition of the Indians is such as to require it, and the obligations of the United States toward them can not be discharged without its application.

" The executive of the territory, in fixing the election districts and appointing voting places, and in establishing the executive office, did not regard the organic law, which excluded Indian reserves from its operation, but embraced several reservations within the districts, and authorized polls to be opened in them. He also established his executive office within the Shawnee country. The territorial legislature, following his example, held its session at the Shawnee mission, and by its enactments embraced some of the Indian reserves within the organized counties, all of which is clearly a violation of treaty stipulations and the act creating the territory.

" Many of the emigrants to, and settlers in, the Territory of Kansas, are engaged in bitter controversy and strife in relation to the institutions to be formed there, as applicable to the condition of the African race ; yet the hostile factions seem to have no sympathy for the red man, but, on the contrary, many of both sides appear to disregard his interests, and trespass upon his rights with impunity."

The relief that was expected from the military arm of the government was not obtained. The commissioner had arraigned the officers implicated in the unlawful seizure of the

site of the city of Leavenworth, and suggested that the gravity
of the offense was such that they should be dismissed from
the service, which fact, and their sympathy for those who
were appropriating unlawfully portions of the Indian reservations, made them unwilling agents. Moreover, they were
sustained by the secretary of war. Some of the civil as well
as judicial officers of the territory became enlisted on the side
of the squatters, having themselves been engaged in transactions neither honorable nor lawful. Another year passed
away—a year of great disorder in Kansas—and in November,
1856, the commissioner of Indian affairs thus alluded to it:
"The general disorder so long prevailing in Kansas Territory,
and the consequent unsettled state of civil affairs there, have
been very injurious to the interests of many of the Indian
tribes in that territory. The state of affairs referred to with
the influx of lawless men and speculators incident and introductory thereto, have impeded the surveys and the selections
for the homes of the Indians, and otherwise prevented the
full establishment and proper efficiency of all the means for
civilization and improvement, within the scope of the several
treaties with them. The schools have not been so fully attended, nor the school buildings, agency houses, and other improvements, as rapidly constructed as they might otherwise
have been. Trespasses and depredations of every conceivable
kind have been committed on the Indians. They have been
personally maltreated, their property stolen, their timber destroyed, their possessions encroached upon, and divers other
wrongs and injuries done them. Notwithstanding all which,
they have afforded a praiseworthy example of good conduct
under the most trying circumstances. They have at no time,
that I am aware of, attempted to redress their own wrongs,
but have patiently submitted to injury, relying on the good
faith and justice of the government to indemnify them. In
the din and strife between the anti-slavery and pro-slavery
parties with reference to the condition of the African race
there, and in which the rights and interests of the red men
have been completely overlooked and disregarded, the good
conduct and patient submission of the latter contrast favorably with the disorderly and lawless conduct of many of their

white brethren, who, while they have quarreled about the African, have united upon the soil of Kansas in wrong doing toward the Indian!" As order and peace seemed in some degree restored, the commissioner expressed the hope that the good citizens of the territory would make haste to repair the injury which the Indians had suffered by the wrong doing of their white neighbors, and that thereafter they would treat the Indians fairly, and resist the conduct of any lawless men who might attempt to injure them. But all appeals in favor of the rights of the Indians were in vain. Within the bounds of the territory, there appeared to be no spot of land occupied by an Indian tribe that was free from lawless intrusion.

In 1860, a treaty was made with the Delaware Indians, by which the tract of land reserved in the treaty of 1854, for their permanent home, was conveyed to the Leavenworth, Pawnee and Western Railroad (excepting only the tracts reserved for the homes of a few individuals), upon the payment of such sum in gold or silver coin, as three commissioners appointed by the secretary of the interior should find to be the value of the land. In July, 1862, another treaty was made with the Delawares, by which the payment for the lands ceded to the railroad company, amounting to 224,000 acres of very valuable land, was changed from gold and silver coin to the bonds of the company, the appraised value of the land being two hundred and eighty-seven thousand dollars, for which sum twenty-eight bonds of the road, calling for ten thousand dollars each, and the twenty-ninth bond for a fraction of ten thousand dollars, were given, and to secure the payment of these bonds, the railroad company gave a mortgage on one hundred thousand acres of the land purchased! Then, on July 4, 1866, still another treaty was made with the Delawares, in which they were made to say that they desired to remove from the State of Kansas, and take up their abode in what is known as the Indian Territory, and the United States having, by treaty with the Cherokees, Creeks, and Seminoles, and the Choctaws and Chickasaws, acquired the right to colonize other Indian tribes within said territory, agreed to sell to the Delawares a home in the same, equal in quantity to one hundred and sixty acres for each of them, the

Indians agreeing to sell all their remaining land in Kansas to the Missouri River Railroad Company; or in default of a sale to it, then the secretary of the interior was authorized to sell the land to other parties; and now we find this once powerful and historic nation of Indians, numbering about one thousand souls, located in the Indian Territory, broken in spirit, a monument of the debasing effects produced by the process of removals to which they have been subjected for three generations.

The ancestors of these Indians were with William Penn at the treaty of 1683 (then known as the Lenni Lenape, or original people), and faithfully observed the conditions of the agreement then made. One of their early sachems, Tamanend, or Tammany, left a name among his people which was treasured with veneration, and they recounted his wisdom and his virtues until his character rose so high with the colonists, that he was in some sense canonized. It was said that his virtues, and exploits both among the white men and Indians, excited so much respect that after his death he was held in such remembrance that the day of his birth was regarded as a holy day. It was among these Indians that Heckewelder and others labored, and from their work arose an interesting community known as the Christian Indians. In that day, as well as now, there was a class of men who were intent on invading the rights of the Indians, and if necessary to accomplish their object, destroying them. Of such, Heckewelder wrote: " I have yet to notice a class of people generally known to us by the name of ' backwoodsmen,' many of whom, acting up to a pretended belief that ' an Indian has no more soul than a buffalo,' and that to kill either is the same thing, have, from time to time, by their conduct brought great trouble and bloodshed on the country. Such, then, I wish to caution not to sport in that manner with the lives of God's creatures. . . . Believe that a time will come when you must account for such vile deeds!—when those who have fallen a sacrifice to your wickedness will be called forth in judgment against you! Nay, when your own descendants will testify against you."

The first treaty made by the United States with any Indian

nation was that of 1778, with the Delawares, at Fort Pitt. They were then regarded as an equal power with the government, and promised each to the other assistance in time of war, and provisional arrangements were suggested for the organization of an Indian state, with the Delawares at its head, and to have a representation in Congress. The Indians agreed to and did furnish troops and supplies, and also fought in the ranks in the war of the revolution. There were among them a number of men of great force of character, and they were perfectly reliable. They were parties to the treaty of Fort McIntosh, in 1785; Fort Harmer, in 1789; Greenville, in 1795; Fort Wayne, in 1803; Vincennes, in 1804; Fort Industry, in 1805; Fort Wayne, in 1809; Greenville, in 1814; Rapids of the Maumee, in 1817; St. Mary's, in 1817. In this process of treaty making the Delawares were found in 1829, on the James Fork of White river, in the State of Missouri, and on the 24th of September, 1829, agreed by a treaty made at their home to remove to the country in the fork of the Kansas and Missouri rivers, the same to be conveyed and *forever* secured to them as a permanent home. When we contemplate these facts, and reflect upon the broken promises and bad faith which has been the lot of these people, it is not surprising that they have wasted away.

The first treaty relation with the Kickapoos was in 1795. They belonged to the quasi Indian confederacy formed many years before. Their location was in Illinois. They were, with other tribes, parties to the treaties in 1803, 1810, 1814, 1815, 1816, 1820, 1821, 1833. By the terms of the treaty of 1833, they were given the country in Kansas where they resided in 1854, when they ceded all their lands in Kansas to the United States, except one hundred and fifty thousand acres, reserved for their permanent home. In 1862, the Kickapoos were induced to make another treaty, in which such of them as desired to do so were given the right to select individual homes, and a small tract was set apart to be held in common by such of the tribe as preferred that course, and the residue of their land was conveyed to the Atchison and Pike's Peak Railroad Company, and thus they, like the Delawares, were divested of their inheritance by a railroad corporation.

The Piankashaw, Wea, Kaskaskia, Peoria, Chippewas of Rouche de Boeuf, Miami, and Wyandot Indians, all of whom had early treaty relations with the government, after having passed through this same process of treaty making as the Delawares and Kickapoos, were finally landed in the Indian Territory (Kansas), where they were to dwell forever. In 1854, they, too, surrendered most of their lands for the use and occupation of citizens of the United States, reserving, however, a small part. From these reserved lands they were, by an omnibus treaty, proclaimed in 1868, in which all were included, placed in the country of the Choctaws and others, there to brood over the injustice and wrong done them by the white race. It is not deemed necessary to go further into this narrative. Suffice it to say, that of all the emigrated tribes which were transplanted under the act of May, 1830, and whose reservations were within the limits of the State of Kansas, there remained in November, 1877, within that state, according to the report of the commissioner of Indian affairs, two hundred and forty-eight Kickapoos, four hundred and fifty Pottawatomies, and sixty Chippewa and Munsees. It is painful to contemplate this phase of the Indian question, and to note the many solemn promises and covenants made to these Indians, at each successive removal, that it should be the last one.

Owing to the complications growing up between the Indians and the whites, within the states, it was admitted in 1825 that the government could not fulfill its obligations to these people, unless they were transferred to a country to the west, which was to be and remain forever outside of any organized state or territory. The Indians yielded to the urgent demands made upon them, and were, under the authority of the act of May, 1830, removed. The fate of those who were at this time located in Kansas, presents matter for the most serious consideration of every friend of justice and humanity. The whole record is one of broken promises and bad faith on the part of our people and government.

The Cherokees, Choctaws, Chickasaws, and Creeks were

enabled, from the time of their removal, to overcome all attempts to make inroads upon them, and "bereave them of their lands;" and through the governments organized by them, have advanced gradually in civilized pursuits, and increased slightly in population. In 1866, treaties were made with some of them, by which, in addition to the right granted to locate and construct railroads through their reservations, a clause was inserted, which may be regarded as dangerous to their interests and their peace in the future. It is the clause providing for the sale, to each railroad corporation, of every alternate section of land, for six miles in width, along the line of the same. Following this, there have been indications, in Congress, of a disposition to open these reservations to the occupation and settlement of the white people. Already this agitation has been hurtful to the Indians. They have, in each tribe, many men of intelligence, who realize the danger. These understand that the organization of Kansas Territory, and the general disorder that immediately followed, and for years grew in volume, was the forerunner of measures that finally disinherited their brethren in that territory, and they are sufficiently intelligent observers of passing events to know that, in their case, in addition to the influences which prevailed in Kansas, there will be added the energy of powerful corporations having lines of railroad built or contemplated through their reservations, in aid of the scheme for opening their country to the occupation and settlement of the whites. These influences argue that civilization can not consent that such a body of land as these tribes possess, shall remain, as much of it is, in a state of nature; that it should be in possession of a race that will subdue the land and bring it into cultivation. They ignore the fact that these lands came from the government, of its own motion, to the Indians for a permanent home, in consideration that they surrendered their homes east of the Mississippi, and that the Indians have, in the most solemn form, the guaranty of the government that the country they now own should be, to them and their posterity, a permanent home forever, and that it should always be, and remain, outside of the limits of any organized territory or state. It is true that the lands owned by the Cherokees, Choctaws, Chickasaws, Creeks, and Seminoles is in excess of what is necessary for their use, and with their consent freely given, portions of it might be disposed of without injury to them. There is, too, a class of their own race to whom it would be a great boon to be located on these reservations. All the Indians east of the Rocky Mountains, and in and west of the mountains also, could be gradually transferred to this Indian territory, and there provided with good homes; and it is believed that the Indians owning it would assent, on fair terms, to an arrangement of this sort; but at this time Congress stands in the way of such a beneficent measure. The Sioux commission of 1876 inserted a clause, in their agreement with the Sioux, for the surrender of the Black Hills, looking to a gradual transfer of the Sioux to the Indian Territory, and sent down a delegation of the Sioux to inspect the country, with a view to that object. When the agreement came before Congress for its approval, that body made haste to strike out that part of it, and expressly directed the president to prohibit such removal. This action of Congress was, no doubt, quite gratifying to the agents of the corporations who have covetous eyes set upon the Indian reservations within the Indian Territory; and it was not displeasing to those opposed to the measure, who reside in Kansas, Missouri, and Arkansas. Some few object to the transfer of northern Indians to the Indian Territory, alleging that the change of climate is disastrous to them, and offer as evidence the sickness and deaths among the Pawnees, Poncas, and Joseph's band of Nez Perces, that followed their removal. There were causes, other than the change of climate, to produce the mortality among these Indians, to which reference is made; and, at the present time, it is presumed that their sanitary condition is much improved. It is not believed there is any thing substantial in this objection. The Cherokees, who were southern Indians, suffered more, in their removal to the Indian Territory, than any other tribe. Indeed, they lost about one-fourth of their number on the sad journey.

There is nothing that has yet appeared that is a valid reason why northern Indians should not be colonized there, and it does seem that the friends of Indian civilization ought to take hold of this matter of the integrity of the Indian Territory, and its dedication to the Indian race, with all their energy. It is believed, as stated, that the civilized nations residing in and owning it, would be willing for the gradual colonization of their brethren within the territory, and, under proper arrangements, would engage to enter into the work, and aid in the civilization of such tribes as might be colonized there. It is a source of profound regret that the Indians in Kansas— the colonized tribes—were dispossessed as they were, and by reason thereof many of them nearly ruined and destroyed; yet this fact, while it reflects forcibly on the conduct of the white race, when dealing with the Indian, should not cause despondency or doubt as to his capability to accept civilization, and under proper care and training become a useful member of society. There are many living examples among our Indian population, not only that the Indian is susceptible of civilization, but that he is capable of taking respectable rank among the educated of our own race. Among the tribes in Kansas, when the pro and anti-slavery parties rushed in to possess the land, there were many then so far advanced as to qualify them for the proper discharge of the duties incumbent on civilized men in well-regulated communities. The treatment that such ones, as well as all the Indians, received from the maddened whites, who in their conduct disgraced civilization and violated every principle of humanity, is a dark stain upon our nation's honor. In fact, the precipitate legislation by which the country was thrown open to the occupation of the white race, in the face of the plighted faith of the government, was a crime, and the whole country has suffered the penalty. In the bitter discussions in Congress and among the people, in relation to the prohibition of the institution of slavery in that territory, which assumed a sectional character, the seed was sown which bore fruit and resulted in our civil war.

CHAPTER VIII.

THE REMOVAL OF INDIAN TRIBES.—THE STORY OF ONE REMOVAL SUBSTANTIALLY
THE STORY OF ALL.—THE REMOVAL OF THE SANTEE SIOUX AND WINNEBAGO
INDIANS.—THE DESTRUCTION OF THE BUFFALO AND SMALL GAME.—ITS EFFECT
ON THE INDIANS OF THE PLAINS.

THE policy of removing Indian tribes from seat to seat, as
the white settlements pressed upon them, which was adopted
at a very early day, has at all times resulted disastrously to
the Indians. It has also been a fruitful source of corruption.
It is believed that there are but few instances in which perfect
good faith, in all respects, has governed in the removal of a
tribe from an old to a new home. In numberless instances
removals have been brought about, not because there was a
necessity for them, but with a view to the plunder and profit
that was expected to result from the operation. A volume
could be filled with details of the most unhappy character;
growing out of those removals, and in what preceded and
followed them, in which the Indians were cruelly treated and
the government defrauded.

A brief extract from a letter written in 1851, to an Indian
agent, by a member of a firm that had grown wealthy in Indian trade, and contracts for transportation and Indian removals, will show not only the watchfulness of persons engaged
in such transactions, but illustrate the mystery of correspondence in relation to operations among the Indians. The extract
is as follows: "During this short session there has been much
excitement, and but little effected in these Indian matters.
Nothing done or moved in the Menominee matters; they are
as before, and most likely will remain so for another year. In
the meantime, if the president requires them to remove west,
the contract for that object will be an object. Colonel Thompson will be at Washington for some time, and so will my
brother. Write to them freely; you will find them right and
true. If that could be carried out as we talked the matter
over, it would result in a good profit. Write to my brother

about this. I have said to him what was proposed between you, Wright, and us. . . . I am compelled to go in the morning to St. Louis, to provide funds for our transportation contract to New Mexico, and write in haste. Will be back in twenty days. We must try and make this business tell well yet."

In 1863, the government removed the Santee Sioux and the Winnebago Indians from Minnesota to the Crow Creek agency, on the Missouri river, about one hundred and fifty miles above Yankton, in the Territory of Dakota. The guard that accompanied these Indians consisted of four commissioned officers, one hundred and thirty-five soldiers, and one laundress—in all, one hundred and forty persons. The number of Santee Sioux transported was thirteen hundred and eighteen. For the transportation and subsistence of these Indians and the guard, there was paid the sum of $36,322.10. The number of Winnebagoes transported was nineteen hundred and forty-five; for their transportation and subsistence there was paid the further sum of $56,042.60—making the whole amount paid the contractors, the sum of $95,864.70.

The Sioux were transported from Fort Snelling to Hannibal, Missouri, on two steamboats; one of the boats stopped there, and the Indians on it crossed over to St. Joseph, on the Missouri river, by rail. The other boat continued to the junction of the Mississippi and Missouri rivers, and thence up the latter to St. Joseph; and here the Indians that crossed over by rail were put upon the boat, and from thence to Crow Creek all of them were on one boat. They were very much crowded from St. Joseph to Crow Creek. Sixteen died on the way, being without attention or medical supplies. All the Indians were excluded from the cabin of the boat, and confined to the lower and upper decks. It was in May, and to go among them on the lower deck was suffocating. They were fed on hard bread and mess pork, much of it not cooked, there being no opportunity to cook it, only at night, when the boat laid up. They had no sugar, coffee, or vegetables. Confinement on the boat, in such a mass, and want of proper food, created much sickness, such as diarrhea and fevers. For weeks after they arrived at Crow Creek, the Indians died at the rate of from three to four per day. In a few weeks, one hundred and fifty had died, mainly on account of the treatment they received after leaving Fort Snelling. They were landed at Crow Creek on the first day of June, 1863. The season was unusually dry; vegetation burnt up, and no crop growing; some corn had been planted, but did not get more than four inches high before it wilted down.

During the summer, the Indians were fed on flour and pork. They got no beef until fall. They suffered for want of fresh beef, as well as for want of medical supplies. In the fall, their rations began to fail, and the issue was gradually reduced, and the Indians complained bitterly. About the first of September, a train of one hundred wagons arrived at Crow Creek, from Minnesota, loaded with goods and supplies for the Indian traders, and the Santee Sioux and Winnebago Indians. The only supplies for the Santee Sioux, brought by the train, was flour. It was understood that when the train left Minnesota, it contained some corn for these Indians, but none came to Crow Creek agency. Some pork was brought, but none of it was issued to the Santee Sioux; but was issued to individual Indians in payment for work. After the arrival of the train, the ration issued to the Indians was flour and beef. The quantity was very short. The beef furnished was from the cattle that hauled the supplies from Minnesota. These cattle had traveled over three hundred miles, hauling the train, with nothing to eat but the dry prairie grass, there being no settlements on the route they came. The cattle were very poor. Some died or gave out on the trip, and such were slaughtered, and the meat brought in on the train for food for the Indians. About the first of January, 1864, near four hundred head of the cattle were slaughtered. Except the dry prairie grass, which the frost had killed, these cattle had no food from the time they came to Crow Creek until they were slaughtered. A part of the beef thus made was piled up in the warehouse, in snow, and the remainder, in like manner, packed in snow outside. This beef was to keep the Indians until the coming June. The beef was black and very poor; indeed, the greater part only skin and bone. Shortly after the arrival of the train from Minnesota, the contractors for supplying the Indians with flour, took about one hundred head of the oxen, selecting the best of them, yoked them up, and sent them with wagons to Sioux City, some two hundred and forty miles, to haul up flour. This train returned in February, and these oxen were then slaughtered and fed to the Indians.

In January, the issue of soup to the Indians commenced. It was made in a large cottonwood vat, being cooked by steam carried from the boiler of the saw-mill, in a pipe, to the vat. The vat was partially filled with water, then several quarters of beef chopped up were thrown into it, and a few sacks of flour added. The hearts, lights, and entrails were added to the compound, and in the beginning a few beans were put into the vat, but this luxury did not continue long. This soup was issued every other day—to the Santee Sioux one day, the alternate day to the Winnebagoes. It was very unpalatable. On the day the Indians received soup, they had no other food issued to them. They were very much dissatisfied, and said they could not live on the soup, when those in charge told them if they could live elsewhere, they had better go, but that they must not go to the white settlements. Many of them did leave the agency, some going to Fort Sully, others to Fort Randall, in search of food. From a description of this nauseous mess, called soup, given by Samuel C. Haynes, then at Fort Randall, and assistant surgeon in the military service, it is seen that the Indians had good cause to leave Crow Creek. He states that there were thrown into the " vat, beef, beef heads, entrails of the beeves, some beans, flour, and pork. I think there were put into the vat two barrels of flour each time, which was not oftener than once in twenty-four hours. This mass was then cooked by the steam from the boiler passing through the pipe into the vat. When that was done, all the Indians were ordered to come with their pails and get it. It was dipped out to the Indians with a long handled dipper, made for the purpose. I can not say the quantity given to each. It was about the consistency of very thin gruel. The Indians would pour off the thinner portion and eat that which settled at the bottom. As it was dipped out of the vat some of the Indians would get the thinner portions and some would get some meat. I passed there frequently when it was cooking, and was often there when it was being issued, and it had a very offensive odor; it had the odor of the contents of the entrails of the beeves. I have seen the settlings of the vat after they were through issuing it to the Indians, when they were cleaning the vat, and the settlings smelt like carrion—like decomposed meat. The Santees and Winnebagoes were fed from this vat; some of the Indians refused to eat it, saying they could not do so, as it made them sick. The Winnebagoes protested against such filthy cooking, and said they could not eat it; they said it was only fit for hogs, and they said they were not hogs."

No clothing having been issued to the Santee Sioux or Winnebagoes since 1862, they suffered much for want of proper apparel, and from this want, as well as from the lack of food, many were induced to go out on a buffalo hunt. Mr. Williamson, the missionary, went with them, although he was fearful they might perish; yet such were their necessities that he encouraged them to go, fearing that if they did not they would starve before spring. About three hundred went out on the hunt in February. Mr. Williamson said that, in his opinion, if all the Santees and Winnebagoes had stayed at the agency during the winter, many of them would have starved to death. They were out about six weeks. On their return they found that the issue of soup had ceased, and the ration consisted of flour and beef; the beef that had been packed in snow during the winter. The ration consisted of about one-fourth of a pound of flour and three-fourths of a pound of beef, per head, per day, during the spring and summer. The flour had been hauled some three hundred miles in wagons, without cover, and from rainfall on the way, such was the condition of the sacks containing the flour, that after all the loose flour was knocked out of them, some of the sacks weighed thirty pounds. This flour was issued to the Indians at ninety-eight pounds to the sack. It was all inferior flour. During the winter of 1864–5, the beef was killed and packed in the same manner for the Santee Sioux, and the result was that many of the Indians left in search of food. It is stated that many of them went to different points where military expeditions had camped, to pick up the scattered corn that had been left by the horses and mules, when fed, for the purpose of eating it, and also to pick up the dead mules and horses to eat. Mr. Williamson states that such treatment had a demoralizing influence on the Indians, many of the women being compelled to prostitute themselves in order to get something to eat.

The Winnebagoes, not by reason of any thing done by them, but because of the massacre of the whites by the Sioux in Minnesota, in 1862, and the excited feeling growing out of that sad affair, were compelled to leave their reservation in that state. Congress, in response to the demand of the people in the region in which they lived, passed an act providing for their removal. They had no previous warning, and remonstrated against this act of injustice, but their protest was unheeded. They were, as stated, taken on boats, and carried down the Mississippi and up the Missouri to Crow Creek. All were dissatisfied with their treatment on the journey, and their location at Crow Creek. Much sickness prevailed, and many died. They were living in Minnesota in peace and quiet, and had been so for years. They had made considerable advancement in civilization. Many of them had farms and houses, and had acquired habits of industry and economy. Such was their dissatisfaction at Crow Creek, that large numbers of them during the summer and fall made their way down the Missouri in canoes, landing at different points, where they managed to live through the winter of 1863–4. It is said that at the time of their forcible removal they were supplied with grain, stock, implements of husbandry, etc., most of which were stolen or destroyed, since they were unable to take their property with them. Little Hill, a Winnebago chief, thus told the story at Dakota City, Nebraska, to a member of the joint committee of Congress, charged with the investigation of Indian affairs in 1865. The chief said:

"You are one of our friends, as it appears. We are very glad to meet you here. Here are some of our old chiefs with me, but not all. And we will tell you something about how we have lived for the four years past. Now you see me here to-day. Formerly I did not live as I now do. We used to live in Minnesota. While we lived in Minnesota we used to live in good houses, and always took our Great Father's advice, and did whatever he told us to do. We used to farm and raise a crop of all we wanted every year. While we lived there we had teams of our own. Each family had a span of horses or oxen to work, and had plenty of ponies; now we have nothing. While we lived in Minnesota another tribe of Indians committed depredations against the whites, and then we were compelled to leave Minnesota. We did not think we would be removed from Minnesota, never expected to leave; and we were compelled to leave so suddenly that we were not prepared; not many could sell their ponies and things they had. The superintendent of the farm for the Winnebagoes was to take care of the ponies we left there, and bring them on to where we went, but he only brought to Crow Creek about fifty, and the rest we do not know what became of them. Most all of us had put in our crops that spring before we left, and we had to go and leave every thing but our clothes and household things; we had but four days' notice. Some left their houses just as they were, with their stoves and household things in them. They promised they would bring all our ponies, but they only brought fifty, and the hostile Sioux came one night and stole all these away. In the first place, when we started from Minnesota they told us they had got a good country for us, where they were going to put us. . . . After we got on a boat we were as though in a prison. . . . We were fed on dry stuff all the time. . . . After we got there [to Crow Creek] they sometimes gave us rations, but not enough to go round most of the time. Some would have to go without eating two or three days. It was not a good country; it was all dust. Whenever we cooked any thing it would be full of dust. We found, after a while, that we could not live there. Many of them [the women and children] died because they could not get enough to eat. We do not know who was to blame. . . . They had a cottonwood trough made and put beef in it, and sometimes a whole barrel of flour and a piece of pork, and let it stand a whole night, and the next morning, after cooking it, would give us some to eat. We tried to use it, but many got sick on it and died. I am telling nothing but the truth. They also put in the unwashed intestines of the beeves, and the liver and the lights, and after dipping out the soup, the bottom would be very nasty and offensive. . . . The pork and the flour that we left in Minnesota that belonged to us, was brought over to Crow Creek and sold to us by our storekeepers at Crow Creek. . . . For myself, I thought I could stay there for a while, and see the country. But I found it wasn't a good country. I lost six of my children, and so I came down the Missouri. When I got ready to start some soldiers came there and told me if I started they would fire on me. I had thirty canoes ready to start. No one interceded with the soldiers to permit me to go; but the next night I got away, and started down the river; and when I got down as far as the town of Yankton, I found a man there and got some provisions; then came on down further and got more provisions, and then went on to the Omahas. After we got to the Omahas somebody gave me a sack of flour, and some one told us to go to the other side of the Missouri and camp, and we did so. We thought we would keep on down the river, but some one come and told us to stay, and we have been there ever since."

Little Hill's narrative is quite lengthy, and in all its parts is corroborated by Big Bear, Little Chief, and Decorah, all Winnebago chiefs. Big Bear, in his testimony, contrasts the treatment of the Indians with what it was " many years ago " when they lived in the State of Iowa, " when the men used to get two pairs of blankets apiece, but we do not know (said he) what becomes of the goods now."

The story of these Indians is a sad but a truthful one; and is, in a certain sense, the story of all Indian removals; for, while precisely the same train of events may not have marred the pathway of all Indians in the process of removal, and the incidents preceding and following, yet all have suffered seriously, many being subjected to barbarous and inhuman treatment. When attempts have been made to remove an Indian tribe with fidelity, and to extend to the Indians on the journey the semblance of such treatment as is due to human beings—such cases being exceptional—disaster, discomfort, and suffering have been experienced. With such incidents repeated frequently in the life of each generation, as tokens of our civilization, should we be surprised that the savage is distrustful of us, and hesitates to accept as genuine our professions of friendship? The joint committee of Congress that investigated the transactions connected with the removal of the Santee Sioux and Winnebago Indians, in reporting upon the case, said: "Of one thing we may be assured, that no government can permit such injuries to go unredressed without incurring the penalty of treaties broken and justice violated." This committee gathered a vast amount of testimony in relation to our Indian affairs in all sections, from the Mississippi river to the Pacific ocean, wherever Indians were located, and, among other things, came to the conclusion that in a large majority of cases Indian wars were to be traced to the aggressions of the whites, and that such wars were very destructive, not only of the lives of the warriors, but of the women and children also, often becoming wars of extermination. The committee say: "The indiscriminate slaughter of men, women, and children has frequently occurred in Indian wars."

As a remedy for existing evils this committee proferred a bill to Congress, creating five boards of inspectors of Indian affairs, each to have a section of country within the states and territories, inhabited by Indians, composed of "men of high character, and organized in such manner and clothed with such powers as to supervise and inspect the whole administration of Indian affairs in its threefold character—civil, military, and educational." The report of the committee, with the testimony taken by it, forms a volume of more than five hundred pages, which may, probably, be found stowed away in the document room at the capitol, in Washington, but the grave matters to which it called attention, have met with the same fate that kindred subjects, in previous and subsequent reports, involving the interests of a race, have received. Congress has signally failed to do its duty in the premises.

The constant agitation of the removal of Indian tribes has a very pernicious influence on the Indians. This agitation is kept up by the white people who live adjacent to and desire to possess themselves of the Indian lands. Unfortunately, Congress seems ever ready to gratify the desire of the whites to bereave the Indian of his home. A few examples of the effect produced by such agitation, are here presented from the annual report of the Hon. E. A. Hayt, commissioner of Indian affairs for the year 1877 :

The agent of the Selitz agency, in Oregon, says : " Hearing, as they constantly do, that the government is soon to drive them from the land they now occupy, in order to make room for the whites who want homes, they sometimes get discouraged, and conclude it is useless to improve what they are so soon to vacate."

The agent of the Grand Rounde agency, in Oregon, says : " The Indians in this agency are kept in a constant state of insecurity by reports of whites with whom they come in contact, to the effect that they are soon to be removed."

The agent at Fort Defiance, Arizona, says : " The Indians are much attached to their homes, and dislike the idea of removal."

The agent of the Kickapoos, in Kansas, says : " Many practical and progressive Indians have been discouraged and deterred from making improvements, upon which they had determined, through fear that they would not be allowed to enjoy the benefit of them."

The agent of the Ottoe Indians, in Nebraska, says : " The subject of removal that has been agitating these Indians for a number of years, has prevented, to a very great extent, active improvements among them."

It will not be necessary to make further quotations from similar reports, to call the attention of all reflecting people to the subject, in order that the bad influences growing out of Indian removals may be understood. As a general thing there is no valid argument in favor of the removal of a tribe, when they are favorably located on land on which they can make their support. Removals simply to oust the Indians and let the whites have their land, must have an end. Every consideration founded in economy, justice, and humanity, demands that the Indian have a fixed and settled home—to be

in fact permanent. Without it his doom is sealed, and the
extinction of the race only a question of time. With a permanent home, fair dealing, and just treatment, the civilization
and elevation of the race in the social scale is assured. Let
it once be proclaimed as the unalterable law of the land that
Indian removals must cease; that the settler's patent is not
more sacred than the Indian title to his land; that his home
is his castle, and the stride of the red man on the road of
progress will astonish his white brother, and ere long, instead
of the constant pressure to remove him from his home, he
will have the confidence and even sympathy of his white
neighbor.

When the commission appointed to endeavor to compose
the trouble with Joseph's band of Nez Perce Indians (in relation to the Wallowa valley, in Oregon, claimed by this
band), held council with them in 1876, and asked them to
abandon their claim to the valley, within which a few whites
were settled, that chief said: "The earth was his mother.
He was made of the earth, and grew up upon its bosom.
The earth, as his mother and nurse, was sacred to his affections, too sacred to be valued by, or sold for silver or gold.
He could not consent to sever his affections from the land
that bore him. . . He asked nothing of the president.
He was able to take care of himself. . . He was disposed
to live peaceably. He and his band had suffered wrong,
rather than do wrong. One of their number was wickedly
slain by a white man last summer, but he would not avenge
his death. But unavenged by him, the voice of that brother's
blood, sanctifying the ground, would call the dust of their
fathers back to people the land in protest of this great
wrong." The attachment exhibited by Joseph for the land
on which he was born, is common to all Indians, and the sentiments uttered by the chief, indicate that with proper helps
toward civilization, the race to which he belongs might become an element in our society, not only bearable, but desirable. When this chief or some of his people, driven to desperation by oppression, and the forcible attempt to compel
them to yield up the Wallowa valley, rose in resistance, took
the lives of some of the white settlers, and then commenced

that masterly retreat toward the British Possessions, such was his military skill and exemplary conduct, pursued as he was by various military commanders, with fresh troops, as to not only create surprise, but impress the reading public with a high appreciation of his character.

There is not at this time a single Indian reservation in any western state, or in any territory, on which intruders may not at all times be found; while in many the "squatters" are almost as numerous as the Indians, and have such force and influence that they can not be, or at least are not, removed. The government has lamentably failed in making good its treaty pledges, that Indians within their reservations shall be undisturbed by the intrusion of the whites. There are, in our past history, a few notable instances where the whites have been expelled, and in more recent years a few spasmodic efforts have been made, rather to appease the Indians for the time being, than to drive out the outlaws; but no persistent and determined course has been adopted to compel implicit obedience to law on the part of the whites, and to fulfill, in good faith, our obligations to the Indians. In addition to the class of persons who "squat" on Indian lands for the purpose of residing and cultivating, or taking the timber from them, there is another large class who invade the reservation to rob and plunder the Indians. The effect, as may well be expected, is to make the Indians restless; to check their progress; to engender strife, often resulting in loss of life; and in such cases, frequently troops move to the scene of disorder, not to drive off the intruders, but to punish the Indians, as though they were the aggressors, and the matter terminates, finally, in the expulsion of the tribe, and its removal to a new home!

The incessant destruction of the buffalo and other animals, as well as the game on the western prairies and the plains, and even in the mountain territories, has been a source of great injury to the native inhabitants. It has deprived the wild tribes of the support on which they had relied from time immemorial, and often induced them to take to the war-path. As well might we expect the farmers in agricultural regions

10

to witness with composure the destruction of their crops by an invading force, as to suppose that the nomad Sioux, Cheyenne, Arapahoe, Kiowa, or Comanche could witness the destruction of the animals and game on which they relied for sustenance, with indifference. When treaties were made, in 1867–8, with these Indians, assigning specific reservations to them, the right to roam and hunt was guaranteed to them in the territory outside of the same. By this right the Indians not only acquired food, but the hides of the buffalo they killed were made into robes, and, with the skins of other animals, were sold, and thus they were supplied with such things as were useful and necessary. Notwithstanding this fact, there has been a systematic and continuous effort to destroy the buffalo, as well as the small animals and game abounding at that time in certain localities. In Dodge's "Plains of the Great West," a recent publication, William Blackmore, a distinguished and intelligent Englishman, who has for many years made excursions over our western plains, wrote the introductory chapter, and in it referred at some length to the destruction of the buffalo. He said:

"Before referring to the Indian tribes, I desire to add my testimony to that of Colonel Dodge, as to the wholesale and wanton destruction, during the last few years, of the buffalo. When one reads of the total destruction, during three years (1872–3–4), of four millions and a half of the 'black cattle of Illinois,' out of which number upward of three million have been killed for the mere sale of their hides, it is at first almost impossible to realize what this slaughter represents, and how much good and nutritious animal food, which would have fed the red men as well as the hardy settlers of the 'Great West,' has been wasted.

"The figures speak for themselves. When in the West, in 1872, I satisfied myself, by personal inquiries, that the number of buffalo then being annually slaughtered for their hides, was at least one million per annum. In the autumn of 1868, whilst crossing the plains, on the Kansas Pacific Railroad, for a distance of one hundred and twenty miles, between Ellsworth and Sheridan, we passed through an almost unbroken herd of buffalo. The plains were blackened with them; and more than once the train had to stop, to allow unusually large herds to pass. A few years afterward, when traveling over the same line of railroad, it was a rare sight to see a few herds of from ten to twenty buffalo. A like result took place still further southward, between the Arkansas and the Cimarron rivers. In 1872, while on a scout for about a hundred miles south of Fort Dodge, to the Indian Territory, we were never out of sight of buffalo. In the following autumn, on traveling over the same district, whilst the whole country was whitened with bleached and blackening bones, we did not meet buffalo until we were well in the Indian Territory, and then only in scanty bands. During this autumn, while riding some thirty to forty miles along the north bank of the Arkansas river, to the east of Fort Dodge, there was a continuous line of putrescent carcasses, so that the air was rendered pestilential and offensive to the last degree. The hunters had formed a line of camps along the banks of the river, and had shot down the buffalo, night and morning, as they came to drink. In order to give some idea of the numbers of these carcasses, it is only necessary to mention that I counted sixty-seven on one spot, not covering more than four acres.

" But this great loss of good and wholesome animal food, all of which, with a little judgment and foresight, could have been utilized, will be better understood by a reference to the statistics of cattle in other countries. On reference to the official agricultural returns of Great Britain, the United Kingdom, and British Possessions, and foreign countries, it will be seen that the wanton and wasteful slaughter for the three years in question (and in making the comparison I am keeping to the *legitimate* slaughter for hides, and not *legitimate* for food), swept away more buffalo than there are cattle in Holland and Belgium, or as many as three-fourths of the cattle in Ireland, or one-half of those in Great Britain.

" The result, therefore, would be the same as if a fearful murrain in one year had destroyed the whole of the cattle in Holland and Belgium, or, in the same time, if either three-fourths of the cattle in Ireland, or one-half of those in Great Britain, had been swept away by a plague as great as that of Egypt.

"The citizens of the United States will better realize this great waste, if they consider that this destruction amounted annually to more than double of the annual drive of the cattle from Texas, which ranges from three hundred and fifty thousand to five hundred thousand head per annum; or that it would have been the same, during the three years, as if half the cattle of Texas, or all the cattle in Canada, had been carried off by some dire disease.

"The mere loss of food, however, is not the only evil which has resulted from the wanton wastefulness. Many of the wild Indians of the plains, deprived of their ordinary sustenance, government rations not being forthcoming, and driven to desperation by starvation, have taken to the war path; so that, during the present war, many of the Cheyennes and Arapahoes, and some of the young braves from the friendly 'Red Cloud' and 'Spotted Tail' agencies, have left their reservations and joined the hostile Sioux under 'Sitting Bull.' The hardy settler and pioneer of the plains, who always looked to the buffalo for his winter supply of meat, has been deprived of this resource, and complains most bitterly of this slaughter for pelts."

Mr. Blackmore pursues this subject at considerable length, and expresses surprise that the government should tolerate it, while seeking to enforce economy in all departments, and suggests, that "as it was allowed," it was a proper source of revenue as well as the seal in Alaska, and that for buffalo, killed annually for the hides alone, a reasonable tax on each hide would have brought millions into the treasury. So far as the destruction of the buffalo deprived the wild Indian of his most desirable and natural food, the deficiency had to be supplied by the issue of rations, thus putting an additional burden of millions on the treasury of the nation.

A vast number of buffalo, as well as deer, etc., and the small game, have been killed by parties visiting the plains for the express purpose of hunting, and such parties, if successful, are profuse in the destruction of such game as falls in their way. In the country surrounding military posts the pursuit of the buffalo and other game is an amusement that the officers engage in, and the visitors to the posts are generally entertained with a hunt. Col. Dodge, in his book, refers to the pleasure of hunting as only an expert could. He thinks there is a vast deal of "enjoyment" in it, especially in a country where game is in great variety. He gives a specimen of a twenty days' hunt in the country south of Fort Dodge, on the tributaries of the Cimarron river, in the month of October, 1872, accompanied by three English gentlemen and an officer of the post. They killed 127 buffalo, 20 deer, 11 antelope, 154 turkeys, 5 geese, 223 teal, 45 mallard, 49 shovel-bill, 57 widgeon, 38 butter-ducks, 3 sheldrakes, 17 herons, 6 cranes, 187 quail, 32 grouse, 84 field-plover, 33 yellow-leg snipes, 12 jacksnipes, 1 pigeon, 9 hawks, 3 owls, 2 badgers, 7 raccoon, 143 meadow-larks, doves, robbins, etc., 1 bluebird, and 11 rattlesnakes— total, 1,262. The next year the same party, diminished by one, went over nearly the same ground, with a bag of like variety, numbering 1,141. The colonel exults at the success of his party, and thinks it might challenge the whole world "to offer a greater variety of game to the sportsman."

The wanton waste that this exhibit of the work of Col. Dodge's company of sportsmen presents, and the effect such destruction must have on the minds of the Indians who were compelled to witness it all, does not seem to trouble him in the least. Mr. Blackmore was one of the gentlemen who made up Col. Dodge's hunting party, and while they can see an impropriety, a wanton waste in the destruction of the buffalo, by those who kill the animal for the pelts, neither of them seems to be at all concerned at the destruction and waste produced by the hunting parties, who go out chiefly for the excitement and amusement growing out of these expeditions. The destruction of the buffalo and the game has, however, the same effect on the mind and temper of the Indian, whether done by professional hunters or by gentlemen who go out on a hunting excursion merely for the enjoyment imparted by the sport. He looks upon the matter in a practical sense. It destroys his means of subsistence, deprives him of the pecuniary aid supplied by the sale of the robes and skins, and fills his mind with mingled feelings of despondency, desperation, and revenge.

In his work, Col. Dodge states that it was his " desire and

intention to have furnished complete and authentic official statistics of the number of hides of buffalo transported over the different railroad routes, and thus obtain a pretty accurate knowledge of the numbers actually killed." To that end he made application, "either direct or through friends, to the officers of the various railroads which bring this product to market." To his very great surprise he states that he soon found he was treading on most delicate ground, the authorities of but one prominent road giving the desired information. After offering reasons which he considered futile why his requests were not complied with, Col. Dodge says that he was "constrained to believe that the refusal is prompted by fears that publicity in this matter might result in some legislation which would interfere with profits." This language seems rather cool, coming from one who, in many years' service on the plains, has done his share in destroying the subsistence of the native population, and thus actively aided in indelibly fixing in the minds of the Indians the impression that the white race is imbued with cruel and bitter feelings toward the red man. To cap the climax, Col. Dodge, like the most of military officers, is ready to join in the denunciation of the Indian as an irreclaimable savage, devoid of any noble impulses; that he will not voluntarily do any thing good; that he must be compelled, by punishment and force; in short, that he must be given over to the army, and by the bayonet receive lessons in civilization.

CHAPTER IX.

THE INDIANS ON THE PACIFIC SLOPE, TEXAS, NEW MEXICO, AND THE TERRITORY EMBRACED IN UTAH, NEVADA, IDAHO, MONTANA, WYOMING, COLORADO, ARIZONA, AND PART OF DAKOTA.—THE INCURSIONS OF WHITES PREVIOUS TO ANY ARRANGEMENT WITH THE INDIANS.—COMPLICATIONS, WARS, AND TREATIES.— DESTRUCTION OF LIEUTENANT GRATTAN'S COMMAND.—HARNEY'S CAMPAIGN.— OPERATIONS OF LIEUTENANT DUNN AND MAJOR DOWLING.—BLACK KETTLE'S VISIT TO DENVER.—CHIVINGTON'S ATTACK ON HIS VILLAGE.—DESTRUCTION OF COLONEL FETTERMAN'S COMMAND.—CAMPAIGN OF GENERAL HANCOCK.— BURNING OF THE CHEYENNE VILLAGE, ETC.

WITH the vast territory which came to the United States at and shortly after the close of the war with Mexico, our Indian population was largely increased. Some of the Indians on the coast in California, and the Navajoes and Pueblo Indians in New Mexico, were sufficiently civilized to be self-supporting; but the greater part of the Indians within our newly acquired territory were uncivilized. Moreover, the Indians east of the Rocky Mountains, and west of Missouri, Arkansas, and Iowa (except those transplanted from the east of the Mississippi), were generally wild horsemen. The excitement through all the states in relation to the gold discovered in our new possessions, induced an immense emigration, which at first was chiefly directed to California, Washington, and Oregon. Many reached the Pacific slope by shipping from our Atlantic seaports to the isthmus of Panama, thence across to the Pacific, and thence by vessel to San Francisco and other places on the coast, and from there into the interior. Large bodies, however, passed to the frontier of Missouri and Iowa, and thence across the plains. This gold-hunting emigration went in advance of any arrangements with the Indians, and was in no sense mindful of their rights. The result was that complications grew up and wars ensued, in which both races suffered. In the progress of time the government sent a board of commissioners to the Pacific slope to make, if possible, such arrangements as would quiet the Indians, and at the same time assure to the emigrants protection. Congress made haste to pass a law granting homesteads to actual settlers. This law was passed before any steps were taken to extinguish the Indian title. These homestead grants stimulated emigration. On portions of the Pacific coast and in New Mexico there was some population other than Indian, but of such very few were natives of the United States. When the "Americans" first entered the country and came in contact with the Indians, they generally met with no opposition. Occasionally a petty theft was committed, and some provisions or stock stolen, and for such offenses the punishment meted out to the savage was death. It was not long before the natives were killed, when met, simply because they were Indians.

As stated, commissioners were sent out by the government to Oregon, Washington, and California, for the purpose of negotiating with the Indians. It would seem from the first official report of Messrs. Gaines, Skinner, and Allen, who were operating in Oregon, that their instructions required that wherever a treaty was made with an Indian tribe, the entire Indian title must be extinguished, and no reservation left on which the tribe should dwell. These commissioners, in their correspondence, said: "We found ourselves compelled, against the wish of the government, as expressed in our instructions, to accede to reservations in the land purchased. . . . The habitations of these people are, so far as regards place, not only permanent but hereditary, and they are possessed of local attachments of the strongest kind." Of the land reserved for the use of the Indians they said: "That these reservations will cause any considerable annoyance to the whites we do not believe. They consist, for the most part, of ground *unfitted* for cultivation, but suited to the peculiar habits of the Indians." These representatives of the government took care to consult with the whites adjacent to the reservations, and since the land within them was unfit for cultivation, and the boundaries were adjusted to their satisfaction, no objection was made. Indeed, the commissioners said, "in most cases we found no desire felt to remove the Indians altogether, as they render themselves useful in many ways, as laborers and servants." Referring to the Indians in western Oregon, the commissioners say: "In their present condition they are peaceful and harmless, and the origin of no other mischief than an occasional petty theft, although subject to certain temptations from intercourse with the whites." Very soon after the occupation of the Oregon territory by our adventurers, they established a provisional government, and one of the first laws enacted by it had a provision in it that no negro, mulatto, or Indian should be a witness in any court against a white man, and the act of Congress organizing the territory provided that "the laws now (then) in force in the Territory of Oregon, under the authority of the provisional government, established by the people thereof, shall continue to be valid and operative therein, so far as the same be not incompatible with the constitution of the United States, and the principles of this act."

The commissioners operating in California, McKee, Barbour, and Woozencroft, at an early day gathered the representatives of sixteen different bands of Indians, at Camp Barlow, on the San Joaquin river, and concluded a treaty with them for their lands, reserving a tract along the foot hills of the Sierra Nevada, for an Indian reservation for these bands, of which the commissioners say, that " while apparently liberal in extent, it is not likely to be ever coveted by the whites, and as a general thing *is of no value* for common agricultural purposes. It is also outside the mining or gold district, and so far as we can ascertain, not more than one Mexican grant, and that of very doubtful authenticity, covers any part of it." The commissioners further say that "the Indians we have met here are, generally, a hale, healthy, good-looking people, not inferior to their red brethren in the southwestern states; and from having among them many who, in early life, were attached to the old missions of this country, have already some knowledge of letters, stock raising, and agriculture. We think they will, therefore, make rapid improvement, when schools, etc., shall be established among them."

The emigration was incessant, and those who came paid no attention to the reservations assigned to the Indians. It did not matter with them whether the land could or could not be cultivated; it was believed that gold was hidden in the earth, and hence it was invaded by the whites. If the Indians manifested dissatisfaction, they were rudely treated, if not killed. It was not long until the respect originally manifested for the "Americans" was supplanted by disgust and hatred. The encroachments of the whites and their unjust conduct toward the natives, finally brought on the Oregon and Washington war, in which the lives of many of our citizens and soldiers, as well as the lives of many Indians were sacrificed, and millions of money expended.

In one of their reports, the California commissioners say: "The common and favorite abode of the Indians in this country was in the valleys and the range of mountains. The greater portion were located and had resided as long as their recollections and traditions went, on the ground now being turned up for gold, and occupied by the gold hunters, by whom they have been displaced and driven higher up in the range of mountains, leaving their fisheries and acorn grounds behind. They have been patient in endurance, until necessity taught them her lesson (which they were not slow to learn, as it is measurably instinctive with the Indians), and thus they adopt from necessity that which was deemed a virtue among the Spartans, and the result is we have an incipient border war; many lives have been lost, and an incalculable amount of property stolen."

That the reader may have an idea of the mode and manner in which the "Americans" introduced their civilization among the Indians on the Pacific slope, two incidents out of many such that occurred, are here given. At an early day a party started up the coast from San Francisco on a gold hunting expedition. They had a vessel loaded with supplies, tools, etc., sufficient for a substantial outfit. After sailing up to near the southern boundary of Oregon, they landed, when a portion of them immediately set out on a tour of exploration, leaving the remainder to discharge the cargo and in due time follow their comrades. About thirty Indians came to the beach, and at the request of the "Americans" proceeded to help unload the vessel. The Indians labored faithfully for the new comers. There were on the vessel two pieces of cannon, and a supply of guns and pistols. In the bay near the landing and close to the vessel, there was a large rock, the top surface of which was above the water, and of sufficient area to accommodate many persons. The cannon, when removed from the vessel, were placed upon this rock and in proper position. When the work was completed, the Indians were requested to come on the rock to receive pay for their labor. As they passed up in Indian file, at the proper moment, the guns were brought to bear upon them, and all but two were killed.

In 1853, Captain Wright surprised a few Modoc Indians, took them to his camp and treated them kindly, and then sent them, with presents of tobacco and calico, to their people, and by this means he opened negotiations for a council to arrange for a treaty. In due time it was agreed that the principal men of the Modocs should meet Captain Wright at a place designated on Lost river, for a preliminary council. On the appointed day some fifty of the chiefs and head men attended. The force of Wright was about equal in numbers, and they were drilled for the occasion. It was agreed that the filling and lighting of the pipe of Wright during the deliberation of the council should be the signal for action. As the wreath of smoke ascended, fifty revolvers were drawn from their concealment, the possessors being distributed among the Indians, and every Modoc save two, was instantly killed. Such incidents as these, and there were many in some degree like them, bore fruit, resulted in retaliation, and finally in a general Indian war.

To meet the complications existing in California, Congress, in the winter of 1852-3, appropriated two hundred and fifty thousand dollars to defray the expenses of removing the Indians in that state to five military reservations of not more than twenty-five thousand acres in each. When the plan was about to be put into operation, it appeared that it was difficult to obtain suitable locations for such reservations, in the regions designated, since there were alleged claims to the lands founded upon Spanish and Mexican grants. The superintendent concluded to purchase the lands embraced in the reservations from those who held such grants, subject to the ratification of Congress. Thus new complications grew up in California, while in Texas, New Mexico, Utah, Washington, and Oregon, Indian affairs were in an unsettled condition, arising out of the constant encroachments of the whites, and resulting in loss of life on both sides. In this condition of things, the commissioner of Indian affairs, in November, 1853, recommended that a board of commissioners, composed of able, practical, impartial, and upright men, be sent without delay to all our remote possessions, with a view to such conventional and other arrangements as should be deemed proper and necessary to place our Indian relations there on a safe, stable, and satisfactory basis. Congress made no provision for such commission, and outbreaks among the Indians continued, resulting in loss of life, destruction of property, and working great demoralization among the natives.

In 1851 it was found necessary to make some arrangement with the wild Indians of the plains and mountains, by which the right of transit through the country claimed by them, should be assured to the multitudes going across the plains to our distant possessions; and on the 17th of September of that year, at Fort Laramie, a treaty was made with the Sioux or Dakota, Cheyenne, Arapahoe, Crow, Assiniboine, Gros Ventre, Mandan, and Arickaree Indians, who claimed most of the country east of the Rocky Mountains, north of Texas and New Mexico, south of the Missouri, and west of the emigrated tribes. By this treaty the boundaries of the territory of each tribe were defined, and they all agreed to abstain from hostilities against each other, and maintain friendly relations. They also agreed that the United States might establish roads and military posts within their limits; and in consideration of these concessions, the government agreed to protect them from depredations on the part of the whites, and to give them in goods suited to their wants, yearly, for fifty years, the sum of fifty thousand dollars, to be divided ratably among them. The Senate amended the treaty to limit the annuity to a period of fifteen years. In the fall of 1852, the commissioner of Indian affairs reported that " notwithstanding the mountain and prairie Indians continued to suffer from the vast number of emigrants who pass through their country, destroying their means of support, and scattering disease and death among them, yet those who were parties to the treaty of Fort Laramie, in the fall of 1851, have been true to their obligations, and have remained at peace among themselves," and this state of things continued until in the month of August, 1854, when, by the folly of a young military officer, then in command at Fort Laramie, it was interrupted. Some bands of the Dakota Indians, parties to the Laramie treaty, were at that time in camp at a point about eight miles from the fort, awaiting the agent, then on the Arkansas, and on his way to these Indians, to distribute to them their share of the fifty thousand dollar annuity. While thus encamped, a Mormon train passed by on its way to Utah, and a cow in the rear, and belonging to the train, left the road and went into the Indian camp. This cow was killed by some of the Indians. The Mormons, on arriving at the fort, reported the fact, when Lieutenant Fleming, in command, ordered Lieutenant Grattan, with a file of soldiers, to proceed to the Indian camp, and arrest the Indian or Indians who killed the cow. At the time there were but few troops at Laramie, and nearly one-half of these were absent on the Platte river cutting hay. Lieutenant Grattan took twenty-nine men and an interpreter, and set out to execute the order. When he arrived at the trading post, near the Indian camp, and told his mission, the trader advised him not to enter the camp, and proposed that he would go in and bring out the chief to see Grattan. The lieutenant replied that he had come to arrest the party that killed the cow, and intended to do so. In addition to the muskets of the men, the expedition had two pieces of cannon, and they were not without stimulant, the interpreter being in such condition that he talked to the Indians in a very indiscreet manner. He told them, among other things, that the soldiers had come there to " cut the d——d hearts out of them ; " that they had come to kill Indians, and intended to do so. The troops went into camp, unlimbered their guns, and fired them, as well as a volley from their muskets. They killed one, and mortally wounded several of a band of Brulé Sioux, when the Indians became aroused and advancing toward the troops, the latter retreated, followed by the Sioux. In the conflict the lieutenant and all his men were killed. The Indians, without waiting longer, for the arrival of their agent, went to the warehouse near by, where their annuity goods were in store, took them, and separated for their homes. Although able to have stormed Fort Laramie, and taken away all its military stores, they did not commit any violence on the fort or its inmates. The secretary of war did state that they had designs on the fort, with the intention to seize all the public and private stores there, but there was no foundation for such statement. On account of this affair Congress authorized an addition of three regiments to the regular army, and then followed General Harney's "Sioux Expedition." The crowning act of General Harney's campaign, and which he pompously styled the "Battle of the Blue Water," took place on the 22d of September, 1855, in northwestern Nebraska or northeastern Wyoming. He heard that a Brulé band of Sioux, of which Little Thunder was principal chief, was with his braves, and women and children, encamped at this point, and moved immediately for them, and at half-past four o'clock in the morning commenced an attack on this unoffending village, the inhabitants of which had no more to do in the affair with Lieutenant Grattan than General Harney had. He threw his cavalry around in the rear of the village, and in the direction the Indians would retreat when he attacked them in front. He says in his official report that the cavalry movement "was executed in a most faultless manner by Colonel Cook, to secure a position to cut off the retreat of the Indians, and was effected without attracting their attention." When General Harney moved upon the village, the Indians commenced a retreat up the valley, precisely in the direction that Cook's cavalry was coming toward them. The Indians halted short of the cavalry, and General Harney held a parley with the chief, in which he (Harney) stated the causes of dissatisfaction, and "that the Indians had massacred our troops under the most aggravated circumstances, and now the day of retribution had come ; that he did not wish to harm him (Little Thunder) personally, as he professed to be a friend of the whites, but that he must deliver up the young men whom he acknowledged he could not control, or they must suffer the consequences of their past misconduct, and take the chances of battle. Not being able, of course, however willing, to deliver up all the butchers of our people, Little Thunder returned to his band. I, immediately after his disappearance from my view, ordered the troops to advance. The skirmishers opened their fire around the bluffs, on the right bank of the stream, in a very spirited manner, and gallantly driving the savages into the snare laid for them by the cavalry, which last troops burst upon them so suddenly and so unexpectedly as to cause them to cross instead of ascending the valley of the Blue Water, and seek an escape by the only avenue now open to them. . . . The result of the affair was, eighty-six killed, five wounded, and seventy women and children captured, and fifty mules and ponies taken. The provisions and camp equipage were all destroyed. The troops were eager from the first for a fray with the butchers of their comrades." General Harney omitted in his report, above quoted, to state that he killed a number of women and children, which he did do. Except this omission, we have his own unvarnished story of how he treated an innocent band of Sioux Indians, who were in nowise involved in the sad affair with Lieutenant Grattan's command. General Harney wore the uniform of a brigadier-general in the United States army, and such was his rank, and yet in this report he admits that he set a trap for these hapless people, who were not a war party, but a band of peaceful Indians, men, women, and children, residing at Ash Hollow, on the Blue Water; that he made demands of the chief, that he knew, however willing, he could not comply with. This, however, is not an isolated case. It is the common practice of our troops, when out on expeditions to kill Indians whenever found, without care to know whether they be guilty or innocent. Serious trouble grew out of General Harney's campaign, and many white people lost their lives, by reason of the complications which followed.

Contemplating the condition of the Indian population in the vast territory to the west, and the rapid flow of our own population into it, and the conflicts which were ever recurring and never ending, the commissioner of Indian affairs, in the fall of 1856, said : " The wonderful emigration to our newly-acquired states and territories, and its effect upon the wild tribes inhabiting them, and the plains and prairies, is well calculated, at the present period, to attract special attention. Not only are our settlements rapidly advancing westward from the Mississippi river toward the Pacific ocean, and from the shores of the Pacific eastward toward the Mississippi, but large settlements have been made in Utah and New Mexico, between the two. Already the settlements of Texas are extending up to El Paso and spreading into the Gadsden purchase, and those of California have reached into the great valley of the Colorado, whilst the settlers of Minnesota are building cities at the very head of Lake Superior, and villages in the remote valley of the Red river of the North, on their way to Puget Sound." The commissioner continued, at some length, to cite the projected railroads, and other improvements, calculated, as they progressed, to affect the condition of the Indians, and operate as a check to their civilization, unless some means were adopted to counteract the injurious effect of these measures, and then he adds : " As sure as these great physical changes are impending, so sure will these poor denizens of the forest be blotted out of existence, and their dust be trampled under the foot of rapidly advancing civilization, unless our great nation shall generously determine that the necessary provision shall at once be made, and appropriate steps be taken to designate suitable tracts or reservations of land, in proper localities, for permanent homes for, and provide the means to colonize them thereon. Such reservations should be selected with great care, and when determined upon and designated, the assurances by which they are guaranteed to the Indians should be irrevocable, and of such a character as to effectually protect them from encroachments of every kind."

The absorbing topic, at this time, in Congress and the country, was the slavery question, and the toleration or prohibition of the institution in our new acquisitions lying south of 36° 30′ north latitude. The partisans in this controversy, which convulsed the whole country, had no dispute in relation to the Indians. It is true they had but recently owned the country about which this fierce controversy was waged; and, although in one way and another, much of it had been wrested from them, no satisfactory arrangement or adequate provision had been made with them for their future protection and care. Treaties with many tribes had been made; but these were not ratified for some time after this period. The pro-slavery and free-soil champions failed to see any thing wrong in this unsettled condition of the Indian race. Indeed, to those who observed closely, it was difficult to decide which of these parties was the most oppressive and cruel in its conduct toward the red man. It was no uncommon thing to see representative men of both parties, while in violent hostility on the question of "free soil," in Kansas, participating in, and enjoying, the plunder taken from the Indians. Such seemed to have as little scruple in invading the rights of the Indians as they would feel remorse in treading on a reptile in their path.

Without going into the detail it may be stated that the flow of population, which continued toward our new territories, did not all, as in the beginning, reach the Pacific slope. Many dropped out of the overland caravans by the wayside, at points where wood and water were found, and ranches sprang up on the plains and toward the base of the mountains, and in the valleys of the rivers. By the Fort Laramie treaty, which defined the boundaries of the several tribes parties to it, the home of the Cheyennes and Arapahoes was bounded as follows: "Commencing at the Red Butte, or the place where the road leaves the north fork of the Platte river, thence up said north fork of the Platte to its source, thence along the main range of the Rocky Mountains to the headwaters of the Arkansas river, thence down the Arkansas river to the crossing of the Santa Fé road, thence in a northwesterly direction to the forks of the Platte river, and thence up the Platte river to the place of beginning." Within these boundaries is embraced most of what is now western Kansas and the larger portion of Colorado. It is an eligible body of land, equal in area to two of our larger states. Several years previous to the commencement of our civil war, gold and sil-

11

ver were discovered in the mountains of Colorado, and thousands, who had only the right to pass through the country, took possession of the land and went to mining. Against the protests of the Indians they opened mines, built towns, and opened farms and roads. They crowded the Indians from the high lands where they lived into the valley of the Arkansas. The Indians had been generous to the white intruders, but when driven from their homes, they became sullen and dissatisfied. The treaty of 1851 gave them the pledge that the United States would protect them against the commission of all depredations upon them by its citizens. They knew very well the wrong done them, and that the stipulations of the treaty had not been complied with. In the language of the commission of 1867–8, known as the Peace Commission : " These Indians saw their former homes and hunting grounds overrun by a greedy population thirsting for gold. They saw their game driven east to the plains, and soon found themselves the objects of jealousy and hatred. They, too, must go. The presence of the injured is too often painful to the wrong-doer, and innocence offensive to the eyes of guilt. It now became apparent that what had been taken by force must be retained by the ravisher, and nothing was left for the Indians but to ratify a treaty consecrating the act. On the 18th of February, 1861, this was done at Fort Wise, Kansas. These tribes ceded their magnificent possessions, enough to constitute two great states of the Union, retaining only a small district for themselves." This reservation lies on both sides of the Arkansas, extending from the mouth of the Sandy Fork to the mouth of the Purgatory. In consideration of this cession the United States entered into new obligations. " Not being able (in the language of the commission of 1867–8) to protect them in the larger reservation, the nation resolved that it would protect them ' in the quiet and peaceable possession ' of the smaller tract. Second, to pay each tribe thirty thousand dollars per annum for fifteen years; and third, that houses should be built, lands broken and fenced, and stock animals and agricultural implements furnished. In addition to this, mills were to be built, and engineers, farmers, and mechanics sent among them. These obligations, like the obligations of 1851, furnished glittering evidences of humanity to the reader of the treaty. Unfortunately the evidence stopped at that point." From the date of this treaty, February 18, 1861, to April 12, 1864, the Cheyenne and Arapahoe Indians were at peace: "On that day (in the language of the commission of 1867–8) a ranchman named Ripley came to Camp Sanborn, and stated that Indians had stolen his stock. Of what tribe they were he did not know. He asked and obtained troops for the purpose of pursuit. Lieutenant Dunn, with forty men, was put under Ripley's guide, with instructions to disarm the Indians found in possession of the stock. Beyond his representation no one knew who Ripley was. That he owned stock his own word was given—no one else said he did. During the day Indians were found. Ripley claimed some of the horses. The lieutenant ordered the soldiers to stop the herd, and ordered the Indians to come forward and talk. Some of them rode forward, and when within a few feet of him, Dunn ordered his men to dismount and disarm the Indians. They, of course, resisted, and a fight ensued. What Indians they were he knew not; from bows and arrows found he judged them to be Cheyennes.

"Dunn getting the worst of the fight, returned to camp, obtained a guide, and a remount, and the next morning started again. In May following, Major Downing, of the first Colorado cavalry, went to Denver and asked Colonel Chivington to give him a force to move against the Indians, for what purpose we do not know. Chivington gave him the men, and the following are Major Downing's own words: 'I captured an Indian and required him to go to the village, or I would kill him. This was about the middle of May. We started about eleven o'clock in the day, and traveled all day and all night; about daylight I succeeded in surprising the Cheyenne village at Cedar bluffs, in a small valley, sixty miles north of South Platte river. We commenced shooting. I ordered the men to commence killing them. They lost, as I am informed, some twenty-six killed and thirty wounded. My own loss was one killed and one wounded. I burnt up their lodges, and every thing I could get hold of. I took no prisoners. We got out of ammunition, and could not pursue them.'

"In this camp the Indians had their women and children. He captured one hundred ponies, which the officer says were distributed among the boys for the reason that they had been marching almost constantly day and night for nearly three weeks! This was done because such conduct 'was usual (he said) in New Mexico.' About the same time, Lieutenant Ayres, of the Colorado troops, had a difficulty, in which an Indian chief, under a flag of truce, was murdered. During the summer and fall occurrences of this character were frequent. Some time during the fall, Black Kettle and other prominent chiefs of the Cheyenne and Arapahoe nations, sent word to the commander at Fort Lyons that the war had been forced upon them, and they desired peace. They were then upon their own reservation. Major E. W. Wynkoop, then of the first Colorado cavalry, did not feel authorized to conclude a treaty with them, but gave them a pledge of military protection until an interview could be procured with the governor of Colorado, who was then superintendent of Indian affairs. He then proceeded to Denver with some of the leading chiefs to see the governor. Colonel Chivington was present at the interview. Major Wynkoop, in his sworn testimony, thus relates the action of the governor, when he communicated the presence of the chiefs seeking peace: 'He (the governor) intimated that he was sorry I had brought them; that he considered he had nothing to do with them; that they had declared war against the United States, and he considered them in the hands of the military authorities; that he did not think it was policy anyhow to make peace with them, until they were properly punished, for the reason that the United States would be acknowledging themselves whipped.' Major Wynkoop further states that the 'governor said the third regiment of Colorado troops had been raised on his representation at Washington, to kill Indians, and Indians they must kill.' Wynkoop then ordered the Indians to move their villages nearer to the fort, and bring their women and children, which was done. In November, this officer was removed, and Major Anthony, of the first Colorado cavalry, ordered to take command of the fort. He, too, assured the Indians of safety. They numbered about five hundred men, women, and children. It was here, under the pledge of protection, that they were slaughtered by the third Colorado and a battalion of the first Colorado cavalry, under command of Colonel Chivington. He marched from Denver to Fort Lyon, thence to Sand creek, and about daylight on the morning of the 29th November, surrounded the Indian camp, and commenced an indiscriminate slaughter. The particulars of this massacre are too well known to be repeated here with all its heartrending scenes. It is enough to say that it scarcely has its parallel in the records of Indian barbarity. Fleeing women, holding up their hands and praying for mercy, were brutally shot down; infants were killed and scalped in derision; men were tortured and mutilated in a manner that would put to shame the savage ingenuity of interior Africa. No one will be astonished that a war ensued which cost the government $30,000,000, and conflagration and death to the border settlements. During the spring and summer of 1865, no less than eight thousand troops were drawn from the effective force engaged in suppressing the rebellion, to meet this Indian war. The result of the year's campaign satisfied all reasonable men that war with Indians was useless and expensive. . . To those who reflected on the subject, knowing the facts, the war was something more than useless and expensive; it was dishonorable to the nation, and disgraceful to those who had originated it.

" When the utter futility of conquering a peace was made manifest to every one, and the true cause of the war began to be developed, the country demanded that peaceful agencies should be resorted to. Generals Harney, Sanborn, and others were selected as commissioners to procure a council of the hostile tribes, and in October, 1865, they succeeded in doing so at the mouth of the Little Arkansas. At this council the Cheyennes and Arapahoes were induced to relinquish their reservation on the upper Arkansas, and accept a reservation, partly in southern Kansas and partly in the Indian Territory, lying immediately south of Forts Larned and Zarah. The object was to remove them from the vicinity of Colorado.

. . . When this treaty came to the Senate for ratification, it was so amended as to require the president to designate for these tribes a reservation outside of the State of Kansas." This provision deprived them of any home at all, except the hunting privilege reserved by the treaty. At the same time (October, 1865) agreements were made with the Kiowas, Comanches, and Apache Indians, and so soon as these treaties were signed, the war of nearly two years' duration ceased at once. Travel on the plains was again safe. What eight thousand troops had failed to give, this simple agreement, which was virtually rendered valueless by the Senate amendment, and bearing nothing but a pledge of friendship, obtained. From that time until the fall of 1866, peace on the part of the Indians prevailed. General Sherman, during this period, traveled without an escort to the most distant military posts, and yet with a feeling of perfect security.

In the year 1866, the Sioux Indians became dissatisfied at the great emigration, through their country, of parties attracted to Montana by the stories of wonderful gold discoveries in that territory. The route called the Powder river route was the popular one, and yet the one that the Indians objected to most seriously. This country, by the assignment of boundaries to the different tribes, by the Laramie treaty of 1851, was recognized as Sioux territory. It was true that by that treaty the Indians conceded the right to the government to locate roads through, and establish military posts in it, and for this privilege they were to receive a share of the fifty thousand dollar annuity, for fifty successive years. This the Senate amended, so that the annuity was to be only for fifteen years. The amendment was never agreed to by the Indians. In fact, it was never submitted to them. The annuity ceased in 1865, and the Indians claimed that the grant then ceased also. They did not object to travel through their country, entirely, but did protest earnestly against the use of the Powder river route, since that was their buffalo range, and its preservation was, in their condition, indispensable. They could not exist, at that time, without the buffalo, as they had no other resource for food. In March, 1866, General Pope, then in command of the department of the Missouri, ordered the establishment of military posts on that route. The Iowa legislature had, by resolution, called on General Sherman for military protection to emigrants going into Montana, and he, in reply, had assured the public that such as went by the Powder river route should find a well-guarded road all the way. During the summer, when troops were ordered to garrison Forts Phil Kearney, McPherson, and Reno, the Indians notified the government that the occupation of the country by troops would be resisted; but the warning was unheeded. An attempt was then made to compose the matter by treaty. In the council, the Indians insisted that the troops must be withdrawn before a treaty was made. This was refused, and some of the Indians did reluctantly sign the treaty, while others declined; and Red Cloud retired from the council, and, placing his hand upon his rifle, said: "In this, and the Great Spirit, I trust for the right." In a short time, a fierce war began. Emigrant travel ceased, the forts were besieged, and the mountains and valleys swarmed with Indian warriors. On the 21st of December, a wood party, from Fort Fetterman, was attacked, when Lieutenant-colonel Fetterman went out from the fort to relieve it. A fight followed, in which every man of our forces was killed. There was a route through the Sioux country to Montana, said to be preferable to this Powder river route, and to the travel on which the Indians offered no objection, but the military had decided that the route they indicated should be kept open. The attempt to do this, kept up hostilities during the year 1867, and in the spring of 1868, in the treaty then made with the Sioux, the government agreed to, and did, abandon her posts, and close up the road on the Powder river route to Montana.

When the trouble began with the Sioux, in 1866, some of them, who desired to avoid war, and were willing to have yielded this route to our travel, came south. They visited the valley of the Republican river, in western Kansas, and thence south as far as Fort Larned. Their movements created uneasiness among the freighters on the plains, and the people in the settlements became alarmed. The military posts also became disturbed. In the fall, the traders on the Arkansas were prohibited from selling arms to the Indians. In January,

1867, Major Douglas, of the Third Infantry, communicated to General Hancock his fears. He did not specify any hostile act of the Indians, but stated that Kicking Bird, a Kiowa chief, and rival of Satanta, said that Satanta talked of war, and said he would commence when the grass grew in the spring. In February, Captain Smith, of the Nineteenth Infantry, in command of Fort Arbuckle, reported to General Ord, at Little Rock, and the report was at once forwarded to the department of the Missouri, that a negro child and some stock had been taken off by the Indians, before he took command. His informant was one Jones, an interpreter. In his letter, he used the following language: " I have the honor to state further, that several other tribes than the Comanches have lately been noticed on the war-path, having been seen, in their progress, in unusual numbers, and without their squaws and children—a fact to which much significance is attached by those conversant with Indian usages. It is thought by many white residents of the territory, that some of these tribes may be acting in concert, and that plundering incursions are at least in contemplation." After enumerating other reports of wrongs (coming, perhaps, from Jones), he said that, in reporting, he had deferred to the views of white persons who, from long residence among the Indians, were competent to advise him, and that his communication was " more particularly the embodiment of their views." This brought ten additional companies of troops to his post.

Captain Asbery, at Fort Larned, reported that a small party of Cheyennes had compelled a ranchman near that post to cook supper for them, and then threatened to kill him because he had no sugar. Finally, on the 9th of February, Jones, the Kiowa interpreter, filed, with Major Douglas, at Fort Dodge, an affidavit that he had recently visited the Kiowa camp, in company with Major Page and John E. Tappan, on a trading expedition. That the Indians took from them flour, sugar, rice, and apples; that they threatened to shoot Major Page, because he was a soldier, and tried to kill Tappan. He (Jones) said they shot at him. He also said that Satanta requested him to say to Major Douglas, that he demanded that the troops and military posts be at once removed, and also that the railroads and mail stages must be stopped at once. Satanta also requested him to tell Douglas that he hoped the government stock was in good condition, as he would be over in a few days to get it. Jones further said, that while at the camp, an Indian war party came in, having with them two hundred horses, and the scalps of seventeen negro soldiers and one white man. All this information was at once dispatched to General Hancock; and a short time thereafter, and before any verification of this startling news, he commenced to organize the expedition which thereafter marched to the Pawnee fork of the Arkansas, and burned the Cheyenne village. The commission of 1867–8 thus refer to these matters:

"On the 11th of March following, General Hancock addressed a letter to Major Wynkoop, then the agent of the Cheyennes and Arapahoes, stating that 'he had about completed arrangements for moving a force to the plains.' He said that his object was to show the Indians that he was 'able to chastise any tribes who molest people traveling across the plains.' Against the Cheyennes he claimed, first, that they had not delivered the Indian who killed a New Mexican, at Fort Zarah; and second, he believed he had 'evidence sufficient to fix upon the different bands of that tribe, whose chiefs are known, several outrages committed on the Smoky Hill last summer.' He requested the agent to tell them he 'came prepared for peace or war,' and that hereafter he would 'insist upon their keeping off the main lines of travel, where their presence is calculated to bring about collisions with the whites.' This, it will be remembered, was their hunting ground, secured by the treaty. On the same day he forwarded a similar communication to J. H. Leavenworth, agent for the Kiowas and Comanches. The complaints he alleged against them are precisely the same contained in the affidavit and statements of Jones and the letter to Captain Asbery. The expedition left Fort Leavenworth on the 13th of April, and proceeded to and up the Pawnee fork of the Arkansas, in the direction of the village of one thousand or fifteen hundred Cheyenne and Sioux. When he came near their camp the chiefs visited him, as they had already done at

Larned, and requested him not to approach the camp with his troops, for the women and children, having the remembrance of Sand Creek, would certainly abandon the village. On the 14th he resumed his march, with cavalry and artillery; and, when about ten miles from their village, he was again met by the head men, who stated that they would treat with him there or elsewhere; but they could not, as requested by him, keep their women and children in camp, if he approached with soldiers. He informed them that he would march up to within a mile of the village, and treat with them that evening. As he advanced, the women and children fled, leaving the village, with all their property. The chiefs and a part of the young men remained. To some of these, visiting the camp of General Hancock, horses were furnished, to bring back the women and children. The horses were returned, with word that the women and children could not be collected. It was then night, and orders were given to surround the village and capture the Indians remaining. The order was obeyed, but the chiefs and warriors had departed. The only persons found were an old Sioux and an idiot girl of eight or ten years of age. It afterward appeared that the person of this girl had been violated, from which she soon died. The Indians were gone; and the report spread that she had been a captive among them, and they had committed this outrage before leaving. The Indians say that she was an idiotic Cheyenne girl, forgotten in the confusion of flight; and, if violated, it was not by them. The next morning General Custer, under orders, started in pursuit of the Indians, with his cavalry, and performed a campaign of great labor, passing over a vast extent of country, but seeing no hostile Indians. When the fleeing Indians reached the Smoky Hill they destroyed a station and killed several men. A courier having brought this intelligence to General Hancock, he at once ordered the Indian village, about three hundred lodges, together with the entire property of the tribe, burned.

" 'The Indian now became an outlaw—not only the Cheyennes and Sioux, but all the tribes on the plains. The superintendent of an express company, Cottrell, issued a circular order to the agents and employes of the company, in the following language: 'You will hold no communication with Indians whatever. If Indians come within shooting distance, shoot them. Show them no mercy, for they will show you none.' This was in the Indian country. He closes by saying: 'General Hancock will protect you and our property.' Whether war existed previous to that time seems to have been a matter of doubt even with General Hancock. From that day forward no doubt on the subject was entertained by any body. The Indians were then fully aroused; and no more determined war has ever been waged by them. The evidence tends to show that we lost many soldiers, besides a large number of settlers on the frontier. The most valuable trains, belonging to individuals as well as the government, among which was a government train of ammunition, were captured by these wild horsemen. Stations were destroyed. Hundreds of horses and mules were taken, while we are forced to believe that their entire loss, since the burning of their village, consists of only six men killed.

" The Kiowas and Comanches deny the statements of Jones in every particular. They say that no war party came in at the time stated, or at any other time. They deny that they killed any negro soldiers, and positively assert that no Indian was ever known to scalp a negro. In the latter statement they are corroborated by all the tribes and by persons who know their habits; and the records of the adjutant-general's office fail to show the loss of the seventeen negro soldiers, or any soldiers at all. They deny having robbed Jones or insulted Tappan. The testimony of the latter was taken, in which he brands the whole statement of Jones as false, and declares that he and Page so informed Major Douglas, within a few days after Jones made his affidavit. We took the testimony of Major Douglas, in which he admits the correctness of Tappan's statement, but for some reason unexplained, he failed to communicate the correction to General Hancock. The threats to take the posts on the Arkansas were made in a vein of jocular bravado, and not understood by any one present at the time to possess the least importance. . . . This completes the case against the Kiowas and Comanches, who are exculpated, by the united testimony of all the tribes, from any share in the late troubles.

"The Cheyennes admit that one of their young men, in a private quarrel, both parties being drunk, did kill a New Mexican, at Fort Zarah. Such occurrences are so frequent among the whites on the plains, that ignorant Indians might be pardoned for participating, if it be done merely to evidence their advance in civilization. The Indians claim that the Mexican was in fault, and further protest that no demand was ever made for the delivery of the Indian.

"The Arapahoes admit that a party of their young men, with three young warriors of the Cheyennes, returning from an excursion against the Utes, attacked the train of Mr. Weddell, of New Mexico, during the month of March, and they were gathering up the stock when the war commenced."

The report from which the foregoing is taken—the report of January 7, 1868—remarks that "though this recital should prove tedious, it was thought necessary, to guard the future against the errors of the past. We would not blunt the vigilance of military men in the Indian country, but would warn them against the arts of the selfish and unprincipled, who need to be watched as well as the Indians. The origin and progress of this war are repeated in nearly all Indian wars. The history of one will suffice for many." Let it be remembered that Generals Sherman, Harney, Terry, and Auger were members of the commission who uttered these words.

The report of this commission makes a lame attempt to exculpate General Hancock from blame in the premises. It says: "He had just come to the department, and circumstances were ingeniously woven to deceive him. . . . If he erred, he can very well roll a part of the responsibility upon others; not alone on subordinate commanders, who were themselves deceived by others, but on those who were able to guard against the error and yet failed to do so. . . . His distinguished services in another field of patriotic duty, had left him but little time to become acquainted with the remote or immediate causes producing these troubles." It is very kind in the commission, of whom several are military colleagues of General Hancock, to offer an apology for his con-

duct; but to thinking people, with the facts before them, no
valid excuse can be given. The truth is, the "selfish and
unprincipled" who manipulated the operations which opened
the way for General Hancock's movement against the Indians, found him quite ready to co-operate with them. He
was extolled in the press of Kansas as he moved across the
state; and the huzzas and acclaim of that portion of the population, and it was quite large, that believed the only good Indian was the dead one, met him on every side. Without attempting to verify any of the stories on which he professed to
base his movements, and all of which were false, or to scan
the motives of those who sought to precipitate a war upon
the Indians, he assumed that they needed discipline and discipline they must have; and in all cases, discipline with the
military arm means punishment, and punishment means
death. It was not his or General Custer's fault that only
six Indians were killed in the campaign. Had it been within
their power the whole village would have been put to the
sword. Military commanders of divisions, as well as post
commanders, seem to have adopted as a maxim that the first
duty they have to perform after assuming command is to
punish the Indians, and their ears are ever open to hear complaints, in order that a foundation may be laid for fitting out
expeditions against the Indians; and the civil officer who un-
dertakes to correct the misrepresentations that are pressed
upon the military commander will be lucky indeed if he do
not incur the displeasure of the man of war. There are exceptions in the conduct of some military officers to what is
here stated, but that fact only proves the general rule. When
the chiefs visited General Hancock, at Fort Larned, in April,
and begged him to desist and forego his expedition until they
could confer with him, he would have given some evidence
that he desired to do right if he had granted their request,
and given them a hearing. He had the stories against the
Indians, and it was but just that he should hear them, but he
declined to do so. The report of January 7, 1868, shows
most conclusively that the stories furnished him were absolutely false, and this he could have known by investigation,
if he had desired to be informed. But he did not desire any

further information than such as Major Douglas furnished him in February. This and the applause and compliments of the people of Kansas, among whom were many of the *"selfish and unprincipled"* who manipulated these things, were sufficient.

CHAPTER X.

MILITARY OPERATIONS AGAINST THE INDIANS IN NEW MEXICO AND ARIZONA IN 1862, 1863, 1864, AND 1869.—DELIBERATE ATTEMPT TO EXTERMINATE THEM.— MASSACRE OF APACHES IN 1871 AT CAMP GRANT, ETC.

MANY army officers claim with unlimited assurance that the military branch of the government is the proper one to have charge of Indian civilization. This claim has no foundation on which to rest. As a rule (to which it is admitted there are exceptions), army officers, when charged with duties in the Indian service, are not only unjust, but absolutely cruel. In order that the reader may have an insight into the humane manner in which our Indian population is treated by the military when acting without restraint, a brief recital will be found in this chapter of operations in New Mexico and the adjacent country, in 1862, 1863, 1864, and 1869.

In the Territory of New Mexico tillable land is nowhere to be found in large bodies. Indeed, there is but little such land. The Indian population resident in the territory at the time it was acquired by the United States, was composed of the Pueblo, Navajoe, Comanche, and Apache tribes. Fragments of Utes and other bands, occasionally made incursions into it. The Pueblos had small reservations, and resided in villages. They had churches and schools. Their form of government was democratic. They selected their officers, made their laws, and by diligence supported themselves. It was said that at this time they were remarkably free from vices, and guiltless of any grave crimes. The Navajoes, in some respects, resembled the Pueblos in their customs, but relied chiefly for support on their flocks of sheep, and the manufacture of their wool into blankets, in which they had quite a commerce. In 1846, the first expedition after the acquisition of New Mexico was made by Colonel Doniphan into the Navajoe country. He was surprised at the quantity and quality of the blankets manufactured by them. The Apaches were a more nervous race, and obtained their subsistence chiefly by the chase, and the mascel which they laid up for winter use. When the barrenness of the country and the profusion of game at the time is considered, it is probable the white man, had his lot been cast in some parts of the territory, and his attention had not been called to the mineral deposits, would have followed the example of the Apache. The fact that there was supposed to be hidden beneath the unfriendly and barren land, "gold and silver, and precious stones," excited the cupidity of the Mexicans long before the territory became the property of the United States; but not to the same extent that our people were moved after the acquisition. The Indians and Mexicans had, however, their troubles and conflicts. The Indians, for injuries inflicted on them and loss of property, retaliated, and frequently stole cattle and sheep from the Mexicans, who in turn would pursue them, not only to reclaim the property, but to rob and murder the Indians. They would also seize the Indian women and children, whom they carried off and sold into slavery.

In 1848–9, our military commander in New Mexico acted on the theory that the only way to have peace with the Indians was to exterminate them. They did not acquiesce in his view, but resisted. Under better counsels our Indian difficulties, in a few years thereafter, were so far composed that comparative tranquillity prevailed, and with just treatment it was discovered that the Pueblo and Navajoe Indians were, to borrow the words of Governor Greiner, about as easily controlled "as a woman's school." The Comanches and Apaches were not so well disposed, especially under the treatment they had received. In 1854 and 1855, there was an occasional foray, with such results as usually follow. As the influx of prospectors and miners increased, difficulties between them and the Indians followed. The "Americans" were aggressive, and the Indians, when wronged, retaliated. Several military expeditions were sent into the country, not to protect the Indians from the aggression of the whites, but to punish them because they did not submit to wrong and injustice. Finally, the civil war broke out, and rebel troops from Texas invaded the territory. General Carleton assumed command in the department of New Mexico, in 1862. He at once commenced to discipline the Indians residing therein. A few extracts from his dispatches will give the reader an idea of the manner in which he performed his work. On the 11th of October, 1862, in a confidential letter addressed by him to Colonel J. R. West, commander of the district of Mesilla, he said: " You will order the following troops into the Mescalaro country to co-operate with Colonel Carson, yet to be independent of him. Captain McClave you will place in command of one expedition, to be composed of his own and one company of your regiment. He will start with this force, increased with twenty good Mexican spies and guides, which you are authorized to employ at reasonable rates, on the 15th of next month, and be absent until the 31st of December. . . You will order Captain Roberts to command another expedition against the Indians. . . There is to be no council held with the Indians, nor any talks. *The men are to be slain whenever and wherever found.* . . If the movements are kept from being made public, so the Indians through the Mexicans may not know of your plans until the troops take the field, it will be better so. . . Both McClave and Roberts will be instructed to keep a journal of every day's march and work; of the estimated courses and distances traveled; of the kind of country passed over; of the watercourses, springs, grass, etc., which they find. The journal will be forwarded to department headquarters as soon as the campaign is over, and copies of them to Washington."

On the 12th of October, 1862, this humane officer instructed Colonel Carson. The gist of the instructions read thus : "You will make war upon the Mescalaro, and all other Indians you may find in the Mescalaro country, until further orders. *All Indian men are to be killed, whenever and wherever you can find them.* . . . If the Indians send a flag of truce, and desire to sue for peace, say to them that you have no power to make peace; that you are there to *kill them wherever you can find them.*"

On the 26th of November, 1862, having heard that a man

12

by the name of Beach was, with others, engaged in the plunder of a band of Mescalaro Indians, and had, as the avails
thereof, a horse and mule, General Carleton directed that he
restore the property, not to the Indians, but to Colonel Carson, and that Beach be forbidden to settle in the country; and
on December 9, 1862, having heard that some parties in Toas
had taken an Indian, whom they found there, and after dosing
him with whisky, saturated his clothes with spirits of turpen-
tine, and then set fire to them, from the effects of which the
Indian died, General Carleton immediately wrote to the judge
of the district, calling his attention to the matter, and said:
" As one of the United States officials in New Mexico, and as
one whose particular calling is to see justice done, I trust I
have but to call your attention to this alleged crime, to awaken
your zeal in the cause of justice and humanity. In many
years' experience, connected with Indians, I think it never has
been my lot to have heard of such horrible barbarity of the
white men toward the Indians." In view of the instructions
of General Carleton to his military commanders, his letter to
the judge, and his banishment of Beach, present him as an
extraordinary compound; but he was a military officer, and
hence above reproach, and beyond criticism. It is clear that
in New Mexico he intended to retain a monopoly of his civilizing process in the hands of the military officers then on
duty there.

On January 2, 1863, General Carleton wrote to General
Lorenzo Thomas, adjutant-general, at Washington, and said
that, when he had "punished" the Indians that infest the
head-waters of the Gila, "the Pino Alta gold mines can then
be worked with success."

February 1, 1863, he wrote General Thomas again, and
stated that "the evidences of rich gold fields and veins of silver, and of inexhaustible mines of the richest copper in the
country, at the head of the Mimbres river, and along the
country drained by the upper Gila, are of an undoubted
character. It seems providential that the practical miners of
California should have come here to assist in their discovery
and development." He added: " I have sent four companies
of California volunteers to garrison Fort West, in the Pino

Alta gold region. I beg to ask authority to let, say, one-fourth of the command at a time, have one month's furlough, to work in the gold mines, on their own account. In this way, the mines and the country will become developed, while the troops will become contented to remain in service, where the temptation to leave is so great."

March 16, 1863, General Carleton wrote General J. R. West, commander at Mesilla, thus: "There must be no peace or conference with any of the Indians living on any of the tributaries of the Mimbres, or the head-waters of the Gila, down so far as Fort Stanton, until they are completely subdued, and not then, until the subject has been duly considered and decided upon at these headquarters. . . . The campaign sweeping the Florida mountains, about which I have twice written you, should be borne in mind. Information should be gathered concerning that region; the best guides employed' and the work done at the earliest practicable moment. This is a settled purpose, and will, I am sure, meet with a prompt and hearty co-operation on your part. Driven from the Gila, the Apache will naturally seek an asylum in these mountains. There the maguey grows, which is their principal food, and in the month of May they will begin to prepare it."

On the 10th of April, 1863, General Carleton instructed the commanding officer at Fort Stanton, that he " be sure *to have slain every Mescalaro who may be met with at large in the vicinity of his post.*"

On the 10th day of May, 1863, General Carleton wrote to General Halleck, general-in-chief, at Washington, and said: " Among all my endeavors since my arrival here, there has been an effort to brush back the Indians, as you have seen from official correspondence, so that the people could come out of the valley of the Rio Grande, and not only possess themselves of the arable lands in other parts of the territory, but, if the country contained veins and deposits of the precious metals, that they might be found. So I re-established Fort Stanton, and at least a hundred families have gone to the vicinity to open farms, and they are commencing to find gold. I established Fort West, and have driven the Indians away from the head of the Gila, and they are finding gold and silver, and cinnabar there. There is no doubt in my mind, that one of the richest gold countries in the world is along the affluents of the Gila, which enter it from the north, along its whole course. . . . You will also see, from the inclosed notes, what signs of mineral wealth are already discovered. . . . If I had one more good regiment of California infantry, comprised as that infantry is of practical miners, I would place it in the Gila country. While *it would exterminate the Indians*, who are a scourge to New Mexico, it would protect people who might wish to go there to open up the country, and would virtually be a military colony when the war ended, whose interest would lead the officers to remain in the New Eldorado. Pray give all this a thought. It is not a chimera, but a subject that is worthy of the government *now*. California, you remember, was not considered as valuable an acquisition until its gold startled the world. Do not despise New Mexico, as a drain upon the general government. The money will all come back again."

During the fall of 1862 and the year 1863, Gen. Carleton issued many orders to the different subordinate commanders in his department, the burden of which was *to destroy, to kill, to exterminate the Indians wherever found.* It is not necessary to reproduce them, since those already given show unmistakably that the object and design was TO EXTERMINATE THE NATIVE INHABITANTS IN NEW MEXICO. A few additional extracts must suffice, and these will fully demonstrate how earnestly General Carleton impressed his views on his subordinates. The following is an indorsement on a letter referred by Gen. Carleton to Col. West, then operating in Arizona. It is dated July 5, 1863, and reads thus: "This letter is respectfully referred to the commander at Fort Craig, who will send company K, 1st infantry California volunteers, to the points mentioned by Major McClave, and this company will be instructed to proceed *with great caution, without noise of trumpets or drums, or loud talking, or the firing of guns, except in battle, to march silently, mostly by night; to build fires of dry twigs, that no smoke may arise from them; to have no fires by night;* TO KILL EVERY INDIAN MAN THEY CAN FIND; to be gone thirty days; to have pack-mule transportation where wagons can not go; to *remember that California troops always find and whip the Indians;* to excel, in this respect, all other California troops."

On the 16th of August, 1863, Gen. Carleton wrote to Col. Riggs at Fort Craig, thus: "The troops must be kept after the Indians not in big bodies, *with military noises and smokes, and the gleam of arms by day, and fires, and talk, and comfortable sleeps by night; but in small parties, moving stealthily to their haunts and laying patiently in wait for them; or by following their tracks day after day, with a fixedness of purpose that never gives up.* . . . Some flour, bacon, a little sugar and coffee, thrown on a pack-mule, with the men carrying, say, two or three days' rations in their haversacks, and it will surprise the country what a few resolute men can do. If a hunter goes after deer, *he tries all sorts of wiles to get within gunshot.* An Indian is *a more watchful and a more wary animal than a deer.* He must be hunted with skill; he can not be blundered upon; nor will he allow his pursuer to come upon him when he knows it, unless he is stronger."

It would be difficult to find language sufficiently strong in which to condemn the inhuman and barbarous treatment which the Indians, in New Mexico, received from the troops in Gen. Carleton's department, and in accordance with his express orders. It is sad, it is humiliating, to know that his operations and the scope and intent of them, were known to the authorities at Washington. He not only corresponded with the adjutant-general and the general-in-chief of the army, but with the secretary of the treasury and the post-master-general freely.

On the 20th of September, 1863, in a long letter to Secretary Chase, he said: "If I can but have troops to whip away the Apaches, so that prospecting parties can explore the country, and not be in fear all the time of being murdered, you will, without the shadow of a doubt, find that our country has mines of the precious metals, unsurpassed in richness, number, and extent by any in the world. Rich copper, in quantity enough to supply the world, is found at the head of the Gila. Some of this copper abounds in gold. Some is pure enough for commerce with very little refining. The gold is pure. I send you herewith a specimen of copper from near Fort West, on the Gila, and two specimens of pure gold, from the Antelope mountains. . . . If it be not improper, please give the largest piece of the gold to Mr. Lincoln. It will gratify him to know that Providence is blessing our country, even though it chasteneth."

On the 13th of September, 1863, Gen. Carleton wrote Mr. Blair, the postmaster-general, and said: "There is no doubt but the reports of these immense deposits of gold are true. As a statesman, you will readily imagine all of the political results which must at once ensue from such startling developments when they obtain publicity. This should not be given them until we have reports from Surveyor-General Clark and a party I sent with him to see precisely into the matter. We know, from various other sources, what that report must be, at least sufficiently to make timely preparations for emergencies which will then at once arise. For myself, there comes no little satisfaction in the thought that, for all the toil through the desert, of the troops composing the column from California, there will yet result a substantial benefit to the country ; that if these brave fellows, who encountered this hardship so cheerfully and patiently, who endured and suffered so much, have not had the good fortune to strike good, hard, honest blows for the old flag, they have at least been instrumental in helping to find gold to pay the gallant men who have had the honor. Somebody had to perform their part in the grand drama upon which the curtain is about to fall. The men from California accepted, unmurmuringly, the role that gave them an obscure and distant part upon the stage, where it was known they could not be seen, and believed they would hardly be heard from; but in the great tragedy so cruelly forced upon us, they tried to perform their duty, however insignificant it might be, and to the best of their ability; and now a finger of that Providence who has watched over us in our tribulation, and who blesses us, lifts a veil, and there, for the whole country, lies a great reward."

The freedom with which General Carleton corresponded with the secretary of the treasury and the postmaster-general, indicates an intimacy that is not to be admired. It is to be hoped they did not fully understand the character of his operations against the Indians in the department of New Mexico. There can be no doubt, however, that the war department had full knowledge in the premises, since he frequently and fully corresponded with Generals Halleck and Thomas, and had express authority from them to commence war against the Navajoe and other Indian tribes. Indeed, his field of operations was extended in 1864, and he operated that year against the Indians in portions of Arizona and Colorado. Our country can not, therefore, escape the dishonor and disgrace of such cruel wrong as was perpetrated against the Indians while General Carleton was in command of the department of New Mexico.

By the treaty of peace with Mexico, the Territory of New Mexico became a part of our possessions, and the United States voluntarily assumed the obligation of taking such care of the native inhabitants as became a government founded on principles of justice and humanity. In 1850, the United States made a treaty with the Navajoe Indians, not for the cession of their right to territory, but simply of peace and friendship. In the treaty the Indians acknowledge that by virtue of our treaty with Mexico, they were lawfully placed under the exclusive jurisdiction of the United States; mutual covenants for peace and friendship followed; also for regulating trade, and the delivery of persons for committing offenses or crimes against either party, and for the reclamation of captives, and the right of citizens of the United States for transit and travel through the Navajoe country. It was also stipulated that the United States should at its earliest convenience " designate, settle, and adjust the territorial boundaries, and pass and execute in their territory such laws as may be deemed conducive to the prosperity and happiness of the Indians." The concluding paragraph of the treaty is in these words : " This treaty is to receive a liberal construction at all times and in all places, to the end that the said Navajoe Indians shall not be held responsible for the conduct of others, and that the government of the United States shall so legislate and act as to secure the permanent prosperity of the Indians."

In 1853, a treaty was made with the Comanche, Kiowa, and Apache Indians. It was not for a cession of their land, but simply for the right of our people of transit and travel through their country. The material stipulations were substantially the same as those in the Navajoe treaty. The seventh article is in these words : " The United States do moreover bind themselves, in consideration of the covenants contained in the preceding articles of this treaty, to protect and defend the Indian tribes, parties hereto, against the committal of any depredations upon them, and in their territories, and to compensate them for any injury that may result therefrom." Such were the existing relations between the government and the Indians, during the time that General Carleton was operating against them, not for offenses committed by them, but for the avowed purpose of driving them out of their own country or exterminating them within it, to the end that mining companies might safely operate in regions where every one that entered therein to dwell was a trespasser, whom, instead of protecting with its troops, the government was in good faith bound to expel. It would seem incredible that any man could be found wearing the uniform of our army, so lost to every principle of justice, so devoid of every sentiment of humanity, as to qualify him for deeds of such enormity as those committed by General Carleton. The reader will remember that in one of his dispatches, General Carleton commends California troops, and designates them as those " who always find and whip the Indians." This statement will serve to remind such that when given an insight into the operations in New Mexico in 1862–3–4, we have substantially the manner in which troops had been operated against the Indians, not only in California, but in all our territories. Is it not time that such inhuman and barbarous conduct ceased ?

There is another phase to military operations in the Indian country. While striving to destroy the natives, military officers seem to have time to correspond with a class of people between whom and such officers there appears to be the most intimate relations. A few extracts from the correspondence of General Carleton will explain this phase. On the 22d of

April, 1863, he wrote to Samuel F. Jones, Kansas City, as follows: " Your letter of March 18, 1863, in relation to gentlemen who have made inquiries of you, whether Fort West is to be permanently garrisoned, as in this event those gentlemen are desirous of investing in, and working the mines of precious metals near the head of the Gila, I have had the honor to receive, and I beg to reply, that unless I am compelled by the Confederate forces to abandon the rich country about Pinos Altas and on the Rio Preita, it will be held permanently. Our troops have already killed Magnus Colorado, his son, his brother, and some sixty of his braves, and I am still prosecuting hostilities against the Gila Apaches, and propose to continue doing so, until people can live in that country, and explore and work the veins of precious metals, which we know abound there, with perfect safety. The country along the Rio Preita, and further down the Gila, gives promise of wonderful richness in gold and silver. I have two companies out now surveying a road from Fort Craig to Fort West."

On the 22d of June, 1863, he wrote to Captain Joseph Walker, of the Walker mines, whom he had, under the promise of military protection, invited into the country, and said: "I am just commencing operations against the Navajoes. I inclose an order which organizes the expedition. You see the new fort will be at Pueblo, Colorado, about twenty-eight miles south of Fort Defiance, and this will be the nearest point for your people to get supplies in case of accident. The sutler there will doubtless have a large stock of goods, and I will tell him about keeping on hand such articles of prime necessity as you might require. I send you a map of the country, so that you may know about where Fort Canby will be situated. I send you another similar map on which you can trace your new gold fields. If I can be of any service to yourself or party it will afford me pleasure to help you. . . . Yourself and your party deserve success for your industry and perseverance. Hoping that each of you will receive abundant reward for your past toil, hardships, and danger, I am," etc.

It is to be observed that General Carleton is writing to men, and inviting and encouraging them to enter and work the mines, in a country in which all who entered were trespassers. Without further comment the operations and conduct of this officer are left to the contemplation of the reader, with such judgment as may be deemed proper and the case demands.

Military operations in Arizona in 1869 will now have a brief notice. General Ord was at this time commander of the department in which that territory was situate. In his annual report of September 27, 1869, General Ord said, that within Arizona Territory he had fourteen military posts "with an average garrison of one hundred and fifty men each, or two thousand one hundred men. There are (said he) in the territory three thousand three hundred horses and mules, and to maintain these troops and animals it costs the government, not including fuel, quarters, medical attendance, arms and accouterments, ammunition, clothing, pay of troops and employes, or stables, at least four thousand dollars per day; add other items, all the more expensive, where, as in southern Arizona, a foot of lumber costs twenty-five cents, and the cost to the government for the troops in Arizona is not far from three millions of dollars per annum. Almost the only paying business the white inhabitants have in the territory is supplying the troops, there being as yet but few mines in the country worked to profit; and I am informed from every quarter, that if the quartermasters and paymasters of the army were to stop payment in Arizona, a great majority of the white settlers would be compelled to quit. Hostilities are, therefore, kept up with a view to supporting inhabitants, most of whom are supported by the hostilities. Of course their support being derived from the presence of troops, they are continually asking for more. There was in Arizona, January 1, 1860, according to the army register, not a single army post or soldier, and there was then more travel across the southern portion of the territory than now, more need of troops there, and more Indians. It therefore becomes a question if this large expenditure can not be reduced by reducing the number of troops in the country to the minimum consistent with the interests of the whole country." It would appear from the foregoing that General Ord was not favorably impressed with the duties of his position as military commander of the district, and hence suggested a reduction and concentration of the troops. Of his operations, he says in his report: "I have encouraged the troops to capture and root out the Apaches by every means in my power, and to hunt them as they would wild animals. This they have done with unrelenting vigor. Since my last report over two hundred have been killed, generally by parties *who have trailed them, for days and weeks, into the mountain recesses, over snows, among gorges and precipices; laying in wait for them by day and following them by night.* Many villages have been burned, large quantities of supplies, and arms and ammunition, clothing, and provisions have been destroyed, a large number of horses and mules have been captured, and two men, twenty-eight women, and thirty-four children taken prisoners. . . . Many of the border men, especially those who have been hunted, or lost friends or relations by them, regard all Indians *as vermin, to be killed wherever met.* . . . The Apaches have but few friends, and, I believe, no agent. Even the officers, when applied to by them for information, can not tell them what to do. There seems to be no settled policy, *but a general idea to kill them wherever found.* I am a believer in that, if we go for extermination." General Ord occupies a high position, as well as rank, in the army. He clearly indicates his distaste for the mode in which the troops are used against the Indians; and yet "if we go for extermination," he is ready to proceed to kill off the natives. According to his report, the work of the year was to explore extensive districts of country, of which white men had little or no knowledge, and which were supposed to be retreats of "hostile" Indians, with a view to their subjugation. He expressed the opinion that there were not, at that time, more than one thousand fighting men of the Apaches left. He has, in his report, this remarkable paragraph: "Colonel John Green, First United States Cavalry, in a recent scout in the White Mountains, a country of which we knew but little, after destroying some villages, killing a number of warriors, and destroying a large quantity of corn, etc., having heard of a village thirty miles north, where the Indians were reported friendly and anxious to appease the troops, sent Captain John Berry, First United States Cavalry, to examine the matter, and if he found them concerned in hostilities, to destroy them." Green thus describes the result: "On the night of April 1st, Captain Berry returned with his command, and reported that when he reached Miguel's village, there was a white flag flying from every hut and every prominent point; that the men, women, and children came out to meet them, and went to work at once to cut corn for their horses, and showed such a spirit of delight at meeting them, that the officers united in saying that if they had fired on them they would have been guilty of cold-blooded murder. Even my chief scout, Manuel, who has no scruples in such matters, and whose mind was filled with taking scalps when he left camp, said he could not have fired on them after what he saw." Miguel expressed a strong desire to go on a reservation, where he could be protected; but Captain Berry knew not where to send him, and probably the chief could not have found a more secluded spot than the recess in the White Mountains where he then dwelt, in a country of which the white man knew but little; and yet, but for the exhibition of his white flags, it is probable that his village would have been destroyed. Many villages that were destroyed by our troops, in the hunt after the Indians, as though they were wild beasts, were as well disposed as the inmates of Miguel's village, and had opportunity been given the inhabitants, would have shown evidence of their pacific disposition equally as satisfactory as that shown by Miguel's Indians.

A reference to the manner in which a friendly band of Apache Indians were massacred at Camp Grant in Arizona, in 1871, by citizens of Tucson, aided by Mexicans, will close this chapter. In February, 1871, a young Apache chief, accompanied by some twenty-five of his band, came to Camp Grant and stated that they desired peace; that he and his people had no home, and could make none, since wherever they were located they had constant fear of the approach of troops. He was advised by a young lieutenant, R. E. Whitman, then in command, to go to the White Mountains, and locate there. The chief replied that those mountains were not the country of his people; that he had never dwelt with the Indians infesting the mountains; that he was an Aravapa Apache, and wanted to dwell in the home of his fathers, where he could raise corn and mescal, which was a principal article of food. Lieutenant Whitman told this chief that while he could make no permanent arrangement with him, that he could bring in his band and he would aid them, and report their wishes to the department commander. The chief left, and about the first of March returned with his whole band. In the meantime, runners from two other small bands had been in, asking the same privilege, and giving the same reasons. These were also permitted to come in with their bands, so that early in March, about three hundred Indians were at Camp Grant. The kindness of the lieutenant, so unusual among military officers, no doubt attracted the Indians to that point. He made a detailed report of the whole matter, and sent the same by express to the department commander, for instructions to guide him. After awaiting more than six weeks, his communication was returned to him without any other reply than to call his attention to the fact that his report was not properly briefed!

The Indians were camped about one-half mile from the military post, and were supplied by Lieutenant Whitman with limited rations. The number increased until over five hundred Indians were in the camp. They were very poor, and nearly naked. They were encouraged by the lieutenant to cut and bring in hay for his post, and in about two months they had brought in about two hundred thousand pounds, carrying it all on their backs. Men, women and children engaged in this work. They also gathered mescal for food. Additional bands, with whom these were intermarried, were preparing to come in. The Indians asked and obtained leave to move their camp further up the Aravapa to higher ground, and where water was plenty. In the meantime, Captain Stanwood took command of the post, and upon investigation and being satisfied the Indians were acting in good faith, on the 24th of April he left with the greater part of his troops to make a scout in the lower part of the territory. The ranchmen in the neighborhood were satisfied with the residence and location of these Indians, and had promised Lieutenant Whitman to employ and give them labor when the season came to gather barley. Lieutenant Whitman became much interested in the Indians, and said officially: " I had come to feel respect for men who, ignorant and naked, were still ashamed to lie or steal, and for women who would cheerfully work like slaves to clothe themselves and children, but, untaught, held their virtue above price. . . I had ceased to have any fears of their leaving, and only dreaded for them, that they might at any time be ordered to do so. They frequently expressed anxiety to hear from the general, that they might have confidence to build for themselves better houses, but would always say, ' You know what we want, and if you can not see him, you can write.' On the morning of April 30th, I was at breakfast at 7:30 o'clock, when a dispatch was brought to me by a sergeant of company P, Twenty-first Infantry, from Captain Penn, commanding Camp Lowell, informing me that a large party had left Tucson, on the 28th, with the avowed purpose of killing all the Indians at this post. I immediately sent two interpreters, mounted, to the Indian camp, with orders to tell the chiefs the exact state of things, and for them to bring the entire party inside the fort. As I had no cavalry, and but fifty infantry (all recruits), and no other officer, I could not leave the fort to go to their defense. My messengers returned in about an hour, with intelligence that they could find no living Indians. The camp was burning, and the ground strewed with their dead and mutilated women and children. I immediately mounted a party of about twenty soldiers and citizens, and went with them and the post surgeon, with a wagon to bring in the wounded, if any could be found. The party returned in the afternoon, having found no wounded, and without being able to communicate with any of the survivors. Early the next morning I took a small party with spades and shovels, and went out and buried all the dead in and about the camp. I thought the act of caring for their dead would be an evidence to them of our sympathy, at least, and the conjecture proved correct, for while at the work many of them came to the spot, and in-

dulged in their expressions of grief, too wild and terrible to
be described. That evening they began to come in from all
directions, singly and in small parties, so changed in forty-
eight hours as to be hardly recognizable, during which time
they had neither eaten nor slept. Many of the men whose
families had been killed, when I spoke to them and expressed
sympathy for them, were obliged to turn away, unable to
speak, and too proud to show their grief. The women whose
children had been killed or stolen, were convulsed with grief,
and looked to me appealingly, as though I was their last hope
on earth. Children who, two days before, had been full of
fun and frolic, kept at a distance, expressing wondering horror. . . Their camp was surrounded and attacked at day-
break. So sudden and unexpected was it, that no one was
awake to give the alarm, and I found quite a number of
women, who were shot while asleep beside their bundles of
hay, which they had collected to bring in on that morning.
The women who were unable to get away, had their brains
beaten out with clubs or stones. . . The bodies were all
stripped. . . I have spent a good deal of time with them
since the affair, and have been astonished at their continued
unshaken faith in me, and of their perfectly clear understanding of their misfortune. . . What they do not understand is, that while they are at peace, and conscious of no
wrong intent, that they should be murdered. . . One of
the chiefs said: 'I no longer want to live; my women and
children have been killed before my face, and I have been unable to defend them. Most Indians in my place would take
a knife and cut his throat, but I will live to show these people that all they have done, and all they can do, shall not
make me break faith with you, so long as you will stand by
us and defend us, in a language we know nothing of, to a
great governor we never have, nor never shall see.' About
their captives, they say: 'Get them back for us; our little
boys will grow up slaves, and our girls, as soon as they are
large enough, will be diseased prostitutes to get money for
whoever owns them. Our women work hard and are good
women, and they and our children have no diseases. Our
dead you can not bring to life, but those that are living we

give to you, who can write and talk, and have soldiers to get them back.' I will assure you, it is no little task to convince them of my zeal, when they see so little being done."

It was not long after this massacre before Lieutenant Whitman was relieved from duty at Camp Grant. In April, 1872, General Howard visited the scene. The Indians showed him the remains of their dead, which had become exposed. There he found the camp utensils, and clothing and blankets strewn around, and the bundles of hay that the women had brought in the night preceding the slaughter. The Indians spoke of Lieutenant Whitman—the attachment they had for him—and asked that he might be restored to the post, to remain with them. But his denunciation of the barbarous, the murderous act, and those engaged in it, had produced much feeling against him, and there was no cordiality between him and the commanding general, in view of which General Howard thought it was better the petition of the Indians be not granted.

This affair at Camp Grant is not an isolated case. Expeditions of the same kind have been often fitted out and set on foot, with results as merciless and barbarous, and men who claim to give tone to the actions of the communities in which they reside, have openly participated in them. Even the governors of territories have organized bodies of men to go out and hunt down the natives, with authority to kill them wherever found; to destroy their villages, take possession of their property as booty, and to receive a premium for all Indian scalps taken. Territorial legislatures have placed upon their journals resolutions organizing bands of men to be employed in "Indian hunting," with rewards for all scalps taken. The legislature of Idaho fixed the price of scalps at one hundred dollars for the scalp of the "buck," fifty dollars for that of the squaw, and twenty-five dollars for the scalp of every thing in the shape of an Indian under ten years of age, provided that each person shall make oath that the scalps were taken by the "Indian hunting" company; thus reducing the hunting down and killing human beings to a level with the destruction of dangerous wild animals!

The removal of Lieutenant Whitman from the post at Camp

Grant has much in it to attract the attention of considerate persons. Here was a military officer who had, by his conduct, secured the confidence of the Indians who survived the massacre; they were attached to him, and so informed General Howard, and desired his return; but his superiors had relieved him, and why? Simply because he had expressed his opinion, without reserve, touching the conduct of the murderous mob that came from Tucson. Instead of commending the lieutenant for his noble conduct, and defending and sustaining him, the military commander of the district transferred him to another post. The massacre was approved by men of prominence and influence in the territory, and these and the military commander were on such terms that the lieutenant must needs be relieved. General Howard, who felt keenly the enormity of the crime against the Indians, was so embarrassed by the influence of the mob, that he could not recommend that the petition of the Indians have favorable consideration.

13

CHAPTER XI.

A BOARD OF PEACE COMMISSIONERS CREATED BY CONGRESS.—TREATIES MADE
WITH THE KIOWA, COMANCHE, CHEYENNE, AND ARAPAHOE, SIOUX, AND OTHER
INDIANS.—FIVE HUNDRED THOUSAND DOLLARS APPROPRIATED TO CARRY
THEIR PROVISIONS INTO EFFECT.—THIS DUTY CONFIDED TO GENERAL SHER-
MAN.—TRANSFER OF GENERAL SHERIDAN TO THE DEPARTMENT OF THE MIS-
SOURI.—HE CONDEMNS WHAT THE PEACE COMMISSION HAD DONE.—HOLDS
THAT THE INDIANS SHOULD HAVE BEEN PUNISHED.—GENERAL SHERMAN CO-
INCIDES IN THIS OPINION.—ACTION OF THE COMMISSION AT CHICAGO.—CAM-
PAIGN AGAINST "THE HOSTILE INDIANS SOUTH OF THE ARKANSAS," ETC.

OWING to the complications then existing, Congress, on the
20th of July, 1867, created a commission, with a view "to
establish peace with certain hostile Indians." This commission was composed of N. G. Taylor, Commissioner of Indian
Affairs; J. B. Henderson, chairman of the Indian Committee
of the United States Senate; J. B. Sanborn and S. F. Tappan,
civilians; and Generals Sherman, Harney, Terry, and Auger,
of the regular army. The commission was authorized "to
call together the chiefs and head men of such bands of Indians as were then waging war, for the purpose of ascertaining their reasons for hostility, and, if thought advisable, to
make treaties with them, having in view the following objects, viz: *First.* To remove, if possible, the causes of war.
Second. To secure, as far as practicable, our frontier settlements, and the safe building of our railroads looking to the
Pacific. And, *Third.* To suggest or inaugurate some plan
for the civilization of the Indians." Also, to examine and
select "a district or districts of country, having sufficient
area to receive all the Indian tribes occupying territory east
of the Rocky Mountains," not then peaceably residing on
permanent reservations, under treaty stipulations, etc., which
district or districts should have sufficient arable or grazing
land to enable the tribes placed on them to support themselves, and that they should be so located as not to interfere
with established highways of travel, and the contemplated
railroads to the Pacific."

At the time of its appointment, the commission stated, in its report, that " war was being openly waged by several hostile tribes, and great diversity of opinion existed among the officials of the government, and no less diversity among our people, as to the means best adapted to meet it. Some thought peaceful negotiations would succeed, while others had no hope of peace until the Indians were thoroughly subdued by force of arms. As a concession to this latter sentiment, so largely prevailing, as well as to meet the possible contingency of failure by the commission, it was, perhaps, wisely provided, that in case peace could not be obtained by treaty, or should the Indians fail to comply with the stipulations they might make for going on their reservations, the president might call out four regiments of mounted troops, for the purpose of conquering the desired peace."

The condition and temper of the Indian tribes east of the Rocky Mountains, at that time, was a natural result growing out of such affairs as Lieutenant Dunn's, at Camp Sanborn ; Major Dowling's, at Cedar Bluffs ; Colonel Chivington's, at Sand Creek ; and General Hancock's, at Pawnee Fork ; as well as other incidents of a like character, of which there were many, together with the constant aggression of the white people upon the reservations and hunting grounds of the Indians. The dispatch of General Sherman, of the 28th of December, 1866, had much to do in stimulating all who were inclined to annoy and harass the Indians. It was addressed to General Grant, and was in these words : " Just arrived (at St. Louis) in time to attend the funeral of my adjutant-general, Sawyer. I have given general instructions to General Cooke about the Sioux. I do not understand how the massacre of Colonel Fetterman's party could have been so complete. We must act with vindictive earnestness against the Sioux, even to their extermination—men, women, and children. Nothing less will reach the root of this case." All who felt disposed to depredate upon the Indians, even to maiming or killing them, seemed to feel that no matter what excesses they committed, the military would shield them.

The commission, at first, found some difficulty in securing interviews with the chiefs and warriors of such tribes as were regarded as hostile ; but finally, through the means afforded at the military posts and Indian agencies, appointments were made to meet certain bands of the Sioux, at Fort Laramie, on the 13th of September; and the Cheyennes, Arapahoes, Apaches, Kiowas, and Comanches, at Fort Larned, on the 13th of October, 1867. On their way to Fort Laramie, on the 12th of September, the commission found, at North Platte, on the Pacific Railroad, a considerable number of Sioux and northern Cheyennes, some of whom had long been friendly, and others who but recently had been engaged in war. This was the first council, and at one time it seemed as if no good would result from it; but it proved otherwise, and a full understanding was arrived at, which, though not reduced to writing, was, by the Indians, faithfully kept. Of this council, in their report made to the president, January 7, 1868, the commission said :

" It was at this council that the hitherto untried policy in connection with Indians, of endeavoring to conquer by kindness, was inaugurated. Swift Bear, a Brulé chief, then and now a faithful friend of the whites, had interested himself to induce the hostile bands to come to this council, and had promised them, if peace were made, that ammunition should be given them to kill game for the winter. This promise was not authorized by the commissioners, but we were assured it had been made, not only by him, but by others of our runners, and that nothing less would have brought them in. These Indians are very poor and needy. The game in this section is fast disappearing, and the bow and the arrow are scarcely sufficient to provide them food. To give one of these Indians powder and ball, is to give him meat. To refuse it, in his judgment, dooms him to starvation ; and worse than this, he looks upon the refusal (especially after a profession of friendship on his part) as an imputation upon his truthfulness and fidelity. If an Indian is to be trusted at all, he must be trusted to the full extent of his word. If you betray symptoms of distrust, he discovers it with nature's intuition, and at once condemns the falsehood that would blend friendship and suspicion together. Whatever our people may have to say of the insincerity and duplicity of the Indian, would fail to express the estimate entertained by many Indians of the white man's character in this respect. Promises have so often been broken by those with whom they usually come in contact; cupidity has so long plied its work, deaf to their cries of suffering; and heartless cruelty has so often sought them in the garb of charity, that to obtain their confidence, our promises must be scrupulously fulfilled, and our professions of friendship divested of all appearance of selfishness and duplicity. We are now satisfied, whatever the criticisms on our conduct at the time—and they were very severe, both by the ignorant and the corrupt—that had we refused the ammunition demanded at the council, the war, on their part, would have resulted in great loss of life and property. As it was, they at once proceeded to their fall hunt, on the Republican river, where they killed game enough to subsist themselves for a large part of the winter, and no act of hostility or wrong has been perpetrated by them since. The statement of this fact, if it prove nothing else, may serve to indicate that the Indian, though barbarous, is yet a man, susceptible of the feelings which ordinarily respond to the exercise of magnanimity and kindness."

While at the North Platte the scouts of the commission apprised it that the Northern Sioux would not be able to meet it at Laramie at the time indicated, and thereupon the meeting at that point was postponed until the 1st of November, and the commission proceeded to a point about eighty miles south of the Arkansas river, where it met, on Medicine Lodge creek, the Kiowas, Comanches, Arapahoes, and Apaches. The Cheyennes, remembering Cedar Bluff, Sand Creek, and Pawnee Fork, with the hospitalities of civilization, as exemplified by Dowling, Chivington, and Hancock, were absent from the first councils, having camped some forty miles distant. They were dubious as to the purposes and objects of the commission. They knew that quite recently troops had been after some of them, and they did not comprehend the change in our policy. Hence they kept at a distance, but sent in small parties to observe what was in progress. In due time the commission made a treaty with the Kiowas, Comanches, and Apaches; and finally, when the

Cheyennes came in, a treaty was made with them and the Arapahoes. These treaties were executed at Council Camp, on Medicine Lodge creek—the first one on the 21st, and the second on the 28th of October, 1867. After the execution of these treaties, the limited annuities due these Indians in the spring of that year, but which had been withheld, were, by permission of the commission, distributed to them. The commission then returned to Laramie to meet the Sioux, but they were not present. A prevalent belief existed among them that we had resolved on their extermination, and hence they were distrustful of the objects of the commission. Moreover, it was too late in the season for those northern Sioux to come to a council, however much they might have desired to do so. Red Cloud sent word to the commission that his hostility was with the view to save the Powder river country from intrusion, it being the only hunting ground left to his people. He assured them that whenever the military garrisons at Fort Phil. Kearney and Fort C. F. Smith were withdrawn, his hostility should cease. As the commission had no authority to make such arrangement, it adjourned to meet in Washington on the 9th of December, first sending a message to Red Cloud to meet it early in the spring; and asked of him a cessation of hostilities until such meeting was had. On the return of the commission, by way of North Platte, the members received new assurances of peace, even friendship, from the Indians there assembled, being the same to whom the ammunition was given at the previous meeting; and, after the board arrived at Washington, it was advised that Red Cloud had accepted the proposition to cease hostilities, and meet them in council, as requested.

On the 7th day of January, 1868, the commission, as we have said, made report of its operations. *In every case of complications existing with the Indians at the date of its creation, and for several years previous to that time, and which was investigated by it, the cause of the difficulty was traced to the wrong-doing of our own people, both civil and military.* In a preceding chapter, extracts are given from its report, and quoted as the language of the commission of 1867–8, and these have, doubtless, already attracted the attention of the reader. Although no treaty had then been made with the Sioux, the commission said, in their report, that " with any thing like prudence and good conduct, on the part of our people in the future, we believe the Indian war, east of the Rocky Mountains, is absolutely closed."

In the spring the commission resumed its duties, and met the Ogallalla and Brulé Sioux, at Fort Laramie, on the 29th of April, 1868, concluded a treaty with them, and thereafter, during the spring and summer, at divers places on the Missouri river, the same treaty was submitted to the Upper and Lower Yanktonais, Uncpapas, Blackfeet, Sans Arc, Two Kettle, Minneconju, Lower Brulé, and Santee Sioux, and was accepted and ratified by them. The general provisions in all these treaties were similar. War between the parties was to cease forever. The honor of the government and the Indians was pledged to this. If bad men, among the whites, committed any wrong against the Indians, the government was to cause the offender to be arrested and punished, and to reimburse the Indians for losses sustained. If bad men among the Indians committed wrong against the whites, the tribe, upon proof, was to deliver up the wrong-doer, to be punished by the United States, and the person injured to be reimbursed out of the annuities. The president was to prescribe rules for ascertaining damages; but no person sustaining loss, while violating the provisions of the treaty, or the laws of the United States, should be reimbursed therefor.

By the treaty with the Kiowas, Comanches, and Apaches, a district of country was set apart for the absolute and undisturbed use and occupation of the tribes named, and for such other friendly tribes or individual Indians, as from time to time they might be willing, with the consent of the government, to admit among them; and the United States solemnly agreed " that no person except those herein authorized so to do, and except such officers, agents, and employes of the government as may be authorized to enter upon Indian reservations in discharge of duties enjoined by law, shall ever be permitted to pass over, settle upon, or reside in the territory described in this (the second) article, or in such territory as may be added to this reservation for the use of said Indians." The territory described in article two, as the reservation thus set apart, is bounded as follows : " Commencing at a point where the Washita river crosses the 98th meridian west from Greenwich ; thence up the Washita river, in the middle of the main channel thereof, to a point thirty miles, by river, west of Fort Cobb, as now established ; thence due west to the north fork of Red river, provided said line strikes said river east of the 100th meridan of west longitude, if not, then only to said meridian line, and thence south on said meridian line to the said north fork of Red river ; thence down said north fork, in the middle of the main channel thereof, from the point where it may be first intersected by the lines above described, to the main Red river ; thence down said river, in the middle of the main channel thereof, to its intersection with the 98th meridian of longitude west from Greenwich ; thence north on said meridian to the place of beginning."

By the second article of the treaty with the Cheyennes and Arapahoes, the following district of country was set apart for their undisturbed use and occupation, together with such other friendly tribes or individual Indians, as from time to time they might be willing, with the consent of the government, to admit among them, to wit : " Commencing at a point where the Arkansas river crosses the 37th parallel of north latitude ; thence west on said parallel—the said line being the southern boundary of the State of Kansas—to the Cimarron river (sometimes called the Red fork of the Arkansas river) ; thence down said Cimarron river, in the middle of the main channel thereof, to the Arkansas river ; thence up the Arkansas river, in the middle of the main channel thereof, to the place of beginning."   The same guaranty is given in this case as in that with the Kiowas, Comanches, and Apaches, that no person, other than those excepted, shall ever be permitted to pass over, settle upon, or reside in the territory set apart to the Cheyennes and Arapahoes as their reservation."

In both treaties the Indians, parties to each, stipulated that they will relinquish the right to occupy permanently the territory outside of the reservations above described, but they all reserve the right to hunt on any lands south of the Arkansas, so long as the buffalo may range thereon in such numbers as to justify the chase, and it is agreed on the part of the government that "no white settlements shall be permitted on any part of the old reservation, as defined by the treaty made between the United States and the Cheyenne, Arapahoe, and Apache Indians, at the mouth of the Little Arkansas, under date of October 14, 1865, within three years from this date" (October, 1867).

The Indians withdraw all pretense of opposition to the building of rail or wagon roads, and the construction of mail stations or other works of utility or necessity, which may be authorized by law; but should such roads or other works be constructed on the lands within the reservations, the government will pay the tribes whatever amount of damages may be assessed by three disinterested commissioners, to be appointed by the president, one of whom shall be a chief or head man of the tribes. The provisions of those treaties are numerous, and contain mutual covenants by the contracting parties. Among them is the following: That no treaty for the cession of any portion or part of the reservations, which are held in common, shall be of any validity or force as against the said Indians, unless executed and signed by at least three-fourths of all the adult male Indians occupying the same, and no cession by the tribes shall be understood or construed in such manner as to deprive, without his consent, any individual member of a tribe of his right to any tract of land selected by him, as provided in the treaty, for a homestead.

In the treaty with the Sioux, there was set apart for their reservation, and guaranteed to them and such other friendly tribes or individual Indians, as from time to time they might be willing, with the consent of the United States, to admit among them, for their absolute and undisturbed use and occupation, the following tract of country: "Commencing on the east bank of the Missouri river where the 46th parallel of north latitude crosses the same; thence along low-water mark down said east bank, to a point opposite to where the northern line of the State of Nebraska strikes the river; thence west across said river and along the northern line of Nebraska to the 104th degree of longitude west from Greenwich; thence north on said meridian to a point where the 46th parallel of north latitude intersects the same; thence due east along said parallel to the place of beginning, and in addition thereto all existing reservations on the east bank of the river." The same guaranties for the prohibition of intruders are incorporated as in the treaty with the Cheyennes and Arapahoes. In this, as in the other treaties, it is stipulated that no cession of any part or portion of the reservation shall be of any validity or force, unless executed and signed by three-fourths of all the adult male Indians occupying and interested in the same, and no cession shall deprive such Indians as have selected homesteads of their rights, without their consent. The provision in relation to building rail and wagon roads, etc., is the same as in the other treaties in all respects.

In the Sioux treaty the United States stipulated that " the country north of the North Platte river, and east of the summit of the Big Horn Mountains, shall be held and considered to be unceded Indian territory, and also stipulated and agreed that no white person or persons shall be permitted to settle upon or occupy any portion of the same, or without the consent of the Indians first had and obtained, to pass through the same; and it is further agreed by the United States, that within ninety days after the conclusion of peace with all the bands of the Sioux nation, the military posts now established in the territory in this article named, shall be abandoned, and that the road leading to them, and by them to the settlements in the Territory of Montana, shall be closed up." And the Indians agreed to relinquish all right to occupy permanently the territory outside of the reservation, as defined in the treaty, but yet reserved the right to hunt on any lands north of the North Platte, and on the Republican fork of the Smoky Hill river, so long as the buffalo may range thereon in sufficient numbers to justify the chase.. It was further agreed that such of the Sioux as should elect to lead the life of nomads, and roam and hunt, should each receive, for the space of thirty years, ten dollars and a suit of clothes each year.

The treaties of Medicine Lodge creek were not ratified by the Senate until in the month of July, 1868, and were not proclaimed by the president until in August, 1868. The treaty with the Sioux was ratified and proclaimed in the latter part of February, 1869.

In their report, the commission recommended the setting apart of two districts of country for the colonization of such Indians thereon, permanently, as had not then a residence on permanent reservations. One of these to be bounded north by the 46th parallel, south by the northern line of Nebraska, east by the Missouri river, and west by the 104th meridian ; the other, east by the States of Missouri and Arkansas, west by the 101st meridian, north by Kansas, and south by Texas. In reference to the treaties concluded previous to the date of their report, the commission said :

" In making treaties, it was enjoined on us to remove, if possible, the causes of complaint on the part of the Indians. This would be no easy task. We have done the best we could, under the circumstances, but it is now rather late in the day to think of obliterating from the minds of the present generation the remembrance of wrong. Among civilized men, war usually springs from a sense of injustice. When we learn that the same rule holds good with Indians, the chief difficulty is removed. But it is said our wars with them have been almost constant. Have we been uniformly unjust? *We answer, unhesitatingly, yes.* We are aware that the masses of our people have felt kindly toward them, and the legislation of Congress has always been conceived in the best intentions, but it has been erroneous in fact or perverted in execution. Nobody pays any attention to Indian matters. This is a deplorable fact. Members of Congress understand the negro question, and talk learnedly on finance, and other problems of political economy, but when the progress of settlement reaches the Indian's home, the only question considered is, ' how best to get his lands ?' When they are obtained, the Indian is lost sight of. While our missionary societies and benevolent associations have annually collected thousands of dollars from the charitable, to be sent to Asia and Africa, for the purposes of civilization, scarcely a dollar is expended, or a thought bestowed, on the civilization of Indians at our very doors. Is it because the Indians are not worth the effort at civilization? Or is it because our people, who have grown rich in the occu-

pation of their former lands—too often taken by force or procured by fraud—will not contribute? It would be harsh to
insinuate that covetous eyes have been set on their remaining
possessions, and extermination harbored as a means of accomplishing it. . . . Would it not be well to so regulate our
future conduct in this matter as to exclude the possibility of
an unfavorable impression?"

As we have stated, the Senate did not ratify the treaties
made in the fall of 1867, until after midsummer in 1868. Indeed, they were not proclaimed by the president until the
latter part of August, 1868. Under the circumstances, the
delay worked great injury. The Indians (Cheyennes and
Arapahoes) had surrendered the reservation they had under
the provisions of the treaty of October, 1865, with the guaranty, however, that no white settlements should be made
upon it for the period of three years from and after October,
1867. The delay in the action of the Senate, and the consequent delay in appropriations of money to carry the new
treaties into effect, the Indians could not comprehend. In
the meantime, white people entered the old reservation, and
began to make settlements on the land. No effort was made
to check this trespass. The Indians were necessarily ousted,
and this made them restless and uneasy. Practically, all that
was left them was the hunting right south of the Arkansas.

Gen. Sheridan, who had been for some time in Louisiana attending to reconstruction matters, having been transferred to
the department of the Missouri, early in the month of April,
1868, visited the military posts on the Arkansas, and when at
Fort Dodge, in Kansas, found encamped in that region many
Indians, composed of Kiowas, Comanches, Cheyennes, and
Arapahoes. These Indians sought an interview with him,
and this he declined to grant, stating to them that he was
simply visiting the military posts to learn their condition and
that of the soldiers, and that he was not authorized to talk
with them. Such is his own statement. It will be noticed
that these Indians were near a military post, and desired an
interview with the commander of the military district in
which they resided. There was no pretense in any quarter,
at that time, that they had any hostile design. They were

practically without a home; had not received the annual annuities due them that spring, under the treaty of 1865, and
no appropriation had been made for fulfilling the provisions
of the treaties of 1867. Indeed, these last were then, and for
nearly four months thereafter, reposing in the pigeon-holes
of the Senate, at Washington, awaiting the action of that
august body. The Indians were destitute. On the 16th of
April, 1868, the commissioner of Indian affairs, in view of
this destitution, had requested the secretary of the interior to
ask Congress for a special appropriation for the relief of these
and other Indians, alike destitute, and the secretary immediately asked Congress for such appropriation. That body took
no action in the matter. The local agents of these Indians
besought the department for aid, and feared deplorable results should Congress fail to respond and make proper provision for these needy Indians. On the 28th of May, the Indian bureau again laid the matter before the secretary, who,
on the following day, implored Congress for prompt action to
save some of the Indians from actual starvation. A third appeal brought forth an appropriation of $500,000, made by a
law approved on the 20th July, 1868, to be expended, not by
the Indian bureau, but by Gen. Sherman. Had Gen. Sheridan deigned to give these starving Indians a hearing when at
Fort Dodge, in April, they would no doubt have stated to him,
with great frankness, their condition and their needs. This
he declined to do, and yet had a willing ear for the stories
told by the people about the fort. He said, in a report of his
tour: "From all I could learn at Fort Dodge, there appeared
to be outspoken dissatisfaction on the part of the Indians, to
removing to their reservations assigned by the treaty of Medicine Lodge creek, of the previous fall. . . . I learned,
from officers and others, that all the tribes considered the
treaty of no importance except to get the annuities promised
in it, and that they did not intend to go on their reservations."
When we call to mind that the treaties (not treaty) of the fall
previous, were then in the pigeon-holes of the Senate, and
were not ratified and proclaimed for more than four months
thereafter, this statement of Gen. Sheridan does not impress
one very favorably with the intelligence of the local officers

at the fort, or their superior, the commander of the department of the Missouri. It is, however, apparent that what he learned about the fort was precisely the sort of information he desired. He had made up his mind in advance, and no doubt before he visited Fort Dodge, in relation to the proper mode of dealing with these Indians. His conclusions, when officially promulgated, were as follows :

"I am of opinion these Indians require to be soundly whipped; the ringleaders, in the present trouble, hung; their ponies killed, and such destruction of their property made, as will render them very poor. . . . The motives of the peace commission were humane, but there was an error of judgment in making peace with these Indians last fall. They should have been punished and made to give up the plunder captured, and which they now hold, and after properly submitting to the military and disgorging their plunder, they could have been turned over to the civil agents. These Indians are now rich in horses, stock, and other property suitable to their comfort in their manner of life. From the best information, the Cheyennes and Arapahoes will average from twenty to two hundred horses to the lodge of six persons; most of this stock has been accumulating in their periodical wars." He adds : " These Indians are better armed than our own people."

Others, who were presumed to know and did know, had said these Indians were poor, and it is difficult to see how they could be otherwise. For several years previous to that time they were almost constantly harassed, their villages burned, and their provisions and property destroyed, and many of their ponies taken from them or killed. The peace commission, when negotiating with them in the fall of 1867, mingling among and dwelling with them for several weeks, were not attracted by this great wealth to which General Sheridan refers, and for the simple reason that the statement was without any foundation. They had no such wealth. The rebuke of the peace commission, in the statement that it meant well, but erred in judgment when it made treaties with these Indians instead of whipping them, and the allegation that they had such wealth, were all stated in an official letter to

Gen. Sherman, for the inspection of himself and his colleagues on the commission, and thus Gen. Sheridan evinced his extreme modesty, as well as his studious regard for accuracy in the preparation of his official papers. In fact, he knew nothing about the temper of these Indians, or their worldly possessions, and yet he wrote of both as though he had personal knowledge in the premises.

Having come to the conclusion, and expressed his belief, that these Indians deserved punishment, before he left Fort Dodge, General Sheridan commenced preliminary arrangements looking in that direction; and took into his employment three men as scouts, and assigned to each a certain district in which to operate, and report to him weekly. As the employment of these men depended on Indian complications, and they were experts in the business, if none existed, they knew well how to originate them. Moreover, they were all imbued with the feelings of their distinguished employer, and ready to respond to his desires, and these were clearly in favor of a case that would serve as a pretext for making war on the Indians.

The last communication of the commissioner of Indian affairs to the secretary of the interior, of the date of June 23, 1868, appealing for aid for these Indians in their destitute condition, was accompanied by a letter from the superintendent of Indian affairs in the district in which the Indians resided. He said: "These Indians, taking it for granted that they had sold their old reservation when they made the treaties (of October, 1867), and expecting soon to be removed to their new homes, did not, to any great extent, cultivate their farms, and made no improvements; and, their treaties not being ratified, they could not be made to understand why this was so, and wonder why they have not been provided with their new homes; and, as the whites are continually trespassing on them, and moving on the ceded country and opening farms, and circulating false rumors relative to the Indians, and the disposition intended to be made of them by the government, the Indians have become excited," and he feared that if they were not removed from Kansas serious conflicts would arise between them and the whites. Such a condition of things as this opened a field for General Sheridan's scouts. This they cultivated, and it was not long until that officer came to the conclusion that the Indians, especially the Cheyennes and Arapahoes, were "hostile," and he began to prepare troops to operate against them. From whence he derived any lawful authority it is difficult to divine. Military officers are, however, on the frontier, and in the Indian country, as a general thing, a law unto themselves, and make war on Indian tribes whenever they please to do so. He had reports of depredations, robberies, and murders committed by Indians, in the most minute form; and these were formidable indeed, since he had experts in that line, under good pay, and whose employment depended on keeping him advised of the fact that there were "hostile" Indians in their districts, committing depredations that required they should be punished. It is an indisputable fact, that for wrong and injury done them, and because of settlements being made on the old reservation by the white people, the Indians, in time, became excited, and some did commit depredations. It may, however, be safely assumed that the detail of these which General Sheridan exhibited, on careful investigation, would bear revision; and it may be affirmed that, in the formidable bill of indictment which he presented against the Indians, there was not an item that he could, if put upon the stand, by his own testimony, have verified. Yet the whole collection was embodied in an official document addressed by him to General Sherman, under date of September 26, 1868, and by the latter laid before his colleagues of the peace commission, at their meeting in Chicago, early in October, 1868. All of the members were present except Senator Henderson and General Harney. The commission was in session several days, and the report of General Sheridan in relation to the depredations of the Indians, and his views as to the necessity of their punishment, as well as the future custody of the Indians, which he urged should be transferred to the war department, were considered. The Indians were not represented, either in person or by counsel. At this meeting of the commission, the military portion, joined by Mr. Sanborn, having the ascendency, passed resolutions that the government should cease to treat with Indians as independent tribes; that the clauses, in the treaties with the Indians, made at Medicine Lodge creek, in October, 1867, allowing them to roam and hunt outside of the reservations, should be at once abrogated; that the Indians should be compelled, by military force, to go on the reservations assigned them by the treaties of October, 1867, and that the Indian bureau should be turned over to the war department!

These resolutions were adopted by a vote of four to two, Commissioner Taylor and Colonel Tappan voting in the negative. On his return to St. Louis, General Sherman immediately advised General Sheridan of the action of the peace commission, and said: " I have sent you by mail every thing in relation to the action of the Indian peace commissioners, at Chicago, and of the interior department, about the Cheyennes, Arapahoes, Kiowas, Comanches, and Apaches, with whom you are now engaged at open war." He informed Sheridan that at the Chicago meeting, one of his colleagues, Colonel Tappan, had " stated that the officers of our army, instead of protecting the Indians against the infuriated whites, had joined the border people in their constant cry of ' extermination,' intimating that you and I had changed over to that creed from interested motives. I denounced this in terms so harsh, that I feel it will not be repeated in my hearing; but he will not hesitate to carry his assertions to other ears, even in Congress, willing to hear any thing to our disparagement." General Sherman was industrious, at the Chicago meeting, in pressing upon his colleagues, what he termed " abundant testimony," against the Indians, but neither he nor any of the members of the commission, except Taylor and Tappan, had one word to say against the " infuriated whites," for their conduct toward the Indians; no condemnation of those who had settled on the old reservation; no steps suggested for the removal of such from it, although the commission had pledged to the Indians, in the treaties of October, 1867, that no settlements should be made upon it for three years from that time. The action of the peace commission, at Chicago, was a complete repudiation of all its

14

previous work, including the many grand utterances embodied in its report of January 7, 1868, and thereupon, without completing the work Congress confided to it, adjourned *sine die*. We shall not attempt to comment on its conduct. The mere statement of the facts is sufficient. The names of the gentlemen who voted affirmatively at Chicago, are: Generals Sherman, Terry, and Auger, of the United States army, and J. B. Sanborn, civilian.

It was specified, in the act of Congress of July 20, 1868, appropriating the sum of $500,000, to be expended under the direction of General Sherman, that the money should be applied in " carrying out treaty stipulations, making and preparing homes, furnishing provisions, tools, and farming utensils, and furnishing food for such bands of Indians with which treaties have been made by the Indian peace commissioners, and not yet ratified, and defraying the expenses of the commission in making such treaties and carrying their provisions into effect." As none of the treaties were then ratified, this fund was applicable to all of them.

On the 10th day of August, 1868, General Sherman, with a view to execute the duties imposed on him by law, connected with the disbursement of this money, issued a general order, with a view to bringing the work into " full harmony with the military interests of the frontier." By this order he designated and set apart two districts of country, which he constituted military districts. The first embracing all the country west of the Missouri river, within the Sioux reservation; the second, the country bounded east by Arkansas, south by Texas, north by Kansas, and west by the 100th meridian. He assigned General Harney to the command of the first district, to have the supervision of the Sioux, and all issues and disbursements to them, subject only to the authority of the lieutenant-general commanding. He made a like assignment of the second district to General Hazen, to have supervision and control of the Cheyennes, Arapahoes, Kiowas, and Comanches, and such other bands as were then, or may thereafter be, therein located, to have the supervision and control of all issues and disbursements to said Indians, subject only to the authority of the lieutenant-general commanding. Out of the appropriation of $500,000, General Sherman set apart $200,000 to and for the use of the Sioux district, to be disbursed by General Harney; and $50,000 to and for the use of the Indians in the second district, to be disbursed by General Hazen.

As early as the 17th of September, 1868, General Sherman, by some process not disclosed in the published documents, but no doubt through correspondence with General Sheridan, became impressed with the opinion that the Cheyennes and Arapahoes were not only hostile, but that they were actually at war with our people, and on that day so wrote to the secretary of war. He alleged that the treaty of Medicine Lodge creek had been broken by them; that the department should invoke the superior orders of the president against any goods whatever, even clothing, going to any part of these tribes, until the matter was settled. He claimed that, as military commander, he had the right, unless restrained by superior authority, to prevent the issue of any goods whatever to Indians outside of their reservations. He seemed to be perfectly oblivious to the fact that these Indians, by virtue of a treaty made with them, by the peace commission, of which he was a member, had a right guaranteed to them to roam and hunt south of the Arkansas, on any land where the buffalo ranged, and he seemed further to have forgotten that no steps had been taken to erect an agency-house, or any other buildings, on their new reservation, and, moreover, that Congress had given to him, and to no one else, the money, and confided to him the initial steps in the fulfillment of the treaty stipulations with those very Indians, thus confiding to him a high trust. The temper he was in when about to enter into the discharge of this duty, may be inferred from a further extract from his letter of September 17, to the secretary of war. He said: "No better time could possibly be chosen than the present for *destroying or humbling* these bands that have so outrageously violated their treaty, and began a desolating war without one particle of provocation; and after a reasonable time given for the innocent to withdraw, I will solicit an order from the president, declaring all Indians who remain outside of their reservations to be declared 'outlaws,' and commanding all people—soldiers and citizens—to proceed against them as such." These are remarkable utterances to fall from the lips of this peace commissioner, who was charged with the authority and supplied with the means to take all needful steps to fulfill our treaty stipulations with the Indians. For some time previous to the 17th of September, the troops of General Sheridan had been, and were then, in motion, and on the 19th of the month, General Sherman again wrote the secretary of war that the Cheyennes and Arapahoes were at war; that the troops could not discriminate between the well disposed and warlike parts of those bands, unless absolute separation be made, and suggested that the "agent" collect all of the former, and conduct them to their reservation, within the Indian Territory, south of Kansas, there to be provided for under their treaty, "say, about old Fort Cobb." He did not appear to understand that their reservation was not in the vicinity of old Fort Cobb, although the peace commission defined the boundaries of it, nor did he remember that he, and not the civil agent, had the money to be expended in making provision for them; and that he had, on the 11th of August, 1868, notified the secretary of the interior, that in the fulfillment of the duties confided to him, he should employ military agents, because he had more faith in their manner of doing business, and because their forms of accounts were more familiar to him, and more easy to be examined and approved. Indeed, on the 10th of August, 1868, he had assigned General Hazen to duty in the district in which the reservation of these Indians was situate. Moreover, about the 20th of September, Colonel Wynkoop, the civil agent of these Indians, ceased to discharge the duties of agent for them, because of the action of General Sherman. Colonel Leavenworth, the agent of the Comanches and Kiowas, had left the Indian country some time previous, and did not return. This was to be regretted, but it did seem that these civil officers could not remain. Military forms and military agents had been adopted by General Sherman, and hence there was nothing for the civil officers to do.

As to the temper of the Cheyennes and Arapahoes, it may be stated that on the 10th day of August, 1868, Colonel Wynkoop wrote to the department that on the day previous he had made an issue of the annuity goods and ammunition to the Cheyenne chiefs and their people; that they were delighted at receiving them, and never before had he known them to be better satisfied. These goods, etc., were limited in amount and due under the treaty of 1865, and should have been issued in the spring, but had, from some cause, been delayed until that time. Several weeks before this issue, a dissatisfied party had started north from the Cheyenne village, on the war-path against the Pawnees, and they, while out, got into diffi-culty with the whites, and committed some excesses and out-rages on the Saline river. The agent, Colonel Wynkoop, hav-ing learned the fact, submitted the matter of these outrages to two of the principal chiefs, Medicine Arrow and Little Rock, and demanded that they deliver up the perpetrators, which they promised should be done; but before sufficient time had elapsed for them to fulfill this promise, the troops were in the field and the Indians in flight. Colonel Wynkoop, in a com-munication detailing the excesses on the Saline, and the demand he had made, remarked that General Sheridan was then at Fort Dodge, organizing an expedition to go in pursuit of the Cheyennes *who had gone south of the Arkansas when the trouble began*, and that the probabilities were that if the troops struck any Indians, it would be the wrong parties.

In a communication from Colonel Wynkoop to the Indian office, after he had arrived at Philadelphia, he said that a " few thousand dollars for subsistence for these starving In-dians at the proper time would have saved millions to the treasury, saved many white men's lives, saved the necessity of hunting down and destroying innocent Indians for the faults of the guilty, and driving into misery and starvation numbers of women and little children, not one of whom but then mourned some relative brutally murdered at the horrible mas-sacre at Sand Creek, and who still suffer from the loss of their habitations and property, wantonly destroyed by Major-Gen-eral Hancock." He concludes his letter thus: "Had each member of Congress seen what I have of the injustice prac-ticed toward these Indians, they would imagine there was not sufficient money in the United States treasury to appropriate for their benefit."

General Sheridan had, for some time previous to his visit to Fort Dodge, been operating with detached squads of troops, and was then preparing a plan for an elaborate campaign. These annoyed and harassed the Indians very much, and wherever possible killed them. In turn the Indians retaliated, killing some whites, and among them some of Sheridan's scouts. His elaborate preparations contemplated in the end a winter campaign against the " hostile Indians south of the Arkansas," to be composed of columns moving from the east, north, and west of the section of country in which he supposed the " hostile " tribes were, and thus force them into the western part of the Indian Territory. He expected with these converging columns to compel the Indians to surrender and be placed on reservations, or chastised into peace. In addition to all the regular troops he could command and draw to his service, he called upon the Osage Indians and invited them to send him warriors to join the expedition, and obtained two hundred of them, whom he attached to the command under General Custer. They were called the Osage trailers. General Hazen, who should have been at Fort Cobb, at farthest, by the middle of September, not as a fighting soldier, but clothed in the garb of " peace," to which service he was detailed on the 10th of August, was, as late as the 18th of October, at Americus, Kansas, inviting the Kaw Indians to supply the expedition with several companies of their warriors, to go out against the " hostile Indians south of the Arkansas." In communicating the offer of the Kaws, General Hazen wrote General Sheridan, and said : " They would be twice the service to you in actually making war, than an entire regiment of equipped cavalry." Indeed, General Hazen became so inspired with the sound of the war bugle, that he seemed willing to surrender his trust and the $50,000 allowed him to entertain the friendly Indians at Fort Cobb, and modestly said : " I would not hesitate, if desired, for a moment, in taking full control of these (Kaws), with the Caddoes, Wichitaws, Shawnees, and Delawares, probably in all four or five hundred." And then, by way of illustrating from a military standpoint, his fitness for the trust to which General Sherman assigned him, to go to Fort Cobb and take charge of the friendly Indians, he said of the Kaw and others, whom he would like to command in the fight against the "hostiles," they "ought to be given all they take from the Indians. They will also want rations, arms, and some pay."

The governor of Kansas also caught the contagion. His very soul was filled with martial ardor, and he not only sup- plied some militia for local posts, but raised a regiment of volunteers and resigned his office to lead it in the combat, and was its colonel.

Last, but not least, General Sherman, one of the peace commissioners, the very one to whom Congress had voted the money to fulfill the stipulations of the treaties that his com- mission had made with the Indians, comes to the front, and on the 15th of October, 1868, wrote to General Sheridan thus: "I have all your dispatches and letters up to date, and do not see wherein I can further assist you or relieve you of unpleas- ant responsibility. I am so conscious of the great difficulty of satisfying public clamor, and of fighting small scattered bands of Indians, well mounted, armed, and equipped, that I want to leave you perfectly free to do what your judgment approves, and yet to assume as much responsibility as possible, to relieve you in case of any delay or temporary failure. . . . I will say nothing and do nothing to restrain our troops from doing what they deem proper on the spot, and will allow no mere vague general charges of cruelty and inhumanity to tie their hands, but will use all the power confided to me to the end that these Indians, the enemies of our race and our civil- ization, shall not again be able to begin and carry on their barbarous warfare on any kind of pretext that they may choose to allege. . . . You may now go ahead in your own way, and I will back you with my whole authority, and stand between you and any efforts that may be attempted in your rear to restrain your purpose or check your troops." In the report of the peace commission, dated January 7, 1868, after reciting all the complications and conflicts with these Indians, from and including the attack on the Cheyenne vil- lage by Chivington, in 1864, up to the date of the report, and in every case tracing the difficulty to the doors of our own race, the commission said: "We would not blunt the vigilance of military men in the Indian country, but would warn them against the arts of the selfish and unprincipled, who need to be watched as well as the Indians." When we call to mind that Congress, with this report before it, with General Sherman's name attached thereto, had confided to him the duty of seeing that the provisions of the treaties were fulfilled, and voted him $500,000 for that purpose; that he had done nothing beyond assigning General Hazen to the command of the district, and placed in his hands $50,000 to be expended for the benefit of the Indians; that Hazen had not then (October 15th) been to Fort Cobb, but three days later (October 18th) was among the Kaw Indians, receiving offers from them to supply warriors to join Sheridan's expedition, and tendering his own services as their commander, the language and conduct of General Sherman are extraordinary indeed. It is not necessary to analyze or criticise either. Every intelligent reader will arrive at his own conclusion in the premises. The subject will be resumed in the next chapter.

CHAPTER XII.

GENERAL SHERIDAN'S OPERATIONS.—MOVEMENTS OF GENERAL CUSTER.—HIS SURPRISE AND DESTRUCTION OF BLACK KETTLE'S VILLAGE, CALLED BY THE MILITARY "THE BATTLE OF THE WASHITA."—HIS RETURN TO GENERAL SHERIDAN'S HEADQUARTERS AT CAMP SUPPLY.—INCIDENTS AND EVENTS OF THE MARCH OF THE COMMAND FROM THENCE, VIA THE BATTLE-GROUND, TO FORT COBB.

GENERAL SHERIDAN left Fort Hayes about the middle of November, 1868, expecting to overtake his invading army at Bear creek. From that point he was to move toward the Indian Territory, but there was an impression that he would not set out thence immediately. The newspaper correspondents with him said he had a large supply of extra horses, and the best outfit that had ever taken the field on the plains. He had, in advance, sent forward 400,000 rations to Fort Dodge, 300,000 to Fort Lyon, and 300,000 to Fort Arbuckle, and thus prepared for his winter campaign.

The one-tenth of this amount of food given to these homeless Indians, would have accomplished all that was necessary, and completely composed and quieted all that were excited, as the small gift to the Sioux satisfied them the fall before. To have supplied these Indians with food would not, however, have been a gift, but the simple performance of an obligation, under the treaties of Medicine Lodge creek. But to have done this would not have met the views of the "ignorant and corrupt," such as criticised the conduct of the peace commission in the case of the Sioux. Nor would it have satisfied General Sheridan. He had decided on a winter campaign, the objects of which were "to strike the Indians and force them on the reservations set apart for them," and if this could not be accomplished, "to show the Indian that the winter season could not give him rest, and that he and his village and stock could be destroyed; that he would have no security, except in obeying the laws of peace and humanity." He had various columns in operation, whom he called "beaters in," but these were not expected to accomplish much, except to crowd the Indians south, and concentrate them in the Washita valley, in the direction of old Fort Cobb. General Sheridan arrived at Camp Supply on the 21st of November, where he found the forces of General Sully engaged in erecting houses, digging wells, and such other improvements as were necessary to protect his supplies. "A furious snowstorm commenced on the same evening, which continued all night and the next day, making the situation very gloomy, especially on account of the non-arrival of the Nineteenth Kansas," which was expected about this time. This was the regiment of Governor Crawford. General Sheridan was much disappointed at the non-arrival of this regiment, since it was his intention to have united it with the Seventh Cavalry (Custer's), and launched both on the Indians at once. Notwithstanding the inclemency of the weather and the absence of Crawford's regiment, General Sheridan ordered General Custer to move his regiment, "storm or no storm," on the morning of the 23d of November. In obedience to orders, General Custer moved promptly on that morning, at daylight, "although the snow continued to fall with unabated fury." For some time previous to this date, California Joe and some other scouts had been out in search of "hostile" Indians, and the Osage allies, or "trailers," had been out on the same errand. Had these scouts discovered the Indian villages on the Washita and so advised General Sheridan? And was this precipitate movement made in such inclement weather, under the apprehension that the Indians might learn that troops were coming from the north, and hence move their villages? In General Sheridan's report of the operations of General Custer, dated November 29, 1868, he says:

"I have the honor to report for the information of the lieutenant-general, the following operations of General Custer's command. On the 23d of November I ordered General Custer to proceed, with eleven companies of his regiment of Seventh Cavalry, in a southerly direction toward the Antelope Hills, in search of hostile Indians. On the 26th he struck the trail of a war party of Black Kettle's band, returning from the north, near where the eastern line of the Pan Handle of Texas crosses the main Canadian. He at once abandoned his wagons and followed in pursuit over to the headwaters of the Washita, and thence down that stream, and on the morning of the 27th surprised the camp of Black Kettle, and after a desperate fight, in which Black Kettle was assisted by the Arapahoes, under Little Raven, and the Kiowas, under Satanta, captured the entire camp, killing the chief, Black Kettle, and one hundred and three warriors, whose bodies were left on the field, all their stock, ammunition, arms, lodges, robes, and fifty-three women and three children. Our loss was Major Elliot, Captain Hamilton, and nineteen enlisted men killed; Brevet Colonel Barnitz badly wounded; Brevet Lieutenant-Colonel Custer, Second Lieutenant E. J. Marsh, and eleven enlisted men wounded.

" Little Raven's band of Arapahoes, and Satanta's band of Kiowas, were encamped six miles below Black Kettle's camp. About eight or nine hundred animals captured were shot, the balance kept for military purposes. The highest credit is due General Custer and his command. They started in a furious snow-storm, and traveled all the while in snow twelve inches deep.

" Black Kettle's and Little Raven's families are among the prisoners. It was Black Kettle's band who committed the first depredations on the Saline and Solomon rivers in Kansas. The Kansas regiment has just come in. They missed the trail and had to struggle in the snow-storm; the horses suffering much in flesh, and the men living on buffalo meat and other game for eight days. . . . If we can get one or two more good blows there will be no more Indian troubles in my department. We will be pinched in our ability to supply, and nature will present many difficulties in our winter operations; but we will have stout hearts and do our best. Two white children were captured; one white woman, and one boy, two years old, were brutally murdered by the Indian women when the attack commenced."

This report was addressed to General Sherman, from the depot on the North Canadian, at the junction with Beaver creek. In transmitting the same to the adjutant-general, at Washington, General Sherman indorsed on it: " This gives

General Sheridan a good initiation. I understand his supply depot to be on Rabbit Ear creek, a little west of south from Fort Dodge, whence he can direct operations; and his very presence there will give assurance that the troops will act with energy, and that nothing will be done but what is right.

. . . The bands of Black Kettle, Little Raven, and Satanta are well known to us, and are the same that have been along the Smoky Hill the past five years, and, General Sheridan reports, embrace the very same men who first began this war on the Saline and Solomon."

The report made by General Custer, of the battle of the Washita, and addressed to General Sheridan, is dated, "In the field, on the Washita, November 28, 1868," one day preceding the date of the report of the latter to General Sherman, and is as follows:

" *General:* On the morning of the 26th instant, this command, comprising eleven troops of the Seventh Cavalry, struck a trail of an Indian war party, numbering about one hundred warriors. The trail was not quite twenty-four hours old, and was first discovered near the point where the Texas boundary line crosses the Canadian river. The direction was toward the southeast. The ground being covered by twelve inches of snow, no difficulty was to be experienced in following the trail. A vigorous pursuit was at once instituted; wagons, tents, and other impediments to a rapid march, were abandoned. From daylight until nine o'clock at night, the pursuit was unchecked; horses and men were then allowed one hour for refreshments; and then, at ten P. M., the march was resumed, and continued until 1:30 A. M., when our Osage trailers reported a village within less than a mile from our advance. The column was countermarched, and withdrawn to a retired point, to prevent discovery.

" After reconnoitering, with all the officers of the command, the location of the village, which was in a heavy strip of timber, I divided the command into four columns, of nearly equal strength. The first, consisting of three companies, under Major Elliot, was to attack in the timber, from below the village; the second column, under Brevet Lieutenant-colonel Myers, was to move down the Washita, and attack in the timber, from above; Brevet Lieutenant-colonel Thompson, in command of the third column, was to attack from the crest, north of the village; while the fourth column was to charge the village from the crest overlooking it from the west bank of the Washita.

" The hour at which the four columns were to charge simultaneously, was the first dawn of day, and notwithstanding the fact that two columns were compelled to march several miles to reach their positions, three of them made the attack so near together as to appear like one charge; the other column was only a few minutes late. There never was a more complete surprise. My men charged the village, and reached the lodges before the Indians were aware of their presence. The moment the charge was ordered, the band struck up ' Garry Owen,' and, with cheers that strongly reminded me of scenes during the war, every trooper, led by his officer, rushed toward the village. The Indians were caught napping for once. The warriors rushed from their lodges, and posted themselves behind the trees and in the deep ravines, from which they began a most determined defense.

" The lodges, and all their contents, were in our possession within ten minutes after the charge was ordered; but the real fighting—such as has rarely been equaled in Indian warfare —began when attempting to clear out or kill the warriors posted in ravines or underbrush. Charge after charge was made, and most gallantly too, but the Indians had resolved to sell their lives as dearly as possible. After a desperate conflict of several hours, our efforts were crowned by a complete and most gratifying success. The entire village, numbering forty-seven lodges of Black Kettle's band of Cheyennes, two lodges of Arapahoes, and two lodges of Sioux—fifty-one lodges in all—under the command of the principal chief, Black Kettle, fell into our hands. By actual and careful examination, after the battle, the following figures give some of the fruits of our victory: The Indians left on the ground and in our possession the bodies of 103 of their warriors, including Black Kettle himself, whose scalp is now in the possession of our Osage guides; we captured, in good condition, 875 horses, ponies, and mules; 241 saddles, some of very fine and costly workmanship; 573 buffalo robes; 390 buffalo skins, for lodges; 160 untanned robes; 210 axes; 110 hatchets; 35 revolvers; 47 rifles; 535 pounds of powder; 1,050 pounds of lead; 4,000 arrows and arrow-heads; 75 spears; 90 bullet molds; 35 bows and quivers; 12 shields; 300 pounds of bullets; 775 lariats; 940 buckskin saddle-bags; 470 blankets; 93 coats; 700 pounds of tobacco. In addition, we captured all their winter supply of buffalo meat, all their meal, flour, and other provisions, and in fact every thing they possessed, even driving their warriors from the village with little or no clothing. We destroyed every thing of value to the Indians, and have now in our possession, as prisoners of war, fifty-three squaws and their children. Among the prisoners are the survivors of Black Kettle and the family of Little Rock. We also secured two white children, held captive by the Indians. One white woman, who was in their possession, was murdered by her captors the moment we attacked them. A white boy, held captive, about ten years old, when about to be rescued, was brutally murdered by a squaw, who ripped out his entrails.

"The Kiowas, under Satanta, and the Arapahoes, under Little Raven, were encamped six miles below Black Kettle's village; the warriors from these two villages came to attempt the rescue of the Cheyennes. They attacked my command from all sides, about noon, hoping to recover the squaws and herd of the Cheyennes. In their attack they displayed great boldness, and compelled me to use all my force to repel them; but the counter charges of the cavalry were more than they could stand. By three o'clock we drove them in all directions, pursuing them several miles. I then moved my entire command in search of the villages of the Kiowas and Arapahoes; but, after a march of eight miles, discovered that they had taken the alarm at the fate of the Cheyenne village and had fled.

"I was then three days' march from where I had left my train of supplies, and knew that wagons could not follow me, as the trail had led me over a section of country, so cut up by ravines and other obstructions, that cavalry could with difficulty move over it. The supplies carried from the train, on the persons of the men, were exhausted; my men, from loss of sleep and hard service, were wearied out; my horses in the same condition for want of forage. I therefore began my return march about eight P. M., and found my train of supplies at this point (it having only accomplished sixteen miles since I left it). In the excitement of the fight, as well as in self-defense, it so happened that some of the squaws and a few of the children were killed and wounded. The latter I have brought with us, and they receive all the medical attendance the circumstances of the case will permit. Many of the squaws were taken with arms in their hands; and several of my command are known to have been wounded by them. The desperate character of the combat may be inferred from the fact that, after the battle, the bodies of thirty-eight dead warriors were found in a small ravine, near the village, in which they had posted themselves.

"I now have to report the loss suffered by my command. I regret to mention, among the killed, Major Joel H. Elliot and Captain Louis M. Hamilton, and nineteen enlisted men; the wounded includes three officers and eleven enlisted men—in all, thirty-five. Of the officers, Brevet Lieutenant-Colonel Albert Barnitz, captain Seventh Cavalry, is seriously, if not mortally wounded; Brevet Lieutenant-Colonel T. W. Custer, and Second Lieutenant T. J. Marsh, Seventh Cavalry, are slightly wounded. Brevet Lieutenant-Colonel F. W. Banteen had his horse shot under him by a son of Black Kettle, whom he afterward killed. Colonel Barnitz, before receiving his wound, killed two warriors. I can not sufficiently commend the admirable conduct of the officers and men.

"This command has marched five days amidst terrible snow storms, and over a rough country covered by more than twelve inches of snow. Officers and men have slept in the snow without tents. The night preceding the march, officers and men stood at their horses' heads four hours, awaiting the moment of attack; this, too, when the temperature was far below the freezing point. They have endured every privation, and fought with unsurpassed gallantry, against a powerful and well-armed foe; and from first to last I have not heard a single murmur; but, on the contrary, the officers and men of the several squadrons and companies seemed to vie with each other in their attention to duty, and their patience and perseverance under difficulties. Every officer, man, scout, and Indian guide did their full duty. I only regret the loss of the gallant spirits who fell in the 'Battle of the Washita.' Those whose loss we are called upon to deplore are our bravest and best."

The camp on the Washita river, where General Custer wrote out the foregoing report, was not less than sixty miles distant from General Sheridan's headquarters, at the junction of Beaver creek and North Canadian river. The communication was made between these points with so much celerity that General Sheridan was enabled to make his report of the "Battle of the Washita" on the 29th of November—Custer's report, on which his was based, being made on the 28th. There was no rail or telegraph communication; and, in view of the fact that the country was broken, the ground covered with twelve inches of snow, and General Custer's horses and men well worn out, the dispatch was extraordinary. After preparing and forwarding his report, General Custer moved, with his command, prisoners, Osage trailers, scouts, and camp followers, to join his chief at his depot, at the junction of Beaver creek and the North Canadian river. On the evening of the 30th of November, a courier arrived at General Sheridan's headquarters, announcing to him that General Custer would camp that night only ten miles distant, and come in on the 1st of December. A correspondent of the New York *Herald*, who was with General Sheridan, wrote:

" Shortly after the sun had passed its meridian (December 1), a cluster of dark and almost undefinable objects appeared on the crest of the hill, about a mile distant, and simultaneously accompanied by shouts and the firing of musketry, announced the approach of the column. On the summit of the hill the head of the column halted for a few moments. Meanwhile General Sheridan took position in the valley, to await the arrival of the column, which was to pass the commanding general in review. All the officers and soldiers not on duty assembled in the vicinity of the post to witness the warlike pageant. The column was now within a short distance of the commanding general; the Indians shouted, the band reiterated the stirring tones of 'Garry Owen,' and the troopers cheered. In response, rounds of huzzas of the troops of the fort shouted welcome and congratulation. In the advance was the Osage Indian trailers. Before leaving camp they had arrayed and decorated themselves in a manner becoming the importance of the occasion. Their faces were painted in the most fantastic and hideous designs. About their persons were dangling the trophies which they had captured in the battle. Spears, upon which were fastened the scalps of their fallen foes, were slung upon their shoulders; from their own painted scalp-locks were suspended long trails of silver ornaments and feathers; over their shoulders hung shields and bows, and quivers full of arrows, while in one hand they held the trusty rifle, and in the other grasped the reins.

"Even the animals which the Osages bestrode were decorated with scalps and strips of red and blue blanket. At the head of the band rode Little Raven, the chief, with a countenance as fixed as stone, yet in his bearing showing indications of an inward self-glorification, which was apparently kept stirring and swelling higher and higher, by the gesticulations and wild notes of the war songs shouted by his warriors, intermingled with whoops and discharge of rifles. In a moment of enthusiasm the chief shouted, 'They call us Americans; we are Osages,' to which sentiment went up a responsive approval. Conspicuous in this party was the young Osage warrior, Koom-la-Manche (Trotter). It was he who, under the impulse of the highest ambition of Indian valor, that singled out the great chief, Black Kettle, the terror of all the Osages, as his victim. After a severe conflict, he reached the crowning point of his efforts, and bore away the ghastly scalp of the terrible chief, as the trophy attaching to his success. With a mark of special attention, this scalp was carefully and fantastically decorated, and hung prominently among the most sacred possessions of the young warrior.

"Following the Indians were the scouts led by California Joe, a veteran pioneer of forty years. Joe is a hirsute-look-

15

ing specimen of humanity, exhibiting an altitude of six feet; a mat of red whiskers hiding two-thirds of his face, and a long, knotty head of hair, well powdered in a series of coats of dust, intermingled with stray blades of grass, leaves, and sticks, as the vestiges of his previous night's slumbers on the bosom of mother earth. Joe was a suitable figure-head for this motley band of curiously clad, adventurous, and rugged men. Next came General Custer, riding alone, mounted on a magnificent black stallion, and dressed in a short blue sack coat, trimmed with the color of his arm of the service, and reinforced with fur collar and cuffs; on his head he wore an otter cap. When General Custer came within fifty yards of the commanding general, he left his position in the column and dashed up to his chief, when a warm and hearty exchange of salutations was made between the commander and his distinguished lieutenant. Next followed the living evidences of the victory—over fifty squaws and their children, surrounded by a suitable guard to prevent their escape. These were mounted on their own ponies, seating themselves astride the animals; their persons wrapped in skins and blankets, and their heads and faces being covered, leaving nothing visible but their eyes. The mothers had their offspring mounted behind them, the papoose being visible only by its diminutive head, peering up over the back of the head of its mother. Without a sigh, without a glance to the right or to the left, these remnants of the band of the once powerful Black Kettle, followed with all the submission of captives. Following these came the keen-sighted sharpshooters, commanded by Brevet Lieutenant-Colonel W. W. Cook, and following these the bravest men in the different companies of the regiment, in columns by platoons, under their proper officers. On a separate line of march from the summit came the wagon train, moving over the hills. In the lead were the ambulances conveying the dead and wounded. The regiment moved up the Beaver about half a mile from the fort, and there went into camp. That night the Osage allies gave a scalp dance, which was kept up to a late hour. . . The scene was one of savage effect. The burning logs in the center, the Indians painted and attired in war costumes, with spears, bows, shields, and all the trophies taken by them about their persons, performed their mysterious contortions of the body and whooped wildly, as if about to engage their foe. Many of our officers and soldiers, among the former Generals Sheridan and Custer, witnessed this scene, and remained until a late hour."

On the 3d of December, the officers of the Seventh Cavalry met to testify by resolutions their sorrow for the untimely death of Major Joel H. Elliot, who was killed in the battle of the Washita, and the respect and estimation in which the deceased was held by his companions in arms. Among other resolutions adopted was one declaring that the gallant bearing of Major Elliot, in the battle of the Washita, "which brought him suddenly to the end of his earthly career, is deserving of the highest praise; that he fell in the attitude of defiant daring, heroically rallying his men, and by example inciting them to deeds of valor worthy of the greatest encomiums that can be bestowed." In point of fact, at that time his colleagues did not know the circumstances under which he fell, or the precise locality where his body, and the bodies of the enlisted men who fell with him, then were. On the 4th of December, 1868, the remains of Captain Louis M. Hamilton, who was killed at the battle of the Washita, were interred with military honors.

Having given the men and animals one week's rest at Camp Supply, on the North Canadian river, General Custer, on the 7th of December, 1868, moved his command, composed of eleven companies of the Seventh Cavalry, ten companies of the Nineteenth Kansas Volunteers, and a detachment of scouts, and some twenty or thirty whites, Osage and Kaw Indians, as guides and trailers—the objective point being Fort Cobb. General Sheridan accompanied the expedition. On the 10th of the month the command reached the Washita, about six miles below the battle-ground of November 27. Here it halted one day to graze the animals, and afford an opportunity to visit the battle-field and learn, "if possible, the exact fate of Major Elliot and his party of seventeen men, who, on the opening of the attack on Black Kettle's village, had pursued a party of fleeing Indians beyond the lines, and had never returned." In a report of the movements of this expedition, dated at Fort Cobb, December 22, 1868, General Custer said:

"So confident was I of their fate (Major Elliot and party) that in my official report of the battle I numbered them in my list of killed. With one hundred men of the Seventh Cavalry, under command of Captain Yates, I proceeded to the battle-field early on the morning of the 11th. The Indians had evidently paid a hurried visit to the scene of the late conflict. The bodies of nearly all the warriors killed in the fight had been concealed or removed; while those of the squaws and children, who had been slain in the excitement and confusion of the charge, as well as in self-defense, were wrapped in blankets and bound with lariats, preparatory to removal and burial. Many of the Indian dogs were still found in the vicinity lately occupied by the lodges of their owners; they probably subsisting on the bodies of the ponies that had been killed, and then covered several acres of ground near by. As ten days had elapsed since the battle, and scores of Indian bodies still remained unburied or unconcealed, some idea may be had of the precipitate haste with which the Indians had abandoned that section of country.

"A thorough examination of the immediate battle-ground failed to discover any thing worthy of special report, except that Indian bodies were found which had not been previously reported in my first dispatch, and which went to prove what we are well aware of now, that the enemy's loss in killed warriors far exceeds the number (one hundred and three) first reported by me. In setting out on our return to camp, Captain Yates was directed to deploy his men in search of the bodies of Major Elliot and his party. After marching about two miles in the direction in which Major Elliot and his little party were last seen, we suddenly came upon the stark, stiff, naked, and horribly mutilated bodies of our dead comrades! No words were needed to tell how desperate the struggle which ensued before they were finally overpowered. . . . The bodies of Elliot and his little band, with but a single exception, were all found lying within a circle not exceeding twenty yards in diameter. We found them exactly as they fell, except that their barbarous foes had stripped and mutilated the bodies in the most savage manner. All the bodies were carried to camp, and there (reached after dark, it being the intention to resume the march before daylight the following day) a grave was hastily prepared on a little knoll, near our camp, and with the exception of that of Major Elliot, whose remains we carried with us for interment at Fort Arbuckle, the bodies of the entire party, under the dim light of a few torches held in the hands of sorrowing comrades, were consigned to one common resting-place. No funeral note sounded to measure their passage to the grave; no volley was fired to tell us a comrade was receiving the last sad rites of burial; yet not one of the living but felt that the fresh earth had closed over some of their truest and most daring soldiers."

The report of General Custer, of December 22d, is quite elaborate. It is not deemed necessary to produce all of it in detail. The next morning the command started on the trail of the Indian villages, nearly all of whom, it is stated, had moved down the Washita toward Fort Cobb. The forest along the banks of the Washita, from the battle-ground to a distance of twelve miles, was found to have been one continuous Indian village. Black Kettle's band being above, then came other tribes, camped in the following order: Arapahoes, under Little Raven; Kiowas, under Satanta and Lone Wolf, and the remaining bands of Cheyennes, Comanches, and Apaches. Nothing could exceed the disorder and haste in which these tribes had fled from their camping-grounds. They had abandoned thousands of lodge-poles, some of which were still standing as when last used; immense numbers of camp-kettles, cooking-utensils, coffee-mills, axes, and several hundred buffalo robes were found in the abandoned camps adjacent to that of Black Kettle's village, but which had not been visited before by our troops. By actual examination and estimate, " it was computed," says Custer, " that over six hundred lodges had been standing along the Washita during the battle, and within five miles of the battle-ground; and it was from these villages, and others still lower down the stream, that the immense number of warriors came, who, after my rout and destruction of Black Kettle and his band, surrounded my command, and fought until defeated by the Seventh Cavalry, about 3 P. M., on the 27th ultimo. It is safe to say that the warriors from these tribes that attempted the relief of Black Kettle and his band, outnumbered my force at least three to one. . . . On returning from the battle-ground to the camp of my command, and when in the deserted camp, which, according to the statement of some of my Cheyenne prisoners, who were brought along with me, was lately occupied by Satanta with the Kiowas, my men discovered the bodies of a young white woman and child, the former apparently about twenty years of age, and the latter probably about eighteen months old. They were evidently mother and child, and had not long been in captivity, as the woman still retained several articles of her wardrobe about her person; among others a pair of cloth gaiters but little worn; every thing indicated that she had been but recently captured, and upon our attacking and routing Black Kettle's camp, her captors, fearing she might be recaptured by us, and her testimony used against them, had deliberately murdered her and her child in cold blood."

The command followed the trail of the Kiowas and other hostiles, for seven days, down the valley of the Washita, over an almost impassable country, " where it was necessary to keep two or three hundred men almost constantly at work, with picks, axes, and spades," before being able to advance with the train. On the 17th, the scouts reported a party of Indians in front with a flag of truce. They bore a letter from General Hazen, at Fort Cobb, of the date of the 16th December. This letter notified the commander of the troops in the field that the writer, General Hazen, had heard that they had reached a point some twenty miles above Cobb, and that all the camps between that point and Cobb were friendly, and had not been on the war-path that season. It advised the commander to communicate with Satanta or Black Eagle, near where he was, and they would readily inform him of the position of the Cheyennes and Arapahoes, and also where General Hazen's camp was. General Custer took a small party and proceeded beyond his lines, and met some twenty of the principal chiefs of the Kiowas, Comanches, and Apaches, who proposed to accompany him to Fort Cobb, the Kiowas assuring him that their village was already near that point, and moving to the post. Not believing in these professions, and learning from his scouts that their entire village was hastening away to the Washita Mountains, General Custer says that, nevertheless, on reaching his camp, he gave rations to the entire party of chiefs and warriors who accompanied him, intending to do no act that might be construed as unfriendly. He states that they all promised to proceed with him to Fort Cobb the following day, except two or three, who were to rejoin the village and conduct it to the fort; but, on resuming the march the next morning, it was found that but three Kiowas and two Apaches remained. These, during the march, expressed a desire to go to their village and change their horses, as well as to give directions about the movement of the village to Fort Cobb. He permitted the Kiowa chief lowest in rank to set out for the village to hasten its march to Fort Cobb, and then placed Lone Wolf and Satanta, the head chiefs of the Kiowas and Apaches, under guard, determined to hold them as hostages for the faithful performance of their people. He said the communication from General Hazen, stating that all the camps referred to were friendly, and had not been on the war-path this season, occasioned no little surprise on the part of those (General Sheridan and himself) who knew the hostile character of the Indians referred to. They knew that these Indians had participated in the battle of the Washita; and they had followed the trail of these tribes from the dead bodies of their comrades slain by them. Moreover, if they needed cumulative testimony, General Custer said they had it, in the statement of Black Eagle, given voluntarily, not to the military, but to the officers of the Indian department, and conveyed by Philip McCusky, their interpreter, to Thomas Murphey, superintendent of Indian affairs. There was other testimony, drawn from conversation with Lone Wolf, Satanta, Black Eagle, and others; and all confirmed by a sister of Black Kettle. General Custer said he had not intimated that he had this testimony to the chiefs he held as hostages, and did not intend to at that time. After reaching Fort Cobb, on December 18th, General Custer said it became evident that the chiefs were attempting their usual game of duplicity, and that their villages were going from and not coming to Fort Cobb. They were all placed under a strong guard, but this did not produce the desired effect. Then it was that General Custer announced to Lone Wolf and Satanta the decision which had been arrived at regarding them. He gave them until sunrise the following morning to cause their people to come in, or to give satisfactory evidence that they were hastening to come in. If no such evidence appeared, both of these chiefs were to be hung, at sunrise, to the nearest tree. At the same time, they were offered every facility to send runners and communicate their desires to their tribes. This, he said, produced the desired effect. By sunrise several of the leading Kiowas came to his camp and reported the entire village on the move, hastening to place themselves under control. General Custer closed thus:

"At this date I have the satisfaction to report that all the Apaches, nearly all the Comanches, and the principal chiefs and bands of the Kiowas, have come in and placed themselves under our control; not to make a treaty and propose terms of settlement, but begging us to pronounce the terms upon which they can be allowed to resume peaceful relations with the government. Of the five tribes which were hostile at the opening of this campaign, three are already in our power. The remaining two, the Cheyennes and Arapahoes, were the principal sufferers at the battle of the Washita, and are no doubt the most anxious of all to abandon the war-path. They are supposed to be concealed in the mountains, forty or fifty miles from this point, awaiting the result of the present negotiations with the three tribes now assembled here. . . . As in the case of the tribes now here, no promise or inducement has been held out. I have made no pretense to be friendly disposed. Whatever I have asked the tribes to do, or accede to, has been in the form of a demand. They have from the commencement of this campaign been treated, not as independent nations, but as refractory subjects of a common government. I have every reason to believe that in a few days, or weeks at farthest, the two remaining hostile tribes, Cheyennes and Arapahoes, smarting under their heavy losses in the battle of the Washita, will unconditionally come in and place themselves under the control of this command, willing to accede to any terms that may be proposed to them. The tribes now here have discarded the arrogant ideas, in the indulgence of which the numerous treaties recently entered into have encouraged them. They now seem to realize that the government, and not a few thieving, treacherous chiefs of predatory bands of savages, backed up and encouraged by unprincipled and designing Indian agents, is the source of all authority. . . . The above, I believe, contains a brief statement of the operations of this command, and the results thereof, up to this date. Every thing indicates a speedy, satisfactory, and permanent solution of the Indian difficulties, so far as the tribes referred to are concerned. . . . In relation to the battle of the Washita, I find, by taking the admission of the Indians now here, and who participated in the battle, that the enemy's loss far exceeded that reported by me in my first dispatch concerning the fight. I reported one hundred and three warriors left dead in our possession. The Indians admit a loss of one hundred and forty killed. This, with the prisoners we have in our possession, makes the entire loss of the Indians, in killed, wounded, and missing, not far from three hundred."

Gen. Sheridan had, as stated, accompanied Gen. Custer from the North Canadian, *via* the battle-ground, to Fort Cobb. On the 19th of December, from Fort Cobb, in advance of the report of the operations of the expedition from Gen. Custer to him, Gen. Sheridan made report to Gen. Sherman. For the information of that officer, Gen. Sheridan advised him that he arrived at Fort Cobb on the 18th of the month, with the command of Gen. Custer, composed of the Seventh Cavalry, and ten companies of the Nineteenth Kansas, and the Osage and Kaw scouts, numbering in all about fifteen hundred. He stated that the command struck the Washita about eight miles south of Custer's battle-ground, distant from Fort Cobb about one hundred and thirteen miles. Here was a rest of one day, during which search was made for the body of Maj. Elliot, which was found—also the bodies of sixteen soldiers killed in the battle. The theory of Gen. Sheridan was

that Maj. Elliot and his troops followed in pursuit of some
fleeing Indians, and the warriors coming up from the camps
below met and surrounded them, and killed and mutilated
them in a horrible manner. They also found the body of
Mrs. Blinn and her child. The Indians enumerated were encamped from " a point about three miles below the battle-
ground, for a distance of six or eight miles. They abandoned
their camps, and fled in the greatest consternation, leaving
their cooking utensils, mats, axes, lodge-poles, and provisions."
This property was burnt. The trail was then taken and followed down the Washita, about seventy-six miles, and thirty-
six from Fort Cobb. This was near the camp of the Kiowas,
who were unconscious of the presence of the command, but
discovered it late in the evening, and hastened to Fort Cobb,
and next morning presented a letter from Gen. Hazen declaring them friendly.

" I hesitated to attack them (said Gen. Sheridan), but directed them to proceed with their families to Fort Cobb.
This they assented to, and nearly all the warriors came over
and accompanied the column, for the purpose of deceiving me,
while their families were being hurried toward the Washita
mountains ; but suspecting that they were attempting to deceive me, as they commenced slipping away one by one, I arrested the head chiefs, Lone Wolf and Satanta, and on my arrival at Fort Cobb, as I suspected, there was not a Kiowa ; so
I notified Lone Wolf and Satanta that I would hang them to-
morrow if their friends were not brought in to-day, and I will
do so. They have been engaged in war all the time, and have
been playing fast and loose. There are over fifty lodges with
the Cheyennes now. They have attempted to browbeat Gen.
Hazen since he came here, and went out and ordered the two
companies from Arbuckle for protection to Gen. Hazen to return. I will take some of the starch out of them before I get
through with them. The Cheyennes, Arapahoes, one band
of Comanches, and the fifty lodges of the Kiowas, are at the
western base of the Washita mountains.

" The following is what I have proposed to do, and I have
submitted it to General Hazen, who approves. I will first
punish the Kiowas if they come; if not, I will hang Lone

Wolf and Satanta. I will send out Black Kettle's sister to-morrow, ordering the Cheyennes and Arapahoes to come in and receive their punishment, which will be severe. She says they will come in, as they are now willing to beg for peace, and have done so already since General Custer's fight. If they do not come, I will employ the Caddoes, the Wichitas, and Asahabet's band of Comanches to go out against them, or will declare them hostile. They have all been working together as one man, camping together, and holding intercourse and trading in captured stock, and they must assist in driving them out of the country or compel their surrender. I will then leave a sufficient force with General Hazen to keep him from being browbeaten. The Comanches are now under my thumb, and the Kiowas will be, I hope; and I hope the Cheyennes and Arapahoes may soon be in the same condition. In the trip down here the distance was one hundred and eighty-seven miles; snow was on the ground most of the way, and the cold, on the high table-lands and the crossing of the rivers, was intense. The country traveled over was terrible; the surface of the earth was defaced by cañons, hummocks, scooped-out basins, making constant labor for the men. I lost some horses; but in this beautiful valley, with splendid grass, will soon have the command in good trim. I am a little sorry that I did not hit the Kiowas; but I did not like to disregard General Hazen's letter, and perhaps we can do as well by other modes. The Indians, for the first time, begin to realize that winter will not compel us to make a truce with them."

While these operations were going on, Lieutenant-Colonel Evans moved from Fort Bascom, up the main Canadian to Monument creek, and there established a depot, from whence he scouted to the head-waters of Red river, and there discovered a trail of Comanches, followed it up, and on December 25th, attacked the party, killing some twenty-five, wounding a large number, captured and burnt their village, and destroyed all their property. General Carr operated on the Canadian, west of the Antelope Hills, and forced the Cheyennes and Arapahoes over into the eastern edge of the Staked Plains, where there was no game; and, being without supplies, they were compelled to surrender, and promised to go on their reservation. The Arapahoes were, it was stated, faithful, and delivered themselves up; the Cheyennes, it was said, broke their promise and did not come in, and General Custer was ordered to move against them, which he did, and came upon them on the head-waters of Red river, apparently moving north.

In the foregoing recital is contained all the material parts of the reports of Generals Sheridan and Custer touching the operations of the troops in the campaign against the " hostile Indians south of the Arkansas." As early as the 19th of September, 1868, Gen. Sherman had officially notified Gen. Grant that he then considered " the Cheyennes and Arapahoes at war," and that it would be impossible " for the troops to discriminate between the well disposed and warlike parts of those bands, unless an absolute separation be made." He said : " I prefer that the agents collect all of the former, and conduct them to their reservation within the Indian Territory south of Kansas, there to be provided for under their treaty, say about old Fort Cobb." He objected to their being collected and held near Fort Larned, and said : " So long as agent Wynkoop remains at Fort Larned the vagabond part of his Indians will remain and cluster about him for support, and to beg of the military." He did not pretend to say what should be done with these, but said it would " simplify our game of war, already complicated enough, by removing them well away from the field of operations." He claimed, further, that the young men of these tribes were committing murders and robberies from Kansas to Colorado. From that time forward Gen. Hazen, who was to operate at Fort Cobb in the interests of peace, considered these Indians as beyond his authority, " till they shall be turned over by Gen. Sheridan, who is now dealing with them." On the 19th and 20th of September, Generals Sheridan and Hazen were at Fort Larned, and held a conference with the chiefs of the Kiowas and Comanches, whom they then regarded as friendly, and who, with their families, were then on the Arkansas. The object was to induce the Indians to go to their own reservation near Fort Cobb, " and thus keep them out of the war." It was arranged at this conference that the Indians should hunt buffalo for ten days, giving these officers time to procure sufficient rations for them to live upon while on their journey, when they were to return to Larned and start for Fort Cobb. On the day the Indians were to have returned to Larned, Fort Zarah was attacked, and for a week after some party or train was daily attacked by Indians, "making it so dangerous" that no communication could be had with the Indian country. "This (said Gen. Hazen) gave the impression to every one that the Kiowas and Comanches had gone to war, yet there was no evidence of the fact." There was no conference held with the Cheyennes and Arapahoes at this time. Gen. Hazen himself did not arrive at Fort Cobb until the 7th of November, 1868. He had previously detailed Col. Alvord, an efficient officer, to repair to Fort Cobb, to learn from that point the status of all the Indians. He found Col. Alvord " with very full information of the Kiowas and Comanches, representatives from both having been in and arranged with him for all their people to come here (Cobb), and their arrival was daily expected." Gen. Hazen came to the conclusion, and said officially, that those Indians " have had no part in any hostilities this season, but have steadily refused to join the Cheyennes and Arapahoes in war, when invited to do so. They give as a reason for breaking their agreement to come in at Larned, that one John Smith, an interpreter at that point, who has great influence with them, told them not to do so, nor to come here, for the troops were laying traps for them at both points, but to move south and west rapidly, to keep out of the war. They are now encamped within reach of this point, on the Canadian and Washita rivers, except a war party of the Kiowas, under Satanta, that has gone to Texas. I apprehend (continued Gen. Hazen) no trouble whatever in managing all these people this winter, except it be in breaking off this old and pernicious habit of marauding in Texas. They say that country was originally theirs; that Texas never negotiated for it, and that they have a right to it still. Gen. Sheridan, still under the impression that these people are at war, may possibly attack them before I can collect them at this point; but I have sent swift runners to prevent this."

In a communication from Col. Alvord to Maj. Ray, commanding the district in the Indian Territory, dated October 30, he says: "The Indians have not understood the non-arrival of Gen. Hazen, and the receipt by them of no supplies. . . . I can not hope to deal favorably with hungry men, to keep hungry hundreds around me, nor succeed in securing the influence of important chiefs and delegations (whom I have every reason to expect here next week), in bringing in their people, unless they are entertained while here, and go back to their camps provided for. I want a good supply of corn and meal, and also flour, especially some coffee, some sugar, and some salt." This paragraph appears in the letter of Col. Alvord to Maj. Ray: "The Indians look with more or less suspicion upon all the soldiers in their country. They do n't like the occupation of this place, nor the movements of troops between the Arkansas and Canadian. The latter, especially, tends to keep them on the plains. It is my belief that the force here and the public property is safer now than if more troops were sent here, and that the principle will hold good that the more soldiers you send here the fewer will be the Indians that remain. . . . I think, too, that it is important to success to have Gen. Hazen here, personally, as soon as practicable, both because the Indians want to know he is here, and that arrangements can be perfected for regular and sufficient supplies."

As early as October 13, General Sheridan had concluded to class the Kiowas and Comanches with the hostiles, and on that day wrote a note from Fort Hays, to the head chief of the Osages, stating that "the Cheyennes, Arapahoes, Kiowas, and Comanches have made war on the white people, and I understand from your superintendent, Mr. Thomas Murphey, that your people are desirous of taking part with the whites in the war. If such are the feelings of your people, I will accept of the services of, say, two hundred warriors, and will furnish provisions after they join General Custer's command, on or near Chalk Bluff creek, about fifty miles south of Fort Dodge, in the big bend of the Arkansas, and will give to them all ponies and other Indian property they may capture." Although General Hazen's "swift runners" and certificates did induce General Sheridan not to hang Satanta, Lone Wolf, and other Kiowa chiefs, the latter did not abandon the idea that they were "hostile."

On the 22d of November, General Hazen wrote to General Sherman, inclosing to him the talk he had with Black Kettle and Big Mouth, at Fort Cobb, on the 20th of the month. He said the Cheyenne chief, Black Kettle, and Arapahoe chief, Big Mouth, came there to ask for peace for their bands. "I inclose their talk. Black Kettle represents a large portion of the Cheyennes, known as the southern Cheyennes, or *those who were at Larned when war commenced*, and Big Mouth speaks for all of the southern Arapahoes. He was accompanied by Spotted Wolf, and Black Kettle by Little Robe. They started in of their own accord, but met one of my scouts, who told them to come on. To have made peace with them would have brought to my camp most of those now on the war-path south of the Arkansas; and as General Sheridan is to punish those at war and might follow them in afterward, a second Chivington affair might occur, which I could not prevent. I do not understand that I am to treat for peace, but would like definite instructions in this and like cases. To make peace with this people would probably close the war, but perhaps not permanently. I would prefer that General Sheridan should make peace with these parties. . . . As soon as the annuities arrive I will have all the Kiowas and Comanches here, except the large band of the latter on the Pecos." This was the 22d of November, and yet General Sherman's military peace agent, General Hazen, was without the annuities for these Indians, and without any definite instructions from his superior, to whom had been confided, by Congress, the duty of fulfilling the treaty stipulations of the Medicine Lodge creek treaties.

General Hazen had a record made of the conversation between him and Black Kettle and Big Mouth, at Fort Cobb, on the 20th of November, 1868. Here it is, word for word, and is the same he forwarded to General Sherman on the 22d November:

Black Kettle, Cheyenne chief: "I always feel well when I am among these Indians—the Caddoes, Wichitas, Waccoes, Keechies, etc.—as I know they are all my friends; and I do not fear to go among the white men, because I feel them to be my friends also. The Cheyennes, when south of the Arkansas, did not wish to return to the north side because they feared trouble there, but were continually told that they had better go there, as they would be rewarded for so doing. The Cheyennes do not fight at all this side of the Arkansas; they do not trouble Texas; but north of the Arkansas they are almost always at war. When lately north of the Arkansas, some young Cheyennes were fired upon and then the fight began. I have always done my best to keep my young men quiet, but some will not listen, and since the fighting began I have not been able to keep them all at home. But we all want peace, and I would be glad to move all my people down this way; I could then keep them all quietly near camp. My camp is now on the Washita, forty miles east of the Antelope hills, and I have there about one hundred and eighty lodges. *I speak only for my own people;* I can not speak for nor control the Cheyennes north of the Arkansas."

Big Mouth, Arapahoe chief: "I come down here a long distance, to this country in which I was born; to these prairies between the Wichita mountains and the mountains on the Arkansas, over which I roamed when a boy, to see all these Indians, my friends, and the white men, who are my brothers, and to have a talk. I look upon you (General Hazen) as the representative of the Great Father at Washington, and I came to you because I wished to do right; had I wished to do any wrong I never would have come near you. I never would have gone north of the Arkansas again, but my father there (the agent) sent for me time after time, saying it was the place for my people, and finally I went. No sooner had we got there than there was trouble. I do not want war, and my people do not; but although we have come back south of the Arkansas, the soldiers follow us and continue fighting, and we want you to send out and stop these soldiers from coming against us. I want you to send a letter to the Great Father at Washington at once, to tell him to have this fighting stopped; that we want no more of it. Although a chief, a kinsman of mine, has been killed, with others, we will forget it, for we wish for peace."

General Hazen: "The Great Father at Washington sent for me when I was away out in New Mexico, because I had been much with the Indians and like them, to come here and take care of all the Cheyennes, Arapahoes, Apaches, Comanches, and Kiowas; to look after them and their agents and their traders; to get them on to the reservation agreed upon a year ago at Medicine Lodge, and see that they were treated aright. Before I could come from New Mexico, the Arapahoes and Cheyennes had gone to war, so that I could not see them; but I saw the Kiowas, Apaches, and Tapparies Comanches at Fort Larned, and I have come here, as I promised them. I am sent here as a peace chief; all here is to be peace; but north of the Arkansas is General Sheridan, the great war chief, and I do not control him; and he has all the soldiers that are fighting the Arapahoes and Cheyennes. Therefore, you must go back to your country; and, if the soldiers come to fight, you must remember that they are not from me, but from that great war chief, and with him you must make peace. I am glad to see you, and glad to hear that you want peace and not war. I can not stop the war, but will send your talk to the Great Father, and, if he sends me orders to treat you like the friendly Indians, I will send out to you to come in. But you must not come in again unless I send for you; and you must keep well out beyond the friendly Kiowas and Comanches. I am satisfied that you want peace; that it has not been you, but your bad men, that have made the war, and I will do all I can for you to bring peace; *then* I will go with you and your agent on to your reservation, and care for you there. I hope you understand how and why it is that I can not make peace with you."

After these Indians had left Fort Cobb, and were well on their way home, General Hazen, on the 26th of November, wrote Major Ray, in command of the Indian Territory district, that "the Kiowas and Apaches had been in, and taken ten days' rations, and to-day have gone back to their camps,

16

some thirty miles up the Washita; some of them, particularly Satanta, grumbling because they could not have every thing at the post. The Cheyennes and Arapahoes, on their way out, talked badly of fight at the various camps they passed. There is the smallest possibility of their doing any thing of the kind; but, to meet this small possibility, I would be glad if you would move Captain Walsh, with two companies of Tenth Cavalry, up to this neighborhood, remaining a week or two, during which time General Sheridan's movement from above will probably develop, when Captain Walsh can return." Black Kettle, on the same evening of the date of this fire in the rear, entered his village and his lodge, to meet his death, which occurred the next morning. That Black Kettle did not talk war, as he went home from Fort Cobb, at the various camps he passed, is proved beyond the possibility of doubt; for General Hazen, in a note to General Sherman, of the date of December 7th, said: "I think I have succeeded in gaining, to a great degree, the confidence of all the Indians down here; and they have been given to understand, from the first, that this is to be a point where every thing shall be at peace, and where the hostile ones even can come and find peace and friends when the war shall cease. They have sent me word, from the hostile camps, to fear nothing from them; that they understand my mission here; *were pleased with the talk I sent them by Black Kettle*, although he was killed the night after his return, and that they will neither molest my animals nor the peaceful people gathered here." More satisfactory evidence of the peaceful disposition of Black Kettle, on his journey home, could not be desired than the testimony sent from the "hostile camps." The subject will be concluded in the next chapter.

CHAPTER XIII.

CORRESPONDENCE AND OFFICIAL REPORTS OF GEN. SHERIDAN AND GEN. HAZEN, TOUCHING THE STATUS OF THE CHEYENNES AND ARAPAHOES.—AN EXAMINATION OF THE CONTENTS OF THESE.—THE OPERATIONS OF GEN. HARNEY AND GEN. HAZEN, ACTING AS INDIAN AGENTS UNDER THE SUPERVISION OF GEN. SHERMAN.

THE command of Gen. Custer, accompanied by Gen. Sheridan, arrived, as stated, at Fort Cobb on the 18th of December. By that time the comments of the press touching the "Battle of the Washita," had reached there, and all were not complimentary. Indeed, some held that it was not a battle, but the assassination of a friendly band of Indians. The presence of Gen. Sheridan had a remarkable influence on the opinion and judgment of Gen. Hazen, the peace chief of Gen. Sherman. That very evening, December 18, he wrote an open letter to Gen. Garfield, in reference to the "Battle of the Washita," in which he said : " I see a great deal said about the killing of Black Kettle ; that he was on his way to his reservation, where he had been invited by the government. These are all fabrications. Some days before he was killed he came to my camp. . . . He made a fair and, no doubt, truthful talk. He said he deplored the war, and wanted peace. That many of his people were on the war path above the Arkansas, and that his band had been at war all summer. They wanted the war confined to Kansas, but we had brought it below the Arkansas, and he wanted it stopped."

The speeches made by Black Kettle and Big Mouth, as recorded by order of Gen. Hazen, and by him certified, are given word for word in the preceding chapter. There is nothing in either to justify his statement to Gen. Garfield. As a rule, army officers do not hesitate to misrepresent the Indians whenever that course is deemed necessary, and Gen. Hazen does not appear to be an exception to the rule.

Gen. Sheridan also felt called upon to speak, and, on January 1, 1869, wrote Gen. Sherman. In the letter he said : " I

see it alleged by Indian agents, that Black Kettle's band was
on their reservation at the time attacked. This is but thirty
miles up the Washita from Fort Cobb. The battle took place
one hundred and twenty miles up the river from Fort Cobb.
It is also alleged the band was friendly. No one could make
such an assertion with any regard for truth. The young men of
this band commenced the war. I can give their names. Some
of Black Kettle's young men were out depredating at Dodge
when the village was wiped out." Even this bold and positive statement was not satisfactory to every person, and the
affair on the Washita continued to be made the subject of
comment by the press. Hence Gen. Sheridan deemed it necessary, in his annual report of the date of November 1, 1869,
to make a specialty of "the military operations in the department of the Missouri, from October 15, 1868, to March 27,
1869." He justified the campaign against "the hostile Indians south of the Arkansas;" insisted that it was a necessity, owing to the system of robbery and murder practiced by
these Indians for many years, and that the blow struck by
Custer on the Washita, fell on the guiltiest of the bands—
that of Black Kettle. He said: "It was this band that, without provocation, had massacred the settlers on the Saline and
Solomon, and perpetrated cruelties too fiendish for recital.
Black Kettle, its nominal chief—a worn out and worthless
old cipher—was said to be friendly; but when I sent him
word to come into Dodge, before any of the troops had commenced operations, saying that I would feed and protect him
and family, he refused, and was killed in the fight. He was
also with the band on Walnut creek when they made their
medicine, or held their devilish incantations previous to the
party setting out to massacre the settlers." To verify this
statement, Gen. Sheridan embodies in his report the affidavit
of Edmund Guerriere, a half breed who lived with Little
Rock's band. This affidavit was taken at military headquarters of the department of the Missouri, on Wichita mountains,
on the 4th of February, 1869, in the presence of the general,
and attested by one of his staff. This affidavit does not, however, connect Black Kettle with any devilish incantations, nor
does it allege that he was in any way involved in the massa--

-cres, real or imaginary, on the Solomon or Saline. It states that Red Nose, of the Dog Soldiers, and Hach-a-mo-a-he, of Black Kettle's band, were the leaders in the massacre, and that as soon as the news came that fighting had commenced, " we moved from our camp on Buckner's fork of the Pawnee, near its head-waters, down to the North fork, where we met Big Jake's band, and moved south across the Arkansas river." This was after the middle of August, 1868.

This affidavit of Guerriere was made February 4, 1869, whereas the village of Black Kettle was destroyed more than two months previous, and hence, even if true, the facts stated in it were not known to Gen Sheridan when the attack on the village was made.

Gen. Sheridan, in pursuit of his effort to fix hostility and guilt on Black Kettle, said in his report of November, 1869, that on their way down the Washita, in December, 1868, they " found in Black Kettle's village, photographs and daguerreotypes, clothing and bedding, from the houses of the persons massacred on the Solomon and the Saline. The mail which I had sent by the expressmen, Nat. Marshal and Bill Davis, from Bluff creek to Fort Dodge, who were murdered and mutilated, was likewise found ; also a large blank book with Indian illustrations of the different fights which Black Kettle's band had been engaged in, especially about Fort Wallace and on the line of the Denver stages, showing when the fight had been with the colored troops, when with white, also when trains had been captured, and women killed in wagons. Still a hue and cry was raised through the influence of the Indian ring, in which some good and pious ecclesiastics took part, and became the aiders and abettors of savages who murdered without mercy men, women, and children, in all cases ravishing the women, sometimes as often as forty and fifty times in succession, and, while insensible from brutality and exhaustion, forced sticks up their persons, and in one instance, the fortieth savage drew his saber and used it on the person of the woman in the same manner. I do not know exactly how far these humanitarians should be excused on account of their ignorance, but surely it is the only excuse that can give a shadow of justification for aiding and abetting such horrid crimes."

It is a lamentable fact that the Indian is a savage, and his modes of torturing his victim are barbarous. It is the mission of civilization to reclaim him from his savage ways. In our warfare with him, however, and especially since Gen. Sheridan has been the chief officer in the department of the Missouri, in our torture and mutilation of the savage, we have, if possible, excelled him in barbarism. And while we have magnified the barbarity of the Indians in their conflicts with us, we have suppressed our brutal conduct in war with them.

In Custer's report of the " Battle of the Washita," he states that he killed " one hundred and three warriors, including Black Kettle himself, whose scalp is now in the possession of our Osage guides," and " have now in our possession fifty-three squaws and their children." He states that " in the excitement of the fight, as well as in self-defense, it so happened that some of the squaws and a few of the children were killed and wounded." How easy it would have been to have given the number of those that were killed and the number wounded, and why was it not done? It is a fact, though not stated, that no male prisoners were taken over ten years of age. All males above that age that did not escape were killed; and why suppress the fact? In Gen. Sheridan's report he states that the number of squaws and children captured was fifty-three, and not fifty-three squaws and their children, and no doubt he is correct. He repeats this number in his report of November 1, 1869. His language is " one hundred and three warriors killed, and fifty-three women and children captured." It is safe to say that there were in the village more than two women for one man in every lodge—more than one hundred women in the village, and yet but fifty-three women and children were captured; hence there were more than fifty women killed. To make the number of warriors killed, Gen. Custer of course counted all the male Indians down to ten years of age that were slain. The barbaric entry into Camp Supply, and the scalp dance that took place, have been referred to in a previous chapter.

As to the evidences offered that Black Kettle and his band were guilty of the excesses on the Solomon and Saline, it is

submitted that Gen. Sheridan overdoes the matter. How did
he know that the Indians ravished women forty and fifty
times in succession? And as to the illustrated book, how did
he know that it represented the operations of Black Kettle's
band? In point of fact, did he find the photographs, daguerreotypes, clothing, bedding, mail, and blank-book in the
village of Black Kettle? In the report of Gen. Custer of
November 28, 1868, he gave a very minute detail of all the
property found in the village, and said that every thing of
value to the Indians was destroyed. He did not mention one
of these evidences of hostility and guilt, which Gen. Sheridan
affirms were found in the deserted village, after every thing
that fire could reach was burned. Had Custer observed any
of them, he would not only have announced the fact, but preserved these relics as evidence against Black Kettle. He said
not one word about this plunder after he returned to Camp
Supply with the trophies of his victory. He was there seven
days, and then moved south again, accompanied by Gen.
Sheridan. It was the 4th of December when they reached
the field of slaughter, on their way to Fort Cobb. A correspondent of the New York *Herald* was with them. He states
that Sheridan and Custer took a survey of the battle-ground,
and the latter reported to the former the details of the " battle," and the position taken by the different columns; that
the ground was well surveyed, and the details of the operation perfectly understood. "As the party entered within the
area of the fight" (said the correspondent), " the alarm of its
approach was the signal for the flight of innumerable beasts
and birds of prey. Thousands of ravens and crows, disturbed in their carrion feast, rose in one dense black mass,
filling the surrounding air with their mournful notes, and,
soaring over the field, seemed to shower down imprecations
in return for their molestation. . . . Entering the space
occupied by the Indian lodges, on all sides lay the ruins of
the village of Black Kettle's band. *The conflagration started
by the troops was so complete that scarcely any thing of a combust-
ible character escaped, and to-day the debris of the village consisted
in broken and burned lodge poles, and small pieces of tanned and
untanned hides.* . . . The former site of the lodges could

be distinctly seen by the pins ranging in a circle and a fire-place in the center. . . . The scene was one of the most intense solitude. The sunlight glistening upon the hoar frost settled upon the grass and trees, lent a tranquil charm to the landscape; the leafless and inert vegetation and painful silence was the picture of desolation." This correspondent was observing and minute in descriptions and details of all that was seen, and yet he does not say one word of those evidences of hostility which Gen. Sheridan asserts were at that time found. Moreover, Gen. Sheridan, on the 19th, and Gen. Custer, on the 22d of December, 1868, made report of their journey from Camp Supply, *via* the battle-ground, to Fort Cobb, and while many facts and incidents are narrated, among them the delay of a day in the region of and visit to the site of the demolished village, but no reference is made to these trophies of hostility and guilt. The correspondent of the *Herald*, the day after the command arrived at Fort Cobb, wrote out in a lengthy letter the details of the journey, with its incidents and events, but said not one word of these relics, which Gen. Sheridan *afterward, and when required by an emergency, asserted were found in the debris of the village.* It is left with the reader to judge whether it be true that Gen. Sheridan did find these trophies in the debris and ruins of the destroyed village on the Washita.

In the report of Gen. Custer, of the 28th of November, 1868, he informed Gen. Sheridan that, on the morning of the 26th, he "struck a trail of an Indian war party, numbering about one hundred warriors. . . . The direction was toward the southeast," etc. The next day, the 29th of November, Gen. Sheridan made a field, and also wrote an official, report of the "battle" to Gen. Sherman, announcing the victory. The first informs his command of "the defeat, by the Seventh Cavalry, of a large band of Cheyenne Indians, under the celebrated chief Black Kettle, reinforced by the Arapahoes under Little Raven, and Kiowas under Satanta," etc. The second informs Gen. Sherman that the command of Custer, "on the 26th (November), struck the trail of a war party of Black Kettle's band, returning from the north, near where the eastern line of the Pan-handle of Texas crosses the main Canadian, . . . and, on the morning of the 27th, surprised the camp of Black Kettle, and, after a desperate fight, in which Black Kettle was assisted by the Arapahoes under Little Raven, and the Kiowas under Satanta, captured the entire camp," etc. It will be noticed that Custer did not say, or even intimate in any form, that the trail he struck was a war party of Black Kettle's band, nor does he say that Black Kettle was reinforced by Little Raven or Satanta, or assisted by these chiefs, or any other Indians. All he did say was that "the Kiowas under Satanta, and the Arapahoes under Little Raven, were encamped six miles below; the warriors from these two villages came to attempt the rescue of the Cheyennes. They attacked my command from all sides, about noon, hoping to recover the squaws and herd of the Cheyennes." He had previously said that the lodges and all their contents were in his hands within ten minutes after the attack; that the real fighting continued several hours, when his efforts were crowned with success. It was after this fighting was all over, and the warriors killed, that the Kiowas and Arapahoes came, hoping to recover the squaws (prisoners) and herd of the Cheyennes. There is nothing in Custer's report to justify Gen. Sheridan in stating that the trail was that of a war party of Black Kettle's band, or that the chief was reinforced during the "battle" by any Indians whatever. In his annual report of November 1, 1869, Gen. Sheridan, in referring to the trail which Custer struck on November 26, 1868, said that it was the trail of a war party which was "composed, as I *afterward* learned from Indians, of Black Kettle's band of Cheyennes." Unfortunately for him, he did not see any Indians until the afternoon of December 1, 1868, while his field order and letter to Gen. Sherman, in which it was stated that the trail struck was that of a war party of Black Kettle's band, were written more than two days previous.

The Kiowa Indians were located on the Washita, a few miles below the village of Black Kettle, at the time Custer surprised and destroyed it. Philip McCusky was the interpreter for these and the Comanche Indians. Black Eagle, a Kiowa Chief, gave McCusky the first information he had

" concerning the action that recently took place on the Washita river, near the Antelope hills," between a column of United States troops and the Cheyenne Indians. This chief stated that a party of Kiowa Indians, returning from an expedition against the Utes, saw, on the 25th of November, on nearing the Antelope hills, on the Canadian river, a trail going south toward the Washita. On their arrival at the Cheyenne camp, they told the Cheyennes about it, but the Cheyennes only laughed at them. One of the Kiowas concluded to stay all night at the camp, and the rest of them went on to their own camps. About daylight the next morning, the camp was attacked by the troops. The Kiowa who was a guest made his escape, and bore the news to the villages below. On the 3d of December, 1868, McCusky, from Fort Cobb, wrote to Thomas Murphey, the superintendent of Indian affairs, residing at Atchison, Kansas, communicating to him, in detail, the report of the affair, as he received it from Black Eagle. It seems pertinent here to ask the question, if Custer did strike a trail, whether it was not the trail of this war party of Kiowas, who were returning from an expedition against the Utes?

As early as the 22d of August, 1868, Superintendent Murphey inclosed to the commissioner of Indian affairs a letter from E. W. Wynkoop, the Cheyenne and Arapahoe agent, touching " the recent Indian troubles on the Solomon and Saline rivers," with the report of a talk had by the agent with the Cheyenne chief, Little Rock, in relation thereto. Mr. Murphey said: " The agent's letter and report are full, and explain themselves. I fully concur in the views expressed by the agent—that the innocent Indians, who are trying to keep in good faith their treaty pledges, be protected in the manner indicated by him ; while I earnestly recommend that the Indians who have committed these gross outrages be turned over to the military, and that they be severely punished."

Colonel Wynkoop suggested in his letter that he might be permitted to take those Indians whom he knew to be guiltless, and who were desirous of remaining at peace, and locate them and their lodges and families at some point in the vicinity of Fort Larned, and there let them be subsisted entirely by the government until the trouble was over—the Indians to have certain prescribed bounds, and a small squad of troops furnished for their protection. He urged that justice to the Indians who had faithfully held to their treaty obligations demanded that some measure of the kind be taken; that policy dictated it, and that it would be economy in the end. He feared that unless some such measure be immediately adopted, to protect and provide for the class of Indians referred to, that they, in case of war, would most likely be the parties who would suffer, instead of those deserving punishment. He was impressed with the importance of early action, since Gen. Sheridan was making provision for his campaign. He said: " If the department acts at all, it must act *quick;* and, in transmitting this letter, I would respectfully beg, if you favorably indorse the same, that you will urge haste."

The talk between Little Rock and the agent was held at Fort Larned on the 19th of August, 1868, the former having returned from a mission on which the latter had sent him to ascertain, if he could, the facts in relation to the depredations and murders committed on the Solomon and the Saline. Little Rock's report was quite full. He informed the agent that a war party left the Cheyenne camps, above the forks of the Walnut, about the 2d or 3d of August, to go against the Pawnees; that it crossed the Smoky Hill near Fort Hays, and thence proceeded to the Saline. Ten lodges of Sioux and four Arapahoes accompanied it. Little Raven's son was one of the Arapahoes. When the party reached the Saline, they turned down the stream, with the exception of about twenty, who, being fearful of depredations being committed against the whites, by the party going in the direction of the settlements, kept north toward the Pawnees. The main party continued down the Saline, until it came in sight of the settlements, where it camped. A Cheyenne, named Oh-e-ah-mohe-a, a brother of White Antelope, who was killed at Sand Creek, and another, named Red Nose, proceeded to the first house. They afterward returned to camp, and with them a captive woman. The main party was surprised at this action, and forcibly took possession of her, and returned her to her home. The two Indians had outraged the woman before they brought her to the camp. The party then left the Saline, and went north toward the settlements on the south fork of the Solomon, where they were kindly received and fed by the white people. They left these settlements, and proceeded toward the north fork. When in sight of the settlements on this fork, the party came upon a body of armed settlers, who fired upon them; they avoided these, and went around, and approached a house some distance off. In the vicinity of it, they came upon a white man alone upon the prairie. Big Head's son rode at him, and knocked him down with a club. The Indian who committed the outrage upon the woman, known as White Antelope's brother, then fired upon the white man, but without effect, while a third Indian rode up and killed him. Soon after they killed a white man and near by a woman, all in the same settlement. At this time the Indians were divided in feeling, the majority being opposed to any outrages being committed, but, finding it was useless to contend against them without bringing on strife among themselves, they gave way, and all went in together. They then went to another house, where they killed two men, and took two little girls prisoners. The party then turned south toward the Saline, and came on a body of mounted troops, by whom they were charged and pursued. The Indians having the two girls dropped without injuring them. Soon after this the pursuit ceased. The Indians proceeded up the Saline some distance, when the party divided, the majority of it going north, toward the settlements on the Solomon. Thirty of them, however, started on their return to their village near Fort Larned. This is the substance of Little Rock's report. The chief then said: " The other day, when I talked with you, you gave instructions what to do; with a great deal of risk and danger I have followed out these instructions, and returned to you with what is straight, and which I have just given you. I want you, as my agent, to give me advice what to do. I do not wish to be at war with the whites, and there are many of my nation who feel as I do, and who are in no way guilty, and do not wish to be punished for the bad acts of those who are guilty."

Col. Wynkoop then asked Little Rock if he knew the

names of the principal men of the party that committed the depredations beside White Antelope's brother? To which the chief replied: "They were Medicine Arrow's oldest son, named Tall Wolf; Red Nose, who was one of the men who outraged the woman; Big Head's son, named Porcupine Bear, and Sand Hill's brother, known as the Bear that Goes Ahead."

Col. Wynkoop then said: "You told me your nation wants peace; will you, in accordance with your treaty stipulations, deliver up the men whom you have named as being the leaders of the party who committed the outrages named?"

Answer by Little Rock: "I think that the only men who ought to suffer and be responsible for these outrages are White Antelope's brother and Red Nose, the men who ravished the woman, and when I return to the Cheyenne camps and assemble the chiefs and head men, I think these two men will be delivered up to you."

Col. Wynkoop: "I consider the whole party guilty; but it being impossible to punish all of them, I hold the principal men whom you mentioned responsible for all. They had no right to be led and governed by two men. If no depredations had been committed after the outrage on the woman, the two men whom you have mentioned above would have been guilty."

Little Rock: "After your explanation, I think your demand for the men is right. I am willing to deliver them up, and will go back to the tribe and use my best endeavors to have them surrendered. . . . I am here in your service; at the same time I am a Cheyenne, and want to do all I can for the welfare of my people."

Before any thing could be accomplished, the troops were in the field, which put an end to any further attempts looking to a peaceful surrender of the principal Indians engaged in the outrages on the Solomon and Saline.

In the same document in which General Sherman, on the 19th of September, officially announced that he regarded the Cheyennes and Arapahoes at war, and suggested that the well disposed should be separated from the warlike parts of the bands, and conducted to the reservation, there to be provided for under their treaty, say at old Fort Cobb, he said: "I can not consent to their being collected and held near Fort Larned." Fort Cobb was not on their reservation, and besides, his peace agent, General Hazen, was not then at Fort Cobb and did not arrive there for fifty days thereafter. Moreover, no provision had then been made for the reception of friendly Indians at Fort Cobb, and at no time was provision made for the Cheyennes and Arapahoes, at that or any other place during the remainder of that year.

While *en route* to Fort Cobb, and about the time General Custer struck Black Kettle's camp on the Washita, Colonel Wynkoop resigned his position as agent for the Cheyenne and Arapahoe Indians, and returned home to Pennsylvania. On the 26th January, 1869, from Philadelphia, he wrote the commissioner of Indian affairs, and said: "I am perfectly satisfied that the position of Black Kettle, at the time of the attack upon his village, was not a hostile one. *I know that he had proceeded to the point at which he was killed, with the understanding that it was the locality where those Indians who were friendly disposed should assemble. I know that such information had been conveyed to Black Kettle, as the orders of the military authorities, and that he was also instructed that Fort Cobb was the point that the friendly Indians would receive subsistence at. . . .* In regard to the charge that Black Kettle was engaged in the depredations committed on the Saline and Solomon, during the summer of 1868, *I know the same to be utterly false, as Black Kettle at that time was camped near my agency on the Pawnee fork.*"

On his return from an official visit to the Osages, Superintendent Murphey, on the 4th of December, 1868, wrote the commissioner of Indian affairs, and said: "I found in the public journals General Sheridan's report of what he calls 'the opening of the campaign against the hostile Indians,' the perusal of which makes me sick at heart. Had these Indians been hostile, or had they been the warriors who committed the outrages on the Solomon and Saline rivers, in August last, or those who subsequently fought Forsyth and his scouts, no one would rejoice over this victory more than myself. But who were the parties thus attacked and slaughtered by General Custer and his command? It was Black Kettle's band of Cheyennes. Black Kettle, one of the best and truest friends the whites ever had among the Indians of the plains."

It does seem that sufficient evidence has been produced to satisfy every candid and fair minded person that Black Kettle was not engaged in any of the excesses on the Solomon and the Saline, or in any excesses whatever during the year 1868, and that General Sheridan's statements to the contrary, are deliberate misrepresentations. Nevertheless, another item of testimony, coming from a military source, will be given, as confirmatory of what has been already offered. In July, 1869, General Carr, after scouting several days in pursuit of hostile Indians, surprised on the 11th of the month a camp of "Dog Soldiers and Cheyennes," near Valley Station, killing some fifty-two, and capturing a number of women and children. The Indians that escaped (the general said) fled without "a single pack; left most of their saddles, and will have no shelter or food, except horse meat, till they can find buffalo. We captured (said Carr) three hundred and fifty animals, eighty-six lodges, forty rifles, twenty pistols, a number of robes and quantities of camp equipage, which was destroyed. . . . We followed them for ten days, and found them at a spring east of the South Platte, near Valley Station, then went back toward the head of Frenchman's fork." General Augur, then commanding the department of the Platte, in communicating this affair to General Sheridan said: "The prisoners report it to be the only body of Indians known on the Republican. *It is the same that fought Forsyth and all other parties on the Republican last year.*"

With a brief recital of the manner in which Generals Harney and Hazen, as representatives of General Sherman in the disbursement of the money placed by him in their hands, to be expended in the fulfillment of treaty stipulations with the Indians with whom the peace commission had made treaties in 1867 and 1868, this chapter will close, and the reader will have in it and the two preceding ones, the plain, unvarnished story of how General Sherman discharged the high trust reposed in him by Congress, and the fidelity with which the stipulations of the treaties with the Kiowa, Comanche,

Apache, Cheyenne, Arapahoe, and Sioux Indians were fulfilled. By General Sherman's general order of August 10,
1868, the officer in command of each district—Harney and
Hazen—were authorized to detail an officer to act as disbursing agent, and to employ such clerical force as was necessary,
and under no circumstances were any purchases, contracts, or
engagements to be made in excess of the actual money placed
in their hands, being the portion of the appropriation of $500-
000 allotted to their respective districts. Reports and returns
were to be made to General Sherman's headquarters, under
the rules prescribed by army regulations for the subsistence
department. Rules for the government of the district commanders were fully prescribed. The $200,000 set apart for
the Sioux district was placed under the control of General
Harney shortly after the 10th of August, 1868. He was then
at St. Louis. On the 23d of November of the same year he
made report of his doings to General Sherman, and was back
at St. Louis on the 14th of December, 1868. This report embraced all his liabilities to the date of it, and the wages of his
employes to December 31, 1868. His indebtedness was stated
by him to be $485,784.21, and being added to the $200,000
which was turned over to him by General Sherman, made the
aggregate of his operations in a little over three months $684,-
784.21. General Harney stated in his report that as soon as
he got control of the $200,000, he proceeded to purchase such
articles of food, agricultural implements, building materials,
etc., as were necessary for the establishment of the agencies.
The supplies thus purchased were, he said, shipped to their
destination, but the early close of navigation found some on
boats, frozen in on their way up the Missouri, and were carried by land to the "reservations." He said the half breeds
from Fort Laramie, and the Brulés of the Platte, were removed to the reservation and located on the Missouri river, at
the mouth of Whetstone, about thirty miles above Fort Randall. At this point he said he had "established an agency,
erected warehouses, a steam saw-mill, etc., agency buildings,
etc., and provided the Indians with sufficient to support them
until the opening of navigation in the spring, together with
cattle, horses, and agricultural implements to enable them,

under the direction of their farmer, to commence operations
in the spring." Upon this reservation, he said, "about one
hundred houses have already been constructed (November 23),
and that, including Spotted Tail's band at the forks of the
White river, it contains a population of 2,500 Indians and
half breeds. A church and school-house are in process of
erection at this point."

The same report states that a reservation had been established for the Two Kettle, Sans Arc, and Minneconju bands,
near the mouth of the Big Cheyenne river, about twelve
miles above Fort Sully. Here, he said, there were erected" com-
modious warehouses, a steam saw-mill, etc., agency buildings,
and the necessary means and subsistence to last throughout
the winter, and until the Missouri opened the next spring, were
provided. A sufficient supply of work oxen and agricultural
implements have been purchased." At this agency, the report said that about two thousand Indians had already
arrived, and messages had been received from the remainder,
saying they "are doing well amongst the buffalo, and assuring
me of their peaceful intentions, and that they will all come in
early next spring and locate on the reservations assigned
them." General Harney said he made no effort to get them in,
since their frequent arrivals "plainly indicated that they would
be on the reservation, in full force, quite as soon as the government could be ready for their support." At the mouth of
Grand river, General Harney said he had established a reservation for the Uncpapas, Cut Heads, and the temporary
location of the Yanktonais and Blackfeet Sioux. At this
point he said: "I have the most important and extensive
agency within the Sioux reservation. A steam saw-mill, etc.,
have been erected here; also, several large warehouses and
six agency buildings have been constructed. The necessary
supplies have been purchased for the support of the Indians
at this upper agency until the opening of navigation in the
spring. The number of Indians already on the reserve is
four thousand five hundred. . . . I have," said the general, "supplied this agency with work cattle and farming implements sufficient to enable the Indians to commence the

17

cultivation of the soil early next season, under the direction of their farmers."

If the statements of General Harney be true, he had accomplished a marvelous amount of work in a very short space of time, especially when we call to mind the fact that the agencies established by him were hundreds of miles apart, with the navigation of the river impeded by low water, an early freeze up, and the rigors of a Dakota winter to obstruct his progress. A tabular statement of his employes, embraced in his report, is a curiosity. His own headquarters (for he was a general in our army) were at Peoria Bottom. There was, at this point, no agency established; nor did any Indians dwell here. Still he had sixteen employes, classified as follows, viz : Commissary, clerk, interpreter, foreman, blacksmith, farmer, butcher, cook, each one; carpenter, herder, each two; laborers four—in all, sixteen. At Whetstone agency, eighteen employes; at Cheyenne agency, thirty-three employes, and at Grand river, thirty-six employes—in all, eighty-seven. These are classified as follows: Teamster and ferryman, each one; superintendent, foreman, blacksmith, and butcher, each two; interpreter, engineer, and cook, each three; clerks, four; carpenter and farmer, each six; herders, fourteen, and laborers, fifty-three. Work oxen and horses, according to the report, are supplied in abundance, and yet but one teamster. About a hundred houses are built at Whetstone agency; also a warehouse, agency buildings, and a steam saw-mill; and a church and school-house are in process of erection, and work cattle and horses are there, and yet but one carpenter, one teamster, and eleven laborers are employed! It is needless to analyze the report at the other agencies, or reservations, as they are termed by General Harney. The reader can do that at leisure. It may be stated, that few evidences remained in 1876 of such improvements as General Harney reported to have been made in the fall of 1868, though if the houses of various kinds, mills, churches, etc., had been permitted to go into rapid decay, it would seem the debris ought to remain as a monument to the marvelous energy that wrought such wonders in so short a time. In 1876, the remains of some timber wheels, in a country where there was no need of them, as well as the remnants of some old "condemned" military wagons, were still visible, to attest the folly of General Harney's attempt to fulfill the provisions of the Sioux treaty of 1868.

It is to be observed that in his report Gen. Harney claims to have had on his three reservations only about nine thousand Indians, out of the whole Sioux nation, and these were, except the twenty-five hundred at Whetstone, Indians who, for years previous, had resided on the Missouri river, and were then living under the provisions of the treaties made with them in 1865. The great body of the Sioux, those residing on the Powder, Tongue, Big Horn, and other rivers, the Rosebud and other streams, and who roamed in the vast country south of the Yellowstone and east of the summit of the Big Horn mountains,(the pacification of whom was the prime object of the treaty of 1868) were not on the Missouri river, and had no lot or part in the rations and supplies that were furnished that fall and preceding winter. The balance-sheet of Gen. Harney is embodied in his report as "an estimate of indebtedness over and above the sum appropriated for the Sioux Indian District, under general order No. 4, dated August 10, 1868." Here it is:

Vouchers approved......................................	$62,142 65
Smith & Peck, for provisions...........................	204,994 87
Smith & Peck, for freight...............................	112,646 49
Boggs & Co., for cattle now being delivered......	55,000 00
John Finn, for cattle now being delivered.........	40,000 00
Pay due employes to January 1, 1869, about......	11,000 00
	$485,784 21

This sum, be it remembered, is in addition to the $200,000 turned over to him by Gen. Sherman, on the 10th of August, 1868. In his report Gen. Harney states that he was "compelled to enter into a considerable amount of indebtedness, but it was absolutely necessary to get up sufficient supplies to last until the opening of the Missouri river, next season, and the parties who undertook to furnish the goods, relying on Congress to make provision for payment, have performed their duty honestly and faithfully. No clothing whatever has been purchased. The purchases consisted mainly of provisions, viz: Flour, corn, bacon, coffee, sugar, and beef cattle, building materials, steam saw-mills, etc. The lateness of the season at which I was enabled to commence operations, made transportation very costly, and is a considerable item in the indebtedness incurred. Two boat loads of provisions were sunk, but were insured, and I have made up for the want of these goods, by purchasing largely of beef cattle, which have just been brought up at this late season. . . . I am perfectly satisfied with the success which has attended the commencement of this work, and can unhesitatingly declare that to insure perpetual peace with the Sioux Indians, it is only necessary to fulfill the terms of the treaty made by the peace commission."

In transmitting Gen. Harney's report to the secretary of war, Gen. Sherman said that the expenses were larger than he had authorized, and asked that Gen. Harney might be permitted to visit Washington to advocate the justice and propriety of his course, and to procure an appropriation of money to cover his past outlays, and to carry into full effect his plan of putting to work in the spring every band of these Indians. He said: " I have no doubt Gen. Harney has laid the foundation for a system which, if persevered in, will, in time, domesticate the larger part of this powerful nation of Indians, and withdraw them from the railroads that have been built across the continent."

It may be safely assumed that the personal knowledge of Gen. Harney as to what was being done at any of the " reservations " where he established agencies, either in improvements or the issue of supplies to the Indians, was very slight. His headquarters were at a point where no Indians were, and the charge of, and duties pertaining to the agencies, were by him relegated to others ; and it is probable that at no time had Gen. Sherman any personal knowledge in the premises. How much money, if any, in addition to the amount he reported as due November 23, 1868, was required and obtained to carry out the enterprise through the winter and spring, may, it is presumed, be ascertained by searching the files of the war department. It does not appear that any further report was ever published of the operations of Gen. Sherman in fulfillment of the treaty stipulations with the Sioux. If the work had been done by civil agents, and in the same manner, no doubt some one would have been curious enough to have called for information, and army officers at that time stationed in the valley of the Missouri would have had a theme on which to dwell with emphasis.

After Gen. Harney retired from the Sioux district, military agents were for some time continued in employment at all the agencies he established. Capt. Poole made his first report as agent of the Whetstone agency on the 20th of August, 1869. He states in it that Whetstone creek extended back into the country but a short distance, was not supplied with running water, and was nearly dry, except in rainy weather. Cottonwood was found on either bank in limited quantities. The valley of the creek bottom was quite narrow, and contained a limited quantity of arable land. A narrow strip of land on the Missouri, he was of the opinion, might be cultivated, but the hills in the rear could not. He reported the number of Indians located at this agency at one thousand souls only, and these were called the "Loafer" band, and composed of individuals who from time to time seceded from the various bands of Sioux and Cheyennes. They were inclined to cultivate the soil and to civilized life, and had among them seventy-seven whites, who had married into the Indian families. He stated that the material for the buildings constructed and in course of construction at this agency was taken from an island in the Missouri river, opposite the agency. He said that most of the agricultural implements turned over to him, and which could not have been in use but a very short time, were " very much worn, and needed repairs; also the wagons, which consisted of a number of very old ones, brought from Fort Laramie, were almost useless, and being very large and heavy, could be used only with oxen. The same is much the case with all the public property, and is so stated in all invoices and receipts rendered by the agent turning over the same." Capt. Poole also stated that the quantity of annuity goods previously distributed was very small—so small that in the subdivision of the same much discontent was exhibited, since the great majority of the Indians received nothing. He further said that no school or mission house; no buildings for carpenter, farmer, blacksmith, miller, or engineer; no agency buildings or residence for physician, had been erected. The employes were engaged at the date of his report in erecting warehouses for storage. One was completed before he took charge, and he had completed a second one, and two more were under way. An office building and a small mess-house were completed. He said nothing of the one hundred houses reported by Gen. Harney as having been built the previous fall. Such is substantially the report of Capt. Poole as to the condition of things at his agency. This paragraph appears in his report: " In stating any plan of benevolence the government may adopt in the future, they recall the promises made by the parties mentioned in the treaty last year, and ask, pertinently, who can they believe now? An agent can do little to regain their confidence, in the face of treaty stipulations so lately unfulfilled."

On the 16th of August, 1869, Capt. George M. Randall, agent at the Cheyenne " reservation," made his first report; and on the 26th of September, 1869, Major J. N. Hearn, agent at the Grand river " reservation," made his first report. Neither of these officers go into details, as did Capt. Poole, and they make no mention whatever of the extended improvements made at Cheyenne and Grand river, the previous fall by Gen. Harney. These same military officers were continued in charge of their respective agencies during the year 1870. Their reports of that year have but little that is specific, and nothing that is encouraging. They state facts, however, which show that in some important matters there was gross neglect on the part of superior officers, either in the interior or war department, or both, and furnish abundant evidence that the civilization of the Indian is not a duty to be successfully pursued by military officers.

The foundation laid by Gen. Harney for the domestication of the Sioux, which was so satisfactory to Gen. Sherman, was for several years pursued under a mixed administration of military and civil agents, and afterward, when all the duties were confided to civilians, there was military interference and dictation from military officers, and the result was that for the six years ending June 30, 1876, there was expended for the support and civilization of the Sioux, on the average, more than two millions of money per year, with scarcely any favorable results or good impressions being made on the greater part of the Indians.

Gen. Hazen, to whom was assigned the conduct of Indian affairs in the southern district, in a communication of the 10th of November, 1868, stated that he received the order assigning him to that district, to have charge of the Indians of the same with whom treaties had been made, about the first of September, and that he had verbal instructions as to his duties on the thirteenth of the month. The order was promulgated on the 10th of August, 1868. He was, by its terms, to repair to Fort Cobb, in the Indian Territory, to take charge of the Indians, and proceed to the fulfillment of their treaty stipulations. As early as September 17, Gen. Sherman had officially declared the Cheyenne and Arapahoe Indians at war, and suggested that the superior orders of the president be invoked against the issue of any goods, even clothing, being given to them. On the 19th and 20th of September, Generals Hazen and Sheridan were together at Fort Larned. General Hazen then understood that these Indians were declared hostile and at war, and afterward, in his correspondence with Gen. Sherman, said : " I have considered them since that time as beyond my authority till they shall be turned over by Major-General Sheridan, who is now dealing with them." This left only the Kiowa, Comanche, and Apache under the supervision of Gen. Hazen, when he assumed his duties at Fort Cobb. He did not get there until the 7th of November. On the 30th of October, Col. Alvord, whom Gen. Hazen had sent to Fort Cobb, wrote Maj. J. P. Ray, holding a military position in the Indian Territory, that the Kiowa and Comanche whom Gen. Hazen had seen at Fort Larned, and who were again to join him (Hazen) at that post, preparatory to moving down to Fort Cobb, " for fear of some trick, and from a dislike to traveling with soldiers, as they state, decided among themselves not to go to Larned, but to come directly here, and they did so accord-

ingly, moving together on the direct trail from Fort Larned
to this place, till they reached the Canadian, where they
camped and sent here to ascertain whether Gen. Hazen was
on time. Finding he was not, and by keeping couriers out,
knowing he was not en route, the Kiowas, hungry, moved
westward to the neighborhood of the Antelope Hills to hunt
buffalo, and they are there now. . . . The Comanches remained on the Canadian, sending hunting parties west."
Black Kettle and other Cheyennes and Arapahoes were, at
that time, just north of the Antelope Hills. They knew from
the Kiowas, who had been at Fort Cobb, that Gen. Hazen was
not there, and hence they remained, for the time being, where
they could hunt buffalo. Black Eagle informed Col. Alvord
that Black Kettle and other chiefs would soon be at Fort
Cobb, to arrange for moving their people down. This could
not be done, however, until Gen. Hazen arrived to attend to
the duties assigned him. Col. Alvord said to Col. Ray:
" The military superintendent (Hazen) and the agent are both
looked for, but are not here. . . . And the promised subsistence is not here." Instead of being at Fort Cobb, Gen.
Hazen was, after the middle of October, among the Kaw Indians, coquetting with them for warriors to join Gen. Sheridan's invading army. Had he been at Fort Cobb, he might
have ascertained that there was no foundation for the charge
of hostility against the Cheyennes and Arapahoes, and been
enabled to give Gen. Sherman correct information as to the
location and disposition of these Indians. It might, perhaps,
have availed nothing, since both Sheridan and Sherman had
decided to make war upon them, and, to justify themselves,
had declared that the Indians were at open war. Gen. Hazen
did not only delay, but when he finally set out for Fort Cobb,
he carried with him the views and feelings of Gen. Sherman
as to the temper and status of the Cheyennes and Arapahoes.

On the 10th of November he made up and forwarded to
Gen. Sherman an estimate of the amount of funds he would
require for six months from November 15, 1868, to ration the
Indians at Fort Cobb. This estimate amounted to $127,700.
He did not include one dollar in the estimate to be applied to
ration the Cheyennes and Arapahoes. On the 20th of No-

vember, a delegation from these Indians, headed by Black Kettle and Big Mouth, visited Gen. Hazen at Fort Cobb, and requested permission to bring their bands there to dwell with him. He declined to permit them to do so.

On the 15th of November, 1868, he made contracts for rations of beef and corn to supply the Indians for six months from that time, to be paid for monthly provided the officer receiving the rations was supplied with funds by the government; if he were without funds the payment was to be deferred until funds were provided. He had $50,000 set apart for his use by Gen. Sherman, and was expressly prohibited, in general order No. 4, from creating any obligation in excess of that sum. Like Harney, among the Sioux, he paid no attention to this limitation upon his action.

On the 7th of December, 1868, he advised Gen. Sherman that Col. Boone, the new agent of the Kiowas and Comanches, was at Fort Arbuckle, on his way to Cobb, but without any annuities, and advised that he do not come among the Indians without them, since so many promises have been made about these annuities and none of them carried out.

Not having much to do in fulfilling the stipulations of the treaties of 1867, with the Indians parties to them, since the Cheyennes and Arapahoes were outlawed, and the Apaches and many of the Kiowas and Comanches were still among the buffalo, Gen. Hazen amused himself in corresponding with Gen. Sherman in relation to the transfer of the Indian bureau to the war department. The Indian agent, in his opinion, was a poor fellow at best, and frequently the chum and partner with the Indian trader. He exalted the horn of the army officer, and presented his fine points and qualifications for an Indian agent, and was satisfied there would be, in the transfer, a great economic advantage. This he illustrated in his own case. " Why," said he, " I will get the ration here for about one-half what was paid for it last year by the Indian bureau, and I think the same has been true in New Mexico, where the army has fed the Navajoes." This was all said on the 10th of November. On December 1, having then some Indians assembled to whom rations were issued, he wrote Gen. Sherman and said: " I am surprised how little money I am getting on with, and I am informed that my expenses are only about one-tenth monthly what it has usually cost to care for the Indians here. I only feed the actual number of Indians present with a ration, all of which they require, while it has been the custom to bear upon the returns a vastly larger number, all of whom a ration was counted against, and so composed that most of the articles could either be neglected or commuted." The contents of this communication were so pleasing to Gen. Sherman, that in transmitting it to the secretary of war, he said: "Gen. Hazen's assertion that he only provides for such as he *knows* to be there, accounts for the other assertion that the subsistence of the Indians costs only one-tenth of former years. I hope the secretary of war will be *careful* to have these papers, as also others of a similar kind, sent heretofore, carefully laid before the committee of Indian affairs of the Senate." He ought to have added, "since they may be valuable in promoting our scheme of the transfer of the Indians to the army."

Shortly after the arrival of Gen. Hazen at Fort Cobb, he received fifteen days' rations for the few Indians that were at that place, and one hundred head of beef cattle from the subsistence department of the army. The first of December may be assumed as the period at which he began to provide food for the Indians at Cobb, and his duties ceased on the 30th of June, 1869. He found he could not obtain the ration at six cents, as he had reported he could, but that the ration of beef and breadstuff, the latter sometimes reduced in quantity, would cost eight cents. He said, however, that for many months in the spring, summer, and autumn, but little beef was required, the buffalo affording ample meat, which the Indians preferred.

In November he wrote Peter Cooper, chairman of the New York Indian Commission, and invited one of the commission, or some person deputed by it, to visit Fort Cobb, and there, with him, study the condition and wants of the Indians. He said the government was assembling, under his direction, from 8,000 to 10,000 wild Indians at Cobb. Mr. Vincent Colyer, the secretary, was, upon this invitation, sent down to Fort Cobb. He was there after midwinter and spent some time. On his departure, he brought away a census or statement of all Indians of both sexes, and all ages, belonging to the Southern Indian District, from actual count and the best authority. This statement was made up by an army officer (Captain Charles G. Penney), and embraced not only the Kiowa, Comanche, and Apache, but the Cheyenne and Arapahoe, and the Wichita and affiliated bands. It was of the date of February 1, 1869, and embraced not only the Indians present, and to whom the rations were issued, but those absent among the buffalo. The number of Indians at that time, of all ages, and including all the bands named, whether absent or present, was 7,638. Of this number, 3,241 were dwelling near Fort Cobb, and 4,397 were absent. General Hazen gave the gross number, on June 30, 1869, at 7,339, of which he estimated as on the reservation 4,339, and absent 3,000. It is believed that the number stated to be on the reservation, or rather near Fort Cobb, on the 1st of February— to wit, 3,241—would be a liberal estimate for the whole period of the administration of General Hazen, although that officer estimated a larger number in the summer, when the Indians would naturally seek the buffalo, the meat of which they preferred. General Hazen reported that when he left, on June 30, 1869, there were supplies on hand sufficient for two months. This being so, he supplied rations for 3,241 Indians for nine months, which would require 884,793 rations; at 8 cents each, these rations would cost $70,783.44. To discharge this bill for rations alone, he had at his command only $50,000, of which he had expended for labor, $3,730; for traveling expenses, $610; for needful things for the Indians, such as clothing, medicine, implements, and two houses built for the chiefs, $4,410—in all, $8,750; leaving, of the $50,000, the sum of $41,250, to be applied to the ration account; and, when so applied, leaving due, on this account, the sum of $29,533.44. In his final report, he states that there is due from the government, on his accounts, $56,106.86, for which he submitted an exhibit in detail; but this is not printed with his report, although referred to in it. As the exhibit is not printed, it can not be analyzed here; but it appears, from the figures, that his indebtedness exceeds the cost of the rations, and the incidental expenses above stated, the sum of $26,573.42.

In his report General Hazen said, that "the feeding of Indians here, the eight months before my arrival, was made a matter of grand speculation, amounting to fraud. An investigation of the matter shows that the United States paid some six times what the service was worth; and, unfortunately, much of this came from what was intended for the Indians' benefit in other ways." The document from which this extract is taken was prepared at Camp Wichita, and it is presumed had special reference to what occurred at the Wichita agency, the Indians of which, after his arrival at Fort Cobb, were under his supervision, and are embraced in those classed as on the reservation, and to whom rations were issued. Henry W. Shanklin was the agent of those Indians, but was not among them, or at the agency, after the 1st of October, 1868, having left because of the confused state of Indian affairs, growing out of General Sheridan's campaign "against the hostile Indians south of the Arkansas." He had under his care while agent, in addition to the Wichita and affiliated bands, the Delawares and Shawnees, then located within what was known as the leased district. The Wichita and affiliated bands on the reservation, by the statement furnished Mr. Colyer, February 1, 1869, numbered 898 souls, of all ages and both sexes. To ration these for one year, at eight cents per ration (General Hazen's price), would cost the sum of $26,221.60. The amount appropriated by Congress, for the year ending June 30, 1868, for the Wichita and other affiliated bands, for expenses of colonizing, supporting, and furnishing them with agricultural implements, stock, clothing, medicine, iron, steel, maintenance of schools, and pay of employes, was $37,800. Of this amount, agent Shanklin expended, during the year, only $24,971.87, divided as follows: For the Indian service, in the district of country leased from the Choctaws, the sum of $14,628.05; colonizing, supporting, etc., the Wichita and other affiliated bands, $5,593.07; pay of superintendents and agents, $2,956.25; pay of interpreters, $400; contingencies, $239.25; buildings at agency, $993.61; vaccination of Indians, $161.65—making the gross sum, as above, $24,971.87; and leaving unexpended, of the appropriation of $37,800, nearly $13,000. The appropriation made by Congress for this same agency, for the year ending June 30, 1869, was, for all purposes, only $15,000, which was made July 27, 1868, none of which, it is presumed, came into the hands of agent Shanklin, since he left the Indian country on the 1st of October, 1868, and did not return. From the foregoing facts, it is submitted that General Hazen was not warranted in asserting that Shanklin paid six times as much as the service was worth, or that, for eight months before his arrival, the agent had made the matter of feeding the Indians a "grand speculation, amounting to fraud." It is shown that to ration the 898 Indians of the Wichita and other affiliated bands would have cost per year, at eight cents per ration, $26,221.60, whereas Shanklin had expended, for all purposes, during his last year, only $24,971.87; and out of this sum, for these Indians only $5,593.07; the residue being expended for the Indian service in the leased district.

Col. Leavenworth, the agent for the Kiowa, Comanche, and Apache Indians, left the Indian country, on the 26th of May, 1868, and did not return, hence he could not have been engaged in feeding Indians, or any operations among them, in the eight months preceding the date of the report of Gen. Hazen, in which he makes this charge.

Col. Wynkoop, the agent of the Cheyennes and Arapahoes, had his agency more than two hundred miles from Fort Cobb, and did not operate in that region at all. He was north of the Arkansas. Moreover, nearly ten months before the date of Gen. Hazen's report, the military had declared Wynkoop's Indians hostile and at war, and thereafter he had no official connection with them, and left the Indian country before Gen. Hazen reached Fort Cobb.

According to the reports of the agents, in 1867 and 1868, of the number of the Indians in their charge, as tabulated in the report of the commissioner of Indian affairs, the Kiowas and Comanches are placed at 4,000; the Cheyennes and Arapahoes at 3,000; and Wichita and other affiliated bands, at 1,175—making the whole number, 8,175. The census and estimates of these same Indians, made by one of Gen. Hazen's military officers, on the first of February, 1869, gave the gross number at 7,638, only 537 less than the returns of the agents. The band of Cheyennes that went north in August, 1868, and those killed at the " Battle of the Washita," on the 27th of November of that year—say 350 in all—added to those in the military statement of February, 1869, would bring up the number to 7,988, only 187 less than the number reported by the agents. In the light of this exhibit, what becomes of the assertion of Gen. Hazen, that he found, on his arrival at Fort Cobb, that the Indians had been greatly exaggerated, and were then " rated at fully double their numbers ? "

The entire appropriations for the support of the Kiowa, Comanche, and Apache Indians, for the year ending June 30, 1868, were $58,000. These were under the care of Col. Leavenworth. The appropriations for the same year, for agent Shanklin's Indians, were, as stated, $38,700, and of which he expended only $24,971.87. Add this sum to the $58,000, and we have the sum of $82,971.87, as the largest possible amount that these agents expended, provided Leavenworth exhausted all his appropriations. Gen. Hazen shows that he had expended and owed for rations, for only nine months, when he had less than one-half of the Indians belonging to these agencies to feed, the sum of $97,356.86. At the same rate, for three additional months, to make up the year, and it would cost him, to feed less than one-half of the Indians, $130,142.48, or $47,214.51 more than the sum expended during the preceding year for all the Indians. This, it would seem, dissipates the boasted economy of Gen. Hazen's Indian management, and stamps with emphasis his statement that he only required one-tenth of the sum that the civil agents had previously absorbed in feeding Indians. He, of course, had no data upon which to base his statements as to the number of Indians the agents had upon their rolls, or the cost of feeding them; and whatever information he obtained was from those who intended to flatter and deceive him, and such stories Gen. Sherman thought it important to impress the secretary of war to be *careful* to have laid before the Indian Committee of the Senate! A reference to them here, and the comparison gone into, is to demonstrate, not only to senators, but to all people, that army officers, when dealing with the Indian question, are not reliable; that their prejudice against civil agents is so deep, that any story, no matter how unfounded, is accepted by them, assumed as fact, and, unfortunately, placed in their reports, and thus made a part of history. It is certain that Gen. Hazen had no facts or information from others, that was reliable, on which to make such sweeping statements as he did in relation to the manner in which Indian agents had discharged their duties previous to his arrival at Fort Cobb. The manner in which Gen. Sherman, either personally or through his military agents, fulfilled his duty, and discharged the high trust reposed in him by Congress, is here left with the reader, without further comment.

CHAPTER XIV.

MILITARY OPERATIONS IN MONTANA IN 1869 AND 1870.—THE DESTRUCTION OF
THE PIEGAN INDIAN CAMP BY COL. BAKER.—MILITARY CORRESPONDENCE AND
REPORTS TOUCHING THE CAMPAIGN.

THE fabulous stories in relation to the mineral treasures in
Montana, which gained currency in 1865, almost frenzied the
people, and induced thousands to rush thither to possess themselves of the product of the mines. The idea that the native
population had any rights there, never for one moment occupied the mind or conscience of those who hurried forward to
these reputed fountains of wealth. The rights and interests
of the Indian were wholly lost sight of. He was treated as an
alien and an outlaw, and wherever found was dealt with accordingly. The natural result was that when the Indian could
he retaliated, and depredations were committed and whites
were killed. Indian resistance and outbreaks were promptly
published, often in a magnified form. Acting Governor Meagher
inaugurated a war against the Indians on his own motion.
He had no authority from the government, but he acted, and
called for one thousand miners, to arm and equip for the campaign. He gave them full license, and guaranteed them all
the property they could take from the Indians, and a liberal
bounty for every Indian scalp.

The Bloods and Blackfeet had for many years been on
friendly terms with the whites, and the agents of the Great
Father. As far as possible, these Indians tried to evade the
scouting parties, and avoid conflicts with Meagher's troops.
They were distinct and did not reside in the same section of
country. With all their caution and friendly disposition, they
did not at all times escape, but suffered in loss of property, and
a number of them were killed.

The Piegans, at least one band of them, that of Mountain
Chief, was disposed to resent and resist injury, and for wrong
done to his band, where he could, he retaliated. Mr. Culbert-
son, a truthful man and long a resident among the Blackfeet,

and intimately acquainted with the Indians in Montana, and with their disposition and temper, stated to Gen. Sully, in a note written him on the 2d of September, 1869, that he had just arrived from the interior, where he had been " since last winter with the Bloods and Blackfeet Indians. These people (he said) are perfectly friendly to the whites, and up to the time I left there, they evinced no disposition to be otherwise." He said of the Piegans that they had lived in almost constant communication with Fort Benton, and that he was surprised to hear of their raids upon the whites, and that his knowledge of their character for a great many years would not permit him to think that there existed a general hostile feeling among them. He supposed that whatever depredations had been committed were by some of the " young rabble over whom the chiefs have no control."

Gen. Sully was then, and had been for some time previous, acting as superintendent of Indian affairs in Montana. Early in August, 1869, he had advised the commissioner of Indian affairs that he apprehended trouble; that the portion of the citizens of the territory who were law-abiding were anxious for peace with the Indians, and would willingly render any assistance in their power to aid the authorities to carry out the laws, if they were backed by military force, but there were not troops sufficient for that purpose. He asked the commissioner to apply for an increase of the military force. He said that war parties of Indians from the Powder river country, the British Possessions, and from Idaho and Washington territories frequently visited Montana, and committed depredations on the whites; that the latter retaliated by killing any Indians they chanced to meet, and sometimes in the most brutal and cowardly manner; he said there was a white element in the territory which, from its rowdy and lawless character, could not be excelled in any section, and the traffic in whisky with the Indians was carried on to an alarming extent. He spoke of the fact that about ten days previous, a harmless old man and a boy about fourteen years old, both Piegans, were murdered in broad daylight in the streets of Benton; that he intended to try to arrest the murderers, but doubted very much

18

if he could convict them in any court; he concluded that nothing could be done to insure peace or order, "until there was a military force strong enough to clean out the roughs and whisky sellers."

On the 22d of September, 1869, General Sully, as superintendent, again wrote to the commissioner of Indian affairs in relation to alleged depredations, supposed to be committed by Blackfeet Indians. Lieutenant Pease, who was their agent, had communicated depredations to General Sully, and expressed the opinion that the Bloods and Blackfeet had nothing to do with the matter; that from what he could learn the depredations were committed by a small band of the Piegan Indians, and that they had moved north. He said in his communication that all the Indians were desirous that the agency should be supported, and the conditions of the treaty of 1868 fulfilled, so that they could be maintained according to promises made them. No part of the $500,000 voted to General Sherman to fulfill treaty stipulations, had been set apart by him to fulfill the stipulations with any of these Indians.

All these communications were referred to the war department, and thence to General Sheridan. That officer responded in a note to the adjutant-general, of the date of October 21, 1869, and said that there had been so few troops in Montana that he had been unable to do much against the Indian marauders, but as the regiments were filling up he thought it would be the best plan to let him find out exactly where these Indians (the Piegan tribe he referred to) were going to spend the winter, and about the time of a good heavy snow, he would send out a party and try and strike them. He named the 15th of January as the time when they would be "very helpless, and if where they live is not too far from Shaw or Ellis, we might be able to give them a good hard blow." He added, "we must strike where it hurts, and if the general-in-chief thinks well of this, I will try and steal a small force on this tribe from Fort Shaw or Ellis, during the winter."

The adjutant-general of the army, under date of November 9, 1869, advised General Sheridan that his communication of October 21 had been submitted to the general of the army, and his proposed action in relation to the punishment of the Piegans, as therein stated, was approved; and on the 15th of November, General Sheridan inclosed the correspondence to General Hancock, with whom, before that period, he had been in private correspondence about the punishment of these Indians, and informed him that authority was given to punish the Piegans if found within striking distance, "and you are authorized by me (said Sheridan) to extend this authority to any of the Blackfeet who may have been engaged in the murders and robberies lately perpetrated in Montana." He adds: " Major Baker, who is now en route to Fort Ellis, is a most excellent man to be intrusted with any party you may see fit to send out. *I spoke to him on the subject when he passed through Chicago.* It will be of no use to make the attempt unless the positions of the villages are well known. The greatest care should be taken to keep the Indians from gaining any information on the subject. It will be impossible to strike these murderers unless the greatest secrecy is maintained."

On the 10th of November, 1869, five days before Gen. Sheridan had officially notified General Hancock that he had authority to punish the Piegans, and extended the authority so as to punish the Blackfeet also, that officer, from his headquarters at St. Paul, communicated to General De Trobriand his desire that the latter should ascertain where the " offending Blackfeet are wintering, and if necessary to pay for information, or to hire guides or scouts for such purpose, you are authorized to do so, reporting to these headquarters what action you have taken." General Hancock adds: " Of course such information would be more valuable if it does not become a matter of notoriety that we are seeking it. If we can get at the Indians during the winter by a quick active march, we might surprise their camps."

The reader has no doubt noted what General Sully said in his dispatches of the 3d of August and 27th of September, 1869. He, though an army officer, was for the time being superintendent of Indian affairs in Montana, and Lieutenant Pease, another army officer, was the agent of the Blackfeet Indians. It is not necessary to repeat their statements.

General De Trobriand was the military commander in Montana. In a lengthy dispatch sent by him to General Hancock, on the 10th of September, he said he had been absent fourteen days traveling, and at military posts. During this time he stated that he " saw many different people, had long talks with most of them, and neglected no opportunity of getting full and reliable information about the *real* facts which gave rise to the excitement in regard to Indian hostilities; what part was to be attributed to exaggerated reports, and what part to interested speculations." He said the facts were those previously narrated, and no more, viz: " The attack on two white men, who died of their wounds at Benton; the execution of two bad Indians, and the murder of two other innocent ones at the same place; the attack on one of the government trains at Eagle creek, between Cook and Benton; the murder of Mr. Clark, and the attempted murder of his son, by a party of Piegans, led by Peter, an Indian brother-in-law of Mr. Clark, the sons of Mountain Chief, Bear Chief, and others not well known. This, as I mentioned previously, is the bloody *denouement* of a long-standing family quarrel." The general then recited some horse-stealing in the direction of the Yellowstone, and expressed the opinion that the party must have divided, or some other Indians must have seized the opportunity of depredating, since at the same time some horses were stolen in another direction. He then said: " These are the only facts so far, for I can not include in the Indian hostilities, the highway robbery of the mail and express, twice repeated, for it was done by white brigands." He further stated that the Blackfeet, Pend d'Orrilles, Bloods, and even part of the Piegans, remained perfectly quiet, protesting that " they have nothing to do with the attacks on the persons and property of white men, that they want no war, but peace, and that they are ready to come and stay on whatever reservation may be assigned them." These assurances General DeTrobriand said came to him through the agencies, " and are so far corroborated by the peaceful attitude of the tribes above named." He expressed the opinion that the responsibility for the hostilities and depredations rested exclusively on a band of Piegans and some roving vagabonds of different tribes, " acting on their own hook, and independently of their own people." From what follows, it is not improbable that had General De Trobriand been enabled to see the band of Piegans referred to, and heard their story, he might with propriety have exculpated them of the guilt of the crimes which he assumes they committed. He does not, however, consider this statement as formidable, probably because of the vast amount of all sorts of crime daily committed by the element among the whites, spoken of by Generall Sully. General De Trobriand said, in his indictment against the Indians : " This is not, altogether, very formidable, but was enough to spread terror between Benton and Helena, and scare the greater part of the territory, as shown by the rush upon me, from all sides, for military protection. . . This caused some commotion and a great deal of talk at Helena. Of course, there was a cry for more troops, and a corresponding blame upon the government for leaving the frontier so unprotected. For it is a remarkable fact, that when there is no apparent danger, and no cause for apprehension, people will think there is *always too much* of military, while if a handful of redskins appear upon the bluffs, shaking their buffalo robes, it turns out suddenly that there is *never enough* of it, according to the same people. In this case I strongly suspect there is some interested scheme on the part of some parties to magnify the danger, exaggerate the reports, and through the general excitement to bring the governor, then just arrived, to issue a proclamation to raise a regiment of mounted volunteers. This, if successful, would have procured some fat jobs for somebody or other, at the expense of the government. But when I broke the subject to Governor Ashley, I found at once that he had seen through the game, and that no proclamation would be issued, at least without real necessity. . . There was another proposition discussed freely, not only at Helena, but along the road to Benton and to Gallatin valley. This was simply an authorization asked by certain men to organize companies to chase and fight the Indians, wherever they might find them. They asked for no pay, no arms, no equipments, no horses, but only for whatever captures they could make from the enemy. This was, I think, still more dangerous to the white farmers than to the red Indians, and no doubt that such bands let loose through the territory would soon make the matters worse than anything else; therefore, it could not be entertained. I do n't believe much in the genuineness of the fear expressed by the people along the road from Helena to Fort Ellis, through the Missouri, the Crow creek, and the Gallatin valley. Every-where I saw them attending to their usual business, traveling with their wives or children, driving isolated wagons with twelve or fourteen oxen, without arms, and without any apparent concern about the Indians. Horses were grazing, as usual, at rather great distances from the ranches, and I found the wife of a farmer traveling alone, on foot, with her carpet-bag, from Morse's store to Foster's bridge. Still, all considered, I am under the impression that if any serious danger was to be apprehended, it would come more properly in that direction, from the Yellowstone river, where hostile Sioux are roaming, more than anywhere else."

The report of Gen. De Trobriand, from which these extracts are taken, was sent to Gen. Hancock just one month before the latter wrote to the former to take steps to ascertain where the Blackfeet Indians were wintering, and it is to be presumed that its contents were not only known to him, but also to Gen. Sheridan long before he sent his dispatch to Gen. Hancock, touching the punishment of not only the Piegan, but also the Blackfeet Indians. The letters of Gen. Sully did not suggest that troops be sent to Montana, to wage war on the Indians, but to guard against disorder and enable the law to be executed. Gen. De Trobriand was the military commander in the territory, and his letter, it does seem, ought to have dissipated any idea that prevailed in the war department or in the mind of Gen. Sheridan, or of Gen. Hancock, that there was any necessity to send troops out to punish the Indians. But the case had been prejudged. No such thing occupied the mind of Gen. Sheridan as the sending of troops to Montana to put down disorder or protect the Indians. All he thought troops necessary for in the territory, was to punish the Indians, and he had seen Major Baker in advance, and he was the man to execute his wishes promptly. Gen. Hancock was advised in the matter, and that Baker was the man, and all this before any authority had come from the general of the army or the war department; and so impressed was Gen. Hancock that long before the authority came from Washington he had written to Gen. De Trobriand to look out and learn where the Indians were wintering.

Major Baker proved himself to be as Gen. Sheridan advised Gen. Hancock he was, the proper man to do the work. Gen. De Trobriand, the chief military officer in Montana, did not seem to take to the idea of a campaign against the Indians. The only one of the Indian bands that those well advised complained of, was that of Mountain Chief, and he had gone north and taken up his abode for the winter in the British Possessions. As Gen. De Trobriand was slow in changing his views, Gen. Sheridan became impatient, and at once sent his inspector-general, Hardie, out to Montana, to report to him the condition of affairs. Of course Gen. Hardie started on his errand imbued with the feelings of his chief, and therefore ready to do and perform all that Gen. Sheridan desired. He made numerous and some of them voluminous reports. Gen. De Trobriand was passive or sent to the rear. Gen. Sully, however, had some opinions of his own. Although this use of troops was avowedly based in the beginning on his September dispatches, he did not so read them, and, being on the ground all the time, he had not seen the necessity for troops to punish the Indians. On January 13, 1870, Gen. Hardie telegraphed Gen. Sheridan that the question then was, " whether chastisement or capture for hostages should be the principal design. Practical result of movement a simple one; if these be, result would probably be killing and capturing both." This is somewhat obscure, probably from an omission of some word or two by the operator. It seems, however, that Gen. Sully had the opinion that while there was no occasion for war, a capture of a few Piegan chiefs as hostages might be well enough. Gen. Hardie explains all this further on in his dispatch. He says : " Under all the circumstances, how far should the opinion of Gen. Sully, as to the scope of operations, govern the military ? I think the military commander (Col. Baker) should be allowed to proceed generally according to the circumstances under which he finds himself in his operations, having in view the fulfillment of promises, etc., and the best interests of the frontier." Gen. Sheridan was prompt in his reply. He did not communicate through the military commander in Montana, which would seem to have been the regular order, but through his inspector-general, and to Col. Baker. He said : " If the lives and property of the citizens of Montana can best be protected by striking Mountain Chief's band of Piegan Indians, I want them struck. Tell Baker to strike them hard." This was on the 16th of January. In reply, Hardie said : " I think chastisement necessary. In this Col. Baker concurs. *He knows the general's wishes;* he will move to-day. . . . Col. Baker may be *relied on* to do all the general wished." Col. Baker moved on the 19th in the direction of the Marias river. Without tracing him on the march, the following brief extract from his report will tell what he accomplished :

" We were obliged to encamp in a ravine on the dry fork of the Marias till the night of the 22d, when we broke camp and marched to the Marias river, arriving there on the morning of the 23d. We succeeded, about eight o'clock, in surprising the camp of Bear Chief and Red Horn. We killed one hundred and seventy-three Indians, captured over one hundred women and children, and over three hundred horses. I ordered Lieut. Doane to remain in this camp, and destroy all the property, while I marched down the river after the camp of Mountain Chief, who I understood was camped four miles below. After marching sixteen miles, I found a camp of seven lodges that had been abandoned in great haste, leaving every thing. The lodges were burned the next morning, and the command started for the Northwest Fur Company's station, arriving there on the 25th. I sent for the chiefs of the Bloods, and had a consultation with them, making them give up their stolen stock. . . . Too much credit can not be given to the officers and men of the command for their conduct during the whole expedition. The result of expedition is one hundred and seventy-three Indians killed, and one hundred prisoners, women and children (these were allowed to go free, as it was ascertained some of them had the small-pox), forty-four lodges, with all their supplies and stores destroyed, and three hundred horses captured. Our casualties, one man killed, and one man with a broken leg, from a fall of his horse." On receipt of this report, Gen. Sheridan thus dispatched Gen. Sherman, on the 29th of January, 1870 :

" In compliance with your permission of November 4, 1869, to punish the Piegan Indians, who have been robbing and murdering in Montana, I have the honor to report the complete success of an expedition sent against them under the command of Colonel E. M. Baker, Second Cavalry, in which one hundred and seventy-three Indians were killed, forty lodges destroyed, also a large amount of winter provisions, and three hundred horses captured, etc. I think this will end Indian trouble in Montana, and will do away with the necessity of sending troops there in the spring, as contemplated." On the 31st of January, by another telegram, Gen. Sheridan supplied an omission in his dispatch of the 29th, thus : " Col. Baker had to turn loose over one hundred squaws. He had no transportation to get them in."

Lieut. Pease was the acting agent at the Blackfeet agency, and these Indians were a part of his charge, not as a military officer, but as an Indian agent. He made report to Gen. Sully, superintendent of Indian affairs, on February 6, 1870. He said :

" I have the honor to state since making my report of January 30, 1870, on the affair between United States soldiers and Piegan Indians, which took place January 23d, that I have visited the camp of Big Jake, of the Piegan tribe of Blackfeet Indians, and have seen and talked with several Indians who were in that camp which was attacked by the soldiers. I have, from these sources, gained the following additional information :

" Of the one hundred and seventy-three killed on the 23d, thirty-three were men ; of these fifteen only were such as are called by them as young or fighting men ; these were between the ages of fifteen and thirty-seven ; the remaining eighteen were between the ages of thirty seven and seventy ; eight of the latter were between the ages of sixty and seventy ; ninety were women, thirty-five between the ages of twelve and thirty-seven, and fifty-five between the ages of thirty-seven and seventy; the remaining fifty-five were children, none older than twelve years, and many of them in their mothers' arms. Out of two hundred and nineteen belonging to Red Horn's camp, only forty-six survived, among them are nine young men who escaped during the attack, and five who were away hunting. The lives of eighteen women and nineteen children (none of them more than three years of age, and the majority of them much younger), some of whom were wounded, were spared by the soldiers. Red Horn himself was killed. At the time of the attack this camp was suffering severely with small-pox, having had it among them for two months."

Gen. Sully, as superintendent of Indian affairs, transmitted the report of Lieut. Pease, the agent of the Blackfoot agency, to the commissioner of Indian affairs, at Washington. He did this in the line of his duty as such superintendent. Vincent Colyer, then the secretary of the board of Indian commissioners, had a desk in the Indian office and had opportunity to examine the reports of Indian superintendents and agents. He saw the report of Lieut. Pease, and, in a letter to Felix Brunot, the president of the board, gave publicity to its "sickening details." This was done on the 22d of February, 1870. When the publication met the eye of Gen. Sheridan, it annoyed him much. In his report of the affair to Gen. Sherman, he had omitted to say one word about the prisoners taken, or the prevalence of small-pox in the camp, and gave as the reason why Col. Baker turned the women and children loose, that he had no transportation to get them in. Hence, Mr. Colyer's publication annoyed him. On the 28th of February, 1870, he addressed a letter by telegraph to Gen. Sherman, and in it said: "I see that Mr. Vincent Colyer is out again in a sensational letter. Why did he not mention that Col. Baker had captured one hundred women and children? This, he suppressed, in order to do injustice to that officer, by deceiving the kind-hearted public, and to further the ends of the old Indian ring, doubtless, in whose interests he is working." After reciting his stereotyped story of Indian barbarities of all kinds, and which is always brought forward when the occasion demands it, he proceeds thus: "It would appear that Mr. Colyer wants this work to go on. I mention these two cases especially (one where the Indians ravished a woman 'over thirty times successively,' and another where they ravished a woman 'over forty times'), because they came under my personal examination, and can give them as an example of what has occurred to hundreds of others." It is submitted that Gen. Sheridan is rather extravagant in this statement of outrages; but, if true, they were not committed by the Indians in Montana. The publication of Mr. Colyer was followed by a general order from Gen. Sheridan's headquarters, at Chicago, of the date of March 12, 1870, to the following effect:

"The lieutenant-general commanding this military division takes great pleasure in announcing to the command the complete success of a detachment of the Second Cavalry and Thirteenth Infantry, under command of Brevet Colonel Baker, of the Second Cavalry, against a band of Piegan Indians, in Montana. These Indians, whose proximity to the British lines has furnished them an easy and safe protection against attack, have hitherto murdered and stolen with impunity, in defiance and contempt of the authority of the government. After having been repeatedly warned, they have at last received a carefully-prepared and well-merited blow. In the middle of winter, the thermometer below zero, when experience had led them to believe they could not be attacked, the blow fell. One hundred and seventy-three Indians were killed, three hundred horses captured, and the village and property of the band totally destroyed.

"The lieutenant-general can not commend too highly the spirit and conduct of the troops and their commander, under the difficulties and hardships they experienced in the inclemency of the weather; and, as one of the results of this severe but necessary and well-merited punishment of these Indians, he congratulates the citizens of Montana upon the reasonable prospect of future security for their property and lives."

When we call to mind that, in the dispatch to Col. Baker, through Inspector-General Hardie, Gen. Sheridan told Baker to strike Mountain Chief's band, and to strike them hard; that Mountain Chief's band was not then in the United States, but in the British Possessions, where they wintered; that the band struck was one against whom no complaint had been made, and at the time was terribly afflicted with the small-pox, this congratulatory order is a most remarkable document. That it is the production of the lieutenant-general of our army is most mortifying.

If the achievement was such a one as to merit the commendation which is bestowed upon it in the general order, a full recital of the details would add to the fame of Col. Baker and his troops. If it gave Gen. Sheridan great pleasure to announce the complete success of the expedition, the troops in his department and the public would enjoy the good news more fully if all the facts were given. Col. Baker was reserved in his report of details; and Gen. Sheridan suppressed, in his order, such of them as referred to the small-pox in the camp, and the Indian women and children being turned loose on the bleak prairie, without food, but scantily clad, and no place of refuge within reach. The exhibit made by Mr. Colyer not only angered Gen. Sheridan, but it made his superior, Gen. Sherman, quite indignant. His wrath was, however, turned against General Sully, and he expressed it thus in a dispatch to Gen. Sheridan: "Gen. Sully, by communicating by telegraph the particulars of the fight, for the use of Mr. Colyer, *did an unofficer-like and wrong act, and this in the end will stand to his discredit.*" This is a most remarkable utterance to come from the very head of the army. It is not only an admission that the deed is of such a nature that it ought not to be told, but it is a notification that punishment awaits the officer, who, in the discharge of duty, makes a report in a case like this that is not agreeable to Gen. Sherman, no matter how truthful the report may be. It would seem that if it be a meritorious act to attack and destroy an Indian village, in which all the indications are that the inhabitants are peaceful, living in quiet seclusion and suspecting no danger, sadly and terribly afflicted with the small-pox, and kill the inmates without regard to age or sex, those who publish "the particulars of the fight" give fame to those who plan, as well as those who execute the order, and merit commendation instead of a mark of "discredit." To plan such expeditions and approve and commend what is done, and yet make it an offense to publish "the particulars of the fight," is to subject officers engaged in such affairs to popular prejudice. Should the people become impressed with the idea that the higher officers of the army regard it as an offense to publish the truthful details of military operations, their usefulness is at an end, and the future of that arm of the service is put in jeopardy. In Gen. Sully's case, the curious inquirer will find, on investigation, that the displeasure of the general of the army did rest upon him. Even Lieut. Pease suffered indignity and was insulted by his superiors because he made the report of the affair on the Marias river, though all he stated was conscientiously done, and from the best information he could obtain. There is no doubt but his report was substantially true.

Annoyed by what was termed unfriendly criticism, on the 12th of March, Gen. Sherman wrote to Gen. Sheridan, and in his communication said: "I think Col. Baker should have reported more exactly the number, sex, and kind of Indians killed; and in view of the severe strictures in Congress on this act, as one of horrible cruelty to women and children, I wish you would require, by telegraph, Col. Baker to report specifically on this point."

On March 18, Gen. Sheridan advised Gen. Sherman that the further report of Col. Baker had not yet been received. His dispatch is lengthy, entering quite fully into his views of his duty and obligation to protect the settlers in the territories, and assumes that he has "nothing to do with the Indians but in this connection." Indeed it would appear that, in his view, such outlaws as Gen. DeTrobriand spoke of as infesting Montana were to be upheld by the troops. He said he had no hesitation in making his choice, and that he would stand by the people over whom he was placed, and give them what protection he could. In taking the offensive, he said: "I have to select the season when I can catch the fiends; and if a village is attacked, and women and children killed, the responsibility is not with the soldier, but with the people whose crimes necessitate the attack." This view is indefensible, and is condemned by all the laws of war. And then the great mistake, even crime, in Gen. Sheridan's administration, is that he accepts the stories of the most disorderly brigands that infest the territories as cheerfully, even more so, than the statements of the most trustworthy citizens. He does not attempt to verify them at all; and when a military expedition is put in the field to chastise Indians, no care is taken to know whether an offense or depredation has been committed, or, if committed, who are the guilty parties. When troops are out, the unalterable rule is, where an Indian trail is struck, to follow it, and if the Indians are overtaken, no inquiry is made as to their guilt, but they are punished. The same course is pursued wherever an Indian village is found. It is destroyed, and its inmates killed without hesitation. *After* the affair is over, and the usual congratulatory proclamation is issued, Gen. Sheridan commences to get up evidence to prove hostility. In this department he has marvelous resources. In the case in hand his dexterity is noticeable. He directed Col. Baker to strike the band of Mountain Chief. That officer, in view of the license that prevailed in the department, struck the first Indians he came upon, and reported that it was the camp of Bear Chief and Red Horn, and yet Gen. Sheridan, with a full knowledge of the Indians struck by Col. Baker, is sufficiently adroit to present the affair in such form to Gen. Sherman that the latter, on the 28th of March, filed the second report of Col. Baker, of March 23d, with the secretary of war, with this indorsement: " This copy of the report of Col. Baker of the killed and captured in his attack on Mountain Chief's Piegan camp is submitted to the secretary of war, with the remark that the officers engaged in that expedition desire a thorough investigation, if you deem the good of the service requires it." On the same day, he wrote to Gen. Sheridan that he had shown the dispatches of that officer, including the second report of Col. Baker, to the secretary of war and the president, and also filed copies of the same with the secretary of the interior. In his letter he said to Gen. Sheridan: " You may assure Col. Baker that no amount of clamor has shaken our confidence in him and his officers, and that if any responsible parties will father the reports that have been so extensively published, we will give them the benefit of an official investigation." A few days preceding, on the 24th of the month, being annoyed by " the particulars of the fight," he said, in a letter to Gen. Sheridan : " It is of course to be deplored that some of our people prefer to believe the story of the Piegan massacre as trumped up by interested parties at Benton, more than a hundred miles off, rather than the official report of Col. Baker, who was on the spot, and is the responsible party. I prefer to believe that the majority killed at Mountain Chief's camp were warriors ; that the firing ceased the moment resistance was at an end ; that quarter was given to all who asked for it ; and that a hundred women and children were allowed to go free, to join the other bands of the same tribe, known to be camped near by, rather than the absurd report that there were only thirteen warriors killed, and that all the balance were women and children, more or less afflicted with small-pox." These " particulars of the fight" which Gen. Sherman has here blocked out, and which he prefers to believe, are the creation of his imagination. Talk about the majority killed being warriors is simply ridiculous ; or that quarter was given to all who asked for it, when it is apparent that no resistance was made, is simply to insult the intelligence of every reader ; to say that the Indian women were allowed to go free to join the other bands known to be camped near by, when Col. Baker said he found only one camp, and that deserted, and the lodges destroyed by him, is, when we call to mind the fact that these helpless people were turned adrift on the bleak prairies, in the middle of winter, without food or shelter, and afflicted with the small-pox, to ignore the truth and smother every impulse of humanity. These unfeeling utterances of the general of the army will stand side by side with that other cruel sentiment of his, uttered in 1866, in these words : " We must act with vindictive earnestness against the Sioux, even to their extermination, men, women, and children. Nothing less will reach the root of the case."

As to the investigation of the affair on the Marias, which General Sherman intimated might take place, if any one would father the stories which were published, no one can doubt that

Colonel Baker had nothing to fear, since General Sherman had already prejudged the case, and any court organized by him would be of such material as he should select, and entertaining his views of the conduct of Colonel Baker. It is strange, however, that Congress did not order an investigation.

The second report of Colonel Baker was made on the 23d of March. It is as follows: "In answer to your telegram, received on the 22d instant, I report that after having made every effort to get the judgment of the officers of the command, I am satisfied that the following numbers approximate as nearly to the exact truth as any estimate can possibly be made; that the number killed was one hundred and seventy-three. Of these there were one hundred and twenty able men, fifty-three women and children; that of captives (afterward released) there were, of women and children, one hundred and forty.

"I believe that every effort was made by officers and men to save the non-combatants, and that such women and children as were killed, were killed accidentally. The reports published in the eastern papers, purporting to come from General Alfred Sully, are wholly and maliciously false, and if he has authorized them, he knew them to be false; if he has given authority to these slanders, I can only suppose that it is that attention may be drawn from the manifest irregularities and inefficiency that mark the conduct of Indian affairs under his direction in this territory. It seems incredible that the false assertion of two officers, General Sully and Lieutenant Pease, neither of whom have made any effort to inform themselves in the matter, should outweigh the reports of those who were engaged in the fight, and who feel that they have nothing to palliate or concede. All the officers of this command ask at the hands of the authorities is a full and complete investigation of the campaign, and less than this can not, in justice, be conceded to them."

In his first report Colonel Baker said that he killed one hundred and seventy-three Indians; that he had over one hundred prisoners, women and children, and these he allowed to go free, as it was found they had the small-pox among them. His first report clearly left the impression that the killed were all males, who were in the combat. In his second report he admits that fifty-three of the killed were women and children, and that his captives afterward released amounted to one hundred and forty, all women and children. He destroyed forty-four lodges, of these seven were sixteen miles away, and were deserted. Hence, none of his killed or prisoners are to be credited to the abandoned camp. The camp of Bear Chief and Red Horn consisted of thirty-seven lodges. One hundred and seventy-three killed, and one hundred and forty captives, gives to the thirty-seven lodges a population of three hundred and thirteen inhabitants. The usual number of persons to a lodge is generally estimated at six, of all ages and both sexes. This would give to the thirty-seven lodges two hundred and twenty-two souls, instead of three hundred and thirteen. Of fighting men the lodge has usually but one, and this to thirty-seven lodges would give thirty-seven, whereas Colonel Baker's one hundred and twenty able men gives more than three fighting men to a lodge. Lieutenant Pease, in his report, states the whole number in the camp to be two hundred and nineteen. Of this number he says five were away hunting, leaving two hundred and fourteen at home when the attack was made. His whole number approximates very nearly to six to each lodge. Lieutenant Pease says that including the nine that escaped, only forty-six survived. He states that eighteen women and nineteen children were spared, and these, with the nine that escaped, makes the number forty-six, as stated by him. His death list is placed at thirty-seven men, ninety women, and fifty children. This makes one hundred and seventy-seven, only four more than the death list of Colonel Baker, though differently classified. It is not seen how any intelligent person seeking the truth can reject the report of Lieutenant Pease and accept that of Colonel Baker. The former had no motive to exaggerate. He made his report in the line of his duty, and by direction of General Sully, who was induced to call for it because of the conflicting reports that reached him. Lieutenant Pease relied much on Big Jake, a chief who was residing on the Marias river at the time. If a reliable Indian, there can be no doubt of the general accuracy of the report, and the

19

classification of inmates of the camp, and the number killed, and the number that was spared. Lieutenant Pease also had conversation with the young men who escaped. They knew the number of the inmates when the camp was attacked, and the whole number is so consistent with the population of Indian lodges that this of itself goes far to confirm belief in the accuracy of the report of Lieutenant Pease. The lieutenant is known to be a careful and reliable man.

The manner in which Col. Baker refers to Gen. Sully and Lieut. Pease, in the report of March 23, evidences a remarkable degree of insubordination. Although these officers were, for the time being, detached from the military service, they were yet officers, and one the superior of Col. Baker, who had no hesitation in charging them with making false statements, and Gen. Sully with inefficiency and irregularity. Such charges, couched in such language, appear to be not only acceptable, but gratifying, to both the lieutenant-general and the general of our army. And yet the breach of order and discipline are so manifest that Gen. Sherman, who is but too ready to make an abstract of the second report of Col. Baker for the press, suppresses the names of Sully and Pease, leaving the rude language in it to be applied generally to such as had commented on Baker's attack on the Piegan camp. He wrote to Gen. Sheridan, on the 28th of March, acknowledging the receipt of Col. Baker's report of the 23d, and said: " An abstract will be given the press, omitting the names of Sully and Pease."

On the 6th of March, 1870, while this Piegan massacre was attracting the attention of Congress and the country, the secretary of the interior addressed a communication to the president, touching the condition of our Indian affairs, in which he said that, from our extreme northern boundary to the Mexican frontier, complaints were received from all the Indian tribes, of what they declare to be a lack of faith on our part, in carrying out the stipulations of our treaties, made with them, and redeeming the promises, which, they allege, induced them to consent to the construction of railroads through their country. He referred to organized bands of whites, in Wyoming and Colorado, etc., who were prepared to move on the Indian reservations, to prospect for gold, etc.; that such contend that the treaties are not binding, and that they intend to go strong enough to take care of themselves. He also referred to an outrage that had but recently occurred in Kansas, where the Osage Indians, on returning home from their winter hunt, found their reservation, not only invaded by whites, but the material of their dwellings carried away, villages destroyed, and their farms, cabins, and stock taken possession of by the "squatters." In relation to Indian affairs in Montana, the secretary said:

" During the summer, frequent complaints were made of thefts of horses and cattle, by different tribes, in Montana. These thefts were believed to be generally perpetrated by some of the younger and more reckless of the Indians, who broke away from the restraints of their chiefs and head men, on the pretext that, as the United States was not performing its promises to them, they were absolved from the obligation to respect property. We have every reason to believe that a scrupulous observance of our engagements with the Indians of the upper valley of the Missouri, during the past two years, would have enabled us to sustain the peaceful chiefs in their authority, so that thefts would have either been prevented, or punished without private revenge, and the source of all the troubles have been thus dried up. The thefts led to private retaliation by the whites, either as punishment for the crimes, or in the effort to recapture property. Lives were taken on both sides, but the most experienced agents and officers are of the opinion that more than five Indian lives were taken for every white man that was murdered, during the season. The disturbances finally led the Indian superintendent to call for additional military force to protect the settlers. It was thought impracticable to do this with the few troops which could be spared from permanent stations or garrisons, and the expedition recently made against the Piegans was chosen by the military commander as a more effective way of correcting the evil. I do not propose to criticise the course or the judgment of either the general or the lieutenant-general of the army, in this matter. . . . I have purposely refrained from any judgment, even upon the manner in which the work was done by the subordinate commander of the expedition, until further reports shall be received. I hold it, however, to be as much due to the officers of the army as to myself, to express the opinion, in which I believe they will concur, that it does not become a civilized nation, even to *consider* the propriety of adopting the mode of warfare, or imitating the horrible barbarities of savage tribes. I am entirely sure that if it shall fully appear that there has been a wanton butchery of unresisting women and children, the condemnation of such cruelty will be as prompt on the part of the superior officers of the army as it would be from ourselves. It is right, also, to say, that the statement of Mr. Vincent Colyer, secretary of the Indian commission, to Mr. Brunot, its chairman, was a simple transcript from the official information at that time received by the Indian office, without exaggeration or diminution. That commission I look upon as being the official advocate of the Indian before the nation, and as it speaks for those who have neither newspaper to show their side of the questions arising, nor representatives in Congress to protect their interests, or tell their story, I think we should as carefully preserve the rights of the commission to speak, as we would the right of a criminal to appear by his counsel in a court of justice. The integrity and entire disinterestedness of the commission are beyond all possible question."

The foregoing sentiments attest the justness and humanity of the secretary of the interior. On one point, however, he was in error, and in another sadly mistaken. He erred in supposing that Gen. Sully's only object in suggesting more troops for the territory, was to protect the settlers. General Sully's suggestion was not to the war, but to the interior department; not as a general in active service, but as superintendent of Indian affairs. He referred to the prevailing disorder in the territory; the incursions made by Indians not residents of it; to the rowdy and lawless white element; the traffic in whisky, and the altercations between whites and Indians growing out of its use; the impotence of the civil authorities; and that, in his opinion, nothing could insure peace and order, until there was sufficient military force to support the civil authorities, and " strong enough to clean out the roughs and whisky-sellers." While the dispatches of Gen. Sully were specific enough, they were perverted by Gen. Sheridan, and read to mean that troops were necessary to make war on the Indians. His plans, for that purpose, were approved by Gen. Sherman, and the war office imbued with them, and hence the erroneous impression of the secretary of the interior, that troops were called for to protect the settlers. In assuming that the higher officers of the army would condemn Col. Baker, if it should appear that he had killed unresisting women and children, the secretary of the interior was sadly mistaken. The attack on this Piegan camp, and the slaughter of its inmates in a barbarous manner, is a well established fact, and yet there has not at any time appeared any indication of displeasure on the part of the superior officers of the army—and there will not be any manifestation of this kind. On the contrary, all that Col. Baker did, has been approved by them, and the approval placed upon record. The truth is, that the general and lieutenant-general habitually instil into the minds of all subordinate commanders, that, in Indian warfare, they should be brutal, even excelling the Indians in barbarity ; and no case has occurred, in all the conflicts between the troops and the Indians, since they have held the high positions now occupied by them, in which they have found any thing to condemn. In many of these conflicts, our troops have excelled the barbarities of savage tribes, and in such the commendation, by public proclamation, has been complimentary, full, and hearty.

CHAPTER XV.

The Sioux war of 1876.—How brought about.—Sitting Bull and his followers turned over to the army February 1, 1876.—Sitting Bull's views.—Seizure of the arms and ponies of the Indians at Red Cloud, Standing Rock, and Cheyenne river agencies.—Military correspondence and comments thereon.

In referring to the war waged against the Sioux Indians in 1876, the commissioners appointed to negotiate for the surrender of the Black Hills and the unceded Indian country, defined in the treaty of 1868, said in their report to the president, made on the 18th of December, 1876, that "it was dishonorable to the nation, and disgraceful to those who originated it." This commission was created in pursuance of an act of Congress, passed August 15, 1876. The reasons which led its members to express so forcibly this opinion were not embodied in the report. Some of them will be given in this chapter.

It will be remembered that by the treaty of 1868, with the Sioux, the country lying between the northern boundary of the State of Nebraska, and the forty-sixth parallel of north latitude, bounded on the east by the Missouri river and west by the one hundred and fourth degree of west longitude, together with the reservations then existing on the east side of the Missouri, was set apart for the absolute and undisturbed use and occupation of the Sioux, for their permanent home. "The United States (to quote the language of the treaty) solemnly agrees that no person except those herein designated and authorized so to do, and except such officers, agents, and employes of the government as may be authorized to enter upon Indian reservations in discharge of duties enjoined by law, shall be permitted to pass over, settle upon, or reside in the same." The treaty also provides "that the country north of the North Platte and east of the summit of the Big Horn mountains, shall be held and considered unceded Indian territory, and (the United States) also stipulates and agrees that no white person or persons shall be permitted to settle upon or occupy any portion of the same, or without the consent of the Indians first had and obtained, to pass through the same." In consideration of these and other covenants the Indians agree " to relinquish all right permanently to occupy the territory outside of their reservation as defined in the treaty, *but yet reserve the right to hunt* on any land north of the North Platte, and on the Republican fork of the Smoky Hill river, so long as the buffalo may range thereon in such numbers as to justify the chase." By the treaty a distinction was made in the annual annuities, between those who settled on the reservation and became farmers, and those who elected to lead the life of nomads, and continued to roam and hunt; and such as did roam and hunt were, for thirty years, to receive a specific money annuity, less in amount per head than the like annuity to the farmers. The latter, when they became settled were, each head of the family, to receive an American cow, and one good well broken pair of American oxen. The former did not receive those. Whether well or ill-advised, the treaty seemed to leave it to the discretion of the Indian whether he should elect to be a farmer or a nomad. Owing to the barrenness of the land within the reservation, and drought, and the blight of the grasshopper, so long as game abounded, many of these wild horsemen naturally followed the chase.

The treaty of 1868 was not the production of the Sioux. It was prepared by the commission, on which were Generals Sherman, Harney, Terry, and Augur. The commission pledged the faith of the United States, and their honor as men, to the faithful fulfillment of its stipulations. In less than three months after the treaty was ratified and proclaimed, and thus became the law of the land, Gen. Sheridan, by order of Gen. Sherman, issued a military order on June 29, 1869, in these words: " All Indians, when on their proper reservations, are under the exclusive control and jurisdiction of their agents; they will not be interfered with in any manner by the military authority, except upon requisition of the special agent resident with them, his superintendent, or the

bureau of Indian affairs, at Washington. Outside the well
defined limits of their reservations, they are under the original and exclusive jurisdiction of the military authority, and
as a rule will be considered hostile."

By the act creating the interior department all power and
authority in relation to Indian affairs, which was then exercised by the secretary of war, was vested in the secretary of
the interior. Hence it is not seen how, when this order was
issued, the military authority could claim such jurisdiction
over Indians outside of their reservations, as it asserts; and it
may safely be stated that there was no law to support this
claim. Moreover, if the claim were supported by existing
law, the Sioux, by virtue of the stipulation in the treaty of
1868, would be protected from the operation of the order,
since the right to roam and hunt in the unceded Indian
country was guaranteed in the treaty. This unlawful order
was, however, inexorably executed until December, 1876. Of
course the Indians did not and could not understand why
they should from time to time be hunted down and punished
for exercising this right, especially as Congress, even as late
as August 15, 1876, appropriated the seventh of thirty in-
stallments to be used in paying Indians who roamed and
hunted, their annuity. To punish them for doing so was a
grave violation of the provisions of the treaty.

While the Sioux were punished for exercising this right,
the whites in small, as well as large bodies, passed through
and prospected in the forbidden territory. The military did
not check these incursions. They were not only permitted
by it, but protected. Among the expeditions were parties
engaged "in the interests of science." These went out from
time to time to explore the Black Hills, and other portions of
the reservation, and were actually accompanied by military
escorts and protection. The Indians protested, but without
avail. The most formidable of these expeditions was fitted
out in the year 1874, and left St. Paul about the last of June.
It was destined to a thorough exploration of the Black Hills,
and was in charge of General Custer. Nothing was said in
Congress about it; no appropriation made for it, and it was
in wanton and flagrant violation of the provisions of the

treaty. General Custer even made application for, and obtained from the Santee agency, about thirty young men of the Santée band of Sioux, to act as scouts. These Indians were surprised when the call was made upon them. They hesitated and expressed regret, but yet obeyed the summons. This expedition incensed the Sioux exceedingly. On its return it was pronounced a successful reconnoissance, and the people were told that there was gold in the Black Hills, and the country much better than hitherto supposed; that timber was plenty, and that water and grass were abundant. The covetous eyes of the white man were thus turned to these hills, and parties began to organize to go into them. The first intruders, who started with the avowed purpose of locating and mining, were driven back, but the idea of occupying the forbidden land was not abandoned. Expeditions were also fitted out to explore and occupy the unceded Indian country. It was also determined to change the line of the Northern Pacific Railroad, which at the date of the treaty was located, and while it crossed the Missouri below the mouth of the Yellowstone, did not ascend that stream a great distance until it was crossed, and thence westward the line was on the north side of the Yellowstone. It was decided to change this line to the south, and ascend on that side. To the nomad Sioux, who roamed and hunted, this change was very objectionable. All these things combined disturbed the Indians, and made them uneasy. Depredations were committed on the Indians, and they retaliated. Stock was taken from and by them. Both Indians and whites were killed. The surveying parties, who attempted to run the new line of the railroad, were driven off. By 1875, many trespassers were lodged in the Black Hills, and early in 1876, the number was greatly increased. In 1875, there was a commission sent to Red Cloud agency to examine charges preferred by Professor Marsh against the agent. Gov. Fletcher, of Missouri, was chairman of this commission. Among the witnesses examined by it were Red Cloud, Sitting Bull of the Ogallallas, Little Wound, and other Indians. In the midst of the questions put to, and answered by Red Cloud, on August 10, 1875, the chief interjected the Black Hills, thus: "Now, as to those Black

Hills. Our Great Father has got a great many soldiers, and I never knew him, when he wanted to stop any thing with his soldiers, but he succeeded in it. The reason I tell you this, is that the people from the states who have gone to the Black Hills, are stealing our gold, digging it out, and taking it away, and I do n't see why the Great Father do n't bring them back." To this, the chairman replied: "The Great Father has ordered these people away from there in five days from now, and if they do not go, he will bring them out with his soldiers."

The next day Sitting Bull, of the Ogallallas, said: "You told me yesterday that the troops would take all the white people away from the Black Hills by the 15th of August, and the young men were all very glad to know that these miners were to be out of the Black Hills before the northern Indians came down to the grand council." (He alluded to a council which was to assemble in September, to treat for the Black Hills.) In reply to Sitting Bull, the chairman said: "We saw Gen. Crook, and he said he had orders from the president to get these miners all out by the 15th of this month, and the miners have all agreed to go by that time."

A month previous to this time Gov. Thayer, of Wyoming, had the coolness to visit Washington to obtain an order for troops to be used in protecting the miners then in the Black Hills, as well as parties on their way there; and in a conference with the president and Gen. Sherman, the president said that the parties in the Black Hills, as well as those going, were acting unlawfully, and ought to be notified of the fact. Hence Gen. Crook's instructions. Gen. Crook did visit the hills, and after a manner advised the miners to go out, first allowing them time to mark off their "claims," so that they could, on their return, possess them again. It was well understood, however, that Gen. Crook's sympathies were with these lawless characters. A few left the hills in good faith; many that feigned to go, soon returned, and a number pursued their mining as though no notice had been given them. In his annual report, made only one month after the time fixed, according to Gov. Fletcher, for the miners to leave, Gen. Crook disclosed very fully his feelings. He said:

"I visited the mining region in July, and, after seeing

many of the miners in their camps, gave them sufficient time to secure their claims against future loss, in case they were eventually allowed to return. They agreed to vacate the country, an agreement I have reason to believe they have observed. In connection with this matter, and having, as I conceive, an important bearing upon it, I would mention the fact that, since I came to the department, there have been over four hundred horses stolen by Indians from settlers along the line of the railroad, which have been trailed on the Sioux reservation. To have followed them with sufficient force to have recaptured the stock, would undoubtedly have resulted in a general war with the Sioux nation; so this stock has never been recovered, but is still in the hands of these Indians, a fact well known not only to the parties who lost it, but to people generally throughout the country.

"Now, when I visited the Black Hills country, and conversed with the miners in regard to vacating, and reminded them that they were violating a treaty stipulation, it was but natural that they should reply that the Indians themselves violated the treaty hundreds of times every summer by predatory incursions, whereby many settlers were utterly ruined, and their families left without means of subsistence; and this by Indians who are fed, clothed, and maintained in utter idleness by the government they (the settlers) help to support. I respectfully submit that their side of the story should be heard, as the settlers who develop our mines and open the frontier to civilization are the nation's wards no less than their more fortunate fellows, the Indians. In any event, unless some arrangement can be made this winter, by which the Indians will be satisfied to cede the mining region, my impression is that serious trouble will ensue when the miners attempt to return, as I believe they will by early spring."

It is doubtless true that some of the settlers lost some stock during the year 1875. They would probably have lost some, had there been no Indians in that region. The Indians also lost stock, but it does not seem clear that, if Gen. Crook's statement that four hundred head of stock were stolen was true, the fact should be put in as an offset to the unlawful occupation of the Black Hills, not by the settlers along the line of the railroad, but by adventurers who did not reside in the country. Moreover, it is strange if the Sioux had stolen four hundred head of stock from the settlers, that no claim was ever filed against the Indians for compensation. In a country where sharp lawyers abound, it is remarkable that the settlers, if they had claims for such depredations upon them, had not filed and prosecuted them, when the treaty provided a full remedy for such cases, and compensation to the injured parties, out of the annuities or other moneys due the Indians. The Sioux commission of 1876, in all their journey among the Sioux, did not hear, from any source or from any person, one word about four hundred horses, or even one horse, being stolen in the preceding year. If any such story had currency at any time, it was no doubt a fabrication; but it was just the kind of news that Gen. Crook was in search of, since his desire appeared to be not to purge the Black Hills of intruders, but to precipitate such a state of things as to compel the Sioux to surrender them.

The instructions to Gen. Crook, in relation to driving the miners out of the Black Hills, have not been published. It is presumed that he was instructed to remove all persons who were there in violation of the Sioux treaty. Section 2118 of the revised statutes clothed the president with all power and authority necessary to remove such persons by military force, and any order that did not, in a case like the one in question, require their removal would be a vain thing. Under the same section, each party who made a claim in the Black Hills was liable to a penalty of one thousand dollars, in addition to being removed. But Gen. Crook seems to have considered the important duty confided to him, in this case, as properly discharged when he gave the intruders sufficient time to secure their claims against loss, and they agreed to vacate the country temporarily. Here is, no doubt, a fair sample of the manner in which military officers of high standing discharge important duties confided to them in the Indian country, in which the interests of the Indians are involved, and hence it would seem to be time to demand a reformation in the military service in the Indian country, if not a total disuse of it. A slight effort—a very slight one—in the right direction, at that time, made in good faith, would have rid the Sioux reservation of all those who were unlawfully in it, as well as all who were intruders in the unceded Indian country. But the sympathy of not only General Crook, but of Gen. Sheridan, was on the side of the outlaws then in the Sioux reservation and unceded country. The latter was at all times ready to stand by those intruding on the rights of the Indians. As early as March, 1870, he had said officially: " I have no hesitation in making my choice. . . . My duty is to protect the people; I have nothing to do with Indians, but in this connection." Such was his frame of mind at that time that he regarded all Indians as "fiends," to be killed, and every lawless intruder was by him esteemed "a pioneer of the frontier."

In less than two months after the annual report of General Crook was made, E. C. Watkins, United States Indian inspector, submitted, on November 9, 1875, a communication to the commissioner of Indian affairs, in relation to " the condition of certain wild and hostile bands of Sioux Indians in Dakota and Montana, that came under his observation during a recent tour through their country," and what he thought should be the policy of the government toward them. He referred (he said) to Sitting Bull's band and other bands of the Sioux nation, under chiefs or head men of less note, " but no less untamable and hostile." He did not name them, but spoke of their roaming " over western Dakota and eastern Montana, including the rich valleys of the Yellowstone and Powder rivers," and making war on the Arickarees, Mandans, Gros Ventres, and others who were friendly. He said:

" Their country is probably the best hunting ground in the United States, a 'paradise' for Indians, affording game in such variety and abundance that the need of government supplies is not felt. Perhaps for this reason they have never accepted aid or been brought under control. They openly set at defiance all law and authority, and boast that the United States authorities are not strong enough to conquer them. The United States troops are held in contempt, and surrounded by their native mountains, relying on their knowledge of the country and powerful endurance, they laugh at the futile efforts that have thus far been made to subjugate them, and scorn the idea of white civilization. They are lofty and independent in their attitude and language toward the government officials, as well as the whites generally, and claim to be the sovereign rulers of the land. They say they own the wood, the water, the ground, the air, and that white men live in or pass through their country but by their sufferance. They are rich in horses and robes, and are thoroughly armed. Nearly every warrior carries a breech loading gun, a pistol, a bow, and quiver of arrows."

The inspector said that these wild Indians are but as a drop in the bucket compared with the great body of the Sioux who he admitted had accepted the peace policy, and were keeping the covenants of their treaty. He said the wild Indians " number, all told, but a few hundred warriors, and are never all together, or under the control of one chief." He suggested that one thousand men " under the command of an experienced officer, sent into the country in the winter, when the Indians are nearly always in camp, and most helpless, would be amply sufficient for their capture and punishment." He said they were the dread of the frontier settler, the luckless white hunter and emigrant, and fortunate was the man "who meets them, if, after losing all his worldly possessions, he escapes with his scalp." As the inspector did not state that he had lost any of his worldly possessions, and as he appeared at Washington with his scalp in its place and secure, it is presumed he was not in the ' paradise ' of these wild Indians, but it is known that he had journeyed through Montana, where the general sentiment then was and had for years been in favor of wresting the unceded Indian country and the Black Hills from the Sioux, and he, no doubt, heard terrible stories about Sitting Bull and the other unnamed ' head men ' who inhabited the valleys of the Yellowstone and Powder rivers, from multitudes of voices, who were anxious for an Indian war, the result of which, in addition to the profits made therefrom, would in some way result in opening the Sioux country to the lawful occupation of the whites.

There was a remarkable coincidence occurred at this time. Generals Sheridan and Crook both *happened* to be at Washington when Inspector Watkins was there. It is not improbable that these gentlemen and the Indian inspector talked about Sitting Bull and other contumacious Indians on his route, and he would naturally have confidence in the judgment of military gentlemen of such large experience as they were, in relation to Indian affairs. It was known that the suggestion of a winter campaign against " hostile " Indians was claimed as an original idea by Gen. Sheridan, as early as September, 1868, and he believed that he had or ought to have it patented as his own, and the feasibility and efficacy of such a campaign would be likely to strike the inspector at once. Not having familiarized himself with the details of the treaty of 1868, the inspector was not aware that these " wild and hostile bands of Sioux" had the right guaranteed to them by its terms to roam and hunt in the valleys where they then were, and in all other parts of the unceded Indian country, as long as game abounded, and hence was forcibly struck with the idea that in the extravagance of their claims and alleged contempt for our troops, they were contumacious, and ought to be punished. In this frame of mind, Inspector Watkins was the very gentleman these military officers would be gratified to meet. They had already determined that military operations were necessary, and the coming winter the appropriate time; still it was important to commit the interior department to the measure. Being convinced that the Indians should be punished, and that the proper time to do it was in the winter, Inspector Watkins said:

" The true policy, in my judgment, is to send troops against them in the winter, the sooner the better, and *whip* them into subjection. They richly merit punishment for their incessant warfare on friendly Indian tribes, their continuous thieving, and their numerous murders of white settlers, or white men wherever found unarmed. . . . The government owes it to these friendly tribes in fulfillment of treaty stipulations; it owes it to the agents and employes whom it has sent to labor among the Indians at remote and inaccessible places beyond the reach of aid in time to save; it owes it to the frontier settlers, who have, with their families, braved the dangers and hardships incident to pioneer life;

it owes it to civilization, and the common cause of humanity." The reasons given by the inspector, though numerous, are stated with great brevity as well as force, inspired, as he no doubt was, by a comparison of opinions with these military gentlemen. The local Indian agents dispersed on the Upper Missouri and in Montana did not seem to be aware of the condition of things as stated by the inspector. Their annual reports, made that fall, have nothing of the sort in them, and from an examination of these it is difficult to escape the conclusion that much that the inspector said was fiction.

After deliberating three weeks on the subject-matter contained in the report of the inspector, the commissioner of Indian affairs, on the 27th of November, 1875, submitted the same to the secretary of the interior, with the recommendation that it be referred to the secretary of war, " for consideration, and such action *as may be deemed best by Lieutenant-General Sheridan, who is personally conversant with the situation on the Upper Missouri, and with the relation of Sitting Bull to the other Sioux tribes.*" The secretary of the interior, on the 29th November, 1875, transmitted the note of the commissioner of Indian affairs, with Inspector Watkins' report, to the secretary of war, for his consideration and action, but expressed no opinion whatever on the subject. On the 3d of December, 1875, the secretary of the interior wrote to the secretary of war, in reference to " the hostile Sioux residing outside of their reservations and remote from any agency," and informed that officer that he had directed the commissioner of Indian affairs to notify said Indians they must remove to a reservation on or before the 31st of January following; that if they neglect or refuse to remove, they will be reported to the war department as hostile Indians, and that a military force will be sent to compel them to obey the orders of the Indian office. Secretary Chandler closed thus : " You will be notified of the compliance or non-compliance of the Indians with this order ; and if said Indians shall neglect or refuse to comply with said order, I have the honor to request that the proper military officer be directed to compel their removal to and residence within the boundaries of their reservation."

On the 6th of December, 1875, the commissioner of Indian affairs, in pursuance of the instructions of the secretary of the interior, issued a letter of instructions to the agents at Red Cloud, Spotted Tail, Lower Brulé, Crow Creek, Cheyenne River, Standing Rock, Devil's Lake, and Fort Peck agencies, directing them to communicate, if practicable, to Sitting Bull and other hostile Indians, the requirements of the government that they remove within the bounds of their reservations on or before the 31st of the next month. The Indians to whom this notice was to be given were nomads, roaming and hunting in the unceded Indian country, by virtue of a right guaranteed to them by the treaty of 1868. Moreover, there was not sufficient food at the agencies during that winter for such Indians as resided adjacent to them.

Agent Howard, of Spotted Tail agency, reportèd, under date of January 3, 1876, that he had sent out runners, and *believed* by that time they had reached the northern camps, and that Sitting Bull was therefore advised of the intentions of the government.

Agent Burke, of the Standing Rock agency, did not receive his instructions until the 22d day of December, and immediately sent some trustworthy and reliable Indian messengers to the " hostile " camps, to notify them of what was required. On December 31st, he wrote this fact to the department, and said : " I have no doubt but a large number of these wild and lawless Indians will come to this agency and accept the conditions of the treaty of 1868. I am strengthened in this belief from the fact that many of them had already sent word to their Indian relations and friends now peaceably settled on this reservation of their intention to do so the present winter or early the coming spring, *in view of which I respectfully invite the attention of the department to the necessity of providing food for their subsistence and maintenance.*" One of agent Burke's messengers returned on Jánuary 30, 1876. When he left the " hostile " country, no communication had been had with the " hostile " Indians, owing to a difficulty between the Two Kettle, Sans Arc, and other bands, and the Fort Berthold Indians. Agent Burke looked, however, for good results from

20

movements he had inaugurated; and urged an extension of time, owing to the trouble referred to, and the great length of the journey to the "hostile" camps at this inclement season.

Agent Hastings, of Red Cloud agency, received the notice on December 20, and replied that Sitting Bull separated in the fall from the "hostile" camp on the Powder river, and started for the Yellowstone. Since then he had heard nothing about his location, but as he was an Uncpapa, suggested that he could be reached with less difficulty from Standing Rock. Crazy Horse and Black Twin, to whom he sent word to come in to the agency, were, he said, then *en route* to Red Cloud agency with their people, but their progress was retarded on account of deep snow. When heard from they were at Bear Buttes. These two chiefs had never been at an agency. He said he had sent couriers to notify the Cheyenne camp, located about one hundred miles beyond Crazy Horse and Black Twin, but had not heard from them. He could not obtain couriers to go north except on a promise of reward.

Agent Bingham, of the Cheyenne river agency, reported that one of the delegations he sent to the camp of Sitting Bull and other wild bands, with the order to them to come to the reservation, or be considered as enemies, returned on the 11th of February, 1876. His messengers reported that the "hostile" Indians received the invitation and warning in good spirit, and without any exhibition of ill feeling. They answered that as they were then engaged in hunting buffalo, they could not conveniently come, but that early in the spring they would visit the agency to dispose of their robes and skins, when the question as to their future movements could be thoroughly discussed. He stated that the Indians referred to were encamped on the Yellowstone, peaceably inclined, and they deny all statements "so extensively circulated," that they intend to make war on the frontier in the spring. In a former communication to the department, of the date of January 26, 1876, agent Bingham said that from such facts as he could obtain from runners, he had no reason to apprehend trouble from the Indians named; that so far as he had information, the Indians had not been so quiet and friendly disposed for a long time, as they were at that period, and the intimation of a renewal of hostilities was a surprise not only to him, but to all the Indians under his charge, who disclaimed all knowledge of any intention on the part of themselves or their less civilized friends, called, he said, for the sake of distinction, "hostile." He said "they blame the newspapers for publishing sensational reports for which there is no foundation, but simply calculated to prejudice the government and its officers against the Indians, who have no means of contradicting such statements, unless through their agents."

The commissioner of Indian affairs having resigned, John Q. Smith, of Ohio, was appointed to that office, and his attention was at once called to the condition of things as they then existed. He learned from the correspondence that had reference to the case that it was the opinion of Generals Crook and Terry, under whom any movement against the Indians would be conducted, in which opinion the general and lieutenant-general concurred, that such a movement at the time referred to (February, 1876), was entirely practicable. He evidently had doubts, and was without any definite knowledge that the Indians had received notice. He came, however, to the conclusion that sufficient had been done to fully commit the department to the policy of restraining, by force of arms, any further outbreak or insubordination on the part of these "hostile" bands, should they not comply and be at the agencies before the 31st of the month, then only ten days distant. Commissioner Smith assumed, of course, that there was ground for the action that had already been taken, and that the Indians were not only "hostile," but in a defiant attitude, and he was not aware that there was no food at the agencies for them should they come in, and it is possible that, in the then state of the case, he was not aware that these Indians had a right, under the treaty, to roam and hunt in the country where they then were.

Promptly on the first day of February, 1876, the secretary of the interior turned over "Sitting Bull and his followers" to the war department, and on February 4, 1876, Gen. Sheridan responded that Generals Crook and Terry were ready, and would move at once against the Indians. Gen. Terry had been at Chicago as early as the middle of December, 1875, in conference with Gen. Sheridan on the subject, and Generals Crook and Sheridan were they not at Washington in November, 1875, where the plan of the winter campaign was evolved, and Inspector Watkins wrote the first letter to the commissioner of Indian affairs suggesting the war? Thus was the Sioux war of 1876, the crime of the centennial year, inaugurated.

In December, 1875, as a preliminary measure, the trader at Standing Rock was ordered to quit selling ammunition to the Indians of the agency. It had been the practice for many of the agency Indians to make a winter hunt, and there was a necessity for their doing so in the winter of 1875–6, since there was a scarcity of rations at the agencies. On the 17th of January, 1876, the commissioner of Indian affairs telegraphed the agents at Red Cloud, Spotted Tail, Standing Rock, Crow Creek, White River, Cheyenne River, Fort Berthold, and Fort Peck, to stop all sales of arms and ammunition to all the agency Indians, and seize any that were liable to reach them. This produced uneasiness and distrust among all the Indians, and hence some of the young men left the agencies and did not return. Subsequently, orders were promulgated that all Indians then absent from the agencies, should, on their return, surrender their arms and their ponies. No exception was made in favor of such bands as were absent, with the knowledge of the agents, and then engaged in hunting. The effect of this order was to surprise the Indians, and many of them refused to submit to it, and not being permitted to come home without a compliance, when the troops were put in motion, these Indians, being regarded as " hostile," were driven back, and many from necessity, others from choice, took refuge with Sitting Bull, and thus his forces were augmented.

In the latter part of February, 1876, Gen. Crook took the field with about thirteen hundred troops, making Fort Fetterman his base. He scouted on several streams and in the valleys, assigning a part of his command, under Gen. Reynolds, to go in quest of the band of Crazy Horse. Agent Hastings had notified the authorities, on the 28th of January, where the village of this chief was, and hence Gen. Crook knew where it was situate. The village was at Bear Buttes, and the Indians were on their way to Red Cloud agency. A number of the Northern Cheyennes were with them. Crazy Horse had been there for some time, the weather being so cold that he could not, with safety, move his women and children. On the 17th of March, Gen. Reynolds attacked and destroyed the village, and captured about eight hundred ponies. The Indians were not aware of the presence of the troops until the attack was made. Crazy Horse recovered his herd the next day. Gen. Crook, in his report of the affair, expressed dissatisfaction at what he regarded as failures on the part of Gen. Reynolds, which he classed thus: "A failure on the part of portions of the command to properly support the attack. A failure to make a vigorous and persistent attack with the whole command. A failure to secure the provisions which were captured, for the use of the troops, instead of destroying them. And most disastrous of all, a failure to secure and take care of the horses and ponies captured, nearly all of which again fell into the hands of the Indians the following morning." And he regarded a farther prosecution of the campaign, at this time, abortive, and his expedition returned to Fort Fetterman, on the 26th of March. This was rendered necessary by the inclemency of the weather. As Gen. Crook could not keep the field with his supply train, and his troops clothed for the occasion and the season, it does seem that Crazy Horse ought to have been excused for not being able to come into Red Cloud agency while the weather was so cold. Gen. Crook did not leave Fort Fetterman again until the 29th of May, when he started out with his force augmented until it exceeded in numbers the army of Gen. Terry. The latter was then in the Yellowstone valley. Gen. Crook moved slowly, awaiting some Indian scouts that did not join him until the 14th of June. On the 17th of June his scouts reported Indians in the vicinity. In due time the Indians and the troops were engaged in what is known as the "Battle of the Rosebud." These were Sitting Bull's Indians, and so skillfully were they handled on the field, that Gen. Crook found it necessary to retire. He claimed that his troops repulsed the attack, and drove the Indians several miles, but, *his* Indian allies refusing to go further, it remained for him to follow the retreating Sioux without rations, and dragging his wounded with him on rough mule litters, or return to his train where they could be cared for, and he determined on the latter course, and marched back to his camp on Goose creek. This failure gave Gen. Crook much uneasiness. His casualties were nine men killed and twenty wounded. It was said, that in the fall of 1875, when he was contemplating, and, in fact, initiating, work, looking to a winter campaign against the Sioux, he expressed the opinion that with five hundred troops he could whip the Sioux nation. In the annual report of Gen. Sheridan, he claimed a victory for Gen. Crook, but was compelled to admit that it was barren of results. He said that it was evident that Gen. Crook had not only the band of Crazy Horse to contend against, but that the " hostile " force had been augmented by young warriors from the agencies on the Missouri, and Spotted Tail, and Red Cloud; and that the agents had not only concealed the fact of the departure of these warriors, but in most cases, they had continued to issue rations as though the Indians were present. He also said that he had feared such a movement from the agencies, and as early as May, had asked that power should be given to the military to have supervision over the agencies, to keep in all who were then there, and all out who were then out and " hostile." There is no doubt that some young men did leave the agencies at the time ammunition was denied them, and joined Sitting Bull; but most of those with him, not of his own band proper, were from those who, being out on the hunt, when the order for dismounting and disarming the Indians absent was promulgated, and hence not permitted to return without submitting to the loss of their arms and ponies, did not return to the agencies. The charges made against the agents by Gen. Sheridan are not sustained by any known facts, and as to the temper of the agency Indians, he had himself assured Gen. Sherman as late as May 29, 1876, that nearly every Indian, man, woman, and child, among them was at heart a friend. This he stated only three weeks before the affair on the Rosebud.

We next have the battle of the Little Big Horn, which took place on the 25th of June, between a portion of the forces of Gen. Terry, under Gen. Custer, and the Indians under Sitting Bull. The result of this sad affair is known to the whole country. The press has designated it a massacre. The attack was made by Gen. Custer, and not by Sitting Bull. It was in broad daylight. Gen. Custer, in pursuance of orders, which met with his own approbation, having invaded the home of the Indian chief. The story is a sad one, and that no quarter was given is regarded as savage barbarity. Are we sure that Gen. Custer would have given quarter had the tide of battle turned in his favor? Let the fate of Black Kettle's band, on the Washita, November 27, 1868, answer. After the sad affair on the Little Big Horn, Gen. Terry withdrew his command to the mouth of the Big Horn, there to refit and await reinforcements, which were at once sent forward to join him. Troops were also sent forward to strengthen Gen. Crook, who, on the 5th of August moved down Tongue river, in search of "hostile" Indians. He lost the trail, and moved his forces south toward the Black Hills. While on the way, Capt. Mills, of the Third Cavalry, on the 8th of September, discovered an Indian village near Slim Buttes, of about thirty lodges, and laid by that night, and the next morning surprised the village, killing some Indians, taking some prisoners, and capturing a number of ponies. This village was located on the Sioux reservation, and inhabited by agency Indians, who had not been in the conflict. From its stores of dried meat, Gen. Crook procured sufficient to supply his troops with food, and thus he was enabled to reach Custer City, in the Black Hills, where supplies forwarded from Camp Robinson met him. He also detailed Col. Merritt, with a column of troops, to scout down the Cheyenne river, and thence to Red Cloud agency, himself and suite preceding them. The errand of Col. Merritt to the agency was to dismount and disarm the Indians there; but, before his arrival, Gen. McKenzie, from Camp Robinson, had anticipated him, and seized the arms and ponies of Red Cloud's band.

Gen. Terry broke up his command, sending Col. Gibbon

back to Montana, and going himself, with the Seventh Cavalry, to Fort A. Lincoln, and from thence down the Missouri to the Standing Rock and Cheyenne river agencies, to dismount and disarm the agency Indians, which was a part of the original plan of the campaign, and, according to Gen. Sheridan, "a final settlement of all further difficulties with the Sioux," provided the Northern Cheyennes and the village of Crazy Horse were killed or captured; and, this done, he said, "the Sioux war, and all other wars of any magnitude in this country, will be at an end forever."

It would seem, however, that there was some work still on hand, since Col. Otis, who had been left on police duty at Glendive, reported a two days' engagement with the Sioux, whom he said he punished severely, and they sued for peace, which being granted, the Indians were paroled, under promise to report at Tongue river. And Col. Miles, who was also on like duty about Tongue river cantonment, had, it was reported, an engagement with Sitting Bull and his followers, in which, after irregular conflicts of several days, over four hundred lodges surrendered, and gave hostages for the delivery of their men, women, children, ponies, arms, and ammunition, at the Cheyenne river agency, on the 2d of December. Sitting Bull and about thirty lodges escaped north. These reports of Otis and Miles were subject, of course, to revision; but, as it was necessary to have some victories for our troops before the close of the year, in which they had been engaged in a most ignoble as well as unfortunate campaign, much prominence was given to them. Gen. Sheridan certified their truth and verity, on the 10th of November, to Gen. Sherman, who was delighted with the news, and congratulated all concerned on the prospect of closing the Sioux war, and expressed delight at the energy and earnestness of Gen. Miles, with the hope that he would crown his success "by capturing or killing Sitting Bull and his remnant of outlaws." Happy the officer who may bring in the head of Sitting Bull, as a star and promotion would surely follow.

The Indians who agreed with Gen. Miles to go into the agency were, in fact, agency Indians, of the Minneconju and Sans Arc bands, who had long desired to return home, but were excluded by the order to dismount and disarm them. They had but few arms, their ammunition was exhausted, and, wearied and worn, they were anxious to get into the agency, and did not belong to Sitting Bull's followers; and there were not four hundred lodges of them. As indicating the actual condition of the agency Indians who were out hunting when the war began, and who could not get home without submitting to injustice and degradation, it may here be stated that, in November, about one hundred and twenty lodges of Uncpapas came to Fort Peck, suppliants for food. They soon heard that Gen. Hazen was on his way to the fort with four companies of troops, and fled southward. When they went out in the spring, they had good lodges, of which not one remained; their ponies were very poor, and they were without food, or ammunition to procure it. One single fact such as this should go far to dissipate the extravagant statements of military men as to the equipment, supplies, and designs of the agency Indians. In relation to these Indians, and their temper and condition, there is something noticeable in the reports of Gen. Terry and Gen. Crook. The former, in the report of his operations in the field, and at Standing Rock and Cheyenne river agencies, says nothing on this point; he simply reports his discharge of the duty assigned him. In view of the fact that, as a commissioner on the part of the United States, he was a party to the treaty of 1868, by which the integrity of the reservation and the unceded Indian country was guaranteed to the Indians, with the undisturbed use and occupation of the same, it has seemed a cruel thing for his superiors to put him in the field to punish the Indians for exercising rights acquired under the treaty. As a good soldier, he must obey orders, there being no alternative other than the resignation of his office. As to Gen. Crook, his reports overflow with charges and allegations against the agency Sioux. He said officially, on September 26, 1876, that, from the date of the treaty of 1868 to the present time, there had been no time that the settlers were free from depredations; that the Indians, without interruption, attacked persons at home, murdered and scalped them, stole their stock, and, in fact, violated every leading feature of their treaty. He said that "the reservations, instead of being the abode of loyal Indians, holding the terms of the agreement sacred, have been nothing but nests of disloyalty to their treaties and the government, and scourges to the people whose misfortune it has been to be within their reach." When it is stated that Gen. Crook, from the date of the treaty with the Sioux, in 1868, until a brief period previous to the time he wrote the above, had been located on the Pacific coast and in Arizona, and hence personally ignorant of the condition, temper, and conduct of the agency Sioux, the reader will know what weight to give to such bold and reckless statements.

It is presumed that the war department was properly informed in relation to the status of the Sioux nation, as well as the object of the expensive military operations in the Sioux country. In a communication to President Grant, dated July 8, 1876, not three months before the date on which Gen. Crook made his sweeping indictment, the secretary of war said : " The present military operations are not against the Sioux nation at all, but against certain hostile parts of it which defy the government. . . No part of these operations is on or near the Sioux reservation. . . The object of these military expeditions was in the interest of the peaceful part of the Sioux nation, supposed to embrace at least nine-tenths of the whole, and not one of the peaceful or treaty Indians has been molested by the military authorities." Gen. Sheridan had said in a letter to Gen. Sherman in May, 1876, that nearly every Indian, man, woman, and child, among the agency Indians, was at heart a friend. In the light of the statements of the secretary of war and Gen. Sheridan, it seems marvelous that Gen. Crook should place in his report such unfounded charges against the Indians of the Sioux agencies.

Although the secretary of war advised the president in July that not one of the peaceful or treaty Sioux had been molested by the military authorities, it appears from the annual report of Gen. Sherman, made on the 10th of November, 1876, that it was a part of the " original plan " of the campaign to dismount and disarm the friendly Indians at the agencies, and this deed of treachery was actually performed at Red Cloud on the 23d, Standing Rock on the 26th, and Cheyenne river on the 28th of October, 1876, by the forces of Gen. Crook and Gen. Terry, assisted by the local garrison at each agency. Was this scheme concealed from the secretary of war? The agreement made by the Sioux commission with the agency Indians, guaranteed to each individual protection in his rights of person, property, and life. The military officers at Red Cloud, Standing Rock, and Cheyenne river were all aware of this provision in the agreement, and some of them, at each place, attested the execution of the paper. Were they aware at the time that they, in the near future, were to be called upon to assist in despoiling these Indians of their property? These are pertinent questions, involving as they do not only the personal honor of each officer, but the character of the service for frankness and open and fair dealing.

The ostensible object of this war was to compel Sitting Bull and his followers to come into an agency, remain upon the reservation, and cease from depredations. If this step were proper, it is quite apparent that the Indians had not such notice as to enable them, if they had been willing, to comply, before they were turned over to the war department. It is not out of place to hear a word on this subject from the Indians. Bear-stands-up, a Brulé chief, went out from Spotted Tail agency to bring home some relatives of his wife, and their women and children. He was moved to do this because of the progress of the war. He returned home on the 25th of June, 1876. He found among the " hostiles " a few northern Cheyennes, some Yanktonais, Arickarees, and Gros Ventres. He must have left the " hostile " camps nearly a month before he returned. He supposed there were of the " hostiles " some two thousand, made up chiefly of those Indians who were excluded from coming to the agencies when the war first began, by the military order requiring them to surrender their arms and ponies. As the troops approached the Indian camps he had great difficulty in getting away. He said the Indians made their soldiers watch the camps and keep the people together. He talked with Sitting Bull and was permitted to move his lodge in the night, and then came very far around to keep out of the way of both Indians and soldiers. Sitting Bull sent word to the agent by him " that he did not intend to molest any one

south of the Black Hills, but would fight the whites in that
country as long as the question was unsettled, and if not settled,
as long as he lived." As soon as the Black Hills question was
settled, he wanted the agent to send him word and tell him
what to do. He said " when the rascality about the Black
Hills was settled, then he would stop his rascality." He did
not want to fight the whites, but " only to steal from them as
they had done from the Indians. The white men steal and the
Indians won't come to a settlement." He said " the government had promised much to the agency Indians that has never
been fulfilled, and it wants to move the agencies again. If
moved, who will occupy the land? It belongs to the Indians.
If good white people will not listen to the Great Father, no
more you young men will listen to your chief." The message
of Sitting Bull closed with this remark : " If troops come out
to him, he must fight them, but if they do n't come out he intends to visit the agency and will counsel his people to peace."
In the latter part of October, Gen. Miles had an interview with
Sitting Bull, at the request of the latter, under a flag of truce.
The chief stated (said Gen. Miles) that " he desired to hunt
buffalo, to trade (particularly for ammunition), and agreed that
the Indians would not fire upon the soldiers if they were not
disturbed. He desired to know why the soldiers did not go
into winter quarters, and, in other words, he desired an old
fashioned peace for the winter. He was informed of the terms
of the government, and on what grounds he could obtain
peace, and that he must bring his tribe in or near our camp.
The interview ended near sunset, without result. . . The Indians appeared again next day, and desired a talk. A council
with Sitting Bull and others followed. Sitting Bull was anxious
for peace, provided he could have his own terms. . . The demands of the government were fully explained to him, and the
only terms required of him were that he should camp his tribe
on the Yellowstone, near the troops, or go into some government agency and place his people under subjection to the government. He said he would come in to trade for ammunition,
but wanted no rations or annuities, and desired to live as an
Indian ; gave no assurance of good faith, and as the council
ended, was told that a non-compliance with the liberal terms

of the government would be considered an act of hostility."
Such is the substance of the interview as detailed by Gen.
Miles.

It is quite apparent, from the purport of Sitting Bull's
views, as conveyed by Bear-stands-up, and also to Gen.
Miles, that he was decidedly an anti-agency Indian, and desired to lead the life of a nomad, but it is not seen that he is
such an outlaw as he has been depicted. He will not fight
any one south of the Black Hills, but if troops come out to
him he must fight them ; he wanted no rations, and desired
to live as an Indian, and if the whites quit their rascality he
would quit his rascality, etc. This is about the substance of
what Sitting Bull uttered, and it seems from it that if white
men did not invade his home there would be no trouble with
him, since he asked neither ammunition nor rations from his
great father. His life since he went into the British Possessions seems to be in accordance with avowals made before he
left his range near the Yellowstone. In the queen's dominions no one has disturbed him, and he has kept the peace.
Here he made no demand that the provisions of the treaty
did not warrant him in making. He had a right to roam and
hunt, and his doing so was no offense. He had a right to annuities as a nomad, which he never received and did not
claim. The order requiring him to go to an agency to dwell
there was in violation of his treaty rights, and the attempt to
execute that order by force was a grave offense. In discussing this question in the New York *Tribune*, Bishop Whipple
said : " I know of no instance in history where a great nation
has so shamefully violated its solemn oath. We first sent an
army into the country which we pledged no white man should
enter to seek for gold. The discovery was heralded by the
press. A greedy host of adventurers flocked to the Eldorado.
The press, the people, and the rulers seemed to have forgotten
that these red men held the title to these lands by the guarantee of a nation's honor, as well as by the undisputed possession of centuries. It was the old story of Ahab coveting
Naboth's vineyard. Ahab excused his conscience by calling
Naboth a churlish old fellow, and he crowned the infamy by
robbery and murder."

The troops of Gen. Terry and Gen. Crook achieved a brilliant victory at Standing Rock, Cheyenne river, and Red Cloud, when they swooped down upon the agency Indians and seized their arms and took their ponies. The military report of the affair at Red Cloud said: "Gen. McKenzie, Fourth Cavalry, with eight companies of the cavalry and part of the Pawnee scouts, left Camp Robinson after dark on Sunday evening, 22d October, and early the succeeding morning surrounded the bands of Red Cloud and Red Leaf, and when daylight dawned, and they saw the condition of things, they surrendered without firing a shot. They were at once disarmed, their ponies taken from them, and the warriors, followed by their families, with their camp equipage and property, brought to the agency, where they were released and put in camp. About seven hundred ponies were captured, with all the arms and ammunition the Indians had about their persons or their lodges." In reporting this bold and brilliant attack on these "hostiles" to Gen. Sheridan, the fact was so gratifying to Gen. Crook that he closed thus: "I feel that this is the first gleam of daylight we have had in this business." A few days after this event, a gentleman not in the military service thus wrote of it to the chairman of the Sioux commission: "To hear Red Cloud tell his story of the treatment he received would make your heart melt with sympathy. It was the most touching recital of wrong I ever listened to. He was told by the military that it was done by order of the president. He asked if his great father had given such an order, and said: 'What have I done that I should receive such treatment from him whom I thought my friend?' My faith in justice being done to the Indians has been obliterated by the course that has been pursued toward this peaceable people."

Gen. Terry stated that the force with which he made a descent on Standing Rock and Cheyenne river agencies was composed of the Seventh Cavalry, three companies of infantry, and a section of artillery. This force was divided into two parts, one of which, consisting of four companies of cavalry, under Major Reno, marched by the right bank of the Missouri to Standing Rock, and reported to Lieut.-Colonel Carlin, Seventeenth Infantry, commanding at the post, who, with his own garrison and Reno's troops, dismounted the Indians on that bank of the river. The other portion, under Col. Sturgis in person, moved on the left bank. It reached the camps on that bank at the same time that Major Reno arrived on the other side, and was equally successful in accomplishing the object of the movement. " Not a shot was fired and no violence was used." Colonel Sturgis' column then marched to Cheyenne agency, to which three companies of infantry from Fort Sully were also brought, reporting to Lieut.-Colonel Geo. P. Buell, Eleventh Infantry, the commander of the post: " This display of force was quite sufficient to effect our object, and the Indians quietly surrendered their arms and their animals. About nine hundred ponies from Cheyenne agency and about twelve hundred from Standing Rock are now on their way to this place (St. Paul), where they will be sold. Without doubt many more will be obtained from Indians who will come in to the agencies for food during the winter." The execution of this piece of vandalism does not seem to impress Gen. Sully in the same manner that the same duty did Gen. Crook at Red Cloud. In a few weeks thereafter five hundred additional ponies were taken from the Indians at Standing Rock, and five hundred more from those at Cheyenne river. The number of ponies seized at the three agencies was seven hundred and eighty-seven at Red Cloud, thirteen hundred at Cheyenne river, and seventeen hundred at Standing Rock. Of these it was said twenty-one hundred were started for St. Paul, there to be sold, of which it was reported more than one-half perished on the road for lack of food. Such as arrived at St. Paul were sold for a mere trifle. About four hundred were driven to Yankton, without food on the way, and there sold for a nominal price. This leaves five hundred of the ponies seized at Cheyenne river and Standing Rock unaccounted for. What was done with these? Those from Red Cloud were taken to Laramie; a portion of them sold at a nominal price, and the remainder taken for a remount for Gen. Crook's Indian allies. The number of arms found with these " hostile " agency Indians proved to be inconsiderable, and the greater part were old guns and pistols. The ammunition they had was quite insignificant in amount.

A gentleman, not of-the army, who was at Cheyenne river when the Indians were dismounted and disarmed, thus wrote of it: "I am not a radical Indian lover, nor-do I hate a class of people that are more to be pitied than punished; but if I ever sympathized with, or grieved for any community, I really did for these poor, hungry, and half-starved Indians, as they came, band after band, some of them actually crying, to deliver to the great, glorious, and free government of the United States, represented by the 'big chief,' commanding the department, acting under order from our brave lieutenant-general, located at Chicago, *their own private property;* theirs by every law, human and divine, and to which our government has no right in the world, no more than it has to my watch or pocket-book; but taken by virtue of the law that might makes right. Failing signally, during the late summer, in conquering, punishing, or himself even fighting the 'hostile' Sioux, General Terry has achieved a most decisive victory over the Indians called the 'coffee-coolers' at this agency. The latter, I presume, compensates for the former. He has now temporarily retired from this part of the country, and will rest on his laurels won at this blood-thirsty agency (?) without firing a gun, and will recuperate at St. Paul, to prepare for a fresh onslaught in the spring, while his subordinates carry on the business of the war and interior departments, in this country, to suit themselves. The question forcibly presents itself: How long is this condition of things to last?"

This is a pertinent question. Such a condition of things, so at war with every principle of justice, ought not to be tolerated for one moment; and such conduct would not be permitted if the people of the United State were aware of the terrible wrong, the overwhelming injustice, visited upon our Indian population. If the public mind was fully enlightened, and the public conscience aroused, to realize, in all its enormity, the cruel conduct of high military officials toward this hapless people, all engaged in it would meet with merited rebuke, and the chief actors be driven from positions for which they are utterly unworthy.

A word as to Sitting Bull, whom General Sheridan has officially stated to be an insignificant warrior, with a few thieving followers. Some have reported this chief as having been schooled among the whites, and being conversant with the English and French languages. He says these are all "strange lies." On being interrogated about these stories, and which he denied, the chief said, "What I am, I am;" and, in his attitude and expression of barbaric grandeur, he repeated: "I am a man. I am a Sioux."

On the 6th of November, 1877, when informed by Major McCloud, of the Canadian police, that he must hold himself ready to move his band to the Red Deer river—that the queen had provided a home for him there—he is reported to have said: "I came to you, in the first place, because I was being hard driven by the Americans. They broke their treaties with my people; and when I rose up and fought, not against them, but for our rights as the first people on this part of the earth, they pursued me like a dog, and would have hung me to a tree. They are not just. They drive us into war, and then seek to punish us for fighting. That is not honest. The queen would not do that." After thanking the queen, he said: "Tell her that I will be a good man; that my people will be good. I will take my people to the Red Deer country; and now I do declare, before you, that I will not make any trouble, or annoy you, or give pain to the queen. I will be quiet. I will never fight on your soil unless you ask me to help you. Then I will fight. Place me where you will, I will be at peace in Canada. But you, who are brave soldiers, and not treaty breakers, thieves, and murderers, you would think me a coward if I did not die fighting the Americans. Therefore, while I go to Red Deer river, now to live in peace, I will come back when my braves are strong [here he almost shrieked], or if they will not come with me, I will come alone and fight the Americans until death. You I love and respect; them I hate; and your queen's soldiers would despise me if I did not hate them. That's all."

21

CHAPTER XVI.

IN referring to the military operations of Generals Terry
and Crook against the Sioux Indians, Gen. Sheridan, in a
dispatch dated November 10, 1876, said that Generals Crook
and McKenzie had then only to hunt up and deal with the
band of Northern Cheyennes and the band of Crazy Horse,
and if successful, of which he had no doubt, the Sioux and all
other Indian wars of any magnitude in this country, would
be at an end forever. Before detailing the military operations against these bands, it seems appropriate to speak of
the Northern Cheyennes and Arapahoes. The peace commission of 1867–8 made a treaty with them on the 10th of
May, 1868. By this treaty they relinquished all right or claim
to any and all territory, except the right to roam and hunt
as long as game abounded in sufficient quantities to justify the
chase. While exercising this right they were to receive like
annual annuities as the nomad Sioux. It was, however,
agreed that a permanent home should be provided for them
on the reservation of the Cheyennes and Arapahoes, south, or
the reservation of the Crows, or the reservation of the Sioux;
and when located on such reservation, school-houses were to
be erected and teachers employed, agency houses and mills
built, and millers, engineers, farmers, and blacksmiths supplied them, and as the separate families located, each was to
receive similar annuities as the Sioux of the same class. The
appropriation of $500,000, made by Congress, July 27, 1868,
to be expended by Gen. Sherman in commencing the fulfillment of the treaties made in 1867–8, had reference to the
treaty with these as well as other Indian tribes. They were
then residing north of the Platte, and had for some time
domiciled with the Sioux of the Red Cloud agency. On the

10th of August, 1868, by military order, Gen. Sherman created the Sioux district, and assigned Gen. Harney to it, and set apart to his use $200,000 of the $500,000. It was expressly declared in the order that the $200,000 was to enable Gen. Harney to fulfill the treaty stipulations with the Sioux. The Northern Cheyennes and Arapahoes were entirely overlooked. No place was designated by Gen. Sherman within the Sioux or any other reservation for their home. In no communication from him to Gen. Harney, or to any other of his military agents, to whom he confided funds to fulfill treaty stipulations, were these Indians named. It does not appear that any of the military agents of Gen. Sherman ever had any interviews with them. From that time forward until September, 1876, when the Sioux commission, in the agreement then made, incorporated them with the Sioux Indians, the Northern Cheyennes and Arapahoes had no fixed home, and hence could only rely upon their right to roam and hunt, and for the exercise of this right, under the military order of June 29, 1869, they were regarded as hostile, and subject, wherever found by military scouting parties, to be treated as such and dealt with accordingly. They had continued from time to time to domicile with the Sioux, of the Red Cloud agency, and received some attention from the agent. An effort was made in 1873, by the interior department, to induce them to join the Southern Cheyennes and Arapahoes, but they declined to do so. In 1874, Congress prohibited the department from giving them any supplies until they should join the southern Indians. Owing to complications which sprung up south of the Arkansas, it was not deemed expedient at that time to attempt their removal. An arrangement was made with them, however, looking to their removal in the future. In 1875, Congress again indicated in the appropriation act, that they should go south before any delivery of annuities was made to them, and the commissioner of Indian affairs, in his report dated November 1, 1875, stated that until such removal there were no funds from which they could be supplied with rations. After the failure of the commission that met the Sioux in the fall of the year 1875, to obtain a cession of the Black Hills, the Indian office decided on the removal of the Northern Cheyennes and Arapahoes, and requested the secretary of war, should the Indians refuse to go, to supply troops to compel them. The matter was referred to Gen. Sheridan, and he expressed the opinion that the change ought not at that time to be made. The secretary of war on the 18th of November, 1875, advised the interior department that such was the opinion of Gen. Sheridan.

At this time Gen. Sheridan was contemplating a war with the Sioux, and this war was inaugurated in February, 1876. In March of that year, a portion of Gen. Crook's command, under Gen. Reynolds, struck the village of Crazy Horse, on the Little Powder river. A large portion of the Northern Cheyennes were then dwelling in this village. Thus they became involved in the war. In the Indian appropriation bill, passed August 15, 1876, Congress again made it a condition that no supplies should be furnished these Indians until they removed south. In all this time no steps had been taken to set apart a home for them south, or anywhere else, and no agency buildings, or other improvements, were provided for them.

In this condition of things, about the middle of September, 1876, the Sioux commission of that year (being then at Red Cloud agency negotiating with the Indians there for a cession of the Black Hills) was waited upon by a delegation of the Northern Cheyennes and Arapahoes, who requested that their people be incorporated with the Sioux, in the agreement about to be made, and which was shortly after executed, and they were made parties to it. The commission had no specific instructions to that effect, but it was apparent that these Cheyennes and Arapahoes had a right to a home on the Sioux reservation (among others), guaranteed to them by the treaty of May 10, 1868, and having indicated a desire to live with the Sioux, who were perfectly willing to receive them, there seemed to be a propriety in making them parties to the agreement. They were unwilling to remove south; they had no association with the Crows, and were friendly to and many of them intermarried with the Sioux. The agreement was executed with the different bands of Sioux residing at the Red Cloud agency, and Northern Cheyennes and Arapahoes, on the 20th of September, 1876. It was executed by the Sioux at Spotted Tail agency, and the Sioux at the agencies on the Missouri, between that time and the last of October, 1876.

In the fourth article of the agreement, it was stipulated that the Indians should select a delegation from each band to visit the Indian Territory, with a view to the selection of a permanent home in that territory, provided that on actual view a suitable location, satisfactory to them, to the Indians in the territory owning the land, and the United States, could be made; and such delegations from Red Cloud and Spotted Tail agencies were selected and visited the country, and were, it was understood, generally well pleased with it. The civilized tribes received the delegations with marked attention and great kindness. On the return of the delegations to the Red Cloud and Spotted Tail agencies (these being the only bands that agreed to send delegates), they were not permitted to make report to the Indians they represented, since officers of the army were then acting as Indian agents at both these agencies, and Gen. Sheridan and Gen. McKenzie, the latter then in command at Camp Robinson, were opposed to the visit of the delegates, or the removal of any of the Indians to the Indian Territory. On the 28th of February, 1877, Congress ratified the agreement made by the commission with the Sioux and the Northern Cheyennes and Arapahoes, first striking out the fourth article, and adding an express prohibition against the removal of any portion of the Sioux Indians to the Indian Territory, until the same should thereafter be authorized by act of Congress. Thus the Sioux were confined to the present Sioux reservation, and both they and the Northern Cheyennes and Arapahoes were, by the third article of the agreement, bound to receive all future subsistence and supplies on said reservation, and in the vicinity of the Missouri river. The law creating the commission of 1876 required that any agreement it made with the Sioux should contain a clause of this kind. The condition was very distasteful to the Indians at Red Cloud and Spotted Tail agencies, since they did not desire to live in, or near the valley of the Missouri river.

In the ratification of the agreement, Congress did not prohibit the removal of the Northern Cheyennes and Arapahoes to the Indian Territory, and yet it did not relieve them from the obligation to receive their future subsistence and supplies at some point on the Sioux reservation, and in the vicinity of the Missouri river. In the Indian appropriation act of March 3, 1877, providing for annuities and subsistence for the Indian tribes for the year ending June 30, 1878, there is not one dollar appropriated to supply the Northern Cheyennes and Arapahoes with the ration stipulated to be given them by the agreement of September 20, 1876. There is an appropriation in their behalf for clothing, and for the pay of a physician, teacher, carpenter, miller, farmer, blacksmith, and engineer, and ten dollars per head to be expended for each of said Indians that may lead a nomadic life, and roam, and hunt!

After the repulse of Gen. Crook, on the Rosebud, on the 17th June, 1876, he moved his troops, by easy stages, in a sort of retreat, passing through the mining camps in the Black Hills, where he separated from his command, and, by way of Red Cloud agency, returned to Fort Laramie. Here he met Gen. Sheridan. He then passed on to the Pacific Railroad, and thence to his home at Omaha. Here he rested until November, before he again resumed offensive operations. His errand was then to hunt up the Northern Cheyennes and Crazy Horse's band of the Sioux, and when these were dealt with, the war, according to Gen. Sheridan, was to be closed. This was Gen. Crook's third expedition. He was, no doubt, aware of the location of these Cheyennes, as well as the location of the band of Crazy Horse. The former were in the Big Horn mountains, and a column of his troops, under the command of Gen. McKenzie, set out in pursuit of their village. On the 24th of November, Gen. McKenzie reached the base of the mountains. Here he rested until about four o'clock in the afternoon, when his scouts were ready to conduct him on his tedious way to the village of the Cheyennes. A correspondent with the troops wrote that the command followed the scouts " through the long, cold night, over mountain and through valley, along steep precipitous bluffs, where a slip or a stumble meant broken bones, or worse.

Until midnight, a bright moon and clear sky favored them, but from that time till daylight seemed an eternity to the scattered, groping, weary command. In many places there was barely room for a single horse to keep the narrow trail, and every few minutes the command would be compelled to halt, and wait for the rear of the column to close up. Wearily dragged the hours, until four o'clock A. M., when it was rumored that the village was only three miles to the front. Another march, and another halt. The scouts were near the village, and the attack was to be made at daylight. Cautiously and silently the long column crept through the broken, ragged valley. Suddenly, while the eastern sky disclosed the gray aspect of approaching day, a scout discovered a dark figure guarding a group of ponies. The figure starts; fires a pistol among them, and flees down the valley, hotly pursued by the cavalry and a body of Indian scouts. Across a stream, and turning to the right, appear, only a few hundred yards in advance, the white steeples of a large Indian village. A wild, prolonged yell broke from hundreds of savage throats, as the Sioux and Pawnee scouts dash into the village, and among the herds of ponies belonging to it. A single rifle shot, closely followed by a rattling volley, told the rear of the column that the ball was opened; and with horses at their utmost speed, down the slippery, dangerous paths, they tore on like a hurricane, to be in at the death. The north fork of Powder river, on which the village was located, is, at this point, a small stream, from fifteen to twenty feet wide, running through a canon varying from a fourth to half a mile in width. On the eastern side, a high, precipitous cliff, of reddish rock, ran nearly parallel to the course of the stream. On the west side, just over the village, was a high, abrupt bluff. Above the village the surface of the ground was broken by broad, deep ravines, running perpendicularly to the stream and the face of the cliffs to the east. Three of these were succeeded by gently-rolling surfaces, gradually rising to the high table-land above, and cut up by numerous small ravines. Along the bed of the stream grew numerous cottonwood trees, the space between that and the bluffs being bare of timber. The attack was a total surprise to the In-

dians, the first intimation of the approach of the column being
the arrival of the herder who had been surprised by the scouts.
The Cheyennes had jumped on their ponies, and were hurry-
ing their squaws and children out of the camp, up the creek,
toward the high ground, for safety, when the troops came
tearing down upon them. Panic-stricken, they fired a volley, and fled, taking refuge among the rocks and ravines,
from which they began to pour a fire on the cavalry, then just
forming for the attack. Some of the Indians had gained the
bluff overlooking the camp, and commanding the immediate
vicinity. The Indian allies charged these, and after a hot
contest, killed all the Cheyennes, and kept possession of the
bluffs, from which they did effective service during the fight.
Some of the Cheyennes still occupied the upper part of the
village, and were directing their fire among the troops. Capt.
Taylor's company of the Fifth Cavalry was ordered to charge
them, and they gave way. The contest, however, lasted all
day." The village was fired, and burned. It was estimated
to contain near three hundred warriors, and twelve hundred
souls. Many Indians were left dead upon the ground.
Many more were killed, but were carried off by their friends.
Eight officers and privates were killed, and about twenty-five
wounded. The winter store of buffalo meat laid up by the
Indians was estimated at 80,000 pounds. This, and 1,200
robes, a large number of saddles, cooking utensils, axes, and
various tools belonging to the Indians, with all their personal
property and clothing, were, with the village, numbering
more than two hundred lodges, burned. Over six hundred
ponies were captured, and given, it was said, to the Indian
"allies." The Cheyennes that escaped were utterly destitute,
scarcely saving even a blanket. The weather was intensely
cold, and it was the opinion among the troops that many of
the Indians that escaped must perish. The Indian "allies"
of Gen. McKenzie, it was said, fought bravely, and did most
excellent service. It was admitted that without their vigilance and aid it was hard to see how the troops could have
accomplished any thing effective. The village was so securely
hidden away, that without the aid of the scouts, the troops
could not have found it. Indeed, it was thought by some

that had not Gen. McKenzie had his Indian "allies," the Cheyennes could have given him a terrible punishment. This work accomplished, Gen. McKenzie did not pursue the winter campaign any further. Knowing, before he set out, the region in which the Cheyennes were, his mission was to surprise their village and destroy it.

Here was an Indian village, hid away in a secluded place, where no white people could reach it. The location was far away from any traveled road, and in the recluse of the mountains. Every indication would go to show that its inmates had not recently been on the war-path, but diligently employed in laying up a winter supply of food, and preparing for market the hides of the buffalo they had slain. These Indians were deprived of any annuities. They had no home on any reservation, but had a right to roam and hunt, and in the country in which they were, this right was guaranteed to them. It is true that in September previous they had been incorporated with the Sioux, in the agreement then made, but the agreement required the approval of Congress before it was binding, and that was not given until the following February, and then Congress modified it, so that, practically, nothing was left them as a home but the hunting right guaranteed by the treaty of May 10, 1868. There was, however, in the agreement of September, 1876, with these and the Sioux Indians, a pledge that each individual should "be protected in his rights of property, person, and life," and this pledge Congress did not disturb. The covenants of this agreement were known to all the military officers at the posts within the Sioux country, and it was known by both Gen. Crook and Gen. McKenzie that the Northern Cheyennes and Arapahoes were parties to the agreement. It is thus that military officers disregard the covenants made by the government with its Indian wards. Under the circumstances, it was a grave offense, it was a crime, to attack this village, kill its inmates, and destroy their property. Such conduct should at all times be disavowed by the government, and such of its public servants as participate in it should be severely dealt with. In transmitting Gen. McKenzie's report of his operations to Gen. Sheridan, Gen. Crook said: "I can not

commend too highly this brilliant achievement and the gallantry of the troops."

Among the Indians who joined in the expedition as " allies "
of Gen. Crook, were Sioux, Arapahoes, and some Northern
Cheyennes. They were from the Red Cloud and Spotted
Tail agencies. They were told by Gen. Crook that he desired
them to join him in an expedition against the Northern Indians—not the Northern Cheyennes. The term "Northern
Indians " was well understood by the Indians at the agencies,
and did not embrace any of the Sioux of the Red Cloud or
Spotted Tail Indians, or the Northern Cheyennes and Arapahoes. They were not told that the object was to surprise and
attack the Northern Cheyennes. At Fort Fetterman, on the
7th of November, 1876, the Indians accompanying the expedition held a council with Gen. Crook. In their speeches
they referred to the agreement made with the Sioux and
Northern Cheyennes and Arapahoes, in September, and spoke
of the delegation sent down from the Red Cloud and Spotted
Tail agencies to explore the Indian Territory. They said that
when this delegation returned, nothing must be done until
they got back ; that when the delegation returned, and " we
come back, we want to pick out an agency and work together." They also said : " We are going with you to fight
the Northern Indians. When you came and asked us to help
you fight these Indians, we said, yes, we'll go with you.
. . . We want good arms, good horses, and plenty of
ammunition." Gen. Crook made them liberal promises, and
they all seemed pleased. Thus they were deceived, and a
part of them induced to join an expedition against their own
people, when they supposed they were going to fight the
Northern Indians.

The Cheyennes, who escaped, had Gen. McKenzie determined to pursue them, it is probable he could not have captured. During the next spring they, or a portion of them,
surrendered to Gen. Miles. It is said that the chief, Hump,
who was the speaker of the party that made the surrender,
handed his belt and gun to the general, and also turned over
all his ponies, saying : " Take these ; I am no longer chief or
warrior." On being asked by a correspondent of the New

York *Herald,* who was with Miles, why he should thus put himself in hostility to the government, Hump replied: "I never went to war with the whites. The soldiers began chasing me about, for what cause I do not know to this day. I dodged as long as I could and hid my village away, but at last they found it, and I had no alternative but to fight or perish. I fought the white chief McKenzie, and would have whipped him and his soldiers, if fresh troops and his Indian allies had not come to his assistance just when they did. As it was we were beaten and lost all our lodges. We had to retreat over one hundred miles, and the weather was bitter cold. We almost perished, but at last reached Tongue river, where there was a big camp. We had not been there long before Gen. Miles came with his foot soldiers, and we had to fight again." At this juncture Hump asked a group of Gen. Miles' officers, "Why did your soldiers come after us?" and not one of them could tell him.

At the time that Gen. Reynolds surprised the village of Crazy Horse, in March, 1876, this chief was on his way to Red Cloud agency. He was, however, by reason of the inclemency of the weather, detained at Little Powder river for a long time, and here Gen. Reynolds struck and destroyed his village. The treatment he received from Gen. Reynolds did not impress him favorably, and hence he did not pursue his journey any further, but remained a nomad. On the return march of Gen. Crook's forces, after Gen. McKenzie had destroyed the Cheyenne village, scouts were sent out in various directions with the hope that the village of Crazy Horse might be discovered; but the troops did not find it. It was more than a month before they returned to Fort Fetterman, and so intensely cold was the weather, that further military operations were abandoned. Some of the agency Indians from Red Cloud and Spotted Tail were, however, sent out in pursuit of Crazy Horse. They found and induced a number of Indians, both Cheyenne and Sioux, to come in from time to time to the agencies. They found Crazy Horse, and while they could not induce any of his band to come in, or obtain any promise from him to do so, yet their influence was such that it wrought a change, and early in May the chief made his appearance at Red Cloud agency with his people. A few days thereafter a council was held, in which the chief said to Gen. Crook: "You sent tobacco to my camp to invite me to come in. I came at once, and since getting in here I have been looking toward the post, and my heart has been happy. In coming this way I picked out a place and stuck up a stick in the ground for a place to live hereafter, where there is plenty of game. All these relations of mine that are here, I would like them to go back with me and stay there." The Young-Man-Afraid-of-his-Horse also spoke. He said: "This was his country, and the treaty allowed them to live here, but if the Great Father said they must leave, they wanted to go north of the Black Hills, where bad white men could not steal their ponies and ruin their country. They wanted a brick school-house and a good minister." High Bear also spoke. He said: "In the first place *we want the interpreter to have courage, and tell the truth.* We have been here for many generations, and this is our ground. I talk for my people. You sent for us to come in, and we knew that some of our people were with you, and we did not wish to fight them, and so we came. I want a place in my country where we can get some game, and a place where I can travel around and chase buffalo, and visit about and be free." The drift of these talks will be better understood when the reader is informed that the matter of removing the agencies of Red Cloud and Spotted Tail to the Missouri was then under discussion, and none of the Indians were favorable to that measure. Spotted Tail closed the conference. He recited the many treaties that had been made with them, and all of which had been broken by the white people and the government. He alluded to the commission that made the agreement of September, 1876, with the Sioux. He said the commission made them promises which were never kept, and concluded with the suggestion " that as there was a new president, he hoped he would help them. So many words," he said, " had been sent to him in time past, and so much had been lost, that he hoped some of them could go to Washington and see him (the new president) face to face. We will," said the chief, "throw away all past treaties and make a new one, which will give us good lands and good schools."

Gen. Crook, in his reply, when referring to the allegation of Spotted Tail, that the promises of the Sioux commission had not been kept, said : "In regard to the commissioners I have had nothing to do with them, and if they do n't keep their word, I can not help it." When we call to mind that the commission, in their agreement with the Sioux and Northern Cheyennes and Arapahoes, pledged the United States to protect each individual Indian in his rights of property, person, and life, and that scarcely one month after the execution of the agreement at Red Cloud agency, Gen. McKenzie, by order of Gen. Crook, took from Red Cloud's and Red Leaf's bands nearly nine hundred ponies and all their arms, burnt about fifty teepees, and temporarily imprisoned Red Cloud, the reply of Gen. Crook places him in a position that no man of honor should desire to occupy. He knew that these acts of vandalism were done by his authority; that they were a part of the original plan of the campaign, and yet in direct violation of the covenants of the agreement. He knew that, at the time of the execution of the agreement at Red Cloud, Standing Rock, and Cheyenne river agencies, the military officers of the local garrisons who witnessed the execution of the instrument, were aware when they did so that very soon it would be violated, in this particular, by the troops. He knew, also, that the commission were kept in ignorance of what was soon to transpire. In the light of such facts, what a commentary on the frankness and honor of the American soldier is the reply of Gen. Crook to Spotted Tail! The commission, when referring to this piece of vandalism in their report, said: "This seizure was unjust and, in view of the facts, cruel to the Indians."

In the month of August, 1877, there was some difficulty at the Red Cloud and Spotted Tail agencies, owing to which the bands of Crazy Horse were dismembered and distributed among other bands, and this chief was arrested and held as a prisoner. On the 5th of September, Gen. Crook telegraphed Gen. Sheridan that Crazy Horse was then a prisoner, and that he had " ordered Bradley to send him off where he will be out of harm's way." He was arrested at Spotted Tail agency, on the 4th of September, and on the evening of the 5th arrived as a prisoner at Camp Robinson, and while being disarmed at the guard-house, was stabbed with a bayonet by a soldier, and died in a few hours thereafter; and thus he was put out of harm's way. It is presumed that the act of the soldier who stabbed the chief was considered, by the officers, a meritorious one, since it does not appear that any proceedings were had against him.

On the 15th of May, 1877, Gen. Sheridan telegraphed Gen. Sherman that the Northern Cheyennes, then at Camp Robinson, desired to go to the Indian Territory, and strongly urged that they be removed to it. The dispatch was referred to the Indian office on the 17th of May, and on the 18th that office advised the adjutant-general that such removal was approved. By what process these Indians had been led to request that they should be transferred to the Indian Territory is not shown. At the time there was a military officer acting as Indian agent at Red Cloud. For several years previous to this time, these Indians were unalterably opposed to going to the Indian Territory, to dwell with the Cheyennes and Arapahoes then residing there. That they were desirous to be separated from the troops of Gen. McKenzie, is no doubt true; but that they sought an alliance with their southern namesakes is not probable. However, in a few days following the date of these dispatches, they were on their way south, conducted by Lieut. Lawton. That officer telegraphed, on the 29th of May, that he was then *en route* to the Indian Territory with 972 Northern Cheyennes, whose removal he was ordered to superintend. On the 5th of August, 1877, these Indians arrived at Fort Reno, and, on the 7th, they were turned over to the agent of the Southern Cheyennes and Arapahoes. The Northern Arapahoes were removed to the Wind river reserve, in Wyoming. It is stated that the Northern Cheyennes, on their arrival at the agency, said that they had come to see how they liked it, and that if they did not like it, they would return north. It will be observed that they were seventy days on their journey. A writer, who met them on the way, said they traveled " quietly and mournfully, for events had forced them to this choice, and they had left their home with the regret of the emigrant. The bucks were mostly mounted. Many of the squaws, however, carried their papooses on their backs, and led ponies that hauled the travois."

In the annual report of the agent for the Cheyenne and Arapahoe agency, in the Indian Territory, for the year ending June 30, 1877, made August 31, 1877, reference is made to the Northern Cheyennes, who had then been there less than one month. The agent said that their connection with his agency had been so brief that he had not been able to form an opinion or fathom the under current that controlled them. He said that there was a marked difference between them and the southern Indians; that they did not yield to the department regulations with such cheerfulness as their southern brethren. He thought, however, that it was not singular that there should be among them a feeling of distrust, as many of them were then in mourning for the loss of sons and brothers in the war, while others were suffering from wounds received in battle. He hoped, in time, by firm and just treatment, to win their confidence. He reported that Lieut. Lawton turned over to him 937, whereas that officer reported on his way that he started with 972.

These Indians were all dissatisfied with their new home. They were wild horsemen, who had never been brought under any agency discipline. At the close of the fiscal year, ending June 30, 1878, the agent reported this tribe to number 970. He said about one-half had refused to affiliate with the Southern Cheyennes, and invariably camped by themselves, away from the other Indians, 'and in all respects acted as if a different tribe. He said they manifested no desire to engage in farming, and in council and elsewhere expressed an intense desire to return north, where they said they would settle down. No difference was made by the agent in the treatment of these and the other Indians. All were required to do certain things, as a condition to the issue of the sugar, coffee, and tobacco ration. The compliance of these Indians with the requirements was of a different nature from that of the others. He thought it might become necessary, in the future, to compel that obedience which he had been unable to obtain by an appeal to their better natures. Had we their view of the case, we should, no doubt, have some reasons, from an Indian standpoint, for their action. Dull Knife's band were among the dissatisfied. These were intermarried with the Ogallalla, or Red Cloud Sioux, and longed to return north and join their friends. So intense was their feeling, that among the Indians they were called the Sioux Cheyennes. They did not conceal the fact that they intended to return north, and such was their temper that on the 5th of September, 1878, the agent informed the commanding officer at Fort Reno of the fact. On the night of the 9th of September, this band, more than three hundred in number, left their lodges and started north. The fact was communicated to the agent about three o'clock the next morning, by one of his Indian police. He immediately dispatched a messenger to Fort Reno, to notify Col. Mizner, and requested him to send out troops and bring them back. The colonel had previously ordered two companies to watch this band, but these camped about four miles from Dull Knife's camp. It was, for some reason unexplained, eight hours after the Indians started, before the troops who had been posted to watch them, knew of their departure! It was said there were eighty-seven warriors in the party. It made a journey of six hundred miles with its camp equipage and its ponies. It was stated that in their progress the Indians did not attack a settler, or any one else, until after they were struck by the troops. They had gone about 120 miles before they were overtaken by the military. Several engagements took place as they passed on through Kansas, and they killed settlers, burnt houses, and committed other atrocities, such as are incident to savage warfare. It is probable they were not aware of the removal of the Sioux from the Red Cloud agency until they had reached northern Nebraska, since their line of march looked in that direction. Here they surrendered to the troops. In their different engagements the band was considerably decimated. The troops, also, lost both officers and men. The *Telegraph* newspaper, of Sidney (Nebraska), of the 25th of January, 1879, stated that when these Indians surrendered in the fall, they claimed that they were assured they should not be taken back to the

Indian Territory. The editor had visited Fort Robinson to obtain information. After being imprisoned more than two months at Fort Robinson, it was agreed upon by the war and interior departments that the Indians should be returned south, to the end that such of them as committed the murders and other atrocities in Kansas might be identified, and put on trial. This was said to be in pursuance of a demand from the governor of that state.

When informed that the government had determined to send them back to the Indian Territory, Dull Knife and his warriors protested. They said they would prefer death where they were than submit to removal. It was midwinter, and terribly cold, and, as a means of reducing them to submission, it was stated that they were for five days deprived of proper clothing, food, and fuel. This was done by the military at Fort Robinson. With the flag of our country floating over the fort, they deprived the Cheyenne men, women, and children of blankets, food, fire, and water for five days, in order to compel them to yield and return to an association they despised! Should such inhumanity be tolerated, and its perpetrators go unpunished? Instead of yielding, the Indians were made more desperate by this attempt to starve and freeze them into submission. Within one hundred feet of their prison-house were several companies of United States troops, and sentinels were kept on duty. These warmly-clad men paced to and fro, with their arms ready for service. Although the Indians had determined to die rather than be carried back, there were apparently at this immediate time no fears entertained by the officers, notwithstanding the interpreter had informed them that the Indians premeditated an outbreak. Strange to relate, that on the evening of the 9th of January, it is said that every available stretcher was overhauled and placed in position where it could be easily brought into use; the attendants were forbidden to retire, and for some reason the troops did not turn in. Moreover, the windows of the prison were left unbarred. About eleven o'clock at night, on a signal given by Dull Knife, every warrior leaped through the windows of the prison-house, and the

22

women and children followed. As the warriors passed from the prison across the grounds of the barracks, and out toward the cold prairie, they fired upon the guard with revolvers, which they had concealed, and four of them were wounded. The main guard, on the report of the revolvers, rushed out, and, following the Indians, shot and killed more than forty of them. Then, as soon as possible, a hundred and sixty cavalry-men started in pursuit, and the sharp bang of their carbines was heard as they pursued the fleeing Indians, who made for the bluffs about three miles distant from the fort. A dispatch from the fort, on the morning of the 10th of January, stated that it was thought not an Indian would be able to escape. The pursuit of the Cheyennes was kept up by the troops, first by one squad and then another, until the 22d of the month. After a few days, there was a disposition to relax, but a dispatch from the fort, on the 15th, stated that Gen. Crook had ordered that the pursuit be continued. On the 16th of January, Capt. Weasels set out with four troops of fresh cavalry. By this time the ranks of the Indians were considerably reduced. He took six days' rations. On the 22d, he closed the campaign. On that day he attacked the remnant of the band, then intrenched in the mouth of a ravine, about twenty miles north of Bluff station, and about fifty miles from Fort Robinson. His troops encircled the Indians, leaving no possible avenue of escape. As soon as the skirmishers approached within striking distance, the Indians fired on them, killing one lieutenant and two privates, and wounding the third. The troops advanced and opened a deadly fire on all sides, and with terrible effect. The Indians, then without ammunition, rushed with desperation toward the troops with their hunting-knives in hand; but before they had advanced many paces a volley was discharged by the troops, and all was over. The bodies of twenty-four Indians were found in the ravine, including, as the dispatch stated, "seventeen bucks, five squaws, and two papooses; nine remained, of whom one buck and five squaws were more or less wounded, and three squaws unhurt." A dispatch to Gen. Crook, of the date of January 23d, said that "the Cheyennes fought with extraordinary courage and firmness, and refused all terms but death." The dispatch of the 15th, from the fort, which stated that Gen. Crook had given positive orders that the pursuit be continued, said, that on the 14th the troops abandoned the pursuit, leaving the Indians in possession of the natural mounds north of Indian creek. The same dispatch stated that "thirty-two Indians, of which twenty-five were bucks and the remainder women and children, had been killed and buried in one common grave." An observer of one burial said: "Let us see the dead and wounded brought into the fort. The soldiers drag out of the army wagons twenty-six frozen bodies. They fall upon the frozen ground like so many frozen hogs. These bodies are pierced by from three to ten bullets each. They are stacked up in piles like cord-wood, the scanty clothing of the women being in some instances thrown over their heads. They are a ghastly pile of God's poor despised children. Their heads have been scalped, and every indignity heaped upon them that more than Indian brutality can invent. The officers account for so many shots being fired into the bodies by saying that 'whenever the wind stirred a blanket, the soldiers fired again to make sure the Indian was dead.' They deny that the soldiers scalped the dead, but it is not shown that other savages were there."

In the annual report of the agent, made in August, 1878, the Northern Cheyennes, then near the agency in the Indian Territory, numbered 970. After Dull Knife and his band escaped, there still remained 650 of these. Hence, the number that left with Dull Knife was 320. We find that a few days after the close of the campaign by Capt. Weasels, on the 22d of January, 1879, there were sent from Fort Robinson to the Pine Ridge agency twenty-two Cheyenne women and thirty-two children, widows and orphans, to dwell with the Ogallalla Sioux, their relatives; and, on the 4th of February, 1879, Capt. Vroom started from the fort with the survivors, being seven Cheyenne men and their women and children, fourteen in number, on his way to Fort Leavenworth, Kansas, to the end that these might be turned over to the civil authorities, to answer for the murders and arsons committed by the band of Dull Knife, on its journey north, in the fall of 1878. Those sent to Pine Ridge and to Fort Leavenworth together numbered seventy-five, who survived of the band of 320 who fled from the agency in the Indian Territory on the night of September 9, 1878.

No man who is familiar with the antecedents of the Northern Cheyennes will assert that the attempt to assimilate them with their southern namesakes was in any sense proper. All conversant with the facts will admit that it was a mistake. For long years in the past, there was no affiliation. They were separate and distinct. Hence, the commission of 1867–8 made a separate and distinct treaty with them. When they had an opportunity, they sought a connection in treaty relations with the Sioux, and were, by the agreement of 1876, incorporated with them. Congress, for years preceding that time, made it a condition that the annuities to be paid them under the treaty of May 10, 1868, should only be paid on their going south, and this they would not do. There was a strong attachment between them and the Red Cloud Sioux, and instead of being sent south in 1877, they should have been allowed to join these Sioux. The only treaty or agreement that guaranteed them rations was the one in which they were associated with the Sioux—that of September 20, 1876. The military have held that Dull Knife's band were moved to break away from the southern agency, in September, 1878, because they were being starved. The agent and the commissioner of Indian affairs say that this is not true. The charge of the military appears to have been based on a letter written by Col. Lewis to Gen. Sheridan, shortly before the outbreak. This officer was stationed at Fort Dodge, nearly 250 miles from the camp of the Cheyennes. He had never visited the Indians, and hence had no personal knowledge in the premises. He, it was said, got his information from a military scout employed at Camp Supply, Indian Territory. In an engagement with Dull Knife's band, as they went north, Col. Lewis fell, and hence can not now speak on the subject. Gen. Pope also states, though he had not the information officially, that when the commanding officer (he does not name him) overtook the Indians, he called Dull Knife to one side, and told him that he did not wish to attack the Indians, and requested the chief to return to the agency without resistance; but the chief replied that the government had not complied with its promises; that they had waited patiently for supplies; that they could not starve, and were going back to their old hunting grounds; that, rather than return to the reservation, they would die in their tracks. In a report made by the commissioner of Indian affairs, on the 16th of November, 1878, he makes such an exhibit of rations furnished as would lead to the impression that the Indians were fully supplied with the beef ration. The agent admits that for several issues preceding the departure of these Indians there was no flour issued to them, but, in lieu thereof, there was an extra issue of beef. It is a fact, however, that the sum appropriated by Congress for the subsistence and civilization of the Arapahoes, Cheyennes, Apaches, Kiowas, Comanches, and Wichitas, for the fiscal year ending June 30, 1879, is $10,000 less than the appropriation for the same purposes was previous to the transfer of the Northern Cheyennes to the Indian Territory. Thus, while the population was increased, the gross appropriation for its support was reduced. Moreover, the annuity of ten dollars per head, which had been regularly appropriated for the benefit of the roaming Northern Cheyennes, up to the end of the fiscal year ending June 30, 1878, was cut off by Congress, and disappears in the appropriations for the year ending June 30, 1879. This item would amount to $9,720, which, had it been appropriated, could, under the discretionary authority as to its use, have been applied to ration these Indians. Whatever the fact may be as to the supply of food, or the cause of leaving the agency and going north, the conduct of the military, in their remorseless and inhuman butchery of these Indians, can find no justification.

CHAPTER XVII.

THE SIOUX COMMISSION OF 1876.—CORRESPONDENCE OF GENERALS McKENZIE, CROOK, AND SHERIDAN, IN RELATION TO THE INDIANS AND THE OPERATIONS OF THE COMMISSION.—THE REMOVAL OF THE COMANCHE AND KIOWA INDIANS FROM FORT SILL TO THE WICHITA AGENCY.—ILLUSTRATIONS OF THE FRANKNESS AND CANDOR OF HIGH MILITARY OFFICERS.

THE officers of the army affirm that, by reason of their intelligence, integrity, business habits, and experience, they are especially qualified for the peculiar duties necessary to the proper care and training of the Indian race. Gen. Sherman states, without hesitation, that to give the care of the Indians to the army is to assure not only fidelity, humanity, and economy in the conduct of their affairs, but that it would eliminate from the Christian influences among them that "cant and hypocrisy," which now pervade the civil service.

In this connection, and by way of illustrating the conduct of high military officers, it is proposed to refer to some matters that occurred in the fall of 1876, when the Sioux commission were among the Indians, negotiating for the Black Hills. It was apprehended by some of the officers at the posts that the commission had some power to, or that its action would, in some way, bring the Sioux war to a close. Unfortunately, the instructions of the commission were such that the question was not touched by it in any of the councils held with the Indians, nor was one word embodied in the agreement it made with the Sioux in reference to the war. The Indians did appeal to the commission to help them "rub the war out;" that it was not an Indian war, but a white man's war. But no authority being found in the instructions to warrant interference, the war phase was not touched. But the military officers were quite anxious on the subject; and the remark that the army had "the matter in hand, and ought not to be interfered with," was frequently heard. The military then had possession of the agencies at Red Cloud, Spotted Tail, and Standing Rock, with army officers discharging the duties of Indian agents. At Cheyenne river the civil agent could not issue a ration of sugar or coffee without the permission of the commander of the garrison. They expected soon to possess all the agencies, and their plans for future operations and the management of the Indians through the military arm were substantially settled, and any step that looked to an interference with these plans was not agreeable to the military gentlemen at any of the agencies, and was very distasteful to the higher officers.

By their instructions the Sioux commission was informed that the president was "strongly impressed with the belief that the agreement which shall be best calculated to enable the Indians to become self-supporting is one which shall provide for their removal, at as early a day as possible, to the Indian Territory, and that the solution of the difficulties which now surround the Sioux problem can be best reached by such removal. The instructions, among other things, said: "Their main dependence for support must ultimately be the cultivation of the soil, and for this purpose their own country is utterly unsuited." If it were deemed necessary to enable the commission to incorporate a clause into the agreement providing for the transfer of the Sioux to the Indian Territory, to send a delegation of the Sioux down to examine the country, authority for that purpose was given in the instructions; and in the exercise of this authority, and deeming it only just to the Indians that they should send a delegation of their best men to the territory to examine the same, provision for that purpose was made in the agreement, and a delegation representing all the bands at both Red Cloud and Spotted Tail agencies was finally sent to and did explore considerable of the territory. Some of the commission had doubts as to the propriety of incorporating such a provision in the agreement, not because it was not deemed desirable, if practicable, to transfer the Sioux to the territory, but it was feared that the Indian nations who owned and possessed it, would not entertain the proposition favorably, and hence that evil might result. As it turned out, the delegation were received with great favor, and wherever they went among the civilized Indians they were greeted with expressions of friendship, and deep interest was manifested in their welfare. The speech of the principal chief of the Creek Indians, welcoming the delegation, made at the council-house at Okmulgee, in the Creek nation, is a model speech, and contained this paragraph, not only of welcome, but of invitation. He said : " We believe our right to our soil and our government, which is best suited to our peculiar necessities, would be safer if all our race were united together here. That is my earnest wish. Then I think the rising generation could be educated and civilized, and what is still better, christianized, which I believe would be the greatest benefit of all. This would be to our mutual benefit and good. I know I express the minds of our people when I give you this welcome to our life of a higher civilization, which is better than the old life so long led by our race in the past."

All the Sioux at the agencies on the Missouri, except the small band of Santee Sioux, expressed an unwillingness to send delegations to visit the Indian Territory, and they were relieved from the obligation. Hence, under the agreement, none of these bands of Sioux, except those at Spotted Tail and Red Cloud, and the Santee Sioux, (had Congress ratified this clause of the agreement,) could have been subject to removal to the Indian Territory. The number at these agencies was about 12,000 or 13,000. They were not all, at the time, prepared to be transplanted, but, under a judicious system of colonization, thirty-three per cent. of them per year could with safety have been removed. If the experiment proved successful, which it is believed it would have been, in a few years, the Sioux of the Missouri valley would have followed, and thus this interesting group of our native population would have been emancipated from the degradation and pauperism that must be their fate if kept on their present reservation, and concentrated according to the suggestions and recommendations of Gen. Sherman and Gen. Sheridan, who urged, in the fall of 1876, that " they be compelled to remove to the Missouri river, near Fort Randall, where they can be guarded and fed at one-half the present cost." The idea of concentrating the Sioux at or near Fort Randall, or any other point on the Missouri or elsewhere, where the soil can not be cultivated successfully, there to be treated like brutes and fed like wild beasts, is simply revolting. Any place that does not offer a reasonable prospect for self-support, by cultivating the soil and herding combined, should not be regarded as their permanent home. It is doubtful whether there be such place within the Sioux reservation.

President Grant approved of the agreement which the commission made with the Sioux, Northern Cheyennes, and Arapahoes, but Congress struck out the paragraph providing for the removal of a portion of them to the Indian Territory. When the delegation returned home from the exploration of the country, the agents then being army officers, the members were not permitted to make report of their proceedings, or the opinion formed of the country explored, to the Indians who sent them on the errand. Generals Sherman, Sheridan, Crook, and McKenzie were all opposed to the removal of the Sioux, or any part of them, to the territory, not in sentiment merely, but their opposition was open and active, notwithstanding the measure was recommended by the president.

That such a measure would meet with opposition from such sources as desired this Indian Territory thrown open to the whites, was to be expected; and this opposition would be powerfully backed by such railroad interests as had covetous eyes upon the territory, and desired land grants therein. Unfortunately, Congress seems to be under the influence of these classes, notwithstanding the scandal and downright corruption that has grown out of land grants in the past.

The first opposition, however, to the proposed transfer of a portion of the Sioux to the Indian Territory, did not come from this class of persons, but from the army. The agreement was executed by the commission and the authorized representatives of the Indians, at Red Cloud agency on the 20th, and at Spotted Tail on the 23d of September, 1876; and the commission left Red Cloud agency, on the 26th of the month, for Sidney, and thence to the Indians on the Missouri. General Crook was at Red Cloud agency on the 20th of September, and left that day for Fort Laramie, where General Sheridan and General McKenzie then were. On the evening of September 24th, General McKenzie returned to

Camp Robinson, of which he was commander. It is situated about two miles from Red Cloud agency. On the 30th of September, he prepared and put in form a document, the substance of which was no doubt agreed upon at Fort Laramie. General Crook knew, before he left Red Cloud, that a conclusion had been reached, and that the Indians were about to execute the agreement. This document of General McKenzie has never been published. It is proposed to incorporate it herein, with the productions of Generals Crook, Sheridan, and Sherman—all apparently based upon it. They are all precious specimens of military literature. The date, as has been stated, is September 30, 1876, and the document is addressed to General Crook, then just arrived at Omaha. It reads as follows:

" *My Dear General:* The state of affairs here is about this. The commission, which was appointed by the secretary of the interior some weeks ago, left here last Tuesday. The Indians have agreed, as I am informed, to move to the Missouri or the Indian Territory, and to send a delegation, from each band, to look at the latter country. They will undoubtedly perform the latter part of their agreement, *i. e.*, send men to the Indian country—a small part, in my judgment, in good faith; but the larger part, in my opinion, to gain time. Just prior to the arrival of the commission, the various bands of Sioux were called on by me to give up such hostile Indians as had returned. They were called on, in pursuance of my instructions from my military superiors; and these instructions were issued, I believe, in accordance with the joint wishes of the secretary of the interior, of the secretary of war, and the general of the army, and with the approval of the president. It was carefully explained to the leaders of the various bands, that this demand was not made simply by me; but at the instance of the highest civil and military officials of the government.

" Now these Indians, in the face of this knowledge, have willfully and obstinately failed to give up any of the parties known to be in any of their camps, and who have been absent engaged in war, and atrocities outside of war.

" Now very soon a part of the gentlemen of this commission, I believe, may be expected back, for the purpose of carrying away, to the Indian Territory, certain of the principal Indians, for the purpose before set forth ; and, unfortunately, many of those who are likely to be taken are the very men who have most conspicuously failed to act loyally toward the government of the United States; and also use, to their utmost, their influence to shield the class of malignant criminals to whom I have referred.

"It is well to mention in this connection, that in my remarks to these Indians, I have taken care to explain that I make this demand, instead of at once proceeding with soldiers to make the arrest, for the reason that the soldiers did not know the individual, and that in the event of a camp being surrounded by soldiers, it was always to be apprehended, that through the folly or wickedness of a few evil-disposed Indians, or even a single individual, to bring on a very serious collision, which might involve the death of many innocent men, and in the end was sure to entail lasting troubles on any Indians who might desire to do right. I will give you but two instances of individual Indians, though they might be multiplied to include the vast majority of them at the Red Cloud and Spotted Tail agencies. Red Cloud and Spotted Tail at the present moment, and have without doubt for weeks, been concealing and endeavoring to exculpate this very worst class of criminals. They are treating with utter contempt my authority as the chief representative of the government of the United States here present, and they are doing this with the full knowledge that my orders are given from the most humane of motives, and given, too, with the belief that such a course has, in similar circumstances, avoided collision with the larger bands of the southern plains, and they are thus acting knowing that my orders are just, and that they are no emanation from myself, but from the very highest officers of the government.

"As for reasons which are deemed wisest, it has been thought best not immediately to act. It seems to be very important that those chiefs be not allowed to leave this country with any civil agents of the government, to look at the Indian Territory, or for any other purpose.

"There is to my mind, from the utter and wide-spread contempt of the highest authority, a temporary existence of martial law, and I believe myself to be justified in preventing at this time any departure of any Indians, under the instructions of any civil officer, no matter what his rank, or any civil official from exercising any authority so far as regards these Indians, or holding any communication with them.

"Now I wish to avoid the possibility of any clash of authority, and therefore wish to urge on you, general, the propriety of procuring from the president the suspension of any action resulting from the agreement of the recent commission, for such period as in your own good judgment may be desirable. I wish to urge on you, and through you in such manner as you may deem most fitting, on our superiors, up to the president, alike the military and civil head of the government, that it would be in my judgment (while believing these Indians ought to be transferred to the Indian Territory as soon as it possibly can be done) utterly wrong in their present condition, as regards arms, and in their present defiant attitude toward the government, to send them there, should they all be willing to go to-morrow. It would be cruel alike to the citizens of the surrounding country and to the Indians, on whom the heaviest weight must in the end inevitably fall.

"In closing I wish to urge on you, and through you on my superiors, and I would very much like my opinion to go to the president, that it is of the greatest importance at once, as a military matter, and as a matter of humanity, as regards soldiers, frontiersmen, and Indians, that there be no further communication with the Sioux at Red Cloud and Spotted Tail agencies, except through the military authorities. With the recent commission I am happy to be able to say that I have had no clash whatever, and endeavored in every way to oblige them."

On the receipt of this most extraordinary document at Omaha, Gen. Crook, on the 2d of October, 1876, forwarded it to Gen. Sheridan, at Chicago, with the following indorsement:

"Respectfully forwarded. I heartily concur in the views of Gen. McKenzie. These agencies are and have been the head and front of all the trouble and hostilities which have been in progress. They are and have been regular depots of recruits and supplies. Many of the very Indians who have been out all summer are now there with the arms and booty of their summer's work, and they do not intend to give up either the arms or the Indians themselves. The parties to the late treaty or agreement are not representative men, and there is no doubt but they are simply doing all they can to gain time. I am certain that unless something positive is done, we shall have to go through the same thing next summer that we have this."

On the 13th of October, 1876, Gen. Sheridan forwarded the communication of Gen. McKenzie, with the hearty indorsement of Gen. Crook, to Gen. Sherman, at Washington City, with this additional indorsement:

" Respectfully forwarded. I have felt deeply the embarrassment brought about by the presence and action of the commission, referred to in this communication, to say nothing about the unfortunate results which may follow. There is scarcely an instance, in the settlement of this widely-extended country, where the Indians have left their places of abode, until after the conclusion of a fierce strife which disabled and broke them down; and the very propositions made by the Sioux to go to the Indian Territory, are sufficient to induce every able-bodied man to take the field; and there is not, in my mind, the slightest doubt that every Sioux Indian capable of bearing arms is now getting ready to take the field in the spring. The paper presented by the commission, and signed by the Indians under protest (at least in their hearts), was only signed to carry them over the winter. The Indians who are out and actively hostile, have been sufficiently encouraged to continue out, believing that they will be joined by all now at the agencies, in the spring.

" There does not seem to have been a thought about where the Indians, amounting to over 30,000, are to be located in the Indian Territory, or the disastrous effect their presence will have on the Indians there, now doing so well. The action of the commission can have no other result than crippling, as it has already done, the action of the military, and produce confusion and calamity."

Gen. McKenzie's document, thus doubly indorsed, and forwarded to General Sherman, was, on the 17th of October, sent to the secretary of war, with copy for the secretary of the interior, thus indorsed by him:

" Respectfully submitted to the secretary of war, with copy for the interior department, and in connection with Lieut.-Gen. Sheridan's letter of September 30, 1876, submitted, with copy, on the 14th instant.

" It is rare that we have in such close connection the frank opinions of three such able men and officers as this paper contains, viz: Generals McKenzie, Crook, and Sheridan. As one who originally negotiated with the Sioux, in the treaty of 1868, and who had much intercourse with them, I must say that I agree with Gen. Sheridan in the belief that the Sioux will never migrate, willingly, to the Indian reservation south of Kansas, in good faith, for the avowed purpose of becoming agriculturists, or to raise stock, as a means of subsistence. They are essentially savage, by nature and tradition, and will never leave the mountain region on the east slope of the Rocky Mountains, without compulsion. The young warriors believe themselves invincible, and are, in fact, dangerous foes, not to be despised. The older men and families may be moved near the Missouri river, where their necessary supply of food can be delivered them at less cost than where they now are, and this will be one step in the direction of weaning them from their habits of war and hunting—the only life they consider becoming their character as warriors. This would leave the eastern slope of the Rocky Mountains to be filled up by miners and grazing farms, north of Laramie, similar to those of Colorado, south of Cheyenne. Near the Black Hills, Custer City, or Deadwood will probably result a settlement of whites, like Denver, able to defend themselves. This would aid the military in the final task of compelling the Sioux to live in a contracted space, like the Kiowas, Comanches, and Cheyennes, now near Fort Sill, and would end this last work of Indian subjugation on the great plains. I submit this case to the careful study of the president and the secretary of the interior."

It is believed that the production of Gen. McKenzie, of

September 30, 1876, has not a precedent in the whole range of military correspondence. A subordinate officer, in command of Camp Robinson, near Red Cloud agency, apparently on his own motion, prepares a document, the intent and design of which was to arrest the progress of the negotiations of the commission created by an act of Congress, acting under instructions from the president, and who, in their councils with the Indians, and in the agreement proposed for execution with them, had kept strictly within the bounds of their authority ; and so intent was he in his purpose, that he appeals to Gen. Crook to procure from the president the suspension of any action growing out of the agreement, which, at the time, had been executed by the Indians, at Red Cloud and Spotted Tail agencies, and the commission had left for other and distant agencies, to submit the agreement to the Indians residing at them. Gen. McKenzie urged his views on Gen. Crook, and through him, on their superiors, up to the president, alike the military and civil head of the government. This was a very bold step, and one which it is believed Gen. McKenzie never would have taken, if he had not known that his immediate superiors stood ready to back him. This was done by both Gen. Crook and Gen. Sheridan. The first heartily concurred " in the views of Gen. McKenzie." The latter was in full accord, and affirmed that the action of the commission could have no other result than the crippling, as it had already done, the action of the military, and thus produce confusion and calamity. Thus McKenzie's document reached Gen. Sherman, but one step from the portals of the executive mansion, and on the 17th of October, 1876, a copy of the budget was transmitted by him to the secretary of the interior, and the secretary of war, with the request that it have " the earnest study of the president and the secretary of the interior."

The secretary of war, it is presumed, was already in full accord with the generals of the army. Gen. Sherman introduces his indorsement thus : " It is rare that we have in such close connection the frank opinions of three such able men and officers as this paper contains, viz : Generals McKenzie, Crook, and Sheridan." The first prepares and dates his paper at Camp Robinson; the second makes his indorsement at Omaha, and the third submits his views from Chicago. They appear to be the opinions of each formed independently and without concert or collusion. When, however, the fact is stated that these "able men and officers" were together at Fort Laramie, from the evening of the 21st to the forenoon of the 23d of September; that the agreement was executed at Red Cloud on the 20th of September, and they were aware of that fact; that the very presence of the commission among the Indians disturbed the military mind very much—there can be no doubt the whole question was discussed at Laramie, and the plan of operations agreed upon, the initiative to be taken by Gen. McKenzie, who then knew that these superiors would indorse and support his suggestions and recommendations. The fact of the caucus at Fort Laramie dissipates entirely the idea of independent thought and action on the part of these "able men and officers." Now as to the statements made by them.

The insubordination which Gen. McKenzie said existed among the agency Indians at Red Cloud and Spotted Tail, was not observed by the commission, nor did they hear of it. The commission arrived at Red Cloud on the 7th of September, and remained there, and at Spotted Tail, until the 25th of the month. The members mixed freely with, and had ample opportunities to arrive at correct conclusions as to the temper of the Indians, and their views, feelings, and desires. They saw nothing and heard nothing to justify the opinion that the Indians were hostile and insubordinate, or that the camps were infested with malignant criminals. They did learn that there were bands of Indians in that region, as well as in the region of Standing Rock and Cheyenne river, who were out and desired to return, but were unwilling to be despoiled of their property, when they did do so, and hence remained away. An incident occurred at Red Cloud, shortly before the commission arrived there, that indicated that the Indians were disposed to carry out the suggestion of Gen. McKenzie. It was this: Sioux Jim, an inferior chief of the band of American Horse, who had been absent from the agency, returned home, when American Horse told him he must surrender himself, and give up his ponies and arms. Jim refused to do this. His chief insisted, and he still refused, when American Horse shot him on the spot, placed the body in his wagon, and bore his remains to Camp Robinson, and turned them over to the military. As to Red Cloud and Spotted Tail, each gave evidence of a desire to comply with the wishes of the government, such as hostile men would not have manifested.

When Gen. Crook followed up his hearty indorsement of Gen. McKenzie's paper with the remark that "many of the very Indians who have been out all summer, are now there with the arms and booty of their summer's work," he stated for fact that of which he had no personal knowledge whatever; and when he asserted that the Indians who were parties to the agreement were "not representative men," he stated that which was not true, and their conduct afterward proved that they were sincere, and not simply acting to gain time.

Gen. Sheridan's indorsement of the fabrications of Gen. McKenzie are followed with the assertion that "the very proposition made by the Sioux to go to the Indian Territory, is sufficient to induce every able-bodied man to take the field, and there is not in my mind the slightest doubt that every Sioux Indian capable of bearing arms is now getting ready to take the field in the spring," and that the paper signed by them "was only signed to carry them over the winter." The fact was, that the proposition to visit the Indian Territory came from the commission, and not from the Indians, and it was one of the most difficult matters to get them to agree to it. Gen. Sheridan also said that the action of the commission on the Indians then out and actively hostile, had been sufficient to encourage them to continue out, believing that they would be joined by all now at the agencies in the spring; and Gen. Crook expressed the opinion that the military, because of what the commission had done, would "have to go through the same thing next summer." Events proved all the statements and predictions of these gentlemen, as to the present status and future designs of these agency Indians, false and unfounded; and Gen. Sheridan himself seemed to

23

have forgotten, in less than a month, all that he had asserted and predicted on the 13th of October, about the agency Indians, when he indorsed and forwarded the McKenzie paper. He even felt free from the "embarrassment brought about by the presence and action of the commission," and said, in a dispatch to Gen. Sherman of the 10th of November, 1876, that Crook and McKenzie had only then to hunt up and deal with the band of Northern Cheyennes and the band of Crazy Horse, and if successful, which he did not doubt, "the Sioux war, and all other Indian wars of any magnitude in this country, will be at an end forever."

Gen. Sherman was a party to the treaty of 1868 with the Sioux, and by it all the Sioux Indians who elected to lead a nomadic life, were not only permitted to do so, but the faith of the government was pledged that no white person should settle in, or, without the consent of the Indians, travel through the vast country called the unceded Indian country. His honor as a soldier, as well as a man, and the honor of the government, was pledged to the Sioux that they should enjoy this hunting right, and such as lived nomads were, for thirty years, to receive a specific annuity. Being at the head of the army, his power was great, and here he had an opportunity to exercise it in behalf of the rights of this hapless people. His disapproval of the McKenzie document and its indorsements would have been an act of simple justice to the Sioux; but he failed in this duty. He not only approved of the document, and the indorsements upon it, but in his comments made to go with it to the secretaries of war and interior, and also to the president for his careful study, he assumes that it will be a meritorious act to wrest from these Indians by force of arms all the rights guaranteed to them by the treaty of 1868.

As to the status and temper of the agency Indians at Red Cloud and Spotted Tail, at the time referred to, instead of being hostile malignants, they were depressed and dejected. This was apparent to the most casual observer; and Red Cloud's salutation to the commission on its arrival, told the whole story. With deep feeling he said: "We are glad to see you; you have come to save us from death."

In referring the McKenzie document to the secretary of war, Gen. Sherman alluded to a communication from Gen. Sheridan, of the 30th of September, which he had previously forwarded. It would seem that Gen. Sheridan was so impatient, that he even anticipated McKenzie's indictment, and on the same day that it was prepared at Camp Robinson, he wrote to Gen. Sherman, from Chicago, and the latter, on the 14th of October, submitted the letter to the war department. The council with the Red Cloud Indians, at which the agreement was executed, convened on the 19th and terminated on the 20th of September. Neither Gen. Sheridan nor Gen. McKenzie was present. They, at that time, were at Laramie. A number of the officers from Camp Robinson were present at the council. That Gen. Sheridan had advices from some one is evident, since he states occurrences that did take place, and puts his own construction on them. Here are a couple of extracts from his letter of September 30th : "It is my opinion that not a single Indian who signed the ultimatum [at Red Cloud] of the commission whose heart and feelings and intentions were not fairly and squarely represented by the Indian who covered his eyes with his blanket when he signed the paper. I wish to state also, in order to show the temper exhibited by the Indians, that Sitting Bull [an Ogallalla Sioux], while in council on the day before the agreement to sign was made, took his rifle in one hand and a horse-whip in the other, and broke up the council by whipping the Indians out of it in the presence of the commission."

Now, it is true that a young chief did draw his blanket over his face when he " touched the pen," which was the token of attaching his name to the agreement. But why was this done ? One of the commissioners during the discussion said at one time: " Your Great Father does not throw a blanket over your eyes;" and at another time : " There is no blanket over any one's eyes now. You must see the trail perfectly straight, so there can be no possible mistake;" and these expressions amused some of the young men, and the young chief threw his blanket over his face, with a jocular remark that caused quite a roar of laughter among the younger Indians.

As to what Sitting Bull did to such as did not understand the matter, it may have seemed abrupt, but there was this in it, and nothing more. The commission pressed the Indians toward the close of the council, on the 19th of September, to get through with their speeches, so that before adjournment the agreement might be executed ; but that was not contemplated by the Indians. There were some points which they desired to discuss further in their own council, and hence it was necessary that the joint council should take a recess. Sitting Bull was the officer appointed by them to act in the character of a sergeant-at-arms, or something of that sort, with certain powers, and among them to do what he did. He adjourned the meeting, and afterward did use a small horse-whip, though not with violence, among some of the young men to disperse them. He did not disturb one of the old men, and was in no wise discourteous to any one of the commission.

On the return of Gen. McKenzie from Fort Laramie, one of the officers of the garrison informed him that Red Cloud, Young-Man-Afraid-of-his-Horse, American Horse, and Black Coal had spoken harshly with reference to the military then about the agency, and it was stated to the chairman of the commission, by an officer of the post, that had Gen. McKenzie been there at the time he would have arrested these Indians, because of their remarks in this connection. The chairman expressed surprise at this statement, when the officer replied that the general would most assuredly have done so. In view of this fact, it seems proper to state here what these chiefs said on the occasion, and this can be done with accuracy, since their remarks were reduced to writing by a competent reporter at the time they were uttered. There was a large influx of troops, both cavalry and infantry, at Camp Robinson, and several companies of the latter were camped within a few hundred yards of the agency. Here is what the Indians said:

RED CLOUD : " We see a great many soldiers here in our country. We know that the duty of these soldiers is to follow people that are bad throughout the western country. We do not like to see them here. I want you to have pity on us, and have them all taken away, and leave us alone here with the agent of the interior department."

YOUNG-MAN-AFRAID-OF-HIS-HORSE: "The soldiers have no business in this country at all, and since I have been here I have always tried to do right. I wish to tell you that I have been very much ashamed ever since the soldiers came here."

AMERICAN HORSE: "You have come here to ask these questions, and at the same time the soldiers are living here in our country, and it seems as if it was a very hard matter for us on account of the soldiers being here. This is the place to hold a peaceful council; it is not a house that was built to fight in. [Referring to the agency buildings.] If they should wish to arrest anybody, they should arrest him and go away to the country at large. I want you to tell this to the soldiers; that the country is very large, and that there are a great many bad men to the north of here, and they ought to go up there after them. We do n't want to know any thing of this kind again. When you go back to Washington I wish you would tell the Great Father these exact words."

BLACK COAL: "This place here is the agency of the government, a place of peace, where we and our people have lived together happily, and behaved ourselves, and we do not understand why so many soldiers come here among us. We have never had any trouble and have behaved ourselves, and wish to have the soldiers sent away as soon as possible, and leave us in peace. The people that live here have both minds and hearts and good sense, but it seems as if the Great Father all at once thought differently, and speaks of us as a people that are very bad. Our only idea has been to live here in peace, and do that which is good for the future of our people."

It is not seen that there is any thing in these utterances that should have offended Gen. McKenzie or any one else. The Indians had been requested by the commission to speak freely on all matters pertaining to their business, and to state wherein they felt aggrieved, if they did so feel. In speaking of the presence of troops and their objection to it, they did not say one word against any officer or soldier personally. The commission, with all the facts before it, concurred with the Indians, and in their report said: "We are impelled to say that it was our unanimous recommendation that all these Indians ought, as speedily as possible, to be placed in the

care of civil agents." From the time that the agreement made
with the Sioux by the commission of 1876, was executed by
the agency Indians at Red Cloud and Spotted Tail agencies,
in September, 1876, until the present period, now more than
three years, the conduct of these agency Indians has been
their most complete vindication against the aspersions and
misrepresentations cast upon them in the document prepared
by Gen. McKenzie, of September 30, 1876, backed by the indorsements of Generals Crook, Sheridan, and Sherman.
Though the covenants of the agreement have been shamefully
violated on our part, these Indians have observed them, and
at all times their bearing has been free from deceit and falsehood. In this regard, when their conduct is compared with
that of the military in charge of them, they are placed on
elevated ground.

In July, 1876, the House of Representatives, by resolution,
called on the president to report to Congress the object of the
military expeditions then operating against the Sioux Indians,
with copies of all correspondence bearing upon the origin and
necessity of these expeditions, together with all military
orders issued by the war department directing the expeditions
under Generals Terry, Crook, and Gibbon. Among the
documents sent to Congress under this call, there is a letter
addressed to the president by the secretary of war, of the date
of July 8, 1876. In this letter, and referring to the military
operations under Generals Crook .and Terry, the secretary
says that the task committed to them is one of unusual difficulty, which has been anticipated for years, and must be met
and accomplished. This, he says, " can no longer be delayed,
and every thing will be done by the department to insure success, which is necessary to give even the assurance of comparative safety to the important but scattered interests which
have grown up in that remote and almost inaccessible portion
of our national domain." The secretary adds that " the present military operations are not against the Sioux nation at all,
but against certain hostile parts of it which defy the government. . . . No part of these operations is on or near the
Sioux reservation. . . . The object of these military expeditions was in the interest of the peaceful parts of the Sioux,

supposed to embrace at least nine-tenths of the whole, and not one of those peaceful or treaty Indians has been molested by the military authorities." There is also among the documents sent to Congress in reply to the call, a letter from Gen. Sheridan, of May 29, 1876, addressed to Gen. Sherman. In this he details the movements of the several columns of troops in the districts assigned to Generals Terry and Crook respectively. He cites the operation of three distinct columns, then in motion, and says: " Gen. Terry will drive the Indians toward the Big Horn valley, and Gen. Crook will drive them back toward Terry; Col. Gibbon moving down on the north side of the Yellowstone to intercept, if possible, such as may want to go north of the Missouri to the Milk river. The results of the movements of these three columns may force many of the hostile back to the agencies on the Missouri river, and to the Red Cloud and Spotted Tail agencies on the northern line of Nebraska, *where nearly every Indian, man, woman, and child, is at heart a friend.*"

In the annual report of Gen. Sherman, of the date of November 10, 1876, after reciting the misfortunes of the troops, and the fall of Gen. Custer, he states that Sitting Bull and his followers having seemed to retreat north, and several small parties of warriors who had been in the Custer fight, having " returned to the several agencies," Gen. Sheridan "*resolved to resume his original plan of dismounting and disarming the friendly Indians at the agencies,* so that hereafter they could not reinforce the hostiles." And the secretary of war, in his annual report, addressed to the president, on the 20th of November, 1876, in referring to the active military operations against the Sioux, and calling the attention of the president to the accompanying report of Gen. Sherman, to which he suggests that it is unnecessary to add any thing, says: " But I wish to bring out in its full prominence the important fact that a vigorous effort is now being made, and so far with success, to disarm and dismount the agency Indians;" and with the success of this measure, he thinks the Indian problem approaches solution, and coincides with Gen. Sheridan in the opinion that " the Sioux war, and all other Indian wars in this country of any magnitude, will be over forever."

Here we have Gen. Sheridan, on the 29th of May, 1876, assuring Gen. Sherman that at the Red Cloud and Spotted Tail agencies at least, if his language does not cover all the Sioux agencies, " nearly every Indian, man, woman, and child, is at heart a friend ;" and the secretary of war, on the 8th of July of the same year, assuring the president that no part of the military operations were on or near the Sioux reservation or against the Sioux nation, but against a refractory and hostile part, not exceeding one-tenth of the whole number; that in fact the expeditions were in the interest of the peaceful parts of the Sioux, numbering at least nine-tenths of the whole nation, and that " not one of these peaceful or treaty Indians had been molested by the military authorities," and yet concealing the fact that the original plan of the campaign inaugurated the February previous, contemplated the seizure of all the horses, mules, and ponies, as well as the arms of the friendly agency Indians, and at the very time that the secretary of war thus wrote to the president, the troops of both Generals Terry and Crook were on their way to commit this act of vandalism, which being accomplished, is with exultation recorded in the annual reports of the secretary of war and the general of the army made the November following.

This robbery of the agency Indians is referred to at some length in Chapter XV. of this work, and the number of horses, mules, and ponies taken is given. Since that chapter was prepared, it has been shown in the testimony taken by the joint committee in December, 1878, that the actual number of ponies taken from the Indians at Standing Rock was 2,000, and not 1,700 ; and the actual number taken from Cheyenne river was 2,200, and not 1,300.* It is believed that, including those taken from Crazy Horse's band in 1877, the number of animals taken at Red Cloud was about 3,000, making in all more than 7,000. These were all disposed of, and for the 2,200 taken from the Indians at Cheyenne river agency, the military returned, as the product of the sale, 450 cows. In the account rendered the Indian bureau, by the war department, it appears that the 2,200 horses, mules, and ponies sold

---

* The Indians claim that at Cheyenne agency 3,072 horses were taken from them.

for $19,412.96, and that the expense of selling them was
$5,683. The residue $13,729.96 was invested in the cows.
The net price yielded from the sale of the animals belonging
to the Indians was $6.25 per head, and the price paid for the
450 cows bought for them was $30.51 per head. Thus it
seems that an expert, well qualified military agent, who is
without "cant and hypocrisy," is absolutely able, with six
head of animals taken from an Indian herd, to return to the
band one cow. The military agent at Standing Rock did not
do quite so well, since there were only returned to the Indians
300 cows, as the product of the sale of 2,000 horses, mules, and
ponies. It is but proper to state that the Indian herds are, in
the main, Indian ponies. These were, however, very superior
animals. Of those taken from Red Cloud agency, it does not
appear that any return has been made of that transaction. It
was stated that the animals of the band of the chief Red
Cloud were taken to Fort Laramie, and 350 of them were
given to the Pawnee scouts, serving under Gen. Crook, for a
remount, and that the balance were sold at about five dollars
per head. In a letter from the chief Red Cloud, written January 14, 1879, he says, in speaking of the military seizure of
the arms and animals of himself and his people, in the fall of
1876: "I ask who got the benefit of all those horses, and all
the robes and rich dresses that were taken out of our tepees?
Were they sold? Did the government get the money? We
did not." In the same letter, the old chief, in speaking of the
condition of the Indians and their needs, said: "I know the
army well, and I know they will never learn us these things.
. . . I do not think the military would bring their hearts
into the Indian work. . . . We can never do any thing
unless we take our hearts with us. . . . One thing I do
know, they are very unreasonable, asking or ordering one
thing to-day and another to-morrow, and if we are not quite
as fast as some hot-headed officer thinks we should be, he
takes our horses, burns our tepees, and the Great Spirit knows
this has often been done when there was no just cause."

In August, 1878, it was, for reasons deemed sufficient, decided to consolidate the Fort Sill and Wichita Indian agencies.
On the 9th of August, the president approved of the measure,

and by it the Comanche and Kiowa Indians were to be re-moved from Fort Sill to the old Wichita agency. When agent Hunt, in pursuance of instructions, removed these Indians, as a precautionary measure, he notified Gen. Pope of the fact, and requested him to send a troop of cavalry to the Wichita agency, to remain there for a brief time. This request was, by Gen. Pope, forwarded to Gen. Sheridan, with an indorse-ment to the effect that he had no troops to fill the order, coupled with a remonstrance against the removal of the In-dians from Fort Sill, since it was to be done *without any suf-ficient reasons known to the military!* On the 14th of Septem-ber, Gen. Sheridan forwarded the papers to the adjutant-general's office, with the following remarks : " I fully indorse the views of Gen. Pope, and am well satisfied, after an ex-perience of more than twenty years, that the principal objec-tion to troops at Indian agencies, and the removal of Indian agencies away from military posts, has, for its main motive, a desire to cheat and defraud the Indians, by avoiding the pres-ence of officers who would naturally see and report it." It will be observed that agent Hunt had nothing to do in this consolidation and removal, except to obey the orders of his superiors, and when he did remove his Indians to Wichita, he requested that a troop of cavalry be sent to the consolidated agency ; and yet the lieutenant-general could see nothing in the transaction but a scheme on his part to get the Indians away from Fort Sill, so that he could cheat them. Mr. Schurz, secretary of the interior, deemed the remarks of Gen. Sheridan as insulting, and requested the secretary of war to inform him that those who determined this measure were, " in point of integrity, honor, and sense of duty, fully his equals, and that to indulge in opprobrious reflections upon their motives, is an act of impropriety so gross that it can not pass without a cor-responding rebuke." This note was sent by the secretary of war to Gen. Sherman and by him to Gen. Sheridan, "for perusal, and to be returned with any remarks he may think proper to make." On the 15th of November, the note was returned by Gen. Sheri-dan, with comments. He said the indorsement made by him, and referred to by Secretary Schurz, was general, and intended to cover operations for a period of twenty years ; and his only object in making it, was to put a stop, if possible, to the appalling waste of army appropriations that attended the removal of Indian agencies, and which called loudly for reform. Referring to the language used by the secretary of the interior, he said : " There can be no excuse for this, but his want of knowledge on the subject, and that does not excuse the stilted tone and the language used."

In order to enlighten, not only the secretary of the interior, but the public, and at the same time vindicate himself, Gen. Sheridan offers a number of instances of the establishment and removal of Indian agencies. The principal ones are here given, in his own language. He says :

" The agency of the Ogallalla Sioux, ten or twelve years ago, was at Fort Laramie, an expensive post, built to control the Indians. The agency was removed from it by the Indian bureau, to avoid the presence of the military. Shortly afterward, the necessity of a military force compelled the bureau to 'ask for troops to be sent to Camp Robinson, and a new post was built there, at an expense which the general of the army can well comprehend.

" The Spotted Tail, or Brulé Sioux, were at the Whetstone agency, on the Missouri river, not far from where Fort Randall had been built, to give it and other interests protection ; but these Indians were removed to Camp Sheridan, two hundred and fifty miles further west ; and being unable, after a time, to get along without troops, a new post had to be established there, at great expense. These Indians have again been moved, and two more posts established. They are now at Wounded Knee and Big White Clay, and by and by the necessity of troops will compel the erection of new posts at each of these locations.

" These removals have cost us hundreds of thousands of dollars, and no one can tell how soon a new change may be made.

" The Indians now at Standing Rock were first located at Grand river, and a military post was requested, and established, to help govern them. Soon afterward, they were removed to Standing Rock, and being unable to do without troops, the post of Grand river had to be removed there."

Gen. Sheridan cites several other agencies, which, he alleges, were subject to the same process of establishment, removal and change, as those here quoted. It is not deemed necessary to present them, since those given above will serve to test the accuracy of his statements, and enable the reader to judge of their sufficiency as a justification for the indorsement he made on the report of Gen. Pope. Referring to the various changes which he specifies in his exhibit, Gen. Sheridan says, that " these removals, which have already absorbed millions of our appropriations in the last ten years, would naturally suggest the inquiry : What was the reason which influenced them ? It could not have been better soil, or less expense, because the soil was no better, and the expense of supply was greater. These changes, and the reports of army officers, from the highest to the lowest (and which are to be found in the office of the general of the army), on the subject of bad management, fraud, and corruption, will furnish the best and most reliable evidence to sustain the remark made."

He repeats that the main cause of the removal of Indian agencies was hostility to army officers, on account of their reports on the civil management of the Indians, and avers that his sole object in making the original indorsement was in the interests of reform, and to put a stop to the " appalling waste of army appropriations," caused by these constant removals of Indian agencies. He then comes back to the matter of his original indorsement on the report of Gen. Pope, touching the removal of the Comanche and Kiowa Indians from Fort Sill to Wichita, and insists that it was a grave mistake, but does not repeat the insinuation that it was wrought out in order that the agent might be enabled to cheat the Indians.

In all that is said by Gen. Sheridan he finds a ready indorser in Gen. Sherman. This is characteristic, since the former has not issued any official document touching Indian affairs, from the time he assumed command of the department of the Missouri, in the spring of 1868, until the present period, that has not been approved by the latter ; and in turn Gen. Sheridan has been prompt to indorse all the utterances of Gen. Sherman. The burden of the military literature of both has been to depict our Indian population in dark colors—a race of barbarous, treacherous, irreclaimable savages—and the Indian service as not only badly managed by the civil agents, but absolutely corrupt. Thus, and by this sort of literature, have the subordinate military officers been educated to decry the Indian and malign the civil agent.

In discussing the question of the consolidation of the Fort Sill and Wichita agencies, and the concentration of all the Indians at the latter, Gen. Sherman admits that the consolidation would be wise, but that Fort Sill is the proper place. He says that to Gen. Sheridan and himself, both being familiar with the country, the removal of the Comanche and Kiowa Indians from Fort Sill to the Wichita agency is proof positive that deceit has been practiced by some one, and that Gen. Pope, as well as Gen. Sheridan, attributes the change to evil motives, but that neither attributes such motives to the president, secretary of the interior, or commissioner of Indian affairs.

In the discussion, the fact is developed that the removal of the Comanche and Kiowa Indians from Fort Sill was first recommended by Col. Alvord. This was done in 1872, but a year or two after the establishment of the agency there. He said in his report that the agency should never have been placed at Fort Sill. The change was afterward urged by the superintendent of Indian affairs, then by one of the Indian inspectors, and again by the board of Indian commissioners. In this connection, it is proper to state that the Comanche and Kiowa Indians were located at Fort Sill and the agency buildings erected by the army officers when these Indians were in their charge. In due time the Indians and the agency buildings were turned over to the interior department. The buildings were so constructed that it was found necessary to prop them up to prevent them from falling, and the stores inside of them had to be kept covered to protect them from rain. When these buildings became utterly unserviceable, and could be used no longer, the question of continuing the location at Fort Sill or transferring the Indians to the Wichita agency became a practicable one, and, after due consideration, the change was determined upon. The propriety of the measure is fully discussed and demonstrated by the secretary of the interior in a letter dated November 29, 1878.

Now as to the sample cases presented by Gen. Sheridan in justification of his sweeping statement that the main object in the removal of Indian agencies from the presence of military posts, was that the agents might have opportunity to cheat them. As to the Ogallalla Sioux, they had not "ten or twelve years ago," or at any other time, an agency at Fort Laramie. Hence none could have been moved from there to avoid the presence of troops. In 1868, when the commission of which Generals Sherman, Harney, Terry, and Augur were members, made a treaty with the Sioux, a definite reservation was set apart for these Indians, and an additional territory outside of such reservation was assigned as a hunting ground for them, but Fort Laramie was not within the limits of either. By this treaty the United States agreed to construct, "at some place on the Missouri, near the center of the reservation," all the necessary buildings for an agency. As all the Sioux could not be concentrated at one point to execute the treaty, a copy of it was left at Fort Laramie for signature, not only of Sioux, but Cheyenne and Arapahoe, and other Indians. Many bands executed it on the Missouri. The Ogallalla Sioux (Red Cloud's band) were the last to sign the treaty. This they did at Fort Laramie. The commission had provided at this place for an issue of some rations to such bands as came in to execute the treaty. It also provided for an issue of rations for a like purpose on the North Platte. During the summer, a special agent was sent out by the interior department to take charge of the Indians in that region, but the military commander at the fort would not permit him to act, or assume any authority in the vicinity of the fort, and when Red Cloud's band had executed the treaty, the same commander at once notified the special agent that "he could not permit any more Indians to come to the post, as Fort Laramie was not within the bounds of the Indian Territory, and if the Indians wanted to communicate with the government, they must go to the new reservation." The question of the location of the agency within the reservation, evidently had not much consideration, and when it became a practical one, it presented many difficulties, which to the present time have not been solved; and hence, now, instead of one agency on the Missouri, and near the center of the reservation, there are within the Sioux reservation five different agencies west of the Missouri, and two, the Crow Creek and Santee Sioux agencies, on the east side of the river. The Ogallalla Sioux were, as late as 1872, residing temporarily on the North Platte, thirty miles southeast of Fort Laramie. A location for an agency was indicated for them on White river, in the fall of 1872, and buildings erected and the Indians removed to it in July, 1873. The military had as much to do in the selection of the site as the civil department. In fact, it is believed that Red Cloud himself indicated it. This was called Red Cloud agency, and is about two miles from Camp Robinson. At this agency, in September, 1876, the Sioux commission found the Ogallalla Sioux and the Northern Cheyennes and Arapahoes, and negotiated with them for the surrender of the Black Hills. The law by which the commission was created, stipulated that no agreement should be valid that did not require the Indians to remove to the Missouri river. At the time of the negotiations, there was, and had been for some time before, a military officer acting as Indian agent. The Indians did not desire to remove to the Missouri, and disliked the stipulation in the agreement which required them to dwell near it. In the fall of 1877, in pursuance of the agreement, the Ogallalla Sioux went to the Missouri river, and from thence, in the spring of 1878, to their present location at the Pine Ridge agency. The last removal was brought about through the earnest solicitation of Gen. Crook, who accompanied a delegation to Washington, whose mission was to ask, on behalf of their people, that the president would permit them to remove from the valley of the Missouri.

The location of the Brulé Sioux, on the Missouri, at what was called the Whetstone agency, was made in the fall of 1868, and by Gen. Harney as the agent of Gen. Sherman. It was an unfit location for the permanent home of any Indians, and the only ones that did come there to dwell were those called the Loafer band, composed of some Sioux and Cheyenne Indians, and some whites who had intermarried with them. Spotted Tail, and the Brulés proper, of whom he was the principal chief, never dwelt there. For several years the Whetstone agency was in charge of a military agent, and he found it necessary to carry the supplies of Spotted Tail and his Indians into the interior. On account of the bad influ-ence of the whites in the valley of the Missouri, the chief held that it would be much better to be back from the river. In 1872, this agency was removed to the interior, in pursu-ance of a promise made to Spotted Tail the previous year, when he, with a delegation of Brulés, visited Washington to petition the president for the removal of the Indians from the valley of the Missouri. The selection of a new location was left with Spotted Tail and his subordinate chiefs, and they designated the point on White river, to which they were removed, and which was known as the Spotted Tail agency. Here the Brulé Sioux resided in 1876. They were an orderly people, and satisfied with their home. In the agreement with the Sioux commission of that year, they were compelled to return to the Missouri to reside. As in the case of the Ogal-lalla Sioux, the law creating the commission required the Brulé and all the other bands to agree in the future to receive their rations and annuities at the Missouri river. Having ex-ecuted the agreement with great reluctance, because of this stipulation, in the fall of 1877, the Brulé Sioux went to the Missouri, and from thence, on their own petition, backed by the urgent request of Gen. Crook, they were, in 1878, re-moved to their present location at the junction of the Rose-bud and White rivers.

The simple statement of the facts touching the original lo-cation, and the subsequent changes, and removal of the Red Cloud and Spotted Tail agencies, shows conclusively that General Sheridan's story, about these transactions, is without any foundation. The changes were not made, by the civil agents, to avoid the scrutiny of the officers of the army into their fraudulent conduct, or for any other reason. Indeed, these had nothing to do with the matter. The military was an active agent in the original location; Congress required the removal to the Missouri to be a condition of the agree-ment with the Sioux, made in 1876; and the change and removal to the Pine Ridge and Rosebud agencies, where the Indians now are, was the result of the earnest petition of delegations of these Indians, made to the president in person, in the fall of 1877, backed by the recommendation of General Crook, who accompanied the delegations to Washington. If these transactions with the Red Cloud and Spotted Tail Indians have, as General Sheridan asserts, cost the army, in following the Indians and the establishment of new military posts, as the locations of the agencies changed, hundreds of thousands of dollars, there has, without any doubt, been an alarming waste of public money. The only military posts established were at Camp Robinson and Camp Sheridan, near the old Red Cloud and Spotted Tail agencies. Aside from the additions made to the post of Camp Robinson, in 1876, and which were in no sense necessary, except as a depot for supplies, and to shelter cavalry horses engaged in the Sioux war of that year, all the buildings ought not to have cost more than $35,000 to $40,000.

The present agency at Standing Rock was originally located at the mouth of Grand river, in the fall of 1868, by General Harney, as the military agent of General Sherman. It was under the control and management of military officers for several years. In 1870, Captain J. A. Hearn, then acting as Indian agent, stated, in his annual report, that the location was "a very poor one; that in high water it was flooded from the Missouri river, and also, in high water, the banks fall away very rapidly, and in a year or two, if the banks continue falling, the buildings will fall into the river." The land was unsuited to cultivation, and the Indians were compelled to go away to distant points, in order to find land on which crops could be raised. Owing to the facts stated, in 1873, the department, at Washington, decided to remove the agency to Standing Rock. Although but four years old, the warehouses were then in a very dilapidated condition, and the agent had commenced to repair them when he received official notice that the agency was to be removed to Standing Rock, and suspended his work.

The agency at Cheyenne river was established in the fall of
24

1868 by Gen. Harney, as the military agent of Gen. Sherman. There was at that time a military post at Fort Sully, but this post was on the east bank of the Missouri, and not on the Sioux reservation. Gen. Harney established the agency on the west bank, and some eight or ten miles above the fort. As he was a military and not a civil agent, it is to be presumed that he did not place it on the west bank and above the post in order " to get away" from the military at the post. These, and a few similar cases, were presented by Gen. Sheridan as a justification for the use of the offensive language to which the secretary of the interior took exception. When examined, it is found that civil agents have had little or nothing to do with the establishment or the removal of these agencies. Except in the matter of the removal of the Ogallallas from Red Cloud (Camp Robinson), and the Brulés from Spotted Tail (Camp Sheridan), to the Missouri, which came of the agreement with the Sioux commission, the credit or censure must be awarded to the officers of the army. And if it be true, as Gen. Sheridan asserts, that such removals in the last ten years have absorbed millions of the army appropriations, he, more than any other, is the gentleman on whom the responsibility must rest, since during that time he has been at the head of the military division of the Missouri. If the military appropriations are thus squandered; if the posts at Camp Robinson and Camp Sheridan, and those on the Missouri above Yankton, have, as Gen. Sheridan asserts, " absorbed millions of the army appropriations" to build them, there is indeed necessity for reform, and Congress, instead of turning to the army for relief from real or imaginary profligacy in the management of Indian affairs, should, in a business way, look into the mode and manner in which the vast sums expended in army disbursements are disposed of, and for what. A thorough investigation into military management, in all its details, at the various posts and in the Indian country, would, it is believed, point to avenues of reform and retrenchment, which, if pursued, would lead to important results. That this is not an idle remark, reference is had to a case or two; and, first, *Fort Sill.* We have the statement of

Gen. Sheridan that he established this post, and it is believed he spent several months there. There is high military authority for saying that the assistant quartermaster who was sent to Fort Sill to build the post, reached there with "an establishment which he traveled with from Fort Harker to the post, of floored hospital tents, cooking-stoves, and teams for his own use that a major-general would never have thought of, and he a captain." He was allowed twenty mechanics. " He organized them into a party of clerks, agents, overseers, and head men, till he had no men to do any work. After hiring them a year and putting up one store-house, that had to be pulled down by his successor, he was relieved." Again, there is the same authority for stating that an assistant quartermaster, since the war, was stationed at *Fort Gibson*, Indian Territory, to build a military post. " He expended $350,000 there, mostly for building the post, yet $30,000, properly applied, would have produced all he could show for the money. The only action ever taken in this case was a letter of thanks from the quartermaster-general, for the efficient manner in which he had performed his duties. He at one time had sixteen young men as clerks, agents, etc., under pay." The same authority— military authority—makes this general remark in connection with the performances of the assistant quartermasters at Fort Sill and Fort Gibson : " These men all get about them a great and costly establishment of aids and helps, that goes far to consume any funds put in their hands. Their head clerks become private secretaries, and are held under pay whether their chiefs are on duty or not. These officers, or at least many of them, have become more costly than useful." These quotations are the exact language of an officer of the army now in service. They are taken from a letter addressed to Mr. Banning, the chairman of the military committee of the House of Representatives, under date of February 6, 1876, and he is informed in the same letter that the assistant quartermasters referred to as operating at Forts Sill and Gibson are still kept in the service. The writer (Gen. Hazen) adds : " I have given but two examples of a dozen I could name." The names of the other ten and the character of their operations as assistant quartermasters were not called for by the military committee, who, as the result of their investigations on the 9th of March, 1876, made a report to the House, urgently recommending the transfer of the Indian bureau to the war department, as a means of insuring honesty, economy, and fairness in the administration of Indian affairs !

CHAPTER XVIII.

THE TRANSFER QUESTION IN THE 45TH CONGRESS.—A JOINT SELECT COMMITTEE
APPOINTED TO INQUIRE INTO THE SUBJECT.—ITS ACTION.—TESTIMONY OF
GEN. SHERMAN AND OTHERS.—REMARKABLE TESTIMONY OF GEN. MEIGS.—
THE COST OF SUPPORTING THE ARMY COMPARED WITH THE COST OF SUPPORT-
ING THE INDIANS, ETC., ETC.

IN the month of February, 1878, the committee on Indian
affairs of the House of Representatives, reported a bill in favor
of the transfer of the care and custody of the Indian tribes
from the interior to the war department. With the report
the committee submitted the testimony of several military
officers as the basis for its action. Prominent among these was
the testimony of Gen. Carleton. The reasons which this officer
gave why the transfer should be made, were the following:
Under the war department which controls the forces operating in the Indian territories, there would, if it had charge of
the Indians, be no conflict of opinion as to what should be
done in given cases; " for, as the fountain from whence might
emanate instructions, whether to commanders, superintendents, or agents, would be one, so the different streams of
authority and regulations descending through these subordinates should be of the same character. In my opinion
(said Carleton) the office of commissioner of Indian affairs
should be abolished, if it be incompatible with the law to
have an army officer .to fill it *ex officio*, contemplating the
placing of the Indian bureau under the direction of the war
department, and organizing it systematically, so that its
operations should harmonize with those of the troops, and
the two run together as parts of the same machine. . . .
I would have not only the head of the Indian bureau an
officer of the army, but each commander of a military department should be an *ex officio* superintendent of Indian affairs
for the Indians in that department, and the commander of
one post nearest any one tribe of Indians in that department

should be the agent *ex officio* for that tribe." Thus the Indians would be remitted to the care and management of commanders of departments and their subordinates without restraint, which is substantially in conformity with the views of Gen. Sheridan. He would have no military officer detailed to preside over an office in the war department, known as the bureau of Indian affairs, but remit the whole matter to the commanding officers of military departments in which Indian tribes are located, who should be *ex officio* in charge of the Indians therein. In Chapter X. of this work some detail is given of military operations in New Mexico in 1862-3-4, and in Arizona in 1869. At that time there were no civil agents in either of these territories, and hence the military operated in Indian matters without restraint. Gen. Carleton was then the commander in New Mexico, and exercised as full and unrestrained authority and power over the Indians as though his views and those of Gen. Sheridan had been embodied in a law of Congress. The reader is especially referred to this detail, since the facts contained in it exhibit Gen. Carleton acting without restraint, and as if, in fact, he was *ex officio* superintendent of Indian affairs for the Indians of New Mexico. In view of his conduct at that time, it is surprising that the committee on Indian affairs should, in the year 1878, present him as authority in favor of the transfer of the Indians to the war department, and embody his views in their report in favor of the measure.

The bill reported passed the House of Representatives. The Senate did not approve of the measure; but, in its stead, a clause was inserted in the army appropriation bill, providing for a joint committee, consisting of three senators and five representatives, with instruction to take into consideration the transfer of the Indian bureau to the war department. This joint committee was authorized to employ a clerk and stenographer, to sit during the recess of, and make final report to Congress, on or before the first of January, 1879. This joint committee was composed of Senators Saunders, Oglesby, and McCreery, and Representatives Scales, Boone, Hooker, Stewart, and Van Vorhes. It took the testimony of many witnesses, addressed letters of inquiry to the secretaries of the war and interior departments, and visited sections of country between the Mississippi river and the Pacific coast, with a view to personal inspection of Indian tribes and agencies; and thus sought to obtain the information desired. On the part of Messrs. Scales, Boone, and Hooker, this was wholly unnecessary, since they were members of the House committee, and united in the report made in February, 1878, recommending the transfer. This joint committee laid before Congress the result of its inquiries, in the shape of two reports, being evenly divided—four in favor, and four against the transfer. The four who favored the measure were Senator McCreery and Representatives Boone, Hooker, and Scales. The four opposed to the transfer were Senators Saunders and Oglesby, and Representatives Stewart and Van Vorhes. All who favored the transfer were Democrats, and from the Southern States; and all who opposed it were Republicans, and from the Northern States. The testimony submitted by the joint committee to Congress covers more than four hundred printed pages. From the perusal of this testimony, it is quite clear that the members who favored the transfer relied mainly on the testimony of the officers of the army to support their view. Indeed, when quoting from the testimony of Gen. Sherman, they said, if space permitted, they could refer " to the statements of many other intelligent and distinguished officers of the army, who are supposed to know, and who, no doubt, reflect the feelings of the army officers generally, on this subject." In this connection, and at this point, the advocates of the transfer, in their report, introduced the substance of the testimony of Gen. Sherman. He concludes thus :

" The war department can employ civil agents for the the peaceful tribes, and military agents for the warlike tribes.

" Christian and civilizing influences can be as well used by the military as the civil.

" There will be less hypocrisy and cant with the military agents than with the civil.

" The military will keep the peace, protect reservations against unlawful intrusions by the whites, and can allow and encourage different Christian denominations to compete in the matter of churches and schools.

" The economy will be in using one set of machinery for both army and Indians, instead of, as now, two.

" In case of transfer, one head of department would have control of all the agencies, and of all troops, so as to apply the remedy on the spot, instead of the system of circumlocution now in practice."

If the reader has perused the chapters in this work detailing military operations against the Indians in New Mexico, in 1862–4; against the " hostile Indians south of the Arkansas," in 1868; against the Indians in Arizona, in 1869; against the Piegans in Montana, in 1870; and against the Sioux and Cheyennes in 1876, and Dull Knife's band of Cheyennes in 1878–9, he is prepared to form an opinion as to the qualification of military officers to exercise Christian and civilizing influences on the mind of the savage. If he has not read the portions of this work alluded to, his attention is respectfully directed to them.

It is very easy for Gen. Sherman to say that the military will keep the peace and protect the reservations against the unlawful intrusion of the whites; but what are the facts? When has he used his influence in that direction? He has been a peace commissioner; he has assisted in making treaties in which solemn pledges have been made with the Indians that the many beneficial provisions embodied in the instruments should be faithfully carried out. Has he ever interested himself in their behalf? On the contrary, has he not time and again thrown the whole weight of his official influence against the very Indians who had a right to expect his aid? Has he not, without cause, made war against tribes to whom he, as a treaty-maker, had pledged peace and protection?

Gen. Sherman seeks to captivate this joint committee by assuring the members that the transfer will work out economy in using but one set of machinery for both army and Indians, instead of, as now, two. In other words, that by the use of military officers, who are under pay at all events, as Indian agents, the salaries of the civil agents will be saved to the government. He, however, in the process of his examination qualifies this, and says that the war department " can employ civil agents for the peaceful tribes, and military agents for the warlike tribes." Assuming that all civil agents and the office of commissioner of Indian affairs were dispensed with, and the duty thrown on army officers, the amount saved in salaries would not exceed $135,000. The quota of farmers, black-smiths, etc., and interpreters at the agencies, can not, at the present time, be dispensed with, whether agents be civil or military. Now, if the military agent do his duty to the Indians, he must be detached from the military service, and how is his vacancy in the army to be supplied? By military regulations troops are not stationary, and when the command moves from one point to another, is this officer, acting as Indian agent, to be left behind? And if not, will not every movement of troops necessitate the appointment of a new agent? Such has been the practice wherever the military has had the temporary care of the Indians. In the summer of 1876, when the Sioux war was in progress, the military deposed the civil, and put in their place military agents at a number of the agencies. At the Spotted Tail agency, between the middle of July, 1876, and the first of May, 1877, there were four different military officers acting as Indian agents at this one agency. This was owing to the shifting of troops from point to point. This feature is not only objectionable, but it is fatal. Conceding that army officers would be suitable persons for Indian agents in other respects, the uncertainty of the tenure by which they would hold the position, is sufficient to settle the question and forbid their employment. There are other objectionable features, such as have at all times in the past proved fatal, and will so prove in the future, should the Indians ever be turned over to the care of the army. The saving of the paltry sum of $135,000, or any other sum, when the fate of a race would be put in jeopardy thereby, should have no consideration.

In the progress of his examination, and with a view to enlighten the members of the joint committee, Gen. Sherman took up and ran over a tabular statement that had a few days previously been prepared at the Indian office, showing the number of Indian agencies, the number of Indians in care of

each, and the disbursements for each agency, and from it
pointed out such agencies and Indians as, in his opinion,
ought to be governed by military force and have military
agents.   There were about seventy-four of these agencies;
and when he had passed them all in review, he indicated only
twenty-five agencies that, in his opinion, required military
discipline and military agents.   Among these were the
Yakama Indians, in Oregon, and the White Earth Chippewas, in Minnesota, to which his attention was called by a
member of the joint committee.   In reply, he said he ran
down the list very hastily, and that he thought, in reference
to these, he was governed by the number of Indians. "Where-
ever (said he) Indians are peaceable, I would not bother
them." So far, then, as saving money by substituting military officers for civil agents, according to Gen. Sherman's own
showing, the amount would be the salaries of twenty-three
agents, at $1,800 each per year, or the sum of $41,400 per year!
The residue of the agents, being more than fifty of them,
would remain civilians.   As to these, the general was asked,
" To whom would these civil agents be responsible?" His
reply was: "To the war department, which would give them
full discretion.   Agents, civil or military, ought to have a
large discretion."   In the course of the examination, Gen.
Sherman stated that he desired the committee " to construe
the present conflict or antagonism to be, not personal, not
a question of honesty, but a natural and necessary conflict of
antagonistic systems."   He, in effect, purged the Indian civil
service, and presented it as free from fraud and corruption,
and reduced the contest to a natural and necessary conflict of
antagonistic systems, and remarked that " the management
of the Indians from 1789 to 1849, a period of sixty years, was
in the hands of the war department.   Since that date, twenty-
nine years, it has been in the hands of the interior department.   Each department can now be tested by its acts instead
of professions."

The four members of the joint committee who united in
recommending that the management of the Indians be transferred to the war department did not exactly agree with Gen.
Sherman in his statement that for sixty years prior to 1849,

the management of the Indians " was in the hands of the war department," but said, in their report, that " our system of Indian management has always been in effect the system now in operation. Even while nominally under the administration of the war department, prior to 1849, the system was very much the same as now." If the fact be so, what is to be gained by recommitting the civilization of this hapless people to the war department? All who feel that our best efforts should be bestowed upon the reclamation and well-being of the Indian race, will admit that there has been at all times something lacking in our treatment of the Indians; and it is not likely that any better results would follow if they were recommitted to the war department than were produced prior to 1849. There does not appear to be any mystery on this question, and yet our statesmen and generals seem to involve it and its results in confusion.

In the year 1876 the committee on military affairs of the House of Representatives took the testimony of sixty army officers touching the propriety of the transfer of the Indians to the war department. In this number were to be found the general, lieutenant-general, all the major-generals, and all the brigadiers but one. The result was a report accompanied by a bill providing for the transfer. In the report the committee said that " previous to the transfer of the Indian bureau from the war to the interior department, in 1849, the disbursements to the Indians were generally made by army officers, under the direction of the commanding officers of the posts, who were acting Indian agents; and as the disbursing officers' commissions, their reputation, and the means of support for themselves and families were at stake, this was sufficient to prevent any attempt at fraud and dishonesty, and the result of this system was what might have been anticipated. It is doubtful if the army officers were ever accused of defrauding the Indians." In the report of the committee on Indian affairs of the House of Representatives, made in February, 1878, and upon which the House passed a bill providing for the transfer of the Indians to the war department, it was asserted, without qualification, " that the control and management of the Indians for seventeen years prior to 1849 belonged exclusively

to the war department." Three members of the joint committee, who recommend the transfer, in the report of January
31, 1879, are Messrs. Scales, Boone, and Hooker, who joined
in the report of February, 1878. In the report of 1879, these
gentlemen say that what was stated by them in the report of
1878 is not true ; that in point of fact the system of Indian
management prior to 1849 was very much the same as now.
These contradictory statements only serve to darken counsel
and confuse those who have no means of consulting the official documents in investigating the question.

A brief statement will dissipate all this confusion. Before
the colonies united, each, as a general thing, acted independently of the others in its dealings with the Indians within its
own limits. There was diversity, and sometimes conflict, as
many of the tribes, in their wandering life, were not confined
to a location within the limits of one colony. In negotiations
the object of the colonists was to compose difficulties as they
arose, and to obtain cessions of lands for occupation and settlement. The amelioration of the condition of the savage
was scarcely thought of. Before the adoption of the constitution, and during the confederation of the colonies, the general government took charge of Indian affairs, and from that
period until the present time all matters pertaining to the
Indians have been substantially under the care of the federal
authorities. In 1775 the Continental Congress created three
departments of Indian affairs—the northern, middle, and
southern—and assigned a board of commissioners to each department. This action had no reference to the civilization of
the Indians, but simply looked to the preservation of peace
with, and to prevent them, if possible, from taking part
against the colonists in the struggle between them and the
parent government, which then seemed inevitable.

In 1785 Congress adopted " an ordinance for the regulation
of Indian affairs," in pursuance of the ninth of the articles
of confederation and perpetual union. By it the Indian
country was divided into two districts, and a superintendent
was created for each. All official transactions between these
superintendents and the Indians were to be "held, transacted,
and done at the outposts occupied by the troops of the United

States," and in any business which could not be done without interfering with the legislative rights of a state, the superintendent was required to act in conjunction with the authority of such state.

In 1787 Congress authorized several of the states to appoint commissioners, who, in conjunction with the superintendents of Indian affairs, were authorized to make treaties, and the superintendents were required to correspond regularly in relation to their official transactions with the secretary of war, "through whom all communications respecting the Indian department shall be made to Congress;" and they were further required "to obey all instructions which they shall from time to time receive from the secretary of war."

Arising out of treaties that were made for cessions of land, annuities became due and payable to the Indians, and the war department became through its agents—the officers of the army—the disbursers of the funds and gifts due to the Indians. At this time the whole office duties connected with Indian affairs were referred to one or two clerks in the war office. There were, in the disbursements, exceptional cases, where the duty was discharged by civilians; but in such cases the work was done under the direction and supervision of the secretary of war. With the expansion of our population, and the progress of treaty making, the business with our Indian wards grew rapidly, but not, so far as the interests of these people were concerned, satisfactorily. Hence, in 1826, the then secretary of war, James Barbour, of Virginia, in a letter to the Indian committee of the lower house of Congress, said of the condition of the Indian population, that "the history of the past presents but little on which the recollection lingers with satisfaction. The future is not more cheering, unless resort be speedily had to other counsels than those by which we have heretofore been governed." The letter from which this extract is taken is one full of lamentation and sorrow, because of the condition of our Indian population. Liberal extracts from it are given in the sixth chapter of this work, to which the attention of the reader is called.

At this period there was neither a commissioner of Indian affairs nor a secretary of the interior. There was no Indian bureau. In 1832, the office of commissioner of Indian affairs was created, and the Indian bureau organized. The same session, and preceding the organization of the bureau, a committee of Congress looked partially into the condition of the business of the Indians, and the management of their affairs, and made report that the system was expensive, inefficient, and irresponsible. In 1834, Congress passed a law, entitled " an act to provide for the organization of the department of Indian affairs." By this act, as well as the one of 1832, the power was vested in the president to prescribe rules and regulations to govern in the execution of both, and he remitted the subject to the secretary of war, with directions to " immediately revise the existing regulations, and prescribe a new set as to the mode in which business shall be done by the commissioner, adapted to the present condition and duties of the office."

The revised regulations made in pursuance of this order were elaborate. Among them was one dividing the country occupied by Indians into three districts, and assigning to each one an officer of the army, to be known as the principal military disbursing officer within his district. Payments were to be made to the Indians by these officers, the assistant quartermasters, and assistant commissaries of subsistence, at the different military posts, and by military officers on duty in any other branch of the service in the Indian country, when thereto required. In cases where it was necessary to employ special commissioners or special agents, deviations from the rule were allowed. Payments of annuities were made to the chiefs of the tribe, or to such persons as the tribe might designate, provided they were of Indian descent, or recognized members of the tribe; and no payment was to be made to any other person or persons, except claimants for depredations, such as were recognized under the intercourse act of 1834. A regulation in relation to the removal of Indian tribes designated the military disbursing agent of the district as the officer to take charge of the Indians, and pay for supplies and services rendered in their removal, assisted by disbursing agents of their own selection, and acting under instructions from them. In all these regulations, the secretary of war was practically the source of power; all things were to be done subject to his instructions and approval. In the process of time, Congress thought it advisable to look into the business management of Indian affairs in the war office at Washington, and this was done by a committee of the House of Representatives in 1842. In its report, the committee said:

" The evidence is submitted as to the general management and condition of Indian affairs. It exhibits an almost total want of method and punctuality, equally unjust to the government and the tribes to whom we have voluntarily assumed obligations which we are not at liberty to disregard. It will be seen that the accounts of millions of expenditures have been so loosely kept as scarcely to furnish a trace or explanation of large sums, and that others have been misapplied, so as to impose serious losses on the Indians and heavy responsibility on the government; that in some books (the only record of these accounts) no entries have been made for a period of several years; and that, where entries have been made, the very clerks who kept them could not state an account from them." In the investment of the funds of the Indians, the committee said there had been great carelessness. State stocks, purchased at prices above par, were paid out by the government, as trustee, at par, when they were worth only twenty-five and thirty cents on the dollar. The report referred to, has much in it going to show the utter indifference right at the fountain head—in the war office—to every thing pertaining to the interests of the Indians. Indeed, there was no restraint to the practice of the grossest irregularities and frauds.

For many years preceding and following this period, the officers of the army were supreme in authority on the Upper Missouri, and there were, between them and the old traders, the most amicable and friendly relations. In the region of Fort Leavenworth the manner in which Indian trade was carried on was well known to the officers in command. Guns worth $7 were sold to the Indians at $30; squaw axes, worth 37 cents, were sold at $2; a double handful of salt, worth 62 cents per bushel, sold at $1; five-gallon kettles, costing 25 cents per pound, sold at $12; a yard of strouding, costing $1.80, sold at $8; a Mackinaw blanket, costing $4, sold at $12; American calico, costing 10 cents per yard, sold at $1; gunpowder, costing 30 cents per pound, sold at $1.50; tobacco, costing 7 cents per pound, sold at $1; vermilion, costing $1.50 per pound, sold at $7; and whisky, costing 25 cents per gallon, sold at $16. Such trade as this was carried on right in the presence of the military officers then acting as guardians of our Indian wards. They saw no objection to it. Indeed, it seemed to gratify them to know that the traders were prosperous. In the purchase of the robes and peltries which the Indians sold at the trading houses, not more than one sixth of the value was paid for them. The result was that colossal fortunes were made by the old traders. Contractors for Indian supplies were not held to a strict accountability; and, when delivered, there was gross neglect in the care of them. Discrepancies in the accounts of disbursing officers were numerous; and, in many cases, actual defalcations occurred.

After Gen. Sherman had invited a comparison of the management of the Indians from 1789 to 1849 with their management from 1849 to 1878, he said to the joint committee that he would not venture to make it, but with the sanction of the members he submitted " some examples to show how awkward is the present system of management by civil agents who find themselves intrusted with the care and maintenance, in time of peace, of a restless, if not a savage race." These examples were the briefs of a number of papers then passing through the war office at Washington, relating to the care, protection, and supply of Indians, a few of which he referred to specially, as illustrating the whole. Here is an example. The agent at Fort Peck, near the British line, made application to the military at the post for assistance to aid in arresting some half-breed Indians from Canada, who had come over to trade with the Indians near Fort Peck agency, and to kill buffalo, and while there interfered with the Indian police at the agency. This application, according to military regulations, was sent to Washington, and when there, turned over by the war department to Gen. Sherman, and by him referred to Gen. Sheridan, at Chicago, and from him to the commander on the Upper Missouri, and from him to the commander from whence it started, at Fort Buford or Fort Benton, who dispatched a detachment of troops to make the arrest, only to find that the half-breeds had gone back to Canada. This Fort Peck case and others like it were presented to the joint committee of Congress by Gen. Sherman, as illustrative of the "impossibility of reconciling the natural and necessary conflict in this double-headed machine of Indian management," and such representations were received and accepted by one-half of the members as a sufficient justification for the recommendation made by them that the management of the Indians and their civilization should be recommitted to the tender care of the army. In regulations requiring such circumlocution and delay in a case like the one stated, there is neither intelligence nor business, and in the affairs of a business firm, if the agents were to adopt similar regulations and be governed by them, the employers would very soon send such agents adrift, and supply their places with men of common sense. The conclusion is irresistible that such regulations are *purposely* made to obstruct the civil agent and embarrass him in his duties, to the end that the civil management may be brought into disrepute because of its inefficiency, and it is absolutely astounding that senators and representatives can, not only listen to such statements with patience, but actually accept them as reasons for dispensing with the civil agents among the Indian tribes. In another case that might have occurred, and many such do occur, the local military officer would have felt that he had full discretion and have acted at once. Had a band of our Indians been charged with some depredation upon the property of a party of white men, no matter how lawless these may have been, or how false the charge, the local post commander would at once have put a squad of troops in motion and sought the Indians, and if overtaken, he would have attacked them, and such as could not escape, would, without hesitation, have been killed.

In his narrative, and as showing the conflict of systems,
25

Gen. Sherman refers to the fact that the agent of the Southern Cheyennes and Arapahoes had, without consulting the military commander at the post, in November, 1878, allowed the chief, Little Robe, and his band, numbering about one hundred and thirty, to leave the reservation to hunt buffalo. He said to the joint committee that a controversy had existed for a long time between the army officers and those of the interior department, as to the right of an agent to give passes to Indians to go outside of their reservations, no matter how peaceably inclined such Indians might be ; the army officers holding that they were, when outside of the reservation, subject to military law. In this case, Gen. Pope had reported the fact, and, of course, objected to the agent exercising such authority ; and Gen. Sherman coincided with Gen. Pope in his view of the case. Gen. Sherman told the joint committee that he held that the " old rule was, and should be," that when the Indians passed beyond their reservation, they became subject to military law. He can find no authority to sustain this position, and if he could, the Cheyennes and Arapahoes are not bound by it, since by the treaty of 1867, made with them by a commission of which he was a member, they had a clear right to go out to hunt in the manner in which they did. Perhaps more than all other causes combined, out of which trouble has grown up with the Cheyennes and Arapahoes, and the Comanches and Kiowas, since the spring of 1869, are those which have grown out of the execution of the unlawful military order issued at that time, in which it was held that these, as well as other Indians, when found outside of their reservations, were declared hostile, and wherever found, were to be dealt with as such.

Gen. Sherman states, to the joint committee, that to remit the management of the Indian tribes to the army, is to assure marvelous economy in the work. How is it possible for such a result to follow? With the ranks full, we have 25,000 soldiers in the army. For the year ending June 30, 1878, with low values for every thing used in its maintenance, the appropriations for the support of the army amounted to $24,583,-186. The number of our Indian wards, exclusive of those in Alaska, is, say, 276,000. The appropriations for the support of the Indian department, for the same year, amounted to $4,-721,275. We have here, for the support of the war establishment, a sum equal to $983.32 per head, per soldier; and, for the support of the Indian establishment, a sum equal to $17.10 per head, per Indian. Military officers, because of their constant talk of the extravagance, as well as corruption, of the Indian service, have much of the responsibility resting on them for the general impression that the Indian bureau is the sink of corruption, and the Indian civil agent the champion scoundrel of the times; and yet here are the figures, and they demonstrate that it requires more than fifty times as much to support a soldier and the war establishment per year, than the sum appropriated to support and take care of an Indian and maintain the Indian service. It may be said that this statement does not present the matter fairly. Suppose that be conceded, and yet the disparity is so great, that it may be well for inquiring minds to look squarely at the gross cost of the military as well as the Indian service.

Gen. Sherman was not the only high military authority that this joint committee called to its aid in the pursuit of knowledge. Gen. Meigs, the quartermaster-general of the army, was on the stand on the 3d of December, 1878. He was asked his opinion as to the propriety of the transfer of the Indians to the war department. His answer was, that it "would be well for the Indians, but ill for the army." He was quite sure that all orders of the executive and Congress would be strictly carried out, and the supplies voted by Congress would be delivered to the Indians, of good quality and in the quantity intended. That was no doubt gratifying to Senator McCreery and Representatives Boone, Hooker, and Scales. But he said they would not be sufficient to feed 250,000 Indians, which he assumed was the number of our wards. He thought the Indian appropriations for the year were about $4,500,000. He said "the cost of feeding 25,000 men in the army was about $2,500,000 per year. It is (said the general) simply a question of arithmetic to see what it will cost to feed 250,000 Indians. It will be about $20,000,000 a year. *I do not think that problem has ever been presented to Congress.*" He said further of the Indian, "his appetite is as good as a soldier's, and if it cost twenty-four cents for a white man's ration to be carried to and delivered to him, I say it will cost twenty-four cents to pay for it for the Indians." In relation to transportation of supplies, Gen. Meigs said: "Our system is perfect, and yet I was a little surprised, in preparing an answer to some inquiries of this committee, to find in some cases that the Indian department has made contracts for transportation at considerably lower rates than we have upon very nearly the same lines. . . . I think some of the Missouri river contracts were considerably lower than ours, although ours were made by public advertisement in the course of the same season. The Indian department got lower prices than we did." This is most marvelous testimony to come from a military officer, at the head of the most important business department connected with the military service. How strange it must have sounded in the ears of his associates, as well as in the ears of those members of the joint committee who had, upon the wild statements of army officers trained under Gen. Sheridan, prejudged the case in favor of the transfer.

As stated, the gross number of our Indian wards, less those in Alaska, is about 276,000. Of these, more than two-thirds are women and children. Probably there are tribes aggregating 110,000 souls that supply their own food and clothing. They have, however, annual annuities coming to them, which are a drain upon the treasury to a certain extent; another portion, and in considerable numbers, in part subsist themselves; another portion produce nothing, and hence can supply nothing toward their own support. Where located, the game has disappeared, and many are confined to reservations that are barren lands. The number of this kind, added to those to whom the ration is supplied in part, it is believed would equal 110,000 Indians to be supplied with full rations. This number, at twenty-four cents per day, for rations for each, would require to feed them one year, the sum of $9,636,000. On this point we are supplied with a very recent practical test by the military department. In August, 1877, the band of the Nez Perces chief, Joseph, surrendered at Bear Paw Mountain, in Dakota, to Gen. Howard. They were turned over by him to Gen. Miles, and in due time sent forward to Fort Leavenworth, where they remained until July, 1878. On the 31st of March, 1878, the war department made up an account against the Indian bureau for the subsistence of Joseph and his band, from August 14, 1877, to March 31, 1878. The period at which they were at Leavenworth, which was the greater part of the time, enabled the war department to ration them cheaper than it could be done at any other place in the West. They numbered four hundred and twenty-one men, women, and children at the time of the surrender. This account covers subsistence for 228 days, and the amount of the bill rendered was $12,565.73. It would require 95,988 rations to feed 421 persons 228 days. The bill would indicate that each ration cost a fraction over thirteen cents. At this rate it would require to ration 110,000 Indians—men, women, and children—for one year, the sum of $5,219,500; which would exceed, by more than $500,000, the entire amount appropriated for the current fiscal year, for the whole Indian service, including money, annuities, rations, clothing, schools, pay of employes, medicines, and all else connected with the Indian service! This bare statement ought to put to shame the host of military gentlemen who make it a specialty to disparage the civil service. And when compared with the extravagant outlay for the support of the army, it ought to seal their mouths forever. The fact is, that with the rapid destruction of the game on which the Indians, until recently, subsisted, and other untoward circumstances surrounding these people, the appropriations for their subsistence should be enlarged considerably beyond the amount which Congress doles out to them, for such period as they are kept upon reservations where they can do nothing toward self-support. The fact that the support and maintenance of the war establishment requires a yearly expenditure of nearly $25,000,000, or $983.32 per head per man, for an army of 25,000 men, would seem to indicate that there is a wide field for reform and retrenchment in this branch of the public service, but Congress does not seem inclined to cultivate it. Some years ago there was some inquiry made in that direction, but the united testimony of army officers was that no reduction could be made in the expenditures of the military establishment. No officer could dispense with his servant, nor could he stand any reduction in his salary, or in his commutation for quarters, etc., when on detached duty away from his command. Some did think that the office of chaplain in the army might be abolished, and others concluded that the company laundress, who was most generally the wife of an enlisted soldier, might be dispensed with, and the privates be required to wash their own clothes! But to touch the pay or perquisites of an officer, with a view to a slight reduction, that was not to be thought of for one moment.

In 1875, Congress did venture on the correction of an abuse of some magnitude, and provided by law that the number of officers employed in the quartermaster's department should be as follows: One quartermaster-general; four assistant quartermasters-general; eight deputy quartermasters-general; fourteen quartermasters, and thirty assistant quartermasters—making in all fifty-seven officers in that department. This action was to correct an abuse that had grown up in the service, whereby, in addition to the regular officers in the establishment, hundreds of the officers of the line were annually detailed to duty as assistant quartermasters. Notwithstanding this provision of law, there were, in the fiscal year 1877–8, upward of three hundred officers of the line acting as assistant quartermasters in excess of the limit fixed in the law of 1875, all of whom were handling and paying out government funds that aggregated millions upon millions!

In the report of the inspector-general, for the year ending June 30, 1875, referring to transportation in the distant territories, where the government supplies its own teams, it is said that "the teamsters, hostlers, herders, etc., for this means of transportation, for the most part are soldiers detailed from the line, often without any knowledge of the work, and against their wishes. . . . These soldiers often maltreat, overwork, and take but little care of their teams; the consequence is that in a short time they require recuperation, or are rendered unfit for further service, and are condemned and sold."

In the annual report of the judge advocate-general of the

date of October 10, 1877, that officer says : " The vice of gambling, as I gather from records of courts-martial and other authentic information, prevails to a very considerable extent in our army. It is, however, not punishable *as such*, but only in certain cases, as when committed by a disbursing officer, or under circumstances rendering some peculiar dishonor on the party. This vice, I need not add, is most demoralizing in its effects, and necessarily tends to relax the bonds of military obligation and duty. Both to put a stop to an immoral indulgence prejudicial to good order and military discipline, as well as to protect young officers having small pay, *who are too often led into it by their superiors in rank*, I would recommend that gambling, or the playing at cards or other games for money or other valuable stake, be absolutely, positively prohibited in the army, by the proper legislation to be sought from Congress."

In the report of the same officer, for the year 1876, it is stated that the number of convictions for crimes and offenses committed in ten months of that year in the army, was *eleven thousand nine hundred and forty-one!* This occurred in a community numbering 25,000 souls, manned and officered by the picked men of the nation, reared at West Point! Can the worst governed and most disorderly city on the continent equal this? Among these convictions, there were for assault and battery, 214 ; for assault with intent to kill, 10 ; for desertion, 347 ; for disobedience of orders, 705 ; for disrespect to superior officers, 289 ; for drunkenness, 1568 ; for drunkenness on duty, 947 ; for larceny, 142 ; for neglect of duty, 526 ; for offering violence to superior officers, 6 ; for selling, losing, or wasting government property, 140, etc.

In the annual report of the second auditor of the treasury for the year 1873, there is this exhibit: " Number of charges raised against officers on account of overpayments, 242 ; number of charges raised against officers on account of double payments, 150." He adds : " Since the last report the accounts of forty-three paymasters have been closed and certificates of non-indebtedness issued. The accounts of thirty-five paymasters have been finally revised, on which there is due the United States $76,541 ; and the accounts of twelve pay-

masters have been prepared for suit, the balance due the
United States aggregating $541,447.87."

In the annual report of the second auditor for the year
1874, that officer says that the number of cases in which
charges were raised during the year against officers and enlisted men for overpayments were 177 ; for double payments,
157 ; credits to officers and enlisted men for overpayments re-
funded, 204 cases ; credits to officers for double payments re-
funded, 46 cases. He adds that cases then under investigation "involve questions of alleged fraud in the preparation
and prosecution of claims, forgery, unlawful withholding of
money from claimants, and overpayments to officers and enlisted men."

In a report made by Vincent Colyer, acting as a special
Indian commissioner in 1869, referring to matters that occurred in his tour, he had, among other items, the following :
" While delayed at Fort Gibson, in the Cherokee country, we
were for several nights in succession awakened from our sleep
by the noisy shouts and oaths of drunken men. Wondering
who could thus disturb the peace of a quiet town like this, and
why the police did not arrest them, I was surprised and mor-
tified to find that it was a party of drunken soldiers from the
fort. On Sunday morning we were sitting by the window in
the house of a Christian friend, soon after service, when our
attention was called to the sudden egress of a number of
peaceable Cherokees and half-breeds from the door of a small
meeting-house. Out they came, tumbling, in the highest degree of alarm, pursued by four drunken United States soldiers. The Cherokees scattered in all directions, when our
'national police' came up reeling, shouting, and swearing,
like all possessed. One of them flourished a revolver, another
a bludgeon, a third had his hat off, shirt sleeves rolled up, and
arms bloody ; and all four looked the picture of riot and disorder. . . . The explanation of this was that the paymas-
ter had been around a few days before."

Capt. Henry E. Alvord, in a report of an extended visit,
in 1872, on a special inspection, referred to the growing evil
of the introduction of liquors among the Indians. The intercourse act forbids this, but there is an exception by which

liquors may be carried to military posts, for the use of officers, under regulations prescribed by the secretary of war. In view of this fact, Capt. Alvord suggests that it is a matter of great importance that the habits of post or district commanders, in this particular, should be known as good. He cites the state of things at Fort Sill, when he was there, and states that the officer in command placed no restriction on the traffic in liquor, and it was, in fact, free to all. " As the result," said he, " a practically open bar was kept while we were at the post, with nightly carousals; soldiers, citizens, and employes frequently seen drunk; and the liquor found its way to the Indians. . . . With such a state of affairs at the military posts, it becomes absolutely impossible to enforce the law elsewhere, and liquor reaches the Indian camps, producing much evil."

On the 12th of December, 1874, the agent of the Navajoe Indians, in New Mexico, wrote the commissioner of Indian affairs, that there was demoralization among both the Indians and soldiers, arising from the fact that the Navajoes were allowed to visit, at their pleasure, the military reservation at Fort Wingate, and asked that the orders of June, 1870, be enforced, and the Indians required to leave the post, and return to their reservation. The order was issued on June 20, 1870, and was to govern in the department of New Mexico. It read thus: " Under no circumstances whatever, will any Indians be permitted to enter any military post or station in this department." In. 1872, the assistant surgeon stationed at Fort Wingate, had written to the post adjutant, that, in consequence of the number of Navajoe squaws being about the post, venereal diseases had become frequent among the troops, so that at that time more than half the sickness among the men was of that character. The assistant surgeon suggested that the commanding officer order all these Navajoe women to leave the post, or should some of them be allowed to remain working for any one at the post, that such regulations be made as would prevent them and the troops from meeting. The suggestion, or recommendation, of the assistant surgeon was not carried out, but he was relieved from duty. As stated, the Indian agent, in December, 1874, informed the commissioner of Indian affairs of the demoralization that existed, and asked that the order of 1870 be enforced.

This communication was referred to the secretary of war, and by him to Gen. Sherman, and thence to Gen. Pope, commander of the department of New Mexico, who indorsed on it, among other matter, the following: "I do not consider the statement of Mr. Arney (the agent) to constitute such a state of hostility as would excuse me in the eyes of the Indian bureau for interfering with the business or pleasure of such Indians as the Navajoes." It will be observed that all the agent desired was the revival of the order of June 20, 1870, which prohibited any Indians entering military posts in the department of New Mexico, and thus put an end to the intimacy existing between the Navajoe women and the troops at Fort Wingate; and this Gen. Pope refused to do for the reason above quoted. He did not feel that he would be justified in interfering with the business or pleasure of such Indians as the Navajoes—notwithstanding he knew well that the intercourse between the troops and the Navajoe women was fearfully demoralizing to both.

Such references and extracts as are contained in the closing pages of this chapter, could be multiplied to the extent of a large volume, but this is not deemed necessary. It is believed that sufficient is presented to enable every reader to arrive at a just conclusion as to the absolute necessity of reform in the management of our Indian wards, and as to whether this reform, and the best interests of our Indian population, both material and moral, could be safely intrusted to the custody of the officers of the army. While deliberating on this question—a momentous one, the fate of a race—I would implore every reader to avail himself of an unerring standard which will work out absolute certainty and a righteous judgment. "Do as you would be done by." "Put yourself in his place."

CHAPTER XIX.

The Ute Indians of Colorado.—The treaty of 1868, and the agreement of 1873 with them.—An examination of the manner in which each party has performed its obligations.—The origin of the present complications, etc.

The Ute nation is composed of the Tabaquache, Muache, Capote, Weeminuche, Yampa, Grand River, and Uintah bands of Ute Indians. Before the United States entered into definite treaty relations with them, these bands roamed over a vast country, occupying, in their excursions, the territory embraced in Western Colorado, Eastern Utah, Northern New Mexico and Arizona, and Southern Wyoming. They also came down through Eastern Colorado, to the buffalo range, on the plains, and made their periodical hunts, at the risk of war with the Cheyennes and Arapahoes, and the Comanche and Kiowa Indians, who claimed as their country the territory over which the great southern herd of buffalo ranged.

In March, 1868, N. G. Taylor, Commissioner of Indian Affairs, Alex. C. Hunt, Governor of Colorado Territory, and *ex officio* Superintendent of Indian Affairs, and Col. Kit Carson, on the part of the United States, concluded a treaty with a few representative men of these bands (among whom were Ouray, Kinache, Ankatosh, José Maria, Nicaagat, Guero, Piah, Suviap, and others), by which it was agreed that a district of country commencing at a point on the south boundary line of the Territory of Colorado, where the meridian of longitude 107° west from Greenwich crosses the same; running thence north with said meridian to a point fifteen miles due north of where the said meridian intersects the fortieth parallel of north latitude; thence due west to the western boundary line of said territory; thence south with said western boundary line to the southern boundary line of said territory; thence east with said boundary line to the place of beginning, " shall be, and the same is hereby set apart for the *absolute and undisturbed use and occupation of the Indians herein named*, and for such other friendly tribes or individual Indians as, from time to time, they may be willing, with the consent of the United States, to admit among them." Following this language, and in the same article of the treaty (the second), these words are found : " *And the United States now solemnly agree that no person*, except those herein authorized so to do, and except such officers, agents, and employes of the government as may be authorized to enter upon Indian reservations in discharge of duties enjoined by law, *shall ever be permitted to pass over, settle upon, or reside in the territory described in this article*, except as herein otherwise provided."

In the next article the Indians agree that they will and do relinquish " all claims and rights in and to any portion of the United States or territories except such as are embraced in the limits defined in the preceding article."

Provision was made for the establishment of two agencies and the necessary buildings ; that the agents should reside at the agency house, and keep an office open at all times, and make diligent inquiry into all matters of complaint presented for investigation by or against the Indians ; and in cases of depredation on the persons or property of either, cause the evidence to be taken in writing, and forward the same, together with their finding, to the commissioner of Indian affairs, whose decision, subject to the revision of the secretary of the interior, should be binding on the parties to the treaty. And if bad men among the whites, or other people subject to the authority of the United States, committed any wrong upon the persons or property of the Indians, the government would, upon proof made to the agent and forwarded to Washington, proceed at once to cause the offender to be arrested and punished according to the laws of the United States, and would also reimburse the injured Indian for the loss sustained ; and if bad men among the Indians shall commit a wrong upon any one—white, black, or Indian—subject to the authority of the United States, and at peace therewith, the Indians agree that they will, upon proof of the fact, made to their agent, deliver up the wrong-doer to the government, to be tried and punished according to its laws; and, in case they willfully refuse to do so, the person injured shall be reimbursed for his loss from the annuities or other moneys due, or to become due, from the United States.

Provision was made for any Ute (being the head of a family), who desired to commence farming, by which he may select a tract of land, not exceeding one hundred and sixty acres, for his homestead, to be held by him and his family so long as he or they may cultivate it. The reservation shall be surveyed, and when this is done Congress shall provide for the protection of the Indian farmer, and fix the character of his title, and he shall be supplied with agricultural implements and seeds, and shall have the instruction of a farmer, and school-houses erected and teachers employed to instruct the children. As an inducement to adopt civilized life, each lodge of Utes shall be supplied with one gentle American cow and five head of sheep.

It was stipulated that all appropriations made under the treaty for beneficial purposes, as well as the annuities, should be divided proportionately among the seven bands of Utes; *provided*, that if any chief of either of the confederated bands make war against the people of the United States, or in any manner violate the essential parts thereof, such chief shall forfeit his position as chief, and all rights to any of the benefits of the treaty; but any Indian of either of the confederated bands who shall remain at peace and abide by the terms of the treaty, shall be entitled to its benefits, notwithstanding his particular chief and band shall have forfeited their rights thereto.

This treaty was not ratified and proclaimed until November 6, 1868, and hence during that year no specific appropriations were made to carry its provisions into effect. On the 8th of June, 1869, Gov. Hunt called the attention of the Indian office to this fact, and said that in many years' experience among Indian tribes " he found delays the most fruitful of all causes which engendered war. An Indian, who is the soul of punctuality, can not comprehend why the officers of a government in possession of unlimited wealth can not be as prompt

as a poor untutored native ; nor can this failure, so often repeated, be explained satisfactorily to him."

On the 12th of June, 1869, Gov. Hunt was relieved by Ed-
ward M. McCook, who succeeded him as governor and *ex
officio* superintendent of Indian affairs. In the annual report,
dated September 1, 1869, Gov. McCook said that his success
in carrying out the plans of the government for the amelioration of the condition of the Indians under his charge " had
been gratifying." He impressed upon the Indians " that the
object of the government was to furnish them *a local habitation forever, free from intrusion,* and to perform faithfully
every obligation of the treaty." The Indians, although unwilling at first, had finally concluded " to accept the situation
and follow the instructions of their white tutors, provided
they might be furnished with suitable stock for agricultural
and pastoral purposes—their own diminutive ponies being entirely unfit for the labors of the farm, and the Texas cattle of
that region being untameable as the buffalo." In consideration whereof he thought " the government had done wisely
in making liberal appropriations for the purchase of American cows and other stock for the use of these people." He
thought the country admirably adapted to grazing, and, as the
Indians were partial to pastoral life, the success of the experiment of colonizing them must, in a great measure, depend
upon this branch of industry. He said the game was fast
vanishing in the mountains, and the buffalo disappearing
from the plains, and that, by reason of the steady march of
civilization, these resources of the Indians would, before many
years elapsed, be entirely cut off, and then the government
must provide further sustenance, or gradually teach them the
dignity and necessity of labor. He thought this was a task
not to be accomplished at once, and, while he saw difficulties
in the way, he felt that much could be done " toward realiz-
ing the dream of eastern philanthropists by the initiation of
a kind and liberal policy, and by integrity and fair dealing
on the part of the agents of the government." He, however, doubted the policy of isolating the Indians in order to
civilize them, and believed the best way to accomplish this
object would be to bring them into direct contact with the

highest standard of civilization, instead of placing them entirely beyond its influence. This standard he believed to be in New England, and said : " I think the settlement of these untutored tribes in the vicinity, say, of Boston, where they would daily be thrown in contact with what is claimed to be the most cultivated community on this continent, would be much more likely to bring about the desired end than a complete isolation from these powerful and beneficent influences."

The number of Indians in Colorado he said was small, and he felt quite sure the people of the territory would not object to their permanent withdrawal therefrom, " in order to advance the great interests which we are led to believe would accrue to the aborigines themselves, and to the whole country, through the transformation of this number of vagrant consumers into industrious citizens and producers of the elements of wealth and property." He closed his report by the expression of the opinion that, by economy, the funds appropriated for provisions, would enable the Indians to pass the winter without suffering.

On the 16th of October, 1869, Gov. McCook made another report, having returned to Denver from a four weeks' tour, in going to, and returning from, the lower Ute agency, and distributing the annuities to the Indians there. He found the distance from Denver to the agency, by the shortest route, about four hundred and fifty miles, a portion of it the worst road he " ever saw." The wagons transporting the goods were eleven days in going from Saquache to the agency, averaging about six and one-half miles per day. He was enabled to obtain additional oxen to attach to his wagons to aid in pulling them " over the pass, or they would never have been able to get through at all." The contractors who carried this freight " through from Saquache, for two cents per pound, informed me (him) that they would not take the contract again for ten."

The governor said he felt a peculiar interest in the success of this lower agency, since many obstacles had been thrown in the way of himself and the agent, by those who were desirous that the location should have been on the border of New Mexico, and so remote from any base of supplies that transportation of material and provisions would have cost more than the purchase price. He found, when at this agency, the saw-mill completed and running, the warehouse finished and ready for the reception of goods, and the other buildings far advanced.

Daniel C. Oaks, an agent, selected a site for the agency on White river, believing that a better place could not be found in the northern part of the Ute reservation. He said the Indians were pleased with this location, and he did not apprehend any difficulty, provided the government was prompt in complying with the terms of the treaty.

The governor advised the department that he had discharged all the old employes, because he was convinced that they had been engaged in dishonest and disreputable practices under the former administration. He said that he was assured by both Indians and whites, that the wants of the Indians in the region of the southern agency, had never before been fully supplied. He felt confident that the agencies he had established would prove a success, and that the system he had inaugurated would go far toward carrying out the designs of the president.

It is not surprising that Gov. McCook was enabled to supply the Indians more bountifully than his predecessor, since he had the expenditure of the first appropriation made to fulfill the stipulations of the treaty of 1868. For this purpose, Congress, on the 10th of April, 1869, appropriated the sum of $122,450, to be expended in provisions, clothing, building agency houses, dwellings for employes, mills, etc., and he had the disbursement of this money. Before that time the appropriations were very limited; and in the last communication from Gov. Hunt, which appears in the public documents, under date of June 8, 1869, he refers the commissioner of Indian affairs to the fact that certain annuities, payable to the one band of Utes with which the treaty of 1863 was made, had never been furnished, as stipulated by the treaty.

On the 10th of August, 1870, Gov. McCook, by direction of the Indian department, made a visit to the White River agency, to inspect the location and the buildings. He took an escort of troops from Rawlings' Springs, and was from that point ten days in reaching the agency at White river. He said, in his report, made September 1, 1870, that he found good camping-grounds and water and grass on the journey, but away from the banks of the streams the whole country was sterile and desolate, the only vegetable productions being sage brush and cactus, "and the only indigenous living creature the horned frog." He found the agency buildings erected "at the mouth of a deep cañon, where the river debouches from the higher range of mountains." He judged from the locality, as well as from what he learned from the Indians, that it was much colder there than twelve or fifteen miles farther down the river. The Indians said their stock could not be kept there on account of the intense cold and the heavy fall of snow. He thought there were in the immediate vicinity of the agency thousands of acres of what appeared to be fertile land, part of it river bottom, part rolling, but all covered with good grass. Although the soil produced good grass, yet it appeared to be largely impregnated with alkali, and the production of cereals and vegetables was an experiment, the success of which was uncertain. His impression was that the proper location for the agency was on the south bank of Bear river, about eighty miles distant from the agency as located. There the climate was more temperate, the valleys broader, the timber more abundant and of better quality, and the place much more accessible. Moreover, the Indians desired that the agency be established at Bear river. The agency buildings having been erected and other improvements made, the governor concluded that the work of civilization must begin at White river.

About the same time that the governor left on his tour of inspection to White river, his private secretary, by his direction, started on the same errand to the southern agency. On his return, September 1, 1869, he made report to the governor. He was generally pleased with what he saw. The condition of the buildings, improvements, and stock was satisfactory. The agency farm had not proved a success, the grasshoppers having destroyed the crop, and in the location

26

there appeared to be, in his opinion, almost insuperable climatic and other difficulties to be surmounted. Yet the secretary concluded his communication thus: "I regard this agency as a success, and if the commissary department is kept well supplied, the question how to keep the southern Utes quiet is solved."

Lieut. Speer, in his report as agent, stated that parties in the southern part of Colorado and in New Mexico sought to thwart his operations. They had, however, but little influence upon the Indians. He had assurances from a number of the chiefs that the Indian children would be sent to school, provided they were supplied with food. This he thought an important auxiliary, and felt convinced that a lasting and permanent peace might be established with these wild Indians.

It will be observed that the site of the southern agency, as well as the one at White river, had the personal inspection of Gov. McCook, in his official capacity as superintendent of Indian affairs in Colorado. From his own statements, as well as those of his agents, there should be no surprise that neither was satisfactory to the Indians. The difficulty and discomfort in journeying to, and the unfavorable surroundings when at the agencies, are apparent; and the extreme elevation of the land and high temperature at White river, and the loss of the first crop at the southern agency, were calculated to make the Indians unhappy, and yet there is not one word in the reports of the agents or in the governor's report, indicating that there was any disorder or serious dissatisfaction manifested by them. In closing the report of his inspection tour to White river, Gov. McCook said: "Any of the country through which we passed was a good country for Indians, for we saw no human habitation from the time we left Rawlings' Springs until we reached White river, and, no matter how much our country may increase in prosperity and grow in population, there is no possibility of this portion of the territory being inhabited by a permanent white population. Except along the valley of the Bear, I saw nothing which would invite occupation by even the most poverty stricken and adventurous of our frontiersmen."

On the 13th of October, 1870, Gov. McCook wrote out his annual report as superintendent of Indian affairs in Colorado. He had before him the reports of his agents, and from the facts stated in these, and his own knowledge, he gathered material for this document. It was addressed to the commissioner of Indian affairs. There were no charges made by the governor against the Ute Indians. They were charged through the Associated Press dispatches during that year with killing some white men in the North Park, to which the governor thus refers: "The Utes were accused of killing the white men who were murdered. So soon as I heard of the murders, I visited the scene of the outrage and satisfied myself that the Utes were innocent." In the second paragraph of this report, the governor said : " I am satisfied that so soon as the Indians thoroughly understand the policy of the department, and believe that the government intends to feed, supply, protect, and instruct them, and enable them to learn those arts which will make them an independent and self-sustaining community, they will come to their reservation and remain there." And, in the closing paragraph, after complimenting not only the commissioner of Indian affairs, but his subordinates in the Indian office, for their uniform courtesy and aid, the governor said: " I desire to say that, with efficient agents and with the kind and energetic assistance and co-operation which you have always given me, I feel satisfied that the experiment just inaugurated, of civilizing the Utes, can be made a success."

In view of the guaranty in the treaty of 1868, by which the government assured to the Utes the undisputed use and occupation of the territory embraced in the reservation, and the language used by Gov. McCook in the extracts just quoted from his report, there are paragraphs in the body of that document that are surprising. In one place he rails at his predecessor, and the officials at Washington, and Col. Carson for making such a treaty, by which there was set " apart one-third of the whole area of Colorado for the exclusive use and occupation of the Ute nation," the greater part of which he said was " the best agricultural, pastural, and mining land on the continent." He said that, while traveling over this ter-

ritory, he " could not help feeling and expressing surprise that
the richest portion of the Territory of Colorado should have
been alienated without any sufficient consideration." In the
exuberance of his surprise, he went on thus : " This Ute reservation includes mines which will pay one hundred dollars
per day to the man, grasses which are luxuriant and inexhaustible, and a soil richer and more fertile than any other
in the territory. The land on the Uncompagre will raise cot-
ton, and this staple has been produced there of as good quality as any raised in the South. Snow only falls for two
months in the year on the worst portions of the reservation
belonging to the Southern agency, and in the Uncompagre
country no snow falls, and yet this great and rich country is
set aside for the exclusive use of savages who will not work
themselves, nor permit others to work." This fact so wrought
upon his mind that he exclaimed : " I believe that God gave
to us the earth, and the fullness thereof, in order that we
might utilize and enjoy His gifts. I do not believe in donat-
ing to these indolent savages the best portion of my territory." He pursues the subject at some length, and closes by
the assertion that he would " allow every American man to go
freely, and without hindrance, wherever the American flag
covers American soil." This declaration, coming from the
governor of Colorado, who was *ex officio* the superintendent of
Indian affairs, was, without doubt, quite gratifying to the
gold hunters and others who had covetous eyes upon the Ute
reservation.

In another part of the report, the governor turned his attention to the army. He said : " I have never seen any troops
stationed in this country affording the needed protection to
our settlers. The great end and aim seems to be to guard the
railroads and take care of themselves. . . . Is the army
stationed on the frontier to guard the iron and the ties of incorporated railroad companies or to protect the people ? . .
I want to see the army out here winter and summer, where
it properly belongs. If winter in this region is too cold for
the soldiers, notify the citizens that they have to take care
of themselves, and they will prepare to do it. . . . I speak
in earnest, and utter the sincere opinion of every honest citi-

zen of this territory, when I say that we do not want any more summer soldiers. If troops are sent down here simply to spend a pleasant summer, trout-fishing, grouse-shooting, and buffalo-hunting, they had better stay away altogether." In another place he complains that the military does not respond with alacrity to calls made upon them, which he intimates is excusable, since it is "no more than human that officers of the army should decline to respect a recommendation of, or act upon a suggestion coming from persons who they regard as possibly inimical to them—that is, civil officers with some military authority." And, finally, he calls the attention of the commissioner of Indian affairs to the fact that he had, in a letter dated January 20, 1870, expressed his belief "that the entire management of Indian affairs should be turned over to the war department."

Notwithstanding the pledge of the government in the treaty of 1868, that no person should settle in the Ute reservation, miners gradually entered it on prospecting tours, and in time they began to locate and work the mines. Gov. McCook had expressed the opinion that every American should be allowed to go freely and without hindrance on the soil where our flag floated, and hence these trespassers had nothing to fear from him, and as time passed, they increased in numbers. While patient, the Utes were not satisfied. Ouray, in 1871, asked that a military post might be established near the southwest corner of the reservation, to the end that the troops might be used to prevent further intrusion, as well as to expel those unlawfully residing on the reservation. In the spring of 1872, Congress authorized the secretary of the interior to enter into negotiations with the Utes for the extinguishment of their title to the southern part of their reservation, which was then overrun by miners and ranchmen; and Gov. McCook, John D. Lang, of Maine, and Gen. McDonald, of Missouri, were commissioned for that duty. On the 28th of August, 1872, these gentlemen met representatives of the Ute nation at the Los Pinos agency. In the opening council, Gov. McCook, the chairman of the commission, said to the Indians that it was the opinion of himself and his colleagues that they had "nothing to ask

except what will be for the good of both the Indian and the
white man." He told them that the authorities of Colorado
Territory having found that "some of the white men of Colorado and New Mexico had gone upon the Ute lands seeking
for gold," had requested the United States to pass a law that
would open negotiations by which, for a consideration, the
Utes would dispose of such lands which were not of value to
them, but very valuable to the white people. Gov. McCook
said : " It is in obedience to the provisions of this act of Congress that the Hon. Columbus Delano, Secretary of the Interior, by consent of the president, appointed this commission. The whole object of the commission can be reduced to
two or three simple propositions : First, we wish to buy
part of your lands, if you desire to sell them, and we propose
to give you a fair price for them. In all these negotiations
we wish the Utes to bear in mind, and our instructions say
implicitly, that the action must be entirely voluntary on your
part, and must meet the approval of the chiefs and a majority
of the Ute people who are in this council. We do not wish
you to be influenced by outside influences, and we must have
your approval before we can do any thing. We wish to have
an expression from the Indians and from your chiefs, and not
from any outside parties."

Mr. Lang followed Gov. McCook. His remarks were interpreted into the Ute language by Mr. Curtis. At the close
of them, Ouray said : " You write down what is said. We
can not. We want Lawrence to interpret. Many of the Indians understand Spanish, and we want Mr. Lang to repeat
what he has said, that all may understand it, and I will interpret it into Ute, that all may get it correct." Mr. Lang
then repeated what he had said.

Mr. Lang. " We sorrowfully say that bad white men want
to drive the Indians from their lands. I want to say to the
Utes, whom I have never met before, that I have been for
thirty years traveling among Indians. I find the Utes are in
the same condition as the other Indians whom I have visited
during those thirty years. I want to say this : I believe the
people are honest, and are anxious to do what they can for
the Utes. They say that the white people are breaking in

upon your land, and are giving trouble to the Utes. The president wants to take care of his white children and of his red children. He asks Gov. McCook, Gen. McDonald, and myself to leave our homes; he believes we are honest men; we do not want your land or your money; he asks us what we can do to make you happy. We believe it a trouble to you to have white men breaking in upon your borders and settling on your land. We have come here to talk with you—to see if you can help us, and if we can help you, in this matter. We know you have been cheated, and wronged, and deceived by bad men. We believe that you have reason to doubt the honesty of all white men, until you have had time to prove whether they speak truth or lies. It is nothing strange to me (and it is the same with our commission) that you are slow in coming together to hear what we have to say. I speak in behalf of the commission, and if I am not correct they will stop me, that we came here as honest men. We do not ask you to believe us until you can have a talk with us, and prove us to be honest men. We believed, at our homes, that the Utes needed help; and when the president and Congress asked us to come here—three thousand miles away from home—we said we would not come; but when they said, ' the Utes are in trouble, we want you to go and talk with them, and they with you,' to see that bad white men shall not drive you from your homes, we consented to come; we want nothing you have, but we come to do you good. We have no railroad in view; no great company of capitalists who want to make money out of your domains; we want you to receive us as brethren; we want to entreat you to be the friends of the government, for the government is a strong friend to you. We want to advise you to every improvement that is adapted to your present situation; and we want Ure (Ouray) to counsel with his wise men, and all to talk with us, at convenient opportunity, that we may counsel what is for your good. You are children of the Great Spirit; we are all one and the same. The Great Spirit has put it into the heart of the president and Congress, and good people, to think of the condition of the Indians. Such is the good heart of the president and Congress to you; old men, young men, and children, he provides for all of you; he sends blankets, provisions, and all such things as you need. Now, I want you to consider that the president and all good people are your friends, and not to decide against the commission and the president, until you find they are not honest men. It embarrasses me to talk to you through two interpreters; but I have said what I have from an honest heart."

Ouray followed, thus: "I understand, and know it was hard for you to go over what you have said. Mr. Curtis talks very well in Ute, but our language is different, and I want all to understand."

Gen. McDonald followed, and said: "I will say to Ure (Ouray) and the chiefs of the different bands of the Utes, and all the people of his nation, that I will not attempt to make a speech. Gov. McCook, who is well known to you, and who is governor of the territory in which your domain is situated, has informed you fully of the object of our mission here. He has read the act of Congress, which has been approved by the president, which is the authority under which we act. Friend Lang, of Maine, one of the commission, who has spent thirty years of his life in the service of the Indians, has expressed the feelings of the president and Congress and the good people of the United States, and in this he has expressed my feelings in full. I feel now that if my mission here will be of any benefit to you and to the white people of the country, I am fully repaid for coming."

Mr. Brunot, at that period chairman of the board of Indian commissioners, was present, and although not a member of this commission to the Utes, was introduced, and made some remarks. He stated that he had come to talk to the Utes about other matters after the council had concluded. He said: "I know the president's heart, and want to tell you that he sent this commission to talk to you for your good, as well as that of the white man. Four years ago there was a treaty made with all the Utes; that treaty marked out some lands that were for the Utes. It was intended for you always to have that land; but after a while Congress finds out that it is a very large piece of land; that white people are getting on the edge of it and in the mountains. Suppose a white man has a farm: he makes a fence around it, and keeps the stock and wild animals out of it. But if it is so large he can not make a fence about it, he sells part of it, keeping the rest to live on, and with the money he buys stock and improves his land. Congress sees that there are white people coming on your land; it will take too many soldiers to make a fence around it. The Utes see how hard it is to keep the whites off, so Congress passed a law and sent this commission to see whether the Utes did not want to sell some of their land, making it smaller, so that it would not take so many soldiers to protect it, and the Utes would not be troubled with the whites coming on it. Congress leaves it all with the Utes to say what they will do. Congress thought when it passed the law it would be good for the Utes to sell a portion of their reservation. It does not compel the Utes to do so. It is just as you please. You must think of it, and do what you think right."

Here Gen. McDonald expressed a desire that Ure (Ouray) should say something, and the chief replied that the Utes did not wish to sell one foot of their land; that was the opinion of all. "For some time," he said, "we have seen the whites coming in on our lands; we have not done any thing ourselves, but have waited for the government to fulfill its treaty. We have come here so that you may see that we are not satisfied with this trespassing on our lands; but we do not want to sell any of them."

Several other chiefs said a few words, when Gov. McCook remarked that the commission desired the evening to talk the matter over among themselves, and an adjournment took place. On the next day the council convened at two o'clock P. M. Gov. McCook informed the Indians that as the commission occupied the time the day before, the members desired the chiefs to talk on that day.

Sapamanore, a Tabequache chief, said that in time past he had talked with Gov. McCook, and thought the treaty was settled, and was to remain. He said: "We thought the land you are trying to buy was given us by treaty for our lands. For that reason we have never thought of going to war or any thing of the kind, and we are contented with the treaty as it is. When we made the treaty, we did not think it was made with common men, but thought it was with people who would abide by the treaty. . . . We believe, and our children who are living and those that will be born shall believe, that the treaty is as it should be, and that nobody can take away our land that we have by the treaty. By this treaty we are here on this reservation, and people are living on land that was ours, and are enjoying it. We do not disturb them on it, and they should not disturb us on this land that is ours. What we are talking about is of great interest to the whites and the Indians, and it should be of equal interest to both. It is business of importance that we are talking about. It is a thing that looks strange to us, that white men who are civilized should be going on our land, and it is strange to us that they are permitted to trespass on it. The whites should be quiet in their own country, and should not be trespassing on land that does not belong to them. Our interest, and all our interest, is to live in peace with all men. . . . For a great many years I have lived in the position in which I am, and my only desire is that we should live in peace. A man who thinks well will always do well. It is the same of the whites and the Indians; they will not forget. A man who is red or white, if he thinks well, will always be just, and do right in all his actions."

Kaneache, a Muache chief, said he did not believe the commission was sent from the States to treat with the Utes, but one that has come of its own accord. To this Gov. McCook replied, that if such was the opinion of the Indians there was no use of the Utes treating with the commission. The chief replied, that the reason he said what he did was because both Mexicans and Americans told him some time before, that Gov. McCook was trying to get the Ute land. The chief added that Gov. Arney, who was then present, was all the time going to Washington and Santa Fé, "and all the time working against us."

Katucheka, a Capote chief, said: "The country where the miners are, we consider as the Capote country. There are a great many passing in our country, and what I want is that they may go in safety, and as they go from house to house they may do it in safety, and not have to be watching the road by which they will return. It is the same both with the Indians and with the whites. I want it to be every-where just as it is when an Indian goes to Denver; he can return in safety without watching the road. We are all one; we were all born of one father and one mother, and it is not right for brethren to be killing each other. All the miners who go into the country misrepresent every thing, and tell us false-hoods. They say the government gives them permission to go there."

The discussion between the commission and the Utes was continued each successive day, until the evening of the 31st of August. The burden of it can be judged by the preceding extracts. The Indians were averse to selling any portion of the reservation, and urged that the intruders should be removed. On the 29th, Gov. McCook, in reply to some remarks of chief Shawano, in relation to the intrusions on the reservation, admitted that gold had been found in the southern portion of it, and that miners had gone there in large numbers. "There are (said the governor) only two ways to meet this difficulty. The first, and we think it the best for both the Utes and the whites, is for the government to extinguish the title of the Utes to it, by paying you a large sum for the mining portion of the reservation. The second is to send soldiers there and drive the miners out. Now, the Capote chief, who has just spoken, said you did not want soldiers in your country. If the miners are an annoyance there, and drive away and kill your game and catch your fish, we think the soldiers would be more of an annoyance. This is a question that has to be met squarely. The Utes do not wish to go to war and drive the miners out, so you have to appeal to the government to do so. I want you to think seriously of this matter."

On the last day this colloquy took place between Gov. Mc-Cook and the chief Shawano and others:

Gov. McCook. "Shawano, are you willing to place yourself in a position where you never can go to Denver again? That is what you are asking of us, that no whites shall go upon your reservation, while the Indian wanders where he pleases. I see Shawano and Piah in Denver every month in the year."

Shawano. "I understand the treaty, that by doing no wrong we can go to the States if we please."

Gov. McCook. "Have these miners been doing any wrong on your reservation?"

Shawano. "It is the same as if the miners were stealing, getting on our reservation."

Gov. McCook. "When you go to Denver do you not steal, when your ponies eat the white people's grass? Grass is just as valuable to your horses, as gold is to the white people."

Shawano. "Being at peace, there is no law that prevents a man going where he wants and getting his living; our treaty is that way, and we can not help saying so."

Gen. McDonald. "Shawano is right. We will accord all to you that you do to the whites."

Shawano. "When I go to Denver I do not disturb anybody. I do not dig up the earth, and I disturb nobody, as these miners do."

Gov. McCook. "Have any of you ever been on the mountain where the miners are? Can your ponies live there, or can any of you make a living there?"

Shawano. "It is a great hunting-ground for us. There are sheep and deer, and it is a matter of great importance to us."

Gov. McCook. "That is not on the mountain where the miners are."

Shawano. "Yes, it is on that mountain."

This colloquy was continued some time, other chiefs participating, when Ouray asked Gov. McCook: "What is your reason for putting all this before us?" To which the governor answered: "Simply I want to tell you that if you insist on the government fulfilling its part, it will insist on you fulfilling your part; that is the letter of the bond." To this Shawano replied: "It is one government; you are a legal man, and why are you talking so much about it?" Shawano then asked this question: "In what part of the territory have the Indians done any harm?" In reply, Gov. McCook said: "What harm have these miners done?" Then the chief Ankatosh put this question: "What did the president say when he sent you to buy our lands? Did he tell you to ask so many questions?"

Finally, and without being able to make any arrangement for the cession of the desired territory, Gov. McCook declared "the council ended, and said we part friends, and all that has been said will be reported to the president."

The commission did report the result of their labors to the commissioner of Indian affairs on the 24th of September. The concluding paragraph of their communication is in these words:

"When we parted with the Indians they manifested the most kind and friendly feeling. We have every reason to believe that the visit of the commission was a timely one, and served to allay any feeling of irritation which might have existed in the minds of the Utes against either the white miners or the government of the United States. It convinced them that the president and Congress fully recognized all the rights conferred and all obligations imposed by the treaty, and would endeavor to discharge their duty toward both the Indians and the white people of the territory in a manner that would be at the same time just and pacific."

In the spring of 1873, an order was issued by the direction of the president for the expulsion of the miners and other settlers then within the Ute reservation, but before the military had entered on the discharge of the duty, this order was suspended. The reason given was that the president had been informed that chief Ouray had intimated that the Utes were willing to resume negotiation for the sale of a portion of their reservation, and he deemed it best to await the result of another council, since, in the event of such council and the sale of a portion of the territory to the United States, it would be a needless hardship to drive out the settlers, who would desire at once to return after the purchase was made, to their former occupations.

On the 2d of July, 1873, Felix R. Brunot and Nathan Bishop, both of the board of Indian commissioners, were designated to constitute a new commission to negotiate with the Utes. The Indian agents at Los Pinos, White River, and Abiquin, the latter in New Mexico, were directed to render the commission all the assistance in their power in securing a full attendance of the different bands of Utes at the Los Pinos agency, where the council was to assemble. Mr. Bishop was unable to attend, and hence Mr. Brunot was the sole commissioner. He arrived there on the 6th of September, 1873, accompanied by his secretary, Mr. Cree, and Dr. J. Phillips, whom he had engaged as Spanish interpreter. The time originally fixed for the meeting had been postponed, and hence there were but few Indians there on the arrival of Mr. Brunot. The journal of the proceedings shows but thirty-two Utes present. These represented the Tabequache, Muache, Capote, Weeminuche, White River, and Denver bands of Utes, and one representative of a band of Apaches. Two bands of Utes were not represented. On the way to Los Pinos, Mr. Brunot met a surveying party, acting under authority of the surveyor-general of Colorado Territory, engaged in sectionizing the land near this agency for settlement. There was also in that region a military surveying party, acting under the direction of the military authorities of the department, and a division of Professor Hayden's exploring party had but recently been some time on the reservation, making surveys and taking observations. Parties of miners were repeatedly in the neighborhood of the agency, and such of them as the Indians came in contact with, said the government was away east in the states, and had no power in the mines; that it could not protect the Indians, and that they did not care whether the Utes sold the mines or not, they were going to stay. All these things were very objectionable to the Indians.

The commission went to work on the afternoon of the day of its arrival. It was not long until the fact was discovered that the Indians misapprehended the purpose and desire of the government, as disclosed by Mr. Brunot. The commission of 1872, as a last resort, asked the Indians to sell only the mines to them, which the Utes understood to mean the mines that were then actually worked, and to include none of the adjacent country, and they supposed that the purpose of the present commission was only to renew this request. They were willing to sell these with the right of way by one road to reach them. Mr. Brunot declined to entertain this proposition. The Indians then said they would sell the portion of the reservation around the head of the Rio Grande, but they would want security that the miners would not go any farther. Mr. Brunot replied that he could not make any agreement to purchase the small piece of country in which the miners were then located. Ouray said that the piece of land they offered to sell was not so small. It was, in fact, large. The mountains were long, and where the miners then were they would sell, but none of the bottom lands. Mr. Brunot suggested that the difficulty in such a contract was that there would always be quarreling as to where the lines were, and hence more trouble than there was at that time. Ouray suggested, to avoid trouble, that the country be surveyed, and the lines marked so that all could see them.

In response, Mr. Brunot said: " It would take five years and one hundred men to do that. What I think (said he), is that the Utes had better sell all the mountain country. Suppose I were to make a contract for where the mines are now, it would take all the Utes and one thousand soldiers to stand around it to see that the miners did not go to the other mountains, and, instead of stopping the trouble, it would make it worse. The mountains west of it, the miners would be hunting mines in. Suppose there are no mines in the part west, and suppose the Utes make a bargain for it."

Ouray. " We can not do what you want."

Mr. Brunot. " But I want you to hear what I have to say. Suppose you sell the mountains, and if there is no gold in them then it would be a benefit to you. The Utes get the pay for them, and the Americans would stay away. But suppose there are mines there, it will not stop the trouble ; we could not keep the people away."

Ouray. " Why can not you stop them; *is not the government strong enough* to keep its agreements with us ? "

Mr. Brunot. " What Ouray says is reasonable. I would like to stop them ; but Ouray knows it is hard to do."

Ouray. " In regard to the mountains around the mines we do not say any thing, but to take in so much land we will not agree to it. We know what the government has to do by the treaty, and we know how you are talking about the trouble. You are a commissioner on the part of the government; we are on our own part. If you do not want to buy, or we do not want to sell, it is all right. The whites can go and take the gold and come out again. We do not want them to build houses there."

Mr. Brunot. "I told you I would not have come if I had not wanted to benefit the Utes. I wanted to befriend you. I do not think I would be doing what was good for the Utes, if I did what Ouray wants. It need not prevent the contract from being made, but I will not make it. I will tell the president, and he may send somebody else, and they may buy just what the Utes want to sell now, and in another year they will find the miners as bad somewhere else, and then they may send somebody else. You understand why I will not agree to it. But it is all right if you do not make an agreement with me. It will not make any difference. I will try and have you protected as well as I can. I will do as I did before. I will ask the president to drive the miners away, as I did last fall; but a thousand other men will tell the president to let them alone. Perhaps he will do as I say, perhaps not."

The discussion between the Ute chiefs and Mr. Brunot continued for nearly a week before a conclusion was reached. A proper location for the agencies, the present and future condition of the Indians, and the invasion of their territory were all discussed. Among other matters, the boundary lines of the treaty of 1868 were discussed, the Indians averring that, as they understood that treaty, the eastern boundary of the reservation as surveyed, was not according to it. Ouray said, the line established by the surveyors, they said, was twelve miles west from Los Pinos, and that was not right. This question of the boundary lines was also discussed before the McCook commission. Ouray was the interpreter when the treaty of 1868 was made, and, from all the facts, there can be no doubt that the Utes misapprehended the territory defined in the treaty, and it is doubtful whether the United States commissioners were not also deceived.

Mr. Brunot finally succeeded, and on the 13th of September, 1873, as commissioner on the part of the United States, entered into an agreement "with the chiefs and people of the Tabequache, Muache, Capote, Weeminuche, Yampa, and Grand River and Uintah, the confederated bands of the Ute nation." By this agreement there was relinquished to the United States "all right, title, interest, and claim in and to the following described portion of the reservation heretofore conveyed to them by the United States, viz: Beginning at a point, on the eastern boundary of said reservation, fifteen miles due north from the southern boundary of the Territory of Colorado, and running thence west, on a line parallel with said southern boundary, to a point on said line twenty miles due east of the western boundary of Colorado Territory; thence north by a line parallel with said western boundary, to a point ten miles north of the point where said line intersects the thirty-eighth parallel of north latitude; thence east, to the eastern boundary of the reservation, and thence south, along said boundary, to the place of beginning; *provided*, that if any part of the Uncompagre Park shall be found to extend south of the north line of said described country, the same is not intended to be included therein, and is hereby reserved and retained as a portion of the Ute reservation."

In the agreement, it was stipulated that the Utes should be permitted to hunt on the land ceded to the government as long as the game lasted and the Indians were at peace with the white people; and the United States agreed to "set apart, and hold as a perpetual trust for the Ute Indians, a sum of money, or its equivalent in bonds, which shall be sufficient to produce the sum of twenty-five thousand dollars per annum, which sum of $25,000 per annum shall be disbursed or invested at the discretion of the president, or as he may direct, for the use and benefit of the Ute Indians, annually forever."

It was stipulated, in the agreement, that all the provisions of the treaty of 1868 should be, and remain, in full force and effect; and the pledge, in that treaty, that no person, except officers and agents of the government, and other persons authorized by law, should ever be permitted to pass over,

27

settle upon, or reside on the Ute reservation, was expressly reaffirmed.

In transmitting this agreement to the department, Mr. Brunot stated that the Utes claimed that the " commissioners who made with them the treaty of 1868, pointed out the Chocitopa Mountain as the eastern line of their reservation; but that now the surveyors said the line was twelve miles west of the agency buildings, instead of the same distance east of the agency, as had been promised at the treaty. They also claimed that the commissioners told them that the southern line of the reservation was upon the highlands south of the San Juan river; but now surveyors had marked a line (the southern line of Colorado) north of the river, which they were told was the limit of their reservation. Both of these lines they desired to have reinstated in the sub-treaty. The Muaches and Capotes wanted to have their agency continued at Cimarron, in New Mexico, and to make its continuance there a condition of even the sale they proposed. None of them were willing to sell any part of the agricultural lands of the reservation. Believing that to purchase the existing mines only, would but postpone, for a few months, the apprehended collision between the whites and the Indians, and, consequently, be of little benefit either to them or the government, I declined to enter into such negotiations. Having no authority on the subject of the lines of the reservation, that question was withdrawn from the council, by the promise that the chiefs should visit Washington to make their representations to the government in person." The tract of land which Mr. Brunot obtained by the agreement contains near four millions of acres. He made, in his communication, several suggestions beneficial to the Utes, which do not appear to have had any consideration, and closed thus: " I desire to express the utmost confidence in the friendly disposition of the Ute Indians, and commend their head chief, Ouray, for his devotion to both the interests of the government and his people."

With the surrender of the portion of the Ute reservation obtained by the Brunot agreement, the Indians had a right to, and did, expect that they would be relieved from any further inroads; that, having given up the mining territory, they would be protected in what was termed the agricultural lands. But this was a delusion. The grazing country was just as much coveted as the mineral, and "ranchmen" intruded to prospect for good locations, where they could herd and graze stock, some of whom now occupy the valleys with their ranches. Hence, it may be said the Ute Indians are not, and can not be, at rest in any part of their reservation; that they have had no progress in farming, and very little in herding, should not surprise any one. There is a desire expressed by many of these Indians to become farmers, and it would seem results in that direction ought to be seen in the immediate neighborhood of the agencies. The sites for these appear to have been located most unfortunately; and, where the original locations were afterward changed, there does not seem to be much improvement. Extreme drought and insufficient means for irrigation are frequently offered by the agents as reasons for a partial or total failure of the crops. At one time, blight comes from the work of the grasshopper, and, at another, the frost is destructive. In 1870, Gov. McCook's private secretary made a report to him, from the Southern Ute agency, in which this paragraph appears: "The agency farm has not proved a success this season, owing to the almost insuperable climatic and other difficulties to be surmounted. A tract of eight or ten acres was planted with oats, potatoes, turnips, etc., all of which might have been an average crop, but for the advent of the grasshoppers. These insects devoured all the farm products above ground, in a single day. I am informed by the agent that a severe frost killed the grasshoppers the same night."

In July, 1878, agent Meeker wrote that one field of twenty acres, three miles from the White River agency, "was sown to wheat last fall, but it was wholly destroyed by grasshoppers and prairie dogs." Numerous extracts from reports of the agents, made from year to year, of the failure of the crops, and the cause thereof, could, if necessary, be produced.

In the annual report of the Indian office for the year 1878, it was estimated that five per cent. of the subsistence of the Utes was obtained by those engaged in civilized pursuits, forty five per cent. by hunting, fishing, root-gathering, etc., and, by the issue of government rations, fifty per cent. The whole number of Indians at the agencies that year was reported at 3,734. Of these, 2,000 were at Los Pinos, 934 at the Southern, and 800 at the White River agency. One-half of the whole number is 1,867. To provide government rations for this number, at twelve cents per day, which is about one-half the amount that an army ration costs in that country, would require the sum of $81,774.60. The entire appropriation for food and clothing, which was granted by Congress, for the year ending June 30, 1878, was only $60,000. Of this sum, only $30,000 were, by the terms of the appropriation act, set off for subsistence. This sum, distributed per capita to the 3,734 Utes, would give to each one, for subsistence, $8.03 per year, or about two and one-third cents per day! If the whole sum were expended for provisions, and no clothing furnished, the per capita for each Ute would be less than five cents per day!

In 1878, the wealth of the Utes was 8,500 head of horses and ponies, 45 mules, 1,372 cattle, and 4,500 sheep, and the value of the robes and peltries sold was $9,500. The revenue of the Indians from this source has fallen off very much. This is the inevitable result of the invasion of the reservation by those unlawfully going into and dwelling therein. It may be observed that the number of the Utes is in excess of those reported at the agencies. The population may be set down at about 4,500.

To say that there has been no violence or disorder among the Utes since they came under treaty relations, in 1868, would be to place them in moral conduct above any society in the United States. To say that they have been remarkably orderly and pacific, is simply to do them justice. There is an almost unbroken chain of evidence in their behalf in the reports of the agents. The reports from the agents, in 1878, contain a reflex of those in preceding years. Agent Weaver, of the Rio Los Pinos agency, in his report for that year, says: "Beyond the excessive and violent demands for rations, and the threat of taking the life of the agent for establishing the agency on the Rio Pinos (to which the Southern agency was removed), instead of the Rio Navajo, as they claim to have been promised them, there is but very little in their conduct to condemn. I blush to say aught about this, when I reflect upon how they have been treated by the government, and imposed upon by individuals."

Agent Abbott, of the Los Pinos agency, says : " With few exceptions, they are a quiet, peaceable, well-disposed people. Quarrels and contentions among them are infrequent, and not a single instance has come to my knowledge of violence or crime committed by them against the person or property of the whites settled along the border of their reservation, or even against the squatters, who knowingly and in defiance of all right and justice, and even the authorities of the government, have encroached upon and taken possession of their most fertile lands."

Agent Meeker, of the White River agency, says, in his report of July 20, 1878 : " These Ute Indians are peaceable, respectors of the rights of property, and, with few exceptions, amiable and prepossessing in appearance. There are no quarrelsome outbreaks, no robberies, and perhaps not half a dozen who pilfer—and these are well known. The marriage relation is strictly observed—at least for the time it continues— and polygamy is practiced to a limited extent. On the whole, this agent is impressed with the idea that, if the proper methods can be hit upon, they can be made to develop many useful qualities, and be elevated to a state of absolute independence."

On the 29th day of September, 1879, agent Meeker and all his male employes at the White River agency were killed by the Indians residing there, and on the same day, fifteen miles away, chief Jack's band of Utes met in battle the command of Maj. Thornburgh, then on its way to the agency, in obedience to a call on the department by agent Meeker for troops. The agent had been injured by one of the chiefs, and hence the call. In the affair between Jack's warriors and the troops Maj. Thornburgh fell. The attention of the whole country has been attracted to this affair, and it has had much discussion, in the absence, however, of any correct analysis of the facts.

In seeking for a solution of the difficulties which culminated in the tragedy at White River agency, several facts lead to the conclusion that agent Meeker, though admitted to be an honest and brave man, was yet not possessed of that degree of patience, combined with firmness, which an Indian agent should have. Moreover, he appeared to be ready to hear and accept complaints and charges of the white people against the Utes as true, without giving them proper investigation.

On the 29th of July, 1878, in a communication to the commissioner of Indian affairs, Mr. Meeker referred to a piece of ground that was sown that season to beets, turnips, peas, and the like, by the help of Mrs. Danforth, the wife of his predecessor, assisting the wife of a disabled Ute hunter. The Indians were out on a hunt when agent Meeker took charge, and he states that he found this ground growing to weeds, and, to save the crop, he hoed it out several times, and carried more than one hundred pails of water to nourish it. When the Utes returned, after an absence of more than six weeks, the wife of the disabled Indian visited the garden, expressed surprise and admiration, and remarked she was much obliged to him. He said he supposed the Indians had wholly abandoned the garden, and, having none himself, he " naturally " concluded he would have some of the products, " but (said he) they have entered into possession, and I have no vegetables of any kind. . . . Of course this style of Indian farming has, under my administration, come to an end."

In the spring of 1879, hunting parties of the White river Utes went north, passing beyond the limits of their reservation, and extending their excursions to the Parks in Western Colorado. In these excursions they killed game, and sold the peltries, etc., to persons who had stores near the northern border of their reservation, and, in exchange therefor, obtained, it was said, among other things, ammunition and whisky. The agent appeared ready to accept all accusations made against the Utes as true, and, early in the spring, wrote the military commander at Fort Steele to arrest all the Utes " bound north, and either hold them or send them back to the reservation. They deserve a lesson."

In July, 1879, Gov. Pitkin, of Colorado, stated, in a dispatch to the Indian office, that reports reached him daily "that a band of White River Utes were off their reservation, destroying forests and game near North and Middle Parks. " They have already (said the governor) burned millions of dollars worth of timber, and are intimidating settlers and miners. . . . I respectfully request you to have telegraphic orders sent troops at nearest post to remove Indians to their reservation. If general government does not act promptly, the State must. Immense forests are burning through Western Colorado, supposed to have been fired by Indians. . . . I am satisfied there is an organized effort on the part of Indians to destroy the timber of Colorado. . . . These savages should be removed to the Indian Territory, where they can no longer destroy the finest forests in the state."

On the 7th of July, the Indian office informed agent Meeker by telegraph of the contents of Gov. Pitkin's dispatch, and said, if true, take active steps to secure the return of the Indians " to their reservation, and, if necessary, call upon nearest military post for assistance." On the same day, and before these instructions were received, agent Meeker had forwarded a dispatch to the Indian office, in which he said that he had been informed that bands of Utes on Snake and Bear rivers, and in Middle and North Parks, were destroying game for the skins, and burning timber, and that he had sent Chief Douglas and an employe to order their return, and had requested the commandant at Fort Steele to cause them to return.

Maj. Thornburgh, the commandant at Fort Steele, after an investigation, wrote, on the 27th of July, that about the 25th of June, a band of Utes from the White River agency made their appearance at a mining camp on the divide, about sixty miles south of his post, and engaged in hunting and trading in the vicinity for about one week, when they departed, as they said, for their agency. After referring to the charges against the Indians, of burning timber, and wantonly destroying game, and intimidating settlers and miners, the commandant said : " I made inquiries, and could not find such a state of affairs to exist ; but did find that the Indians had killed a great deal of game and used the skins for trade. The miners they visited in this section were not molested, but, on the contrary, were presented with an abundance of game. No stock was molested, and, so far as I can learn, no one attributes the burning of timber to these Indians." Much game is killed in that region by white hunters, miners, and pleasure seekers, the parks of Western Colorado being every season frequented by many of the latter. From the camp fires of these classes, carelessly abandoned without being extinguished, many forest fires originate. Agent Meeker appeared ready to believe that the Utes were guilty, especially when such men as the governor said they were.

On the 8th of September, 1879, Mr. Meeker sent a communication to the commissioner of Indian affairs, detailing what occurred in relation to the plowing of a piece of ground near the agency. He said that when the plowing commenced, three or four Indians objected, claiming that their tents and corrals were upon it, and they desired to occupy it. He offered to remove their corrals with his employes, and showed them other places to locate, of which, he said, there were many equally as good, but they refused. He told them that if he were to remove the agency buildings two or three miles away, they would come and claim equal squatters' rights there also, and they replied that he had land enough plowed, and they wanted the rest for their horses. The Indians would listen to nothing, he said, and he ordered the plow to proceed. The strip laid off was a half a mile long and one hundred feet wide, and when the plowman ran one furrow through and came to the upper end, two Indians came out with guns and ordered him not to plow any more. This was reported to agent Meeker, and he directed the plowing to proceed. When the plowman, in obedience to this order, had made a few rounds, he was fired upon from a cluster of sage-brush. Then the agent ordered the plowing stopped, and called chief Douglas in consultation. The chief said that since the Indians who claimed the land wanted it, the agent ought to plow somewhere else. Then agent Meeker sent for Jack, the rival chief, who lived about ten miles away, whom, he said, had a larger following than Douglas; and this chief and his friends came to the agency, and the subject was discussed at length. The conclusion reached was, that the ground laid off might be plowed, but no more. The agent said he wanted to plow at least fifty acres, and finally the Indians said he could plow as much as he proposed. But this was either not understood, or not assented to, by the claimants, who had their corrals on the land, and when the plow started again, they threatened vengeance if any more than the original plat was plowed. The plow ran most of the forenoon, when the plowman becoming alarmed, work ceased, and Jack and his men were again sent for, and another council was held. At this council it was agreed that the agent should plow half the tract he indicated, and inclose the balance, provided he would remove the corrals, dig a well, help build a log cabin, and supply a stove, to which he assented. The agent, in the close of his report, said: "Altogether, there were not more than four Indian men engaged in this outbreak, properly there was only one family, the wife of which speaks good English, having been brought up in a white family. The remainder were relatives, and beside were several sympathizers, but by no means active. . . . Plowing will proceed, but whether unmolested, I can not say."

On the 10th of September, the agent telegraphed to the department, and said: " I have been assaulted by a leading chief, Johnson; forced out of my own house, and injured badly; but was rescued by employes. It is now revealed that Johnson originated all the trouble stated in letter of September 8th. . . . Plowing stops; life of self, family, and employes not safe; want protection immediately; have asked Gov. Pitkin to confer with Gen. Pope."

On September 15th, the war department, at the request of the Indian office, ordered that a detail of troops be sent from the nearest military post, sufficient in number " to arrest such Indian chiefs as are insubordinate, and enforce obedience to the requirements of the agent, and afford him such protection as the exigency of the case may require; also that the ringleaders be held as prisoners until an investigation can be had." On the same day the Indian office informed the agent that troops were ordered, and directed that on their arrival he should cause the arrest of the leaders in the late disturbance, and have them held until further orders. The agent replied that the dispatch of the 15th was received, and would be obeyed.

On the 25th of September, 1879, Maj. Thornburgh, then at Fortification creek, and *en route* to the agency, sent a dispatch to agent Meeker. He said : " In obedience to instructions from the general of the army, I am *en route* to your agency, and expect to arrive there on the 29th instant, for the purpose of affording you any assistance in my power in regulating your affairs, and to make arrests at your suggestion, and to hold as prisoners such of your Indians as you desire, until investigations are made by your department. I have heard nothing definite from your agency for ten days, and do not know what state of affairs exists—whether the Indians will leave at my approach or show hostilities. I send this letter by Mr. Lowrey, one of my guides, and desire you to communicate with me as soon as possible, giving me all the information in your power, in order that I may know what course I am to pursue. If practicable, meet me on the road at the earliest moment."

On September 27th, agent Meeker wrote Maj. Thornburgh as follows : " Understanding that you are on the way hither with United States troops, I send a messenger, Mr. Eskridge, and two Indians, Henry (interpreter), and John Ayersley, to inform you that the Indians are greatly excited, and wish you to stop at some convenient camping place, and that you and five soldiers of your command come into the agency, when a talk and a better understanding can be had. This I agree to, but I do not propose to order your movements, but it seems for the best. The Indians seem to consider the advance of the troops as a declaration of real war. In this I am laboring to undeceive them, and at the same time to convince them they can not do whatever they please. The first object now is to allay apprehension.".

On September 26th, Maj. Thornburgh telegraphed to his department commander, from Bear river : " Have met some Ute chiefs here. They seem friendly, and promise to go with me to the agency. Say Utes don't understand why we have

come. Have tried to explain satisfactorily. Do not antici-
pate trouble."

On September 28th, Maj. Thornburgh sent to the agent the
following : " I shall move my entire command to some convenient camp near and within striking distance of your
agency, reaching such point during the 29th. I shall then
halt and encamp the troops, and proceed to the agency with
my guide and five soldiers, as communicated in your letter of
the 27th instant. Then and there I will be ready to have a
conference with you and the Indians, so that an understanding may be arrived at, and my course of action determined.
I have carefully considered whether or not it would be advisable to leave my command at a point as distant as that desired by the Indians who were in my camp last night, *and
have reached the conclusion that, under my orders, which require
me to march this command to the agency, I am not at liberty to
leave it at a point where it would not be available in case of trouble.*
You are authorized to say for me to the Indians, that my
course of conduct is entirely dependent upon them. Our desire is to avoid trouble, and we have not come for war. I requested you in my letter of the 26th [25th] to meet me on the
road before I reached the agency. I renew my request that
you do so, and further desire that you bring such chiefs as may
wish to accompany you."

In the narrative of Miss Josephine Meeker, she says
that the Indians at the agency first heard of the advance of
troops when Maj. Thornburgh's command was sixty miles
away. The fact was communicated by an Indian runner, who
came in under great excitement. The next day the Indians
held a council, and called on her father, and requested him to
write Maj. Thornburgh, and ask him to send in five officers
" to compromise and keep the soldiers off the reservation."
In agent Meeker's letter of September 27th, to Maj. Thornburgh, he made known the wishes of the Indians, and their
request, and said that he agreed to it. The two Indians who
accompanied Eskridge, the messenger who bore the letter of
the agent to Maj. Thornburgh, returned to the agency on
Sunday morning, the 28th of September. After their arrival
Miss Meeker states that a council was held at the camp of

Douglas, and also at the agency; that the American flag was flying over the tents of the chief; that the other tents and the women were all moved back, and the Indians greatly excited. The fact that the troops were advancing toward the agency was no doubt known to the two Indians who came.in that morning, and by them communicated to the Indians, and hence the excitement. On Monday, the 29th, Eskridge returned. Miss Meeker states that he said " the troops were making a day and night march, and wanted it kept a secret; *that Thornburgh wanted it to be given out to the Indians that he would meet five Utes at Milk creek, fifteen miles from the agency, on Monday night, and desired an immediate answer.* Thornburgh was expected to reach the agency on Tuesday, at noon, with the troops." At this juncture, Miss Meeker says, " the Indians, who at first were angry, brightened up, and Douglas sent two Indians with one white man, Eskridge, to meet Thornburgh."

The agent himself had the information from some source, during the forenoon of the 29th, that Thornburgh was to leave his troops fifty miles away, and come to the agency. He telegraphed the department at Washington, on that day, and said : " Maj. Thornburgh leaves his command fifty miles distant, and comes to-day with five men. Indians propose to fight if troops advance. A talk will be had to-morrow." The dispatch from which this extract is taken, discloses the fact that the agent was disturbed in mind. In it he states that Capt. Dodge, Ninth Cavalry, was at Steamboat Springs, with orders to break up Indian stores, and keep the Utes on the reservation ; that there was a brisk trade in guns and ammunition, and when Capt. Dodge begins to enforce the law, there will be no living at the agency without troops. On the same day, but, without doubt, after agent Meeker had sent this dispatch to Washington, he received Maj. Thornburgh's note of the 28th of September, and to this he replied at once. His note is dated September 29th, 1 P. M.

He says : " I expect to leave in the morning, with Douglas and Serrick, to meet you ; things are peaceable, and Douglas flies the United States flag. If you have trouble in getting through the cañon to-day, let me know. We have been on guard three nights, and shall be to-night, not because we know there is danger, but because there may be. I like your last programme; it is based on true military principles." In none of the published dispatches are the circumstances surrounding the agent, or operating on his mind disclosed, at the time he wrote and sent either of the dispatches of the 29th September. It is, however, clear that he could not have received the dispatch of Thornburgh of the 28th before he sent his dispatch to Washington. It is apparent, that the messenger, whom he sent with his note of 1 P. M., September 29th, was but a short distance on his way when the scene changed at the agency. Miss Meeker says, that "just before Eskridge left with the Indians (to meet Maj. Thornburgh), a runner was seen rushing up to the tent of Douglas with what I since learned was news of the soldiers and Indians fighting." To quote her words: "Half an hour later, twenty armed Indians came from the camp of Douglas, and began firing. I was in the kitchen with my mother washing the dishes. It was after noon. I looked out of the window and saw the Utes shooting at the boys who were working on the new building." During the afternoon, the agent and all his male employes, eight in number, were killed, the agency buildings sacked and fired, and the women and children seized and carried to the south.

Maj. Thornburgh's command entered the Ute reservation on the afternoon of September 28th. He was then, it was said, twenty-five miles from the agency. On the morning of the 29th, when about to enter a cañon, and fifteen miles from the agency, Lieut. Cherry, who had been sent forward with an advance guard to reconnoitre, was fired upon. The fact being communicated to Maj. Thornburgh, he withdrew his troops, and placed them in line of battle, with orders, it was said, to await the attack of the Indians. The warriors, about one hundred in number, soon delivered a volley, and the work of carnage began. These warriors were said to have been from Jack's band.

It was stated that Jack and ten of his warriors were at Maj. Thornburgh's camp on the evening of the 25th, and, at that time, there is some reason to believe that the chief was then not aware that the troops had been called for by the agent. It is known that Mr. Meeker considered it important that the fact that he had called for troops should be concealed from the Indians, and had so telegraphed Gov. Pitkin. On the 26th, it is said that Jack met and conversed with an employe bearing a dispatch to Capt. Dodge, and inquired of him why the troops were coming to the reservation.

It is to be observed that Jack and his following had no part or lot in the difficulty that grew out of the dispossession of the Indian family who had their tents and corrals on the land that agent Meeker plowed. Jack was called in consultation twice about this matter, but neither he nor any of his people had any personal interest in the controversy. Indeed, but few of Douglas' Indians had any interest in it. The council with the agent, at which he was urged to send a messenger to Maj. Thornburgh, and request him to camp his troops and send in some of his officers to a conference, was not attended by any of Jack's band. It does not appear that any of them were aware that such a request had been sent.

The difficulty with the Indian family, in relation to the removal of their tents and corrals, and the plowing of the ground, was settled before the 8th of September, the agent agreeing to remove the corrals, dig a well, help build a log-house, and furnish a stove—all of which he said he had previously promised; and nothing was left but the punishment of chief Johnson, for his assault on agent Meeker, and of his son for shooting at the plowman. The conduct of this chief and his son could not be overlooked. Both merited punishment; and, in the sixth article of the treaty, provision is made for such cases. On the commission of any wrong or depredation upon the person or property of any one, white, black, or Indian, by any of the Utes, upon proof of the fact and notice given to the confederate bands of Utes, they agree that they will deliver up the wrong-doer to the United States, to be tried and punished according to its laws. A demand made in pursuance of this article, on the head chief, Ouray, or even on Douglas, to whose band Johnson and his son belonged, would, no doubt, have been complied with, and the guilty parties turned over to the United States for trial and punishment. Instead of following the provisions of the treaty, troops were called for. It was eighteen days before Maj. Thornburgh reached the reservation, and before he had crossed the line the agent agreed with the Indians that it were better for him to encamp his troops at some proper point, and come in with a few of his officers for conference and consultation. This suggestion, Maj. Thornburgh said he could not consider; that, under his orders, he was required to march his command to the agency. It is true that he learned from his orders that he was going to White river to arrest insubordinate Indians, and enforce obedience to the requirements of the agent. The agent said to Maj. Thornburgh that the Indians considered his advance as a declaration of real war. " They want you to camp your troops, and that you and five soldiers come into the agency, when a talk and better understanding can be had. This I agree to." Ute chiefs had also been to see Maj. Thornburgh. He found them friendly, but uneasy, and tried to explain matters to them. He does not state how.

General Adams, a former agent of those Indians, was sent into the interior of the reservation, in pursuit of such Utes as had the captive women and children. After a tedious, and in some sense a dangerous journey, he succeeded in the rescue of all of them; and a commission, consisting of General Hatch, General Adams, and chief Ouray, was constituted to investigate the case, and demand the surrender of the Utes that participated in the murder of agent Meeker and his employes. The commission indicated twelve Indians as guilty of the murders committed at the agency, and demanded that these be surrendered to the United States. It was at one time supposed the demand would be complied with. Indeed, some of the parties, the dispatches stated, were in the possession of the commission; but General Hatch and General Adams said they must have all or none, and hence the commission came away without any of those indicated as guilty, and whom they had demanded. If it be true that such was the action of these gentlemen, it would seem they are not averse to a war with the Utes. To have retained such as were in their power would most probably, in time, have brought those remaining.

The news carried by the Indian runner to Douglas' camp on the 29th of September, that the troops and the Indians were fighting, was calculated to inflame the minds of the warriors who heard it. They had understood that Maj. Thornburgh would camp his troops, and come in to a conference, as they had suggested, and had shown symptoms of delight when this was told them. To have this good news not only dissipated, but to learn that a battle was going on, filled them with indignation. They realized that deception had been practiced upon them, and believed that the agent and his employes were parties to it, and in their savage wrath they slew all of them. This was murder, and all the warriors who participated in it should, upon trial and conviction, be punished. It is now said that the female captives, while in the possession of the Utes, were brutally treated, and their persons violated. In Miss Meeker's narrative, published October 29, 1879, there is no intimation of any thing of the kind. If true, the guilty parties should be punished. If prudent counsels prevail, these criminals may be secured and turned over to the proper authorities without war.

It is, however, quite clear that Generals Sherman, Sheridan, and other military gentlemen are anxious for a campaign against the Utes. By the Chicago dispatches of the 2d of October, 1879, Gen. Sheridan was represented as saying, that while he knew not what course would be pursued if the Indians *immediately* surrendered to Gen. Merritt, yet should they not do so, "they will be *exterminated*, as the attack on Maj. Thornburgh was a piece of the basest treachery, which *the military officers will resent, if it is in their power.*" And Gen. Sherman, at the dinner of the New England Society, in New York, on December 22, 1879, in referring to the Utes, said : "They have been ordered to deliver up twelve Indian murderers, and they can't do it. But these Indians must submit, and deliver up these murderers, *or take the consequences.*" And the consequences were that they must "*disappear from the face of the earth.*" On the 3d of January, 1880, Gen. Hatch telegraphed the authorities at Washington that the-

Indians demanded were not then in the power of Ouray, and had not been since the 26th of December. He said in the dispatch that when the Utes were assured that there was no other way to *avoid destruction,* they would decide to turn over the Indians demanded.

If all be true that is said in relation to the Ute reservation, a portion of it at least is the most valuable mineral country in the United States, and many covetous eyes are fixed upon it. The Utes have a title to the territory within this reservation, and the government of the United States has solemnly pledged its faith and honor that they shall not be disturbed in the quiet enjoyment of their country. Many propose to wrest this country from these Indians by violence; others, to declare the rights of the Utes forfeited by reason of the conflict with our troops, and the killing of the agent. Such do not recognize any rights in the Indian that the white race is bound to respect. All persons holding such views, and urging them, deserve severe rebuke and condemnation. If a suitable location could be found and secured, where these Indians could succeed as farmers, and with their consent fairly and honorably obtained, they were removed to such location, it would no doubt be to the advantage of the youthful Indians of the present generation, as well as the whole tribe in future time, to transplant them. But the cry that "*the Utes must go,*" and the sad affair at White river, and the conflict with the troops of Maj. Thornburgh, be made the occasion and excuse for their banishment, should not only be discountenanced, but firmly resisted. And the savage cry for exterminating them, so freely indulged in by military officers, should be sharply, speedily, and effectually rebuked. Officers who indulge in such talk dishonor their government.

In the annual report of Gen. Sherman, completed early in November, 1879, he devotes considerable space to the Ute Indians, and states that they are of the worst class, and occupy the roughest part of our country, for farming, grazing, or for military purposes. He embodies in his report the letters of Maj. Thornburgh to agent Meeker, dated September 25 and 28; also, the letters of agent Meeker to Maj. Thorn-

28

burgh, dated September 27 and 29, which he says are the last
letters that passed between them. He states that he gives
these letters entire, because he believes "that Maj. Thornburgh acted, from beginning to end, exactly right." He
adds: "So did agent Meeker; and the crimes afterward committed rest wholly on the Indians."

In point of fact, Gen. Sherman is in error when he assumes
that agent Meeker's letter of September 29 (1 P. M), was received by Maj. Thornburgh. On the 11th of October, as
Gen. Merritt's command emerged from the cañon, on its way
to the agency, the body of Dresser, the employe who bore the
agent's letter, was found in the mouth of an old coal mine.
He had been wounded, and had taken refuge in this mine,
and there died. The letter of September 29 was found in his
pocket. Hence, Maj. Thornburgh was only in possession of
one letter from the agent, and, in that, he was informed that
the Indians considered his advance "as a declaration of real
war."

It is submitted that Gen. Sherman is not justified in saying that the Ute Indians are of the worst class. This is a
sweeping charge, covering both their mental, moral, and physical condition. In the discussions in which they engaged
with the McCook commission, in 1872, and with Mr. Brunot,
in 1873, with reference to the surrender of a portion of their reservation (to be found in these pages), they compare favorably
with the representatives of the government, in the frankness
and business-like manner in which they dealt with the questions; and the patient snbmission with which, at all times,
they have borne the wrong and injury they have received from
those who have intruded upon and overrun their reservation,
while the government has failed to protect their rights, and
fulfill its treaty obligations toward them, should shield the
Utes from such an unjust charge. That these Indians are
very poor and ill-clad, and withal ill-fed, is no doubt true;
but it does not follow that they are bad, or of the "worst
class."

Among the crimes for which the general of the army holds
the Utes responsible, is the killing of Maj. Thornburgh and
such of his command as fell on the 29th of September, 1879.

Let this matter be looked at calmly and impartially. Maj. Thornburgh was ordered to the Ute reservation, for the purpose of affording the agent assistance, and to make arrests at the agent's suggestion, and to hold as prisoners such Indians as might be indicated. He is advised by the agent, as he approaches, but before he reaches the boundary of the reservation, that the Indians desire him to stop and camp his troops, and come in with a few officers, to the agency, for a conference, and to this Mr. Meeker said he agreed. Maj. Thornburgh replied *that his orders from the general of the army were such that he could not comply.* He said he was, by his orders, required to march his command to the agency. The Indians had protested; they considered this an invasion of their country, a challenge to battle, an act of real war, and, as such, they accepted it. As Gen. Sherman was the author of the order, and Major Thornburgh, in attempting to execute it, did, in the opinion of his superior, "exactly right," it seems clear that the calamity came from the attempt to perform what was required by the order. If some discretion had been given to Maj. Thornburgh, and, in the exercise of this, he had complied with the request of the Indians, to which the agent agreed, and camped his troops before, or even soon after he had entered the reservation, every one will admit that no battle could have taken place between the Indians and the troops, and hence no occasion have arisen for the tragedy at the agency. In his testimony before the joint committee of the Forty-fifth Congress, Gen. Sherman admitted that a large discretion should be allowed in the Indian service. In his instructions to Maj. Thornburgh, his orders were imperative, and that officer was in the line of his duty in attempting to execute them. Let the responsibility for the sad calamity at Milk creek, and the afflicting tragedy at White river agency, on September 29, 1879, rest upon the proper party.

A delegation of the Ute Indians is now at Washington, and inquiry and investigation are being had in the interior department, and by the House committee on Indian affairs, as to the origin of the trouble with the White river Utes. It would be idle to express any opinion as to the scope of the investition or conclusions that may be reached. One of the results. that many will desire is that the Utes be removed from Colorado. In this the government should move slowly, and provide in advance a suitable tract of land where these people can by cultivation of the soil make their own support. The government should not act prematurely, because of the unreasonable and imperious demands of the governor of Colorado, backed by the senators and representatives from that State, or be swayed by the pressing clamor of the hosts of men who now have interests in the mines there, re-echoed by other hosts who stand ready to enter into the Ute country. The Ute mind should be reached, and the Indians made sensible of the fact that their true interests will be promoted by removing from the mountains of Colorado to a tract of country were they may become independent, self-supporting farmers, and this done, their free consent could be obtained for the surrender of their present reservation. For this surrender they should have assured to them a perfect title to the home to which they may be transplanted, and, in addition, a fair money consideration.

Letter of Hon. George W. Manypenny
to the
Cincinnati *Gazette*
in Regard to
TREATMENT OF THE INDIANS
January 31, 1867

A WORD ABOUT INDIANS.

COLUMBUS, *January* 31, 1867.

In your issues of the 15th and 17th insts. you published some "startling disclosures" furnished by your Washington correspondent, "H. V. N. B.," in the nature of extracts from a report made by a Commission consisting of Senators Foster, Doolittle, and Nesmith, appointed in the spring of 1865 to visit the whole Indian country and inquire into the condition and management of our Indian affairs in general. Your correspondent states that the report of this Commission was suppressed because of the disgraceful nature of the facts developed, and that it has been lying in the Government Printing Office for more than a year, "carefully withheld from all." The statement of this fact is not very creditable to the American Senate, and it is amazing how a respectable Commission of that body could submit to such indignity, and quietly acquiesce in the suppression of a report made by them, and containing such a narrative of "robbery and general rascality," such gross frauds against the helpless denizens of the forest, involving, as they do, not only the honor of the government itself, but that of all its good citizens.

Aware that Senators Foster, Doolittle, and Nesmith had been deputed to the duty referred to nearly two years ago, it has often been a query with me whether they had made a report of their doings, and if so. what had become of it. Having some knowledge of the powerful influence exercised by the lobby at Washington in matters pertaining to Indian affairs, I will not be surprised to be told that *it* had made herculean efforts to suppress such a report; but it is a matter of surprise that the Commission. all having seats in the Senate, could be induced to submit quietly to the suppression of their report; and this surprise is increased when the fact is stated that, so far as the world knows, no member of the Senate—a body to be selected, according to the theory of the fathers, from the ablest and best men in the respective States—was found to call the attention of the people of the United States to this report, and thus arouse their attention to the heinousness of the crimes therein exposed. Shameful as the facts in these statements are, from a somewhat familiar knowledge of Indian affairs in former years, I am prepared to say that the treatment of Indian tribes is much worse, in the general, than the reader will infer from reading the extracts given from the Senatorial Commission's report in your columns.

We are accustomed to read, at short intervals, terrible stories in the newspapers about the depredations and murders committed by Indians, but we never get the other side of the question; the one side is highly colored, but we never get the other side.

Indian massacres and depredations are terrible, and their mode of warfare to us civilized people very revolting; notwithstanding, I have no hesitation in saying that no "Indian massacre" occurs, no "Indian depredation" is committed, without cause, and that cause, viewed and judged by Indian law, is defensible. Some act previous to the massacre or depredation has been committed by the whites justifying the subsequent conduct of the Indians, according to their law, notwithstanding the Indians may destroy the property or take the lives of innocent whites, for they do not recognize individual responsibility for crimes committed, but take compensation or visit retribution on the race or tribe to whom the offenders belong. Thus it is not unfrequent that the injury and wrong done to Indians by unprincipled whites is revenged by the murder of purely innocent and unoffending persons, without regard to age or sex.

If the reckless and unprincipled white men who push themselves into the Indian country in advance of the regular settlements, and the more reckless scoundrels who contrive to get up Indian disturbances for the gain that is found in Indian wars, were all excluded from the Indian country, it would be a rare occurrence when we should be startled with "Indian hostilities."

This body of men, though unknown to the country generally, is formidable, being in all their acts backed up by the Washington lobby, whose pockets are periodically filled with cash which flows in as the result of these "Indian depredations," "Indian hostilities," &c., &c., produced by the infamous conduct of the body of men referred to in their intercourse with the Red Men.

If Indian agents and employés were all honest men, and the reckless and unprincipled class of men to whom I have referred were kept from the Indian country—driven out, if need be, by force when necessary—the Indian would be regarded by the mass of men in a different light from what he now is. With proper treatment and effort I feel very certain the Indian could be domesticated and civilized. Twelve years ago the tribes in Kansas, who had emigrated within the twenty years preceding from Ohio, Indiana, and other States, were much further advanced in civilization than they now are. But the disorder which succeeded the introduction of the whites was very fatal to the interests and well-being of the Indians; and in all the conflicts there between the New England colonists and those from the South in reference to the negro population, I think it would be difficult to show an instance wherein the Indians of that territory were injured and their rights trampled upon, and there were many such, in which there was not perfect harmony of action between these otherwise belligerent parties.

I repeat, as my firm conviction, that with proper instruction, attention and care, and the assurance of a permanent home, many—a majority of the present Indian youth—could be domesticated and civilized, and made reasonably useful members of society, and that like effort through a few generations would make them all such members, with no greater per cent. of worthless ones than there is in white communities.

But how can the Indian, under present treatment, be expected to be otherwise than he is? What is his condition? Who cares for him or his? *Where has he a friend?* As things stand now he is viewed as a monster to be exterminated, and no voice is lifted up in his behalf.

In the testimony furnished the Senate Commission, and with which the *Gazette* was supplied, it is asserted by intelligent Indian agents and army officers on duty in the Indian country, that a very small proportion of the money annuities nominally paid by the government to the Indians is received by them. To the question " What proportion actually reaches the Indians?" Colonel Sprague says: " Very little, if any." Gen Carlin says: "A very small proportion." Gen. Hoffman replies: "I have no doubt they have little or no benefit from it," (the annuities.) Gen. Sully says: "It is my opinion that very little of it (the annuities) reaches the hands of the Indians." Gen. R. B. Marcy says "that a great portion of the money which has been sent out for payment to the Northwestern Indians during the past ten years has never reached them."

Indian Agent Harlan says: "More than ninety-nine per cent. was actually paid to the traders, and less than one per cent. to the Indians." Agent Ward says: "In my belief the proportion of money which actually reaches the hands of the Indians, if any, must be very limited."

So much for the manner in which the ample annuities annually appropriated for the Indians are disposed of, as testified to by army officers and Indian agents, notwithstanding the law requires these annuities *to be distributed and paid per capita to the Indians of the tribe to whom the money belongs.* These army officers and Indian agents are in the Indian country for the purpose of protecting the rights and interests of the Red Man, and yet such are the baleful influences surrounding them that they testify that very little of the hundreds of thousands—yes, millions—appropriated from year to year for Indian purposes ever reaches the hands of the Indians. The influence of the lobby is even more potent in the Indian country than at Washington.

There the most scandalous depredations are committed on the Indians, and daily they are despoiled of their property, and they obtain no redress. Here is an illustration, to be found in the official proceedings of Congress on the 2d of March, 1865:

Mr. Harlan, a Senator from Iowa, said that he had been told, when in Kansas the preceding summer, that in the three years previous there had been driven from the Indian country west of the Kansas not less than sixty thousand head of beef cattle belonging to the Indians; and, in continuation, he remarked that one of the Kansas Senators said that the estimate is entirely too low; "that, in his opinion, the number of cattle driven out will not fall short of one hundred thousand head."

Mr. Doolittle asked: "Have not those cattle gone to the use of the army of the United States?"

Mr. Harlan replied: "I think some of them have. Perhaps I ought not to utter a mere belief without proof, but still I do believe that a large number of these cattle have been taken from the Indians by contractors and sold to the quartermasters, and a large number bought at nominal sums, and stolen and driven out through Kansas and sold on private account."

Mr. Lane, of Kansas, said the Kansas Legislature had investigated the question of cattle stealing from the Indian country, and that the people of Kansas "estimate the number of cattle taken from the Indians, not by Kansas men, but by the employés of the general government, at one hundred thousand head within the last two years."

A conversational debate occurred between a number of Senators, occupying several pages of the *Congressional Globe*, from which the foregoing extracts are taken, in all which it is agreed that the cattle were stolen from the Indians; but when the Indian appropriation bill was acted upon, which was the question under consideration, (and this cattle stealing was incidentally brought into the debate,) the matter passed away as a dream, not impressing even one Senator with its enormity, or the obligation resting on the United States to indemnify the Indians for their property.

With reference to the home of the Indian, it may be said he has none. A reservation may, by solemn treaty, be set apart to-day for the use and occupancy of a particular tribe "FOREVER," and before the ink is scarcely dry upon the parchment, the whole thing is abrogated, and the tribe compelled to seek a new home. And even during the existence of a treaty, intruders pay no attention to it, but habitually trespass upon the reservation and despoil the Indian of his property, and, if not submissive, take his life. In fact, let him turn his face in what direction he may, he finds the white man confronting him as an enemy.

Not long since I read an extract from the report of Major General Hazen, Acting Inspector of the Platte Department—an officer holding a distinguished position in the army of the United States—wherein he styles the Indian of the plains a "dirty beggar and a thief, who murders the weak and unprotected, but never attacks an armed foe." This general then goes on for quantity in abuse of the Indian race, and concludes that "the white man owes the Indian nothing. He is in the way of natural evolutions of progress, and when government pays what is to him a reasonable compensation for his title to the territory, or for privileges in it, the debt is perfectly canceled, as when a corporation pays the assessed value of the site of a public school." Such sentiments as the above, however common, are not creditable to a federal military officer, and the fact that he is permitted to utter them without rebuke from his superiors is a sad commentary on the times.

But a few evenings since I heard an eminent divine deliver a lecture. It was made up of observations on the Pacific coast. In speaking of the people in that region, he had a word about the

Indians, whom he designated (properly) as low and filthy, and added that there was but one voice among the white people on that coast, and that was for extermination. But the lecturer failed to utter a single word in condemnation of this horrible sentiment! What he stated is not only true of that region, but it is the sentiment of the whites within and bordering on the whole Indian country. If the same divine had been in California before its conquest and acquisition to the United States, he would have found the mission Indians there in a comparatively happy and prosperous condition, with vast flocks and herds about them. Alas, what is their condition now? Degraded and miserable.

Moreover, let the reader ask himself what interest does the religious world give at this day to the condition and prospects of the Indian tribes? My reply would be, let the emanations from the hundreds and thousands of Christian pulpits in the land, in the various religious exercises from one end of the year to the other, answer. How very, very, very seldom is the poor Red Man remembered, and how often—very, very, very often—forgotten?

When all things are taken into consideration, is it to be wondered at that the Indian is a degraded savage?

Originally, the Indian Bureau was a part of the War Department, and when the Interior Department was organized some eighteen years ago, it was taken from the War and assigned to the Interior Department; and the habit is very common among army officers to express the opinion that, however the effort to civilize the Indian may terminate, all the current abuses in the administration of Indian affairs may be corrected by placing the bureau back under the control of the War Department. Inspector General Marcy represents this class, and in his testimony before the Senate Commission, wherein he urges the restoration of the bureau to the War Office, he says : "If any one objects to the system I have recommended, I would ask him if he has ever heard of a single instance where the Indians were ever defrauded of a dollar of their annuities during the time they were disbursed through military channels."

General Marcy no doubt entertains the opinion above expressed honestly; but he is in error. The plunder of the Indian tribes has had a continuous growth, and had not its origin with the separation of the bureau from the War Department—far from it. Simultaneous with that separation the government acquired California, Washington, Oregon, Utah, and New Mexico, with the vast tract embraced within our lately organized territories, and thereby Indian population and Indian annuities were rapidly and wonderfully augmented. Civil officers took the place of the military in paying these annuities, but the pile to steal from increased, and has continued to increase, until it may be said the annual distributions are now millions on millions; whereas they were but a small sum, comparatively, prior to 1849. The ratio in increase of fraud and stealing has probably exceeded the increase in the annuities.

It is further argued by the advocates for the restoration of the Indian Bureau to the War Department, that thereby Indian wars will be avoided. That is all sheer nonsense, if we judge the future by the past. The Seminole war in Florida and the Black Hawk war in the Northwest (the two great wars) occurred when the War Department had control of the bureau, and since the change the authority of the military in the Indian country has never been successfully disputed. For the last few years it has had undisputed sway. In 1864 and 1865 the War Department expended upwards of thirty millions in Indian wars; how much in 1866 I do not know. In the latter part of 1865 and during the year 1866 we know that the business of making treaties with the Indians was almost, if not entirely, confided to gentlemen of the army, and the press of the country assured us, time and again, how wonderfully successful these military commissioners were in making treaties; that all was peace, and there would be no more Indian wars. But now, at the beginning of 1867, it bursts upon us from all quarters that a general Indian war is imminent; our troops are slaughtered in sight of the forts, and general alarm prevails on the frontier.

Considering the gravity of the situation, we are told by the Washington newsmongers that the Senate Committee on Military Affairs has come to the conclusion to report a bill restoring the Indian Bureau to the War Department; and this is to be the remedy for existing evils. It is also said that General Grant, Secretary Stanton, and the President all agree to this, and that it will be speedily done.

Now, Mr. Editor of the *Gazette,* let me invoke your instant and energetic opposition to this measure, believing, as I do, that it ought not to be consummated. It will do no good; it will not stop Indian war; it will not prevent the robbery of the Indians; it will not benefit the whites on the frontier, nor will it in any shape mitigate the condition of the Indians.

That a radical reform in Indian management is demanded, no man can doubt; but that reform will not be achieved by putting the Red Man under the discipline and treatment of the army. I would much prefer, as a reformatory measure, the withdrawal of the army from the whole Indian country; believing, as I do, that military posts therein serve no good purpose, and that the influences going out from them are vicious in the extreme.

If Congress were to go to work and make the Indian Bureau what it should be—a full department, with a Secretary who should be a member of the Cabinet, participating in the deliberations of the Executive councils, and invested by law to organize a military or police force sufficiently numerous to keep order in the Indian country without reference to, and independent of, the War Department or military commanders—the beneficial effects resulting therefrom would soon be apparent. The analogy for this is to be found in the revenue cutter system under the orders of the Treasury Department, and independent of the navy. The army should only go into the Indian country on some great emergency, and when called there by the Department of Indian Affairs.

Many of the ever-recurring and never-ending difficulties that happen in the management of Indian affairs grow out of matters that are acted upon and decided at Cabinet councils, upon the representation of outside parties, (having interests that are concealed from view,) who make their statements to the President, or some one of his Secretaries, and in which the existence of the Indian Bureau and its head are entirely ignored. Hence the great importance of placing the chief officer in charge of the Indians in the Cabinet. Then, let the country awake to its responsibilities on this subject; let statesmen and divines, let all feel and realize that the Indian is the ward of the government; that he is a human being, having rights to be respected, and that obligations rest upon the people of the United States in relation to him. Let our law-makers understand that the Indian is entitled to and *must have a fixed and permanent home;* and that he is not to be driven from that home by any schemes, pretexts, or devices whatever. Let it be further understood, as an unalterable sentiment among the people, that Indian stealing and oppression in all forms is odious; that a man cannot be a leading member of the Senate or House of Representatives in Congress and habitually—nay, at all—dabble in Indian plunder; that an individual cannot hold an Indian agency a few years and retire from it rich; that sharp men on the frontier cannot with impunity rob and plunder the Indians at their pleasure; but let the people be educated up to the point that they will readily, and with one voice, denounce such men as scoundrels, and exclude them from respectable society.

When that day arrives, and the whole country is awake to its duty in the matter, the honest settlers on the frontier will have no cause of alarm or fear, the Indians will have peace, and a new order of things in our Indian relations will prevail.

This article is already too long, I fear, for your columns. As, however, it is but seldom that anything in behalf of the Indian appears, feeble as this is, I hope you will give it a place.

Very respectfully,

GEO. W. MANYPENNY.